love your
library

15 377 127 0

130

210

Contents

Introduction

Barcelona has a panache that is all its own. A radiant pop art sculpture by Lichtenstein towers alongside a dark and sombre neoclassical arcade; serried ranks of apartment blocks in the Eixample occasionally explode in a proliferation of Modernista colour and pizzazz; and local festivals incorporate both the *sardana*, a sedate traditional Catalan dance involving gentle bouncing on tiptoes, and the *correfoc*, a reckless, firework-wielding rampage through the streets.

The city is captivated by all things modern but never turns its back on the past. Much of its appeal stems from a respect for heritage that gives it the best-preserved medieval quarter in Europe. You could spend a day mooching around this labyrinth, escaping the heat in shadowy alleyways while seagulls wheel overhead in an azure sky, without ever feeling the need to tick off museums or head for the beach.

In fact, we suggest you do just that. This book is packed with recommendations for sights and museums large and small, famous and obscure. But to really appreciate what keeps visitors returning time and again, you won't always need it.

Correfoc p215

ABOUT THE GUIDE

This is one of a series of Time Out guidebooks to cities across the globe. Written by local experts, our guides are thoroughly researched and meticulously updated. They aim to be inspiring, irreverent, well-informed and trustworthy.

Time Out Barcelona is divided into five sections: Discover, Explore, Experience, Understand and Plan.

Discover introduces the city and provides inspiration for your visit.

Explore is the main sightseeing section of the guide and includes detailed listings and reviews for sights, museums, restaurants ⑩, cafés, tapas and bars ⑩ and shops ⑩, all organised by area with a corresponding street map. To help navigation, each area of Barcelona has been assigned its own colour.

Experience covers the cultural life of the city in depth, including festivals, film, LGBT, music, nightlife, theatre and more.

Understand provides in-depth background information that places Barcelona in its historical and cultural context.

Plan offers practical visitor information, including accommodation options and details of public transport.

Hearts

We use hearts 💙 to pick out venues, sights and experiences in the city that we particularly recommend. The very best of these are featured in the Top 20 *(see p10)* and receive extended coverage in the guide.

Maps

A detachable fold-out map can be found on the inside back cover. There's also an overview map *(see p8)* and individual streets maps for each area of the city. The venues featured in the guide have been given a grid reference so that you can find them easily on the maps and on the ground.

Prices

All our **restaurant listings** are marked with a euro symbol category from budget to blow-out (€-€€€€), indicating the price you should expect to pay for an average main course: € = under €10; €€ = €10-€20; €€€ = €20-€30; €€€€ = over €30.

A similar system is used in our **Accommodation** chapter based on the hotel's standard prices for one night in a double room: € = under €100; €€ = €100-€200; €€€ = €200-€300; €€€€ = over €300.

Discover

Park Güell

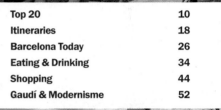

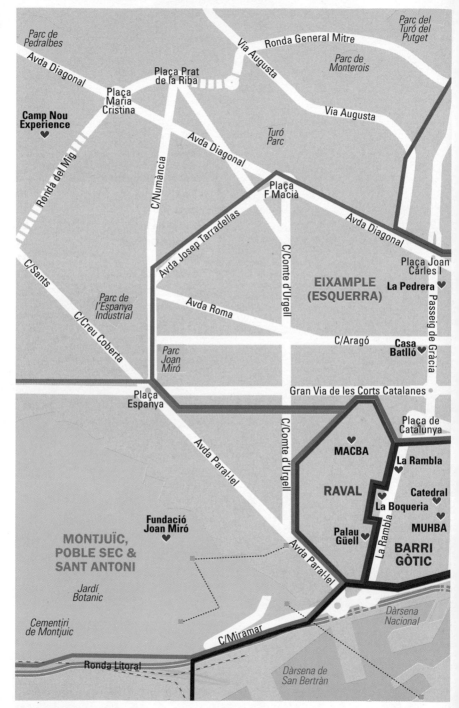

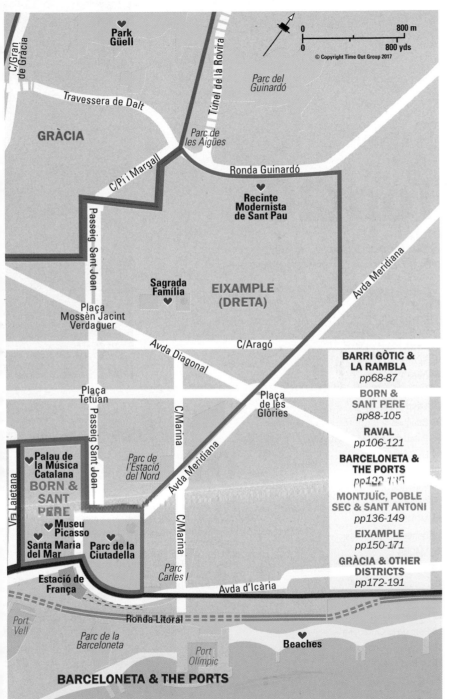

Park Güell

Parc del Guinardó

C/Gran de Gràcia

Túnel de la Rovira

Travessera de Dalt

0 800 m

0 800 yds

© Copyright Time Out Group 2017

GRÀCIA

Parc de les Aigües

C/Pi i Margall

Ronda Guinardó

Recinte Modernista de Sant Pau

Passeig Sant Joan

Avda Meridiana

Sagrada Família

EIXAMPLE (DRETA)

Plaça Mossèn Jacint Verdaguer

Avda Diagonal

C/Aragó

Plaça Tetuan

Plaça de les Glòries

Passeig Sant Joan

C/Marina

Avda Meridiana

Palau de la Música Catalana

Parc de l'Estació del Nord

Via Laietana

BORN & SANT PERE

Museu Picasso

C/Marina

Santa Maria del Mar

Parc de la Ciutadella

Parc Carles I

Estació de França

Avda d'Icària

Port Vell

Ronda Litoral

Parc de la Barceloneta

Port Olímpic

Beaches

BARCELONETA & THE PORTS

BARRI GÒTIC & LA RAMBLA
pp68-87

BORN & SANT PERE
pp88-105

RAVAL
pp106-121

BARCELONETA & THE PORTS
pp122-135

MONTJUÏC, POBLE SEC & SANT ANTONI
pp136-149

EIXAMPLE
pp150-171

GRÀCIA & OTHER DISTRICTS
pp172-191

9

Top 20

*From Modernisme to La Mercè,
we count down the city's finest*

01

Sagrada Família *p158*

Gaudí's unfinished basilica is a fantastic riot of colour and maverick architecture, its walls erupting with flora and fauna. Love it or hate it, it is Barcelona's most emblematic building and a must-see. The plans for its completion were burnt by anarchists long after Gaudí's death, but decades of research have gone into making the building as faithful as possible to his designs.

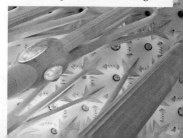

02

Museu Picasso *p97*

Though born in Málaga, Picasso moved to Barcelona as a teenager, and this museum focuses on those early years. With the exception of the entire *sala* devoted to his spectacular *Las Meninas* series, these rooms do not contain a parade of his greatest hits, but instead give a fascinating insight into his development as a young artist, and the accomplishment of some of his very early paintings is jaw-dropping.

Ajuntament de Barcelona

Museu Picasso

03

Camp Nou Experience *p180*

The huge and hallowed Barça stadium –
where the likes of Messi, Ronaldinho and
Maradona have worked their magic – is a
must for die-hard footie fans (and appears
every year in the top three most-visited
Barcelona attractions). Entrance includes
the club museum and a tour of the players'
tunnel and dug-outs, along with a peek
into the President's box.

04

Casa Batlló *p156*

There are many interpretations of the
fantastical façade of Gaudí's Casa Batlló,
but most agree that its shimmering tiles
represent the scales of the dragon slain by
St George (Catalonia's patron saint), and
the skeletal balconies are intended to
evoke the bones of its victims. Nowadays
you can visit the interior, which is
predictably more sober than its shell, but
its sinuous curves are still unmistakeably
the work of Gaudí.

05

Beaches *p130*

There are a few valiant souls who brave the
water around Christmas time, but for most,
the sea is warm enough to swim in from
late spring to early autumn. Seven
kilometres of sand await, with something
for everyone, whether your bag is kayaking,
gay nudism, rock pooling or volleyball.
Barceloneta's *xiringuitos* (beach bars) offer
thumping beats and cruising crowds, while
at the far north are the family-friendly
sands of Platja del Llevant.

06

Palau de la Música Catalana *p98*

A fierce contender for Barcelona's prettiest building, this Modernista flight of fancy was designed by a contemporary of Gaudí's and has functioned as a concert hall ever since. The façade is really quite special, but it's also worth getting a guided tour of the auditorium if you can, or – even better – catching a concert while you're here. Failing that, wander through the lobby to the high-ceilinged café at the back.

07

La Rambla *p74*

Barcelona's golden mile is a long boulevard of street performers, card sharps, hawkers, buskers, human statues and bewildered-looking tourists. Though these days it has more in common with Oxford Street than the Champs-Élysées, it's still a must-see, and beyond the Mexican hats and flower stalls are some fine buildings and a whole host of attractions from La Boqueria food market (*see p84*) to the surprisingly tasteful Museu de l'Eròtica (*see p78*).

06

08

Park Güell *p177*

Gaudí's 'garden city' project was never completed, but instead he bequeathed the wonderful Park Güell to the city. What is termed the 'monumental' zone of the park is now fenced off and ticketed and includes the fairy-tale gatehouses, the famous 'dragon' (actually a giant lizard), and the hypostyle market, topped with the vast terrace and winding tiled benches that form the backdrop for so many holiday snaps.

08

09

09

Fundació Joan Miró *p143*

Joan Miró was born and grew up in Barcelona, where he honed his surrealist skills at the same art school that Picasso attended. His huge, colourful artworks have a universal appeal, but this stark white Le Corbusier-influenced museum building is a draw in itself, along with the view of the city that it commands from its position on Montjuïc. The Miró also hosts some of the best temporary exhibitions in the city.

10

Catedral de Barcelona *p77*

Gaudí's Sagrada Família is often wrongly described as a cathedral, but the real thing is this Gothic fantasy in the heart of the Old City. Built on the site of a Roman temple, it took centuries to complete, and its façade wasn't added until the early 20th century. This element of medieval fakery doesn't detract from its appeal, however, and it graces a thousand postcards.

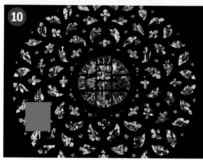

10

11

MUHBA *p79*

The Museu d'Història de Barcelona, to give it its full name, encompasses various buildings; the 15th-century Casa Padellàs, which houses most of the displays of archeological findings, prints and so on; the Santa Àgata chapel; and the splendid Saló del Tinell, once the seat of the Catalan parliament. The *pièce de résistance*, however, is the extraordinary underground labyrinth of Roman remains, which runs from the Plaça del Rei as far as the cathedral.

12

Santa Maria del Mar *p100*

Known as the 'people's cathedral', the 14th-century basilica of Santa Maria del Mar was erected by locals who volunteered their labour, and built it in record time. It's an incredible sight, deceptively large inside, with columns that rise to a dizzyingly high vaulted ceiling and a vast rose window on the front façade. It was twice gutted by anarchists, and it's to this that it owes its clean lines and simplicity.

11

13

MACBA *p111*

Richard Meier's hulking white behemoth of a museum signified a grand turnaround in the fortunes of the Raval, and still shines as a beacon of modernity outside as well as in. It houses the city's main collection of contemporary art (which, in this instance, means 'post World War II'), and while its permanent holdings focus on Catalan and Spanish artists, temporary exhibitions have a more international flavour.

14

Recinte Modernista de Sant Pau *p163*

One of Barcelona's lesser-known gems, the Hospital de Sant Pau (as it was until a few years ago) was designed by Modernista architect Domènech i Montaner as a place where the sick could recover more quickly through the power of beautiful surroundings, a popular belief at the time. It comprises a series of dazzling garden 'pavilions', each of which was once a ward, while the dirty aspects of hospital life happened underground.

14

15

Festes de la Mercè *p221*

There is no shortage of neighbourhood festivals throughout the year, but La Mercè is where the entire city erupts in a week of music, fireworks, dancing and very, very late nights. Held around 24 September, the feast day of Barcelona's patron saint, the Virgin of Mercy, it brings together the best of all the cultural quirks of Catalan festes – papier mâché giants, fire-breathing dragons, human castles and *sardana* folk-dancing.

16

Palau Güell *p113*

From street level, it's hard to believe that Gaudí was behind this sombre medievalist townhouse, but the riot of colour on the rooftop terrace bears all the trademarks of his technique. Built on a narrow strip of land and hemmed in on both sides, its construction is a miracle of architectural cunning, the rooms facing into a graceful central hall, topped with a dome pierced with shafts of light.

15

PLANNING A TRIP TO BARCELONA?

From budget to boutique, the best hotels in Barcelona uncovered.

17

La Boqueria *p84*

Europe's biggest food market is a feast for the senses. Despite its location on La Rambla and the fascination it holds for visitors, it's still the first choice for locals, particularly for produce hard to find anywhere else. Beat your way past the crowds at the front for a taste of local life – preferably viewed from one of the market's various tapas bars.

18

Parc de la Ciutadella *p94*

The verdant Parc de la Ciutadella is the perfect combination of elegant landscaping and spaces intended for nothing but fun. There are playgrounds for little ones (including one for children with disabilities), a boating lake, a waterfall, zoo, picnic area, giant sculptures, statues and acres of grass for romping, juggling and bongo-playing. Be sure to visit its rose garden in spring.

19

Primavera Sound *p213*

Barcelona's indie festival par excellence has built such a reputation internationally that Catalans are substantially outnumbered by music fans pouring in from around the globe for the likes of Radiohead, Arcade Fire, New Order, PJ Harvey and Patti Smith. There are so many acts, and such a multitude of stages, each with a different focus, that you'll need to schedule with military precision.

20

La Pedrera *p160*

'La Pedrera' means 'the stone quarry' and was originally the nickname used by a scornful public who weren't quite ready for Gaudí's undulating apartment block. More recently, its genius has been fully appreciated, and its interior given over to various exhibition spaces, the better to appreciate the maritime-inspired design. No visit is complete without a trip to the roof to walk among the warrior-like chimneys.

Itineraries

Get the most out of the city in the time you have available

ESSENTIAL WEEKEND

Budget €350 for two
Getting around Walking, metro, bus, taxi

DAY 1

Morning

Start the day with a quiet stroll down La Rambla, the city's most famous boulevard, before the crowds, the living statues and the pickpockets arrive. Halfway along, duck into **Cafè de l'Òpera** (*see p83*) for coffee and a breakfast *ensaïmada*, a spiral of flaky pastry dusted with icing sugar.

Another couple of hundred yards or so down La Rambla, heading towards the sea, you'll see the **Plaça Reial** off to your left. Turn in to admire its elaborate lamp posts, an early council commission for Gaudí; then, exiting from its northern side, head right along C/Ferran to the grand **Plaça Sant Jaume**, skirting round the back of the Generalitat to the **Cathedral** (*see p77*). Take time to mooch around its magnificent cloister and take the lift up to the roof for a great view of the city. Come out of the Cathedral and head east, crossing the Via Laietana to the **Palau de la Música** (*see p98*). Take a guided tour or simply marvel at the fantastical Modernista façade.

La Rambla

Afternoon

Having worked up an appetite, head down into the Born proper (with a quick look at the roof of the **Mercat de Santa Caterina** (*see p93*) en route and tuck into some tapas outside the majestic **Santa Maria del Mar** at **La Vinya del Senyor** wine bar (*see p103*). It's a skip and a hop to the **Museu Picasso** (*see p97*), an easy place to while away a couple of hours.

After this, wander down to the **Port Vell** (*see p132*). For the best view over the harbour, go up to the rooftop café of the **Museu d'Història de Catalunya** (*see p133*), where you can sip an early-evening beer before heading up Passeig Joan de Borbó to the seafront.

Mercat de Santa Caterina

Port Vell

Evening

In this part of town there are several excellent seafood restaurants: try **Can Majó** (*see p128*) or **Kaiku** (*see p129*). And if you can't bear to go home afterwards, you could always join the glossy crowd for a late-night cocktail at fashionable **CDLC** (*see p238*), on the fringe of the beach.

Sagrada Família

DAY 2

Morning

To start a day of Modernisme, Barcelona's answer to art nouveau, have coffee and a pastry at La Rambla's branch of the **Escribà** patisserie (*see p170*), with its tiled façade, delicate stucco and wrought iron. From here, walk up to **Plaça Catalunya** and continue straight ahead for the elegant **Passeig de Gràcia**, a showcase for all things Modernista. Note the Gaudí-designed hexagonal paving tiles, along with Pere Falqués' elegant wrought-iron lamp posts.

Unless you get sucked into some of the street's blend of swanky boutiques and major chains, it's a five-minute walk to the contrasting masterpieces of the **Manzana de la Discòrdia** (*see p155*). This block houses three extraordinary buildings designed by the holy trinity of Modernisme: Gaudí, Domènech i Montaner and Puig i Cadafalch. Another five minutes further up is Gaudí's **La Pedrera** (*see p160*). Backtrack to the **Casa Batlló** and then take a metro to Gaudí's most famous work, the spectacular **Sagrada Família** (*see p158*). While all of these buildings are now open to the public, entrance fees are high and queues are long, but the façades alone merit a visit.

Afternoon

Time for lunch. While the Sagrada Família area is strangely bereft of decent restaurants, the adjacent **Avda Gaudí** has several spots with outdoor terraces at which to grab a *bocadillo* and a beer. Post lunch, continue along the avenue for the extravagant **Recinte Modernista de Sant Pau** (*see p163*), an unsung Modernista tour de force by Domènech i Montaner, than take bus H6 from the northwest corner to Gaudí's unmissable **Park Güell** (*see p177*).

Evening

Sticking with the Modernista theme, the deep-of-pocket will love dinner at **Casa Calvet** (*see p162*), a great, if pricey, restaurant set in a Gaudí-designed townhouse. Otherwise, head back to the many restaurants along the **Passeig de Gràcia**. Both are a cab ride from Park Güell; and you're then well placed for other nightlife options if you're not yet ready for bed …

Park Güell

BUDGET BREAK

Budget €90 for two
Getting around Walking

Morning

Els Quatre Gats (*see p82*) may not have the cheapest coffee in town, but it is a great way for some sedentary sightseeing over breakfast. Set in Puig i Cadafalch's Modernista Casa Martí, it was a stamping ground for Picasso, Gaudí and other luminaries of the period. From here it's a short walk to the **Cathedral** (*see p77*), the church and cloister of which are free to enter until 12.45pm. Behind the cathedral is the **Temple d'August** (*see p80*, free to enter), where you can see four soaring Corinthian columns of the Roman temple that once stood here.

Temple d'August

Afternoon

Back in the direction of Els Quatre Gats is **Mercè Vins** (*see p81*), a little pocket of Catalan authenticity, with a great-value set lunch for €12. After this, walk up to **Plaça Catalunya**, beyond which begins the **Passeig de Gràcia**, a long boulevard of grand designs and flagship shops. Many of the greatest Modernista buildings are along here, and although punitively expensive to enter, are almost as rewarding to look at from outside. Look out for Gaudí's **La Pedrera** (*see p160*) and **Casa Batlló** (*see p156*), as well as the **Casa Amatller** (*see p157*) and the **Casa Lleó Morera** (*see p165*). Take any street off to the left and you'll hit the leafy Rambla de Catalunya, its pedestrian section a long line of café terraces. Try **La Bodegueta** (*see p164*) for a pick-me-up.

Evening

Wander back down to Plaça Catalunya, and **La Rambla** (*see p74*), and just down on the right is the **Palau de la Virreina** (*see p80*), which often has free exhibitions. Just beyond it is **La Boqueria** market (*see p84*). One of Barcelona's great attractions in its own right, it's a riot of colour, smells and noise. Continue down La Rambla until you meet C/Ferran, and head left for dinner at **Can Culleretes** (*see p80*), for good food at bargain prices in an unbeatable location.

La Boqueria

FAMILY DAY OUT

Budget €220 for two adults, two children
Getting around Walking, bus, funicular

Morning

Those with very young kids should start the morning at **La Marelle** (C/Mendez Nuñez 4, 93 007 1295), a bright, multilingual 'kids' café' with toys and games on the edge of the Born. With older kids, head round the corner to the **Plaça Sant Pere** where there are plenty of places for breakfast in the sunshine.

From here it's a five- or ten-minute walk to the verdant **Parc de la Ciutadella**, a great place to spend a morning, with a decent-sized zoo (*see p99*), a boating lake, outdoor cafés, various playgrounds and some superb climbing trees.

Parc de la Ciutadella

Sagrada Família, Museu de la Xocolata

Afternoon

Backtrack slightly to the **Bar del Convent** (*see p102*) for a light lunch. It's a lively café with toys for tiny tots and tables outside in the former cloister, an enclosed space big enough for a run around. The building next door houses the **Museu de la Xocolata** (*see p99*), an enjoyable stroll through the history of chocolate, ending with a display of the enormous chocolate sculptures that traditionally form part of a Catalan Easter. End in the café, where you can revive flagging energy levels with steaming mugs of the brown stuff.

Evening

Back on Passeig Picasso, catch the H14 bus to its final stop on Avda Paral·lel and from there take the funicular railway up the hill of **Montjuïc**. At the top you could take a cable car to the castle (*see p146*) or wander over to the **Fundació Joan Miró** (*see p143*), always a hit with kids for the bold use of colour and surrealism. Afterwards follow the signs for the **MNAC** (*see p144*), below which sits the **Magic Fountain** (*see p142*), a fabulously kitsch display of music and colour. It's easy to get back into town from the nearby transport hub of Plaça Espanya.

IN PICASSO'S FOOTSTEPS

Budget €120 for two
Getting around Walking

Morning

Start at one of the many café terraces of the **Pla del Palau** in the Born. Picasso and his family moved here in 1895, to C/Reina Cristina 3. Just over the road is **La Llotja** (*see p96*), which then housed an art school where Picasso studied.

From here, cross Via Laietana to **C/Mercè 3**, the next Picasso family home, now destroyed. This area was an insalubrious red-light district and later inspired his masterpiece, *Les Demoiselles D'Avignon* (1907). Continue along C/Mercè and cross La Rambla to the site of Picasso's bedsit-studio at **C/Nou de la Rambla 10**, opposite Gaudí's Palau Güell. Some have suggested that the bright colours and fragmented mosaics of the terrace chimneys might have sown the seeds of Picasso's cubism.

Back on La Rambla, walk up and right on C/Cardenal Casañas and then left at C/Petritxol. The **Sala Parès** gallery (*see p87*) was a meeting point for the fin-de-siècle set of Barcelona and also exhibited the work of the young Picasso in 1901.

Afternoon

From the gallery it's a short walk to the most famous symbol of Picasso's days in Barcelona: **Els Quatre Gats** (*see p82*). It's no gastro temple but has a decent set lunch for €14. After lunch, head back down **Portal de l'Àngel**; on the corner of Plaça Nova, opposite the Cathedral, is the **Col·legi d'Arquitectes**. Its façade is decorated with a graffiti-style triptych of Catalan folk scenes, from a design drawn by Picasso while in exile in the 1950s. It celebrates both the Senyera (Catalan flag) and the *gegants* (giants, *see p72*). After this, head over to the Born for an afternoon at the **Museu Picasso** (*see p97*).

Evening

Take an early evening stroll down C/Princesa to the entrance of the **Parc de la Ciutadella** (*see p94*). Turn right before the gates and halfway along Passeig Picasso stands Antoni Tàpies' *Homage to Picasso* (1981). This water-covered glass cube contains Modernista furniture cut through by iron beams and draped cloth, and reflects the importance of industry and

Col·legi d'Arquitectes

the working-class rebellion during Picasso's time in Barcelona. Quotations by Picasso decorate the bottom of the sculpture, including: 'A painting is not intended to decorate a drawing room but is instead a ... of attack and defence against the enemy.' Turning ... he Born, you'll find a wealth of dining options on the **Plaça Comercial**.

▶ *Budgets include transport, meals and admission prices, but not accommodation or shopping*

La Llotja

When to Visit

Barcelona by season

Thanks to its cultural riches, Barcelona can be enjoyed at any time of year. But each season brings its own character and atmosphere to the city, not to mention a calendar full of special events and festivals (*see pp210-225* Events).

Spring

Barcelona's high season starts earlier and earlier, and by Easter, hotels have seen their prices rise and their rooms fill. The weather can be changeable around this time of year, and most rain will fall in March and April, although showers tend not to last too long. Watch out for the feast day of **Sant Jordi** (*see p215*) at the end of April when red roses decorate the city's many statues and paintings of George in all his dragon-slaying glory. The increasingly popular **Primavera Sound** (*see p213*) happens at the end of May.

Summer

Barcelona does not normally get as hot as, for example, Madrid, but it is humid in summer, which can be debilitating. July and August are busy times for tourists, but the streets are notably free of traffic, since Catalans melt away to their families' second homes after **Sant Joan** (*see p218*) to recover from several weeks of nighttime festivities. Complete with terrace parties, urban beaches and a Vitamin D-induced buzz, the city is at its finest in summer.

Primavera Sound

Festes de la Mercè

Sardana dancing *p215*

Santa Eulàlia

Autumn

The sea stays warm enough to swim in well into September, and occasionally October, and temperatures are comfortably mild. November can be rainy, but is a quiet month with lower prices. Lots of festivals take place in September and October: one of the best is **Festes de la Mercè** (*see p221*), which marks the end of the hot summer.

Winter

December and January throw up some beautifully sunny days and can be surprisingly mild. **Christmas** is a magical time in Barcelona (*see p224* Christmas & New Year Celebrations), but the downside is that many places close for a couple of weeks. February is a quiet month, though it can feel quite cold and overcast. The festival of **Santa Eulàlia** (*see p223*) helps to gear up for **Carnaval** (*see p225*), where everything is completely over the top.

Barcelona Today

The city in flux

Over the last couple of decades, Barcelona has undergone a massive makeover to emerge from being an overlooked backwater to one of Europe's most popular cities. Around the turn of the millennium, however, the most dramatic change was that seen in the population, with a sixfold increase in foreign residents. This multiculturalism has contributed to the city's coming of age and yet, unlike elsewhere, there has been almost no xenophobic backlash. Meanwhile, the issue of Catalan independence rumbles on, fuelled by a central Spanish government that seems to do everything in its power to stoke the fires of nationalism.

Catalan independence flags

Influx of immigrants

For someone visiting Barcelona for the first time in, say, 15 years, the most striking change is in the city's human face. In 2000, the city had just 46,000 foreign residents; today there are 262,000, or 16 per cent of the population (43 per cent in the Old City, the part most tourists visit). In 2000, the word 'immigrant' was still used to refer to people from elsewhere in Spain and from the southern provinces of Murcia and Andalucía in particular. Now the immigrants hail from all over the world, although they divide roughly into three groups of more or less equal numbers: Europeans, Latin Americans and North Africans. Recent years have also seen a significant influx of people from Asia, principally China and Pakistan. Some 75 per cent of immigrants to the city are under 40 and close to a third have a university education.

This nascent multiculturalism has contributed to what might be described as Barcelona's coming of age as a modern city, transforming it from a provincial, inward-looking town to a global city. As in many European capitals, your waitress is as likely to be from Bratislava as Barcelona, the shop

Multiculturalism has contributed to Barcelona's coming of age as a modern city

Foreign residents now make up a sixth of the city's population.

assistant from Ecuador or Colombia, and your taxi driver from Eastern Europe or Pakistan.

These immigrants have injected new cultures, new languages and new cuisines into the city's life and, despite this rapid transition from being a largely Catalan-Spanish city to an international one, there has been little of the xenophobia that is on the rise in other European cities. The race card is not the vote winner that it is, for example, in France. The Plataforma per Catalunya (PxC) campaigned against immigration in both the 2010 and 2012 elections, but with minimal political success, and by the election of 2015 had almost no profile at all.

Room for improvement

However, Barcelona's coming of age has not been problem-free. Air pollution regularly exceeds World Health Organisation limits, particularly nitrous oxide pollution produced by diesel engines. The city seems reluctant to crack down on car use, despite excellent and affordable public transport and a rapidly expanding network of cycle lanes. Homelessness, too, is becoming endemic, with an estimated 1,000 people sleeping rough in the city every night and another 2,000 in shelters. Poverty has created an underground economy of marginalised people, who, for example, collect cardboard boxes from the Chinese clothing wholesalers, and then sell them on to be shipped back to China for recycling. Illegal immigrants, mostly Africans, criss-cross the city with shopping trolleys collecting scrap metal or sell pirated DVDs, sunglasses and handbags down by Port Vell. Prostitution is widespread and, much to the city authorities' chagrin, highly visible, especially in popular tourist areas such as La Rambla. Police and NGOs estimate that over 80 per cent of the city's prostitutes have been trafficked and are, in effect, sex slaves. Several of the city's stag party websites offer a trip to a local *puti club* as part of the package.

The city seems reluctant to crack down on car use, despite excellent and affordable public transport and a rapidly expanding network of cycle lanes

March for independence on La Diada Nacional de Catalunya.

Bag-snatching continues to plague the city and, thanks to a legal loophole, goes largely unpunished, but overall Barcelona is a safe city. There is little violence, and public drunkenness and the anti-social behaviour that comes with it are rare, among the residents at least.

In another sign of the times, Barcelona has become another city where absentee foreigners are buying up property in far greater numbers than the locals, often negatively affecting the life of the neighbourhood.

Independents' day

The other big change in recent years has been in the political landscape. Having previously occupied the political margins, the Catalan independence movement took centre stage in 2012 and continues to dominate the scene, with a series of spectacular demonstrations, often over one million strong. The momentum was fuelled by the Madrid government's attitude: as it vacillated between provocation and indifference, it served as the secessionists' greatest recruiting sergeant.

The 2014 Catalan regional election was billed as a plebiscite on independence but the *indepes* failed to win 50 per cent of the popular

Art Attack

Shops and street artists are coming together to brighten up the city

Call it art, call it vandalism. Either way, the city council wasn't pleased when shopkeepers and artists got together to do something about the spraypaint tagging that plagues Barcelona. The city's taggers aren't fussed about where they spray – ancient doors, historic monuments and, above all, the steel shutters that cover shopfronts. The city's clean-up brigades wash the tags off walls but can't touch the shutters, which are at least partly the responsibility of the shopkeepers. So two groups, Persianas Lliures (Free Roller Blinds) and Enrotlla't, approached shopkeepers with the idea of selecting an artist on their books to paint their shutters, with the degree of artistic licence to be agreed by the two parties. In one weekend, Enrotlla't painted 47 shutters in the Gràcia district. To the taggers, who perhaps see themselves as artists too, the painted shutters are out of bounds and they remain tag-free. Terrific. A civic solution to a civic problem, and one that brightens up the built environment.

Terrific, that is, unless you're the council, which has started fining shopkeepers €600 a time for what it regards as vandalism. But Jordi Llobell, Enrotlla't's founder, argues that its mission is to encourage the best art. 'The shopkeepers can visit our website (www.enrotllat.org), see the work of the various artists and choose the one that is most to their taste,' he says. 'It's a huge contradiction that the city won't let us paint in public spaces, even with the owners' permission, when the same council mounts expensive exhibitions about graffiti in galleries.' However, through an initiative called Murs Lliures (Free Walls) city districts have begun ceding spaces where graffiti artists can work unmolested.

vote and only managed to cobble together a pro-independence government through the unlikely coalition of the centre-right nationalists and a small far-left party. Since then, the government has been developing parallel institutions such as a 'foreign ministry' and a tax department as part of what it calls the process towards independence, while spending millions on promoting the international profile of Catalonia as an independent state-in-waiting. A referendum is planned for 2017, but unless it's sanctioned by Madrid, which seems hardly likely, it won't be legally binding. Besides, the appetite for independence has begun to wane, perhaps out of weariness at the lack of progress, with recent polls showing barely 45 per cent in favour.

Calatrava's communications tower – built for the 1992 Olympic Games – is a symbol of the city's regeneration at that time.

The prospect of an independent Catalonia having to leave the European Union, as Brussels insists it would, is also a factor. Catalans, and most Spaniards, are deeply pro-European and the prospect of being a small state cut off from the mainstream is not an appealing one, least of all to business in the region. Many multinationals have chosen to locate their Spanish or European headquarters in Barcelona to have access to the Spanish and European markets, not to be isolated from them.

There has never been as much enthusiasm for independence in Barcelona as there has in smaller Catalan towns and villages. In 2014, the city elected Ada Colau as mayor in spite of her disavowal of the independence project. Colau is a product of the city's long and sometimes violent tradition of radical, communitarian politics. Colau's group – not a party as such – stood on a platform of social issues such as housing, jobs and education (issues that had been pushed aside amid the nationalist fervour), and won. The group has now extended itself beyond the city and aims to contest the next regional election on a similar platform. Were it to win, the sovereignty dispute would probably cease to be the dominant theme of Catalan political life.

The appetite for independence has begun to wane, perhaps out of weariness at the lack of progress

The city's changing face

Physically, the city has changed little since its Olympian transformation in the 1980s and '90s. Spain's long-running financial crisis has called time on Barcelona's love affair with signature architecture. Even before her death, Zaha Hadid's Spiralling Tower had been put on ice, as was Sir Norman Foster's reworking of FC Barcelona's Camp Nou stadium and Frank Gehry's tower at the site of the new high-speed rail station at La Sagrera. The only building of any note constructed in the last decade is the vast and gleaming W Hotel at the southern end of Barceloneta beach.

The economy continues to be buoyed up by tourism and the lucrative conference circuit, but there is growing friction between residents and visitors, whose numbers have increased tenfold in as many years. Although the city authorities have introduced a moratorium on new hotels and are cracking down on illegal holiday apartments, visitor numbers in 2016 broke all records, especially from the UK, despite the Brexit-weakened pound. Furthermore, although people are coming in greater numbers, they are spending less. If Barcelona is to avoid becoming another Venice, a victim of its own success, it will need to prioritise quality over quantity.

Spain's long-running financial crisis has called time on Barcelona's love affair with signature architecture

The grid-like Eixample has seen little new architecture in recent years.

Eating & Drinking

Tradition rubs shoulders with innovation

Barcelona's dining scene has proved itself remarkably resilient to recession, and while most other sectors have struggled through the last decade, the city's restaurants have thrived, increased in number and expanded in scope – although it's as difficult as it ever was to bag an unreserved table at a good restaurant on a Friday night. Bars and cafés also seem to be weathering the crisis, with few closures and no perceptible slowdown in business. This is partly explained by local habits. Catalans tend not to entertain at home, so the bar is as crucial a meeting place as ever, while restaurants are kept afloat by the continuing brisk trade in lunchtime *menús del día* for the workers – the sandwich habit has never really caught on in Spain.

Fideuà

Catalan cuisine

Catalan cooking is defined by certain characteristics, such as the *sofregit* and *picada* (*see p42*) that form the base for so many dishes. The former is the foundation for soups, stews, rice and noodle dishes, and for most traditional sauces; it's the first thing in the pot. The latter gets stirred in a few minutes before the dish in question has finished cooking, and fills in all the gaps in flavour and texture. The Catalans also mix fruit with meat or fowl: duck or goose with pears, and apples stuffed with minced pork are specialities of the Empordà region of Catalonia, and *allioli* thickened with puréed apple or quince is a common accompaniment to roast rabbit or pork in the Pyrenees. Local cooks also combine seafood and poultry and/or meat in the class of dishes called *mar i muntanya*, or 'sea and mountain'.

(*see p42*)

In the know
Price categories

All our restaurant listings are marked with a euro symbol category, indicating the price you should expect to pay for a standard main course. The final bill will of course depend on the number of courses and drinks consumed.

€ = under €10

€€ = €10-€20

€€€ = €20-€30

€€€€ = over €30

Albert Adrià at Tickets

New ideas

At the luxury end of the dining spectrum, many of Barcelona's top chefs have adapted to the effects of economic uncertainty by creating diffusion lines – some are now offering catering for people to eat at home, and others have opened lower-key, more affordable eateries. As ever, superchef Ferran Adrià's influence played a part, particularly in tapas bar **Tickets** (*see p148*), which he helped his brother Albert set up. Albert now also has the more affordable **Bodega 1900** (C/Tamarit 91, 93 325 2659, www.bodega1900.com) across the road, among other restaurants. Chef Carles Abellan has closed his flagship, Michelin-starred Comerç 24, but never stands still, and has opened several other ventures around town, the most popular of which is still **Tapas 24** (*see p165*), with **Suculent** (*see p116*) close behind it.

An increasing number of great mid-range restaurants have expats at the helm, such as the excellent **Caravelle** (*see p115*) in the Raval; **Les Tres a la Cuina** (*see p178*) and **Café Godot** (*see p176*) in Gràcia, and **Lascar 74** in Poble Sec (*see p148*).

Drink up

After the welcome comeback of Moritz beer, brewed in Barcelona and preferred by many to the ubiquitous Estrella, came an explosion in craft beers, now widely available everywhere and no longer confined to tap rooms such as **Garage** (*see p170*). Shandy (*clara*) is also popular, here made with bitter lemon and very refreshing in summer. Sangría is rarely offered outside tourist traps.

Catalan wines are becoming better known internationally as they improve, and it's worth looking out for the local DOs, as well as the commonplace Penedès (*see p38* Catalonia Uncorked). Most wine drunk here is red (*negre/tinto*), apart from the many cavas, which run

TAPAS

BERBERECHOS	6.50	
BOQUERONES	3.80	
BUÑUELOS DE BACA.	5.50	
ENSALADILLA	3.50	
EMPANADA	4.30	
SARDINITAS	5.90	
MEJILLONES	5.40	
SEPIETAS SALT	S/M	
PIMIENTOS P	4.40	
GIRGOLAS	4.90	
JAMON DE JABUGO		
Y MAS ...	11.50	

❤ Best bars

Dry Martini *p170*
Old-school bartenders and generous measures.

Ginger *p86*
Local wines, cocktails and excellent music.

Paradiso *p102*
Enter through the fridge to find this little speakeasy.

**In the know
Cañas all round**

If you want draught beer, ask for a *caña*, which is a small measure; tourists invariably request *cerveza*, which is a bottled beer.

Catalonia Uncorked

The region's love affair with wine

Around 25 years ago, an all-Catalan wine list would have been brief. It would have listed cava and a handful of decent reds and whites from the Penedès region; probably a white from a single producer in Alella, near Barcelona; a celebrated dessert wine made near the beach resort of Sitges; and, just possibly, an example or two of the unusual fortified wine called *vi ranci*, literally 'rancid wine' (for its sour character), from an obscure region called the Priorat. Anything else would have been for local consumption only, not deserving of a wider audience.

Today, the Penedès is almost as well known for table wines – many of them produced by the massive Torres firm – as for sparklers. The Priorat has turned into one of the most famous wine regions in Europe, notable for its full-bodied (and pricey) reds. The Empordà *denominación*, which encompasses much of the Costa Brava, is Spain's most exciting up-and-coming wineland. And bottlings from areas that few outside the immediate vicinity had even heard of a couple of decades ago – Conca de Barberà, Costers del Segre, Montsant, Pla de Bages, Terra Alta – are finding space on wine-shop shelves and in restaurants all over the world.

For better or for worse, many of the newer wines of Catalonia are based on classic French varieties, which means they are intense and extracted and full of oak. Chardonnay, cabernet sauvignon, merlot, sauvignon blanc, pinot noir, syrah: you'll find them all here, but naturally some are better than others. More interesting are the whites made from indigenous varieties such as macabeo, perallada and especially xarel·lo, the three traditional cava grapes, and from garnatxa blanca (grenache blanc). A usually insipid cultivar, known as picpoul in southern France but called picapoll in Catalonia, produces an unexpectedly charming white in Pla de Bagès.

For reds, ull de llebre (hare's eye), the local name for tempranillo, yields some pleasant wines, but the great successes are garnatxa and carinyena (carignan). The latter is at the heart of many of the Priorat's finest reds, and both grapes do very well in the area, in neighbouring Montsant and in the Empordà, where the results are less concentrated but often more elegant. Add together all these varieties and you'll end up with an all-Catalan wine list that would be unrecognisable from a quarter of a century ago.

▶ *To explore the Penedès and Priorat regions yourself, see p206 Wine Country.*

from *semi-sec* ('half-dry', but actually pretty sweet) to *brut nature* (very dry). Freixenet is the best known, but there are better cavas, including Parxet and Llopart.

Coffee in Barcelona is mostly strong and mostly good. The three basic types are *solo* (also known simply as *café*), a small strong black coffee; *cortado*, the same but with a little milk; and *café con leche*, the same with more milk. An *americano* is black coffee diluted with more water, and *carajillo* is a short, black coffee with a liberal dash of brandy. Decaffeinated coffee (*descafeinado*) is popular and widely available, but specify *de máquina* (from the machine) unless you want instant (*de sobre*).

Tea is pretty poor and generally best avoided. If you can't live without it, ask for cold milk on the side ('*leche fría aparte*') or run the risk of getting a glass of hot milk and a teabag.

Tapas tips

Tapas are not especially popular in Barcelona, though there are some excellent options, including **Bormuth** (*see p103*), **Tapas 24** and **Quimet i Quimet**. The custom of giving a free tapa with a drink is almost unheard of in Catalonia.

Slightly different from the archetypal Spanish tapas bars are *pintxo bars* their Basque origin means that the word is always given in Euskera – such as **Euskal Etxea** (*see p103*). A *pintxo* (be careful not to confuse it with the Spanish term *pincho*, which refers to a very small tapa) consists of some ingenious culinary combination on a small slice of bread. Platters of them are usually brought out at particular times, often around 1pm and again at 8pm. *Pintxos* come impaled on toothpicks, which you keep on your plate so that the barman can tally them up at the end. Sadly, Brits hold the worst reputation for abusing this eminently civilised system by 'forgetting' to hand over all their toothpicks.

♥ Best tapas

La Cova Fumada *p131*
Family-run, chaotic and utterly authentic.

Tapas 24 *p165*
Return to the classics from a Michelin-starred chef.

Quimet i Quimet *p149*
Barcelona's favourite tapas bar is the size of a wardrobe.

A *pintxo* consists of some ingenious culinary combination on a small slice of bread.

Without a decent grasp of the language, tapas bars can be quite intimidating unless you know exactly what you want. Don't be afraid to seek guidance, but some of the more standard offerings will include *tortilla* (potato omelette), *patatas bravas* (fried potatoes in a spicy red sauce with garlic mayonnaise), *ensaladilla* (Russian salad), *pinchos morunos* (small pork skewers), *champiñones al ajillo* (mushrooms fried in garlic), *gambas al ajillo* (prawns and garlic), *mejillones a la marinera* (mussels in a tomato and onion sauce), *chocos* (squid fried in batter), *almejas al vapor* (steamed clams with garlic and parsley), *pulpo* (octopus) and *pimientos del padrón* (little green peppers, one or two of which will kick like an angry mule, in a vegetable Russian roulette).

Order, order

The concept of 'rounds' is unknown here; instead, drinks are tallied up and paid for when you leave. There are some exceptions, mostly in tourist-oriented or very busy places, where you may be asked to pay as you order, particularly if you sit out on the terrace. To attract a waiter's attention, a loud but polite *'oiga'* or, in Catalan,

❤ Best seafood

Can Majó *p128*
Traditional fish dishes on a seaside terrace.

Kaiku *p129*
Paella with a difference.

La Paradeta *p102*
Shellfish picked from a gleaming display and cooked to order.

In the know
A lot of bottle

Tap water is perfectly safe but quite heavily chlorinated in Barcelona (despite recent improvements), so most people drink bottled. Spaniards often prefer their water served at room temperature; ask for it *fría* if you want it chilled.

'*escolti*' is acceptable. On the vexed question of throwing detritus on the floor (cigarette ends, olive pits and so on), it's safest to keep an eye on what the locals are doing.

Kitchens usually open around 1.30pm or 2pm and go on until roughly 3.30pm or 4pm; dinner is served from about 9pm until 11.30pm or midnight. Some restaurants open earlier in the evening, but arriving before 9.30pm or 10pm generally means you'll be dining alone or in the company of other foreigners. Reserving a table is generally a good idea – not only on Friday and Saturday nights, but also on Sunday evenings and Monday lunchtimes, when few restaurants are open. Many also close for holidays, including about a week over Easter, and the month of August. We have listed closures of more than a week wherever we can, but restaurants are fickle.

Moritz beer was first brewed in Barcelona in 1856. Production stopped for nearly three decades from 1978, but the tipple is now firmly back on the drinks menu.

The price is right

For US and UK visitors particularly, eating out in Barcelona is not as cheap as it used to be, but low mark-ups on wines keep the cost relatively reasonable. The majority of restaurants serve an economical, fixed-price *menú del día* at lunchtime; this usually consists of a starter, main course, dessert, bread and something to drink.

Laws governing the issue of prices are often flouted, but, legally, menus must declare if the ten per cent IVA (VAT) is included in prices or not (it rarely is), and also if there is a cover charge (generally expressed as a charge for bread).

Pimientos del padrón can kick like an angry mule, in a vegetable Russian roulette

**In the know
Tipping tips**

Catalans, and the Spanish in general, tend to tip very little, often rounding up to the nearest euro, but tourists should let their conscience decide.

Catalan Dishes

A primer of local cuisine

Here is a selection of dishes considered to be classically Catalan. It's also worth noting that many dishes apparently from other cuisines – risotto, canelloni, ravioli – are entrenched in the Catalan culinary tradition. Two names borrowed from the French are foie (as opposed to *fetge/hígado* or foie gras), which has come to mean hare, duck or goose liver *mi-cuit* with liqueur, salt and sugar; and *coulant*, like a small soufflé but melting in the centre. For a full glossary of food terms, see *p311*.

a la llauna 'in the tin' – baked on a metal tray with garlic, tomato, paprika and wine

allioli garlic crushed with olive oil to form a mayonnaise-like texture, similar to *aïoli*

amanida catalana/*ensalada catalana* mixed salad with a range of cold meats

arròs negre/*arroz negro* 'black rice', seafood rice cooked in squid ink

botifarra/*butifarra* Catalan sausage; variants include *botifarra negre* (blood sausage) and *blanca* (mixed with egg)

botifarra amb mongetes/*butifarra con judías* sausage with haricot beans

calçots variety of large spring onion, only available from December to spring, and eaten chargrilled with *romesco* sauce

carn d'olla traditional Christmas dish of various meats stewed with *escudella*, then served separately

conill amb cargols/*conejo con caracoles* rabbit with snails

crema catalana cold custardy dessert with burned sugar topping, similar to crème brûlée

escalivada grilled and peeled peppers, onions and aubergine

escudella winter stew of meat and vegetables

espinacs a la catalana/*espinacas a la catalana* spinach fried in olive oil with garlic, raisins and pine nuts

esqueixada summer salad of shredded, marinated salt cod with onions, olives and tomato

fideuà/*fideuá* paella made with vermicelli instead of rice

mar i muntanya a traditional Catalan combination of meat and seafood, such as lobster and chicken in the same dish

mel i mató curd cheese with honey

pa amb tomàquet/*pan con tomate* bread with tomato, oil and salt

picada mix of nuts, garlic, parsley, bread, chocolate and little chilli peppers, often used to enrich and thicken dishes

romesco a spicy sauce from the coast south of Barcelona, made with crushed almonds and hazelnuts, tomatoes, oil and a special type of red pepper called *nyora*

samfaina a mix of onion, garlic, aubergine and red and green peppers (similar to ratatouille)

sarsuela/*zarzuela* fish and seafood stew

sofregit a base for many sauces, made with caramelised onion, tomato and olive oil, occasionally with sugar

sípia amb mandonguilles/*sepia con albóndigas* cuttlefish with meatballs

suquet de peix/*suquet de pescado* stew made with fish (generally monkfish), shellfish and potatoes

torrades/*tostadas* toasted *pa amb tomàquet*

xató salad containing tuna, anchovies and cod, with a *romesco*-type sauce

Crema catalana

WORLD'S FAVOURITE
CITIES SINCE 1968...

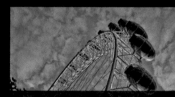

WHERE NEXT?

Shopping

From mainstream malls to backstreet boutiques

As is the case in most other major cities around the world, the high-street chains grow ever more ubiquitous in Barcelona. However, although the credit crunch has picked off many small start-ups, plenty of alternatives remain. Barcelona is still known for its old specialist shops, many of which have been family-run for generations; there's nowhere better to browse for just the right votive candle or handmade soap. Fashion is another strong point: head up Passeig de Gràcia and beyond to the Avinguda Diagonal for high fashion and couture, or trawl the Born, the Raval and Gràcia for an ever-changing line-up of local designers selling from hole-in-the-wall shops.

Survival mode

Strolling down the golden retail belts of Portal de l'Angel, Rambla de Catalunya or Passeig de Gràcia, you would never know there's been a recession, and indeed new designers regularly set up shop here. Down the side streets, however, owners of small shops have had to adapt to survive with food and wine shops such as **Formatgeria La Seu** (*see p87*) and **Vila Viniteca** (*see p105*) holding regular tastings or taking part in food markets. Small designers have sought safety in numbers, forming collectives and making their clothes in workshops attached to the storefront. Vintage stores are also growing steadily in popularity, particularly in the Raval and Gràcia, with many stocking repurposed garments on the side.

Large malls continue to thrive and multiply: the latest is the Richard Rogers-designed **Las Arenas**, constructed from the former bullring on Plaça Espanya.

♥ Best shops

La Boqueria *p84*
Chaotic and colourful, this huge food market is a sight in itself.

Flors Navarro *p166*
Open 24/7, the sweetly scented flower market makes for an unearthly late-night stop.

El Ingenio *p87*
A wonderfully old-fashioned joke and toy shop, where Barna's *capgrossos* ('fat-heads') are made.

Casa Gispert *p104*
Follow your nose to Casa Gispert, which has been roasting nuts and coffee for over a century.

Las Arenas *p138*

Small is beautiful

It is Barcelona's wealth of tiny independent shops that really makes it unique as a shopping destination, although it can be hard to see how the shops devoted to a single obscure speciality such as felt dolls, knives or retro vinyl can possibly survive. Look out for the dressmakers and one-off fashion boutiques in the Born; the indie art galleries of the upper Raval; the traditional artisans, antique shops and speciality food stores of the Barri Gòtic and the quirky jewellery workshops and vintage clothes shops of Gràcia. These shops are also among the most photogenic in the city, often holding treasures such as the ancient butter-making machinery in **Formatgeria La Seu**, the old toasting ovens at **Casa Gispert** or the medieval Jewish baths at **Caelum** (*see p86*).

The wealth of tiny independent shops makes the city unique

Els Encants *p166*

Market forces

In the Ajuntament's book, a revamped local market is the first step on the road to urban regeneration. The latest is the stunning new designer home for the **Els Encants** flea market (*see p166*), but this was true for the **Mercat de Santa Caterina** in Sant Pere and the **Mercat de la Barceloneta**, both spectacular pieces of architecture in their own right and the catalysts for reinventing previously downtrodden neighbourhoods. In an attempt to fuse modern and traditional approaches to shopping, the new markets tend to hold far fewer actual stalls than before, with more space turned over to supermarkets and restaurants. The largest of the current projects is the complete overhaul of the **Mercat Sant Antoni**, set to include three new subterranean floors, while retaining its spectacular iron Modernista shell. Meanwhile, its stalls have been moved to provisional buildings on the Ronda de Sant Antoni between C/Casanova and C/Urgell.

> **In the Ajuntament's book, a revamped local market is the first step on the road to urban regeneration**

In the know
Museum finds

Museum shops are some of the best places to find great presents, or books on art, design and architecture. In particular, try the **MACBA** (see *p111*), **CaixaForum** (see *p141*) and **Museu d'Història de Barcelona** (see *p79*).

Paradigm thrift

The Spanish have always been wary of the second-hand concept, and there are few charity shops and – until recently – fewer flea markets (the rambling Els Encants, in its fancy new incarnation, is one exception). This seems to be changing, not, as one would imagine, because of the recession, but because of the rise of vintage shops and the whole hipster retro concept. This is bad news for IKEA but good news for the planet. Good, and regular, flea markets include **Lost & Found** (www.lostfoundmarket.com), which is usually held at the beach, and **Flea Market Barcelona** (www.fleamarketbcn.com), which normally happens in the Raval – check the websites for details and dates. C/Riera Baixa in the northern part of the Raval is a short strip of vintage clothes shops, and you'll find several others in this area.

Shopping practicalities

Most shops don't open until 10am and close for lunch from 2pm; after lunch, they're usually open from 5pm until about 8pm. Many small shops also close on Saturday afternoons and all day on Monday. Note that if you're paying by credit card, you usually have to show photo ID, such as a passport or a driving licence.

The rate of sales tax (IVA) depends on the type of product: it's currently ten per cent on food and 21 per cent on most other items. In any of the 700 or so shops that display a Tax-Free Shopping sticker on their door, non-EU residents can request a Tax-Free Cheque on purchases of more than €90.15 (see www.aena-aeropuertos.es or www.global-blue.com for further information). Before leaving the EU, these must be stamped at customs and can immediately be reclaimed in cash at the airport branches of La Caixa bank or Global Blue (or from refund offices in your home country).

Bargain hunters should note that the sales (*rebaixes/rebajas*) begin after the retail

In the know
Bargain fashion

One of Barcelona's hotspots for bargain clothes shopping is C/Girona. In particular, the two blocks between C/Ausiàs Marc and Gran Via de les Corts Catalanes are crammed with remainder stores and factory outlets of varying quality. By far the most popular is the Mango Outlet (C/Girona 37, 93 412 29 35).

Louis Vuitton is just one of the designer names to be found on Passeig de Gràcia.

orgy of Christmas and Epiphany, running from 7 January to mid February, and return during July and August. Taking goods back, even when they're faulty, can be difficult. For consumer rights, *see p301*.

Where to shop

Barri Gòtic

The Saturday afternoon hordes head to the big-name chain stores that line Avinguda Portal de l'Àngel and C/Portaferrissa, but there are plenty of less mainstream retail options. It's possible to spend hours browsing antiques on C/Banys Nous, where tiny shops specialise in furniture, posters or textiles. The streets around Plaça Sant Jaume house some lovely, old-fashioned stores selling hats, candles, traditional toys and stationery. For something more modern, try the independent boutiques on C/Avinyó, which offer affordable, streetwise fashion and household items with a twist.

It's possible to spend hours browsing antiques on C/Banys Nous

Born and Sant Pere

The streets leading off the Passeig del Born form a warren of stylish little boutiques offering quality, rather than quantity. Hip music, intimidating sales assistants and heartbreaking prices are part of the shopping experience, but so are gorgeous clothing, shoes and accessories from a clique of fast-rising local and international designers. Nearby C/Argenteria was named after its denizen silversmiths, and a handful of shops there follow the tradition, selling affordable, if mainstream, trinkets.

Raval
The Raval's shopping, concentrated on the streets between the Boqueria market and Plaça dels Àngels, has a youthful bent: head to C/Riera Baixa and C/Tallers for second-hand clothing and streetwear, and C/Bonsuccès for specialist record shops. C/Doctor Dou and C/Elisabets feature some trendy boutiques and shoe shops; the latter also has a couple of design stores. C/Pelai, along the Raval's top edge, has an impressive number of shoe stores.

Barceloneta and the Ports
Barcelona's seafront shopping is concentrated in the shopping centre of Maremagnum, which houses a large, if sterile, collection of high-street fashion stores that are at least open late.

Eixample
Passeig de Gràcia is home to enough high-fashion and statement jewellery to satisfy a footballer's wife. Chanel, Dior, Stella McCartney and friends are present and correct, as are many Spanish luxury brands. A stone's throw away, the tree-lined Rambla de Catalunya offers high-street fashion and cute kids' boutiques.

Gràcia and other districts
Independent shops rule in bohemian Gràcia: head to C/Verdi or the streets around Plaça Vila de Gràcia and – increasingly – the streets north of here, for quirky little boutiques selling clothing, accessories and gifts.

In the know
Out-of-town outlets

Designer bargain-hunters should make the half-hour pilgrimage out of the city to **La Roca Village** (93 842 39 39, www.larocavillage.com). More than 50 discount outlets will tempt you with designer apparel from brands such as Missoni, Versace, Diesel and Armani.

Hip music, intimidating sales assistants and heartbreaking prices are part of the shopping experience

Gaudí & Modernisme

Meet Antoni Gaudí, devout Christian and visionary architect

Over the last century or so, the public images of architect Antoni Gaudí and the city of Barcelona have virtually blended into one. Crazy paving and splintered shards of tile, surrealist distortions marching across rooftops like injured golems, kaleidoscopic explosions of garish colour: the city has almost grown to be defined by the creations of its most famous architectural son. Images of Gaudí's buildings are commonly used by television companies and publishing firms as shorthand for the city's exoticism; a handful have become local icons. Gaudí's work has transformed Barcelona into a virtual pilgrimage site, with many visitors praying at the feet of the high priest of kitsch. But while some commune directly with buildings pinned by many as masterpieces, others see the architect's work as a collection of mere freak shows. Who's right?

▶*About the author*
Gijs van Hensbergen is the author of Gaudí *and* The Sagrada Família *(see p313).*

La Sagrada Família

In pursuit of a quarry

On the surface, Gaudí can appear to be a shameless showman, an attention-grabbing eccentric. But behind the raw energy and daring is an innate sense of design. Without it, the buildings might have survived, but they surely wouldn't have endured. Like the city in which he worked, Gaudí seduces us with first impressions that help to foster the illusion that everything is simply skin-deep. But there's more to both Gaudí and Barcelona than that.

To discover the flesh and bones that underpin a Gaudí structure, there's no better place to start than **La Pedrera** ('the quarry'), which is the generally accepted nickname for the Casa Milà (*see p160*) on the Passeig de Gràcia. Perhaps more than any other Gaudí building, this rocky behemoth demonstrates that behind the showman lay a skilled, radical engineer. Unlike almost all his architectural rivals, Gaudí came from *menestral* (artisan) stock, and was reared among the working-class craftsmen of Catalonia.

Born in 1852 in provincial Reus, now about two hours south of Barcelona by train, Gaudí drew his early inspirations not from other architects but from his boilermaker father's dexterity in creating three-dimensional space, and what he later called 'the great book of nature'. From early in his life and career, Gaudí could think just as comfortably with his hands as with his head. These twin skills are visible at La Pedrera. Built between 1906 and 1909 as a luxury apartment block, its undulating forms echo the swell of the Mediterranean and the rocky crags of the nearby Collserola hills.

A century ago, La Pedrera qualified as enormously avant-garde. Newspapers of the time were filled with cartoons of the building, which some nicknamed a 'Zeppelin hangar'. Even today, it still appears curious. However, in the interpretation centre, Gaudí's rationale

You can dine in Modernista surroundings at Casa Calvet (*see p162*).

Unlike almost all his architectural rivals, Gaudí came from artisan stock, and was reared among the working-class craftsmen of Catalonia

Strange Truths

Some little-known facts surrounding Barcelona's favourite son

As a child, Gaudí was so badly afflicted by rheumatism that he would ride around on a donkey.

As a young man, he was oddly preoccupied with fashion, and would have his hats and kid gloves specially made.

For much of his life, he lived chiefly on nuts and lettuce leaves dipped in milk.

The word 'gaudy', contrary to popular belief, has nothing to do with Gaudí and dates back to Shakespeare.

On 11 September 1924, Catalan National Day, he was arrested for refusing to speak to a policeman in anything but Catalan.

Gaudí also refused to speak in Spanish when he was introduced to King Alfonso XIII.

He was a reluctant draughtsman and would instead make models using whatever was to hand, from vegetables to mud.

The Pokémon film *The Rise of Darkrai* featured a building based on the Sagrada Família and an architect called Gaudy.

His belief in the superiority of the Catalan people led to an insistence that the model for Jesus on the Sagrada Família could be no other nationality.

Picasso and Gaudí enjoyed a mutual loathing.

He was suspicious of spectacle-wearers and felt that poor eyesight would be cured with exercise.

George Orwell called the Sagrada Família 'the most hideous building in the world'.

Gaudí used the corpses of stillborn infants to make casts for the *Massacre of the Innocents*.

For various bird and animal figures, he would chloroform live creatures and use them as casts.

He was a firm believer in homeopathy and vegetarianism.

After he was hit by a tram, several cab drivers refused to take his unconscious body to a hospital, suspecting he was a beggar who would be unable to pay.

In 1987, the Alan Parsons Project released an album called *Gaudí*, inspired by his life and work.

is explained with a collection of models, plans, drawings and scaled-down versions of his structural 'toys'. No aspect of Gaudí's life and career is more deceptively simple than the architect's revolutionary idea that gravity and God, working hand in hand, could shape the way we build. Take a chain, hold it in two hands, invert its natural swaggy shape with a mirror and, lo and behold, you have a catenary

The roofscape of La Pedrera is both uplifting and disturbing (see p160).

arch, one of nature's most resistant and structurally efficient shapes.

Climb the spiral staircase and head out on to the roof, and you enter a fairytale landscape of sci-fi chimneys and playful towers. Initially spirit-lifting, they grow increasingly disturbing with reflection, like other-worldly centurions. This is Gaudí the Catholic at work; even the wealthiest tenants needed moral guidance, he thought, perhaps more than most. Like the building's privileged former residents stealing a few moments of peace and quiet up on the roof, we're caught in a kind of purgatory, between heaven and the everyday 'hell' below.

With Gaudí, everything had the potential for spiritual meaning. However, his buildings could also be fantastically practical. Go back down to the recently restored 'Pis' – Catalan for flat – and marvel at how the naturally lit spaces flow from one end to the other. There's just one dividing

Climb the spiral staircase and head out on to the roof, and you enter a fairytale landscape of sci-fi chimneys and playful towers

line: the kitchen's sliding doors, separating the
worlds of service and noisy children from the
bourgeois parents' plumped-up cushions and
the serious demands of social intercourse and
hard-headed business. In the office, the framed
stock and share certificates speak plainly of the
Catalan gift for business that underpins this
appetite for fancy. Gaudí was such a product
of his time and place that it's impossible
to imagine his works being conceived and
completed in any other era.

His master's choice

Gaudí's rise went hand in hand with Catalonia's
growing sense of its identity. The Renaixença,
a literary and artistic movement that promoted
all things Catalan, needed an appropriate and
defining architecture. Gaudí was on hand to
create it, providing Catalonia's politicians
and ruling elite with just what they needed:
made from expensive materials, such as onyx,
tortoiseshell and exquisite cast bronze, and
with a design that artfully triggered 'imperial'
echoes while mixing the Ruskinian obsession
with craft and the decadent perfume of the
fin de siècle. No building offers as enticing a
window into this world as the **Palau Güell** (*see
p113*), a masterpiece also notable for the fact
that when Gaudí started building the palace
in 1886, he found, in the shape of Don Eusebi
Güell, his patron for life.

Palau Güell was placed symbolically at the
crossroads of two very distinct worlds, just a
stone's throw from La Rambla and the exclusive
Liceu opera house. On the street, prostitution,
criminality and urban decay prevailed. But
behind the closed gates of the Palau, the smell
of incense, associated with the religiously
observant *haut monde*, fugged the air.

Shuttered windows prevented the young
Güell children from peering across the street at
the brothels, drinking dens, regular fights and
the teenage Picasso up to his harmless pranks.

The owner of Palau Güell
(*see p113*) became Gaudí's
patron for life.

Little has changed since its construction; the palace still has a heavy, morbid atmosphere. It's more uplifting to see what the patron and his architect achieved together when they left the Palau's oppressive atmosphere and emerged into the open air: specifically at **Park Güell** (*see p177*), high above Barcelona in the Collserola hills.

Built between 1900 and 1904 as a private development for luxury housing, it's one of the most delightful gardens you'll ever find. But embedded in the fabric of this city retreat – its landscape shaped by mosaic dragons, rubble-built road bridges and grottoes – is a serious message, which Gaudí and Güell hoped might be transmitted to all who visited. The gardens were regarded by both men as sacred: wander the length of the serpentine bench, covered with a riotous explosion of *trencadís* (broken tiles), and look out for the secret graffiti scratched in by Gaudí as invocations to the Virgin Mary and

Two privately owned buildings have recently been opened to the public – the Casa Vicens townhouse (*see p174*) in Gràcia, and the Torre Bellesguard (*see p186*), at the foot of Tibidabo.

asa Vicens

prayers to God. Gaudí even lived here for a time; his former house is now open as a museum, and offers a privileged view of his furniture and his spartan, profoundly religious lifestyle.

Other Gaudí buildings dot the city, some more spectacular than others. The undulating marine-life surface of **Casa Batlló** (*see p156*) is best seen, floodlit, at night. The wonderful restaurant at the **Casa Calvet** (*see p162*) affords visitors the opportunity to taste fine Catalan cuisine while admiring the simplicity and practicality of an industrial space. The Dragon Gate at the **Pavellons de la Finca Güell** (*see p185*) is a masterpiece of ironwork, while the **Col·legi de les Teresianes** (*see p184*) shows off Gaudí's powers of invention using just the humble brick. But over them all, visible from the Park Güell, stand the dramatic spires of Gaudí's expiatory temple, the **Sagrada Família** (*see p158*).

The temple, started in 1882 and now planned for completion some time around 2030, was Gaudí's life's work. But don't be fooled by the entrance: the Darth Vader sculptures date from the 1970s on. Around the far side at the Nativity façade, and down in the basement museum, we encounter the real Gaudí. There is something monstrous, almost megalomaniacal, about the level of ambition. The scale overwhelms, but the sheer creative range overpowers. Gaudí hoped here to illustrate the whole of Catalan creation and the Catholic faith. Plaster casts of human bodies, chloroformed chickens, fishing boats, stars, octopuses, palms and Christmas trees melt together in a concert of stone.

However, this isn't Gaudí's greatest architectural achievement, not quite. For that, you need to take a short ride (15 kilometres) to Santa Coloma de Cervelló, and the crypt at **Colònia Güell** (*see p196*). All of Gaudí's genius is distilled into this enchanting symphony built from rubble, discarded tiles, overburnt brick and rough-hewn stone. It's an exquisite sight.

Casa Batlló's intricate facade can be appreciated both by day and at night (*see p156*).

There is something monstrous, almost megalomaniacal, about the level of ambition

Explore

STARAVOITAVA

Getting Started

The evocative beauty of the Old City is so alluring that many visitors remain willing captives of its labyrinthine streets, entranced by the atmosphere and wealth of ancient buildings. It's a shame to miss out on the rest of the city, however, such as the architectural glories of the Eixample, the hills of Montjuïc and Tibidabo, and the Forum district, which has emerged bright and bold from the ashes of a post-industrial wasteland.

An overview of the city

Barcelona, like any other city, is defined by its geography, but in this case the definition is precise: sea, hills and rivers constrain its area. The city squeezes into the remaining available space, a dense and sometimes confusing tangle of streets and houses. In this guide we have divided Barcelona into a number of defined districts, shown on the overview map (*see p8)* and the neighbourhood maps at the beginning of each Explore chapter.

We begin the Explore section with the **Barri Gòtic** (Gothic Quarter, *see pp68-87*), the medieval heart of the city. The boundaries to this ancient quarter are the pedestrian boulevard La Rambla, the transport hub of Plaça Catalunya, and Via Laietana.

Crossing Via Laietana brings you to the **Born & Sant Pere** (*see pp88-105*). These old

❤ **Time to explore**

For idle wandering
Barri Gòtic *p70*, Montjuïc *p138*, La Rambla *p74*

For art attacks
Fundació Miró *p143*, MACBA *p111*, Museu Picasso *p97*

For communing with nature
Parc de la Ciutadella *p94*, Parc del Laberint *p188*, Park Güell *p177*

For communing with God
Catedral de Barcelona *p77*, Sagrada Família *p158*, Santa Maria del Mar *p100*

For Gaudí and friends
Manzana de la Discòrdia *p155*, Palau de la Música *p98*, La Pedrera *p160*

For grown-up kids
Camp Nou Experience *p180*, Font Màgica *p142*, Tibidabo funfair *p183*

For escaping the crowds
Monestir de Pedralbes *p185*, Museu Frederic Marès *p78*, Recinte Modernista de Sant Pau *p163*

Monestir de Pedralbes *p185*

commercial districts are given a green boundary by the Parc de la Ciutadella, with the heavy traffic using the Ronda Sant Pere marking the division between the Old City and the Eixample.

Crossing La Rambla from the Barri Gòtic plunges the visitor into the **Raval** (*see pp106-121*), once notorious and still an edgier part of town than many of Barcelona's sometimes over-designed districts, though much changed in recent times.

Once upon a time Barcelona turned its back on the sea, cut off by a railway line and put off by toxic waste dumped into the water. All that changed with the 1992 Olympics, and today **Barceloneta & the Ports** (*see pp122-135*) offer a marine respite to city dwellers. To find the big blue, the basic idea is to head downhill: Barcelona slopes gently down to the shore.

The hill of **Montjuïc** (*see pp136-149*) offers a welcome escape from the heat and crowds of the city, and some of the city's best galleries and museums too.

It's easy to tell when you've left the Old City and entered the **Eixample** (*see pp150-171*): narrow streets and alleys become broad, traffic-clogged, geometrically precise roads. Barcelona's 'Extension' encloses much of the Old City, stretching from Montjuïc, around the Raval and the Barri Gòtic, to finally finish as Sant Pere's cap. It's here that you'll find most of the city's Modernisme masterpieces.

Beyond lies the area we've called **Gràcia & Other Districts** (*see pp172-191*), which includes once-independent towns swallowed up as Barcelona has spread: despite this you'll find each area retains a distinct and separate identity.

And finally, Catalonia offers an incredibly varied landscape that includes unspoilt beaches, snowy peaks and film-set-worthy medieval villages, as well as the compact cities of Girona and Tarragona. We've included some easily accessible highlights of the region in **Day Trips** (*see pp192-207*).

♥ Best views

1881 *p134*
A fabulous café-terrace looking out over the Port Vell.

Carmel bunkers *p187*
Climb up to the Civil War anti-aircraft batteries for a city panorama.

El Corte Inglés *p166*
The view from the top-floor café is one of Barcelona's better-kept secrets.

Montjuïc *p138*
The cable car, the castle and Martinez are just some of Montjuïc's vantage points.

Monument a Colom *p133*
One for the brave, at the foot of La Rambla

In the know
Keep your bags close

Bag snatchers and pickpockets are quite common. Don't carry unnecessary valuables and beware anyone trying to clean something off your shoulder or sell you a posy. Those wanting to swap a coin for one from your country are also wont to empty out your wallet.

Carmel bunkers p187

Getting around

Barcelona is deceptively small, and by far the easiest way to get around town is walking – the Old City can be crossed on foot in about 20 minutes – although public transport is swift, efficient and cheap. The metro is quick and serves most areas, but it's worth checking a street map first, because you may find you are only a couple of blocks away and it's quicker to walk. Buses reach the parts of the city not covered by the metro and run through the night. An ongoing remodelling of the system means that buses beginning with V run 'vertically', from sea to mountain, while buses beginning with H run 'horizontally', between the rivers Besos and Llobregat. For more information on public transport, *see p296*.

Discount schemes

As well as the discount schemes described below, a ticket on the **Bus Turístic** (*see p301*) also includes a book of coupons valid for admittance to many of the city's museums and attractions. Be aware, too, that many attractions are cheaper if booked online (and normally this method avoids the need to queue).

Articket

The Articket (www.articketbcn.org, €30) gives free entry to six major museums and art galleries (one visit is allowed to each venue over a period of six months): Fundació Miró, MACBA, the MNAC, Fundació Tàpies, the CCCB and the Museu Picasso.

In the know
Useful apps

FC Barcelona Official All things Barça, with live games and match facts.

BCN Paisatge Glorious visual details around the city, from old shop fronts to street art.

BCN Visual Old photos accessed from an interactive map of the city.

TMBAPP (Metro Bus Barcelona) Interactive transport map.

Barcelona Card

This pass (www.barcelonacard.com, €20-€60, with a 10% discount online) allows two to five days of unlimited public transport and gives discounts at sights, cablecars and airport buses. It's sold at the airport, tourist offices and El Corte Inglés.

Sights and museums

Barcelona emerged triumphantly from a crippling recession with visitor numbers soaring, and many stalled projects are finally seeing the light of day. There was a spate of new openings, from the grand municipal projects such as the **Born Centre de Cultura i Memòria** (*see p96*) and the long-awaited **Museu del Disseny** (*see p190*) to little quirky spaces such as the **Hemp Museum** (*see p78*). Other new spaces include the **Can Framis** art space (*see p190*), the recently unearthed Roman **Domus de Sant Honorat** (*see p78*), the **MEAM** (Museu Europeu d'Art Modern, *see p96*) and the kitsch-but-fun **Gaudí Experiència** (*see p174*).

In addition to the newcomers, several of the city's most iconic buildings have opened or are about to open to the public for the first time. These include Gaudí's **Casa Vicens** (*see p174*) and **Bellesguard** (*see p186*), and Puig i Cadafalch's **Casa de les Punxes** (*see p157*).

On top of that, many existing museums and galleries have revamped their collections, and the **Palau Güell** (*p113*),

Can Framis *p190*

Casa de les Punxes *p157*

the **MNAC** (*see p144*), the **Museu Frederic Marès** (*see p78*) and the **Museu Marítim** (*see p134*) have all undergone extensive overhauls. Richard Rogers' reworking of the Les Arenes bullring into a leisure and office complex is now complete, while the **Fundació Foto Colectània** (*see p96*) has moved to larger premises in the Born. The **Carmel Bunkers** (*see p187*), the evocative anti-aircraft batteries on top of the Turó de la Rovira hill, have been spruced up and now have information panels for visitors.

Many projects, though, proved too expensive in the final tally. Norman Foster's proposed Gaudí-inspired overhaul of the Camp Nou stadium was thrown out and replaced with a more sober design by Japanese Nikken Sekkei – work is due to begin in 2017 – and Frank Gehry's dizzying makeover of La Sagrera station has quietly been dropped.

▶ *For information on walking, cycling and other tours, see p298.*

Tourist information

The biggest and most helpful tourist office is at Plaça Catalunya, underground but clearly signposted (in the central ring, but on the same side as El Corte Inglés). There are banks of informative leaflets, and staff can help with reserving or buying tickets for various sights around town, as well as passes and maps for public transport. For details of other tourist offices, *see p308*, and for further information see www.barcelonaturisme.com.

In the know
Free Sundays

Note that municipally owned museums are free from 3pm on Sundays, and many are also free one day a month. Check individual websites for details.

Barri Gòtic & La Rambla

The central third of the Old City's triptych, the Barri Gòtic (Gothic Quarter) contains the most well-preserved medieval quarter in Europe, dotted with some astounding Roman remains. Neither as glacially cool as the Born nor as bohemian as the Raval, it's nonetheless an essential port of call. Save for the dramatic destruction of a huge part of the medieval core for the construction of C/Jaume I and C/Ferran (1849-53) and Via Laietana (1909), its ancient splendour has survived the last 500 years or so virtually intact.

History is written in stone here; the wealth of historical remains is such that visitors soon become as blasé as the locals about the large sections of Roman wall they might encounter at the back of a curry house, in a café or in a lift shaft leading down to the metro.

❤ Don't miss

1 La Rambla *p74*
The famous mile-long boulevard of shops, cafés and street performers.

2 Catedral de Barcelona *p77*
A Gothic, Disneyesque confection that stands at the medieval quarter's highest point.

3 MUHBA *p79*
The city's history museum, with extensive Roman remains running underground.

4 La Boqueria *p84*
Europe's largest food market, in a historic building.

5 Gran Teatre del Liceu *p249*
An elegant opera house with a storied past.

In the know
Getting around

The streets are so narrow in the Barri Gòtic that it's near impossible for cars to pass, let alone public transport. It's most easily accessed from Jaume I metro to the east or Liceu metro to the west.

Plaça Sant Just *p76*

EXPLORING
THE BARRI GÒTIC

The Cathedral & around

The first settlement of this 2,000-year-old city was a Roman camp set up on the gentle hill of Mons Taber, the highest vantage point on the coastal plains. Now the imposing square of **Plaça Sant Jaume**, this is where the Roman forum was built, at the crossroads of the main thoroughfares of the *cardo maximus* and the *decumanus*, which roughly correspond to the lines traced by C/Call to C/Llibreteria and C/Bisbe to C/Ciutat today. Dominating the forum was the **Temple d'August**, four columns of which can still be seen in C/Paradis. The square now hosts the **Ajuntament** (city hall; *see p76*) and the **Palau de la Generalitat** (Catalan regional government building; *see p79*), and forms the civic heart of the city. It has also provided the stage for demonstrations, speeches and key political moments, such as the proclamation of the Catalan republic in 1931.

Leading off the square, C/Bisbe has one of the area's most photographed features: the neo-Gothic **Pont dels Sospirs** (Bridge of Sighs). It's a pastiche from 1928, when the idea of this area as a 'Gothic Quarter' took off. Other alterations from the same period include the decorations on the **Casa dels Canonges** (once a set of canons' residences, and now Generalitat offices), on the other side of the bridge. Further down C/Bisbe is the **Plaça Garriga i Bachs** and Josep Llimona's monument to the martyrs of 1809, dedicated to the *barcelonins* who rose up against Napoleon and were executed.

In Pla de la Seu you'll find the **Catedral de Barcelona** (*see p77*), Barcelona's Gothic cathedral, dedicated to the city's patron saint, Eulàlia. In C/Santa Llúcia, in front of the cathedral, is the **Casa de l'Ardiaca**; originally a 15th-century residence for the archdeacon (*ardiaca*), it has a superb tiled patio. The broad square at the foot of the steps leading up to the cathedral is **Plaça Nova**, which houses an antiques market every Thursday (*see p86*) and is a traditional venue for festivals, concerts and *sardana* dancing. On the southern flank of the square is *Barcino*: a 'visual poem' by Joan Brossa, installed in 1994, it refers to the ancient name for Barcelona, supposedly given by the Carthaginians after Hannibal's father, Hamil Barca. Directly above is the Roman aqueduct. The final archway of the city's two aqueducts, dating from the first century AD, is preserved inside the tower that defended the north-eastern side of the city gate.

Fast forward two millennia to the opposite side of Plaça Nova, dominated by one of the

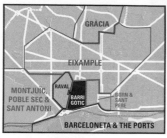

BARRI GÒTIC & LA RAMBLA

Restaurants

1. Belmonte
2. Cafè de l'Acadèmia
3. Can Culleretes
4. Chicken Shop
5. El Gran Café
6. Matsuri
7. Mercè Vins
8. Ocaña
9. El Paraguayo
10. Peimong
11. Els Quatre Gats
12. Les Quinze Nits
13. Rasoterra
14. Shunka
15. Tokyo

Cafés, tapas & bars

1. Ácoma
2. Bar Celta
3. Bar Pinotxo
4. Cafè de l'Òpera
5. Čaj Chai
6. Federal
7. Ginger
8. La Granja 1872
9. Milk
10. Polaroid
11. El Portalón
12. Taller de Tapas
13. La Vinateria del Call

Shops & services

1. Almacenes del Pilar
2. Alonso
3. Antiques Market
4. L'Arca
5. Caelum
6. Cereria Subirà
7. Flora Albaicín
8. Formatgeria La Seu
9. Herboristeria del Rei
10. El Ingenio
11. La Manual Alpargatera
12. Sala Parés

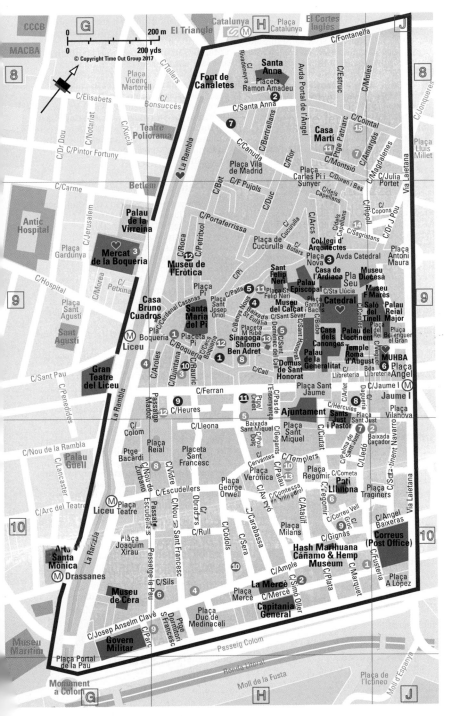

CCCB

MACBA

8

0   200 m   El Triangle   Catalunya   H   Plaça   El Cortes
0   200 yds   Catalunya   Inglés
© Copyright Time Out Group 2017

G

C/Fontanella

J

C/Rivadeneyra

C/Tellers

Plaça
Vicenç
Martorell

C/Elisabets

C/Bonsuccés

Font de
Canaletes

Santa
Anna

Placeta
Ramon Amadeu

C/Santa Anna

Avda Portal de l'Àngel

C/Estruc

C/Moles

C/Comtal

8

Plaça
Lluís
Millet

Pça Patriarc

15

C/Amargós

C/Magdalenes

Via Laietana

C/Llonqueres

C/Dr Dou

C/Notariat

C/Pintor Fortuny

C/Xuclà

La Rambla

Teatre
Poliorama

Betlem

C/Canuda

C/Bertrellans

C/Flor

Casa
Martí

Pge Patriarc

11

7

C/Montsió

Plaça Vila
de Madrid

C/Bot

C/F Pujols

C/Duc

7

Plaça
Carles Pi i
Sunyer

C/Duran i Bas

C/dels
Capellans

C/Ripoll

C/Copons

C/Dr J Pou

C/Julià
Portet

Plaça
Antoni
Maura

C/Carme

Antic
Hospital

C/Jerusalem

Palau
de la
Virreina

C/Roca

C/Petritxol

C/Portaferrissa

C/Pi

C/Arcs

C/Cucurulla

Plaça de
Cucurulla

C/dels
Capellans

C/Sagristans

14

Col·legi d'
Arquitectes

Avda Catedral

3

Plaça
Nova

Museu de
l'Eròtica

12

Plaça
Gardunya

Mercat
de la Boqueria

3

C/Morea

C/Petxina

C/Hospital

Plaça
Sant
Agustí

9

Sant
Agustí

Casa
Bruno
Cuadros

C/Cardenal Casañas

Santa
Maria
del Pi

Plaça
Pi

C/Palla

Sant
Felip
Neri

Palau
Episcopal

Plaça St
Felip Neri

5

11

4

Museu
del Calçat

Baixada St Eulàlia

C/Sant Sever

Casa de
l'Ardiaca

Pla
Seu

Casa
Garriga
Bachs

C/Sta Llúcia

C/Bisbe

Catedral

Museu
Diocesà

Museu
F Marès

Saló
del
Tinell

Palau
Reial
Major

C/Banys Nous

Plaça
Sant
Josep
Oriol

C/Petritxol

M

Liceu

Boqueria

Pla
Boqueria

1

Placeta
Pi

Sinagoga
Shlomo
Ben Adret

12

C/Cecs

C/Boqueria

1

C/M Ribe

Domus
de Sant
Honorat

Palau
de la
Generalitat

C/del
Call

Casa
dels
Canonges

C/Sant Domènec del Call

13

C/Sant Honorat

Temple
Romà
d'August

Plaça
del
Rei

Palau del
Lloctinent

Plaça
Berenguer
el Gran

C/Veguer

MUHBA

Plaça
Àngel

C/Àroles

C/Quintana

C/Aurici

10

Gran
Teatre
del Liceu

La Rambla

C/Sant Pau

C/Penedides

C/Nou de la Rambla

Palau
Güell

C/Lancaster

Passatge
Madoz

9

C/Heures

12

C/
Colom

C/Lleona

Baixada
Sant Miquel

Púgol
Crèdit

11

5

Pça de
l'Ensenyança

C/Pas de
l'Ensenyança

Plaça Sant
Jaume

C/Artet

Ajuntament

Sant
Just
i Pastor

C/Hércules

8

Daguería

C/Jaume I

M

Jaume I

Plaça
Vilanova

C/Dagueria

Plaça
Sant
Miquel

C/Ciutat

7

Plaça
Sant Just

2

Baixada
Caçador

C/Arc del Teatre

Ptge
Bacardí

Plaça
Reial

C/Nou de Sant Francesc

C/Nou de
Zurbano

8

C/Obradors

Placeta
Sant
Francesc

C/Escudellers

C/Gegants

C/Paul
Dofó

C/Cervantes

C/Templers

Plaça
Verónica

C/Palau

10

13

Plaça
Regomir

C/Cometa

C/Palma de
Sant Just

Pati
Llimona

C/Lledó

Plaça
Traginers

M

Liceu

Plaça
Teatre

Passatge Escudellers

C/Nou de Sant Francesc

C/Rull

Plaça
George
Orwell

C/AviYó

C/Comtessa
de Sobradiel

C/Ataülf

C/Regomir

6

C/Correu Vell

C/Àngel
Baixeras

Plaça
Joaquim
Xirau

La Rambla

Passatge de la Pau

C/Codols

C/Sera

Plaça
Milans

C/Gignàs

Correus
(Post Office)

C/Fusteria

10

Arts
Santa
Mònica

M

Drassanes

Museu
de Cera

6

C/Sils

Ptge Dormitori
S Francesc

Plaça
Duc de
Medinaceli

10

C/Ample

Hash Marihuana
Cáñamo & Hemp
Museum

Plaça
Mercé

C/Mercé

La Mercé

C/Simó Oller

C/Plata

C/Marquet

Plaça
A López

Museu
Marítim

Govern
Militar

C/Josep Anselm Clavé

C/Parc

Capitania
General

Passeig Colom

Plaça Portal
de la Pau

Monument
a Colón

G

Ronda Litoral

Moll de la Fusta

H

Plaça de
l'Icteneo

Moll d'Espanya

J

first high-rise blocks in the city: the **Col·legi d'Arquitectes** (Architects' Association) is decorated with a graffiti-style sand-blasted triptych of Catalan folk scenes, designed by Picasso while in self-imposed exile in the 1950s, and executed by Norwegian artist Carl Nesjar. The middle section depicts the *gegants* (giant figures who lead festival processions) and figures holding palm branches; the left-hand section (on C/Arcs) symbolises the joy of life, while the right-hand section (on C/Capellans) depicts the Catalan flag. There are also two interior friezes depicting a *sardana* dance and a wall of arches.

In front of the cathedral, on the right as you leave, the **Museu Diocesà** (*see p78*) houses an excellent collection of religious art . Around the side of the cathedral, meanwhile, is the little-visited but fascinating **Museu Frederic Marès** (*see p78*).

Further along is the 16th-century **Palau del Lloctinent** (Palace of the Viceroy); now restored, it was the local headquarters for the Spanish Inquisition, from where the unfortunates were carted off to the Passeig del Born to be burned. Another exit leads you to the well-preserved **Plaça del Rei**, site of the **Museu d'Història de Barcelona** (MUHBA; *see p79*). The buildings surrounding this medieval palace square formed the **Palau Reial Major** (not to be confused with the Palau Reial in Pedralbes). Parts of the palace are said to date back to the tenth century; there have been many

remarkable additions to it since, notably the 14th-century **Saló del Tinell**, a medieval banqueting hall that is a definitive work of Catalan Gothic. It is here that Ferdinand and Isabella are said to have received Columbus on his return from America. The palace includes some of Barcelona's most historically important buildings: the Escher-esque 16th-century watchtower (**Mirador del Rei Martí**) and the **Capella de Santa Àgata**, which houses the stone where the breasts of Saint Agatha were allegedly laid when the Romans chopped them off in Catania.

The Call

The narrow streets centred on C/Call once housed a rich Jewish ghetto (*call*), although the street names were Christianised after the 1391 pogrom. At the corner of C/Sant Domènec del Call and C/Marlet is the medieval synagogue, now restored and open to the public. Proving the regenerated interest in the Call, in 2008 the **Centre d'Interpretació del Call** research centre opened in Placeta Manuel Ribé (93 256 21 22, closed Mon, Tue, Thur) as part of the Museu d'Història de Barcelona; it has a small selection of medieval Jewish artefacts on display.

Near the centre of the Call is the beautiful little **Plaça Sant Felip Neri** and its fine Baroque church, whose façade was damaged by Italian bombing in one of the grisliest incidents of the Civil War. Over 200 people were killed, some 30 of them refugee children taking shelter in the church; the shrapnel damage is still visible. This square is another 20th-century invention; the shoemakers' guild building (which, until recently, housed the charming but ill-fated **Museu del Calçat shoe museum**) was moved here in 1943 to make way for the Avda de la Catedral, while the nearby

---

In the know
Artistic temperament

When Picasso heard that Joan Miró was being considered for the commission on the Col·legi d'Arquitectes, he said that he could easily 'do a Miró', hence the style.

💙 **Time to eat & drink**

Morning coffee and a pastry
Cafè de l'Opera *p83*

Home-made cakes
Federal *p83*

Picnic supplies
La Boqueria *p84*

Locally grown produce
Belmonte *p80*

A great wine list
Ginger *p86*

💙 **Time to shop**

Espadrilles fit for a pope
La Manual Alpargatera *p87*

Gloves in a kaleidoscope of colours
Alonso *p86*

The best jamón ibérico in town
La Boqueria *p84*

Old-school toys and games
El Ingenio *p87*

tinkers' guild was moved when Via Laietana was driven through the district.

Close by are attractive **Plaça del Pi** and **Plaça Sant Josep Oriol**, where you'll find great bars and artisanal markets. The squares are separated by **Santa Maria del Pi**, one of Barcelona's most distinguished Gothic churches, with a magnificent rose window and spacious single nave. Opposite is the 17th-century neoclassical retailers' guildhall, with its colourful 18th-century sgraffiti.

Snaking up to C/Portaferrissa from the Plaça del Pi is **C/Petritxol**. One of the most charming streets of the Barri Gòtic, it is known for its traditional *'granges'* (former dairies) offering hot chocolate and cakes, and also houses the **Sala Parés**, the city's oldest art gallery; Rusiñol, Casas and the young Picasso all exhibited here (*see p87*). On the other side of C/Portaferrissa, heading up C/Bot, is the **Plaça Vila de Madrid**, where you'll find the excavated remains of a Roman necropolis and an information centre (93 256 21 22, closed Mon, Wed, Fri), along with a rare expanse of city-centre grass (fenced off). Between here and the Plaça Catalunya is the little Romanesque church of **Santa Anna**, begun in 1141 and containing an exquisite 14th-century cloister.

Head back along C/Santa Anna to emerge on the city's most crowded shopping street,

the pedestrianised **Portal de l'Àngel**, crammed with high-street chains and the odd curiosity, such as the **Santa Anna drinking fountain**.

From here, duck into C/Duran i Blas to see four arches from a Roman aqueduct exposed in 1988 when a neighbouring building was demolished; they date from the first century AD and brought water from the River Besòs. Back out on Portal de l'Angel, the end of the street is signposted by the famous five-storey-high **Cottet thermometer**, added in 1956 by the optician's shop beneath and greatly admired at the time as a technological marvel. A few metres away is the entrance to C/Montsió, which holds the world-famous **Els Quatre Gats** café (*see p82*), legendary haunt of Picasso. It's housed in Puig i Cadafalch's richly sculpted **Casa Martí**.

In the know
A fountain of faces

Decorated with scowling bearded faces, the **Santa Anna drinking fountain** dates from 1356 and was later covered in Noucentista painted tiles. It's located to the rear of the Real Cercle Artístic, housed in the Palau Pignatelli.

❤ La Rambla

Whether you catch it on a Saturday night full of sombrero-wearing stags or early in the morning when the kiosk-holders are bursting open their fresh stacks of newspapers, one thing is for sure: you won't get La Rambla to yourself. And, indeed, why would you want to? In the absence of any great buildings or museums, it's the people who provide the spectacle: from flower-sellers to living statues, operagoers to saucer-eyed clubbers, market shoppers to tango dancers, all human life is here.

However, there's no escaping the fact that, these days, it's mostly tourists who walk the golden mile from Plaça Catalunya down to the harbour. The business of extracting as much of their money as possible, whether by fair means or foul, has had an inevitable impact on the character of the boulevard, filling it with fast food outlets, short-stay apartments, identikit souvenir shops and pickpockets. After a lot of bad press, the council is desperately trying to smarten up the city's famous boulevard, and the prostitutes, sex shops, card sharps and fortune tellers are gradually being squeezed out. Even the famous human statues and street artists have been subjected to quality control.

La Rambla started life as a seasonal riverbed, which explains both its snaking trajectory, broadening out at the sea end, and also its name, which derives from *ramla*, an Arabic word for sand. The river ran along the western edge of the 13th-century city; after it became an open sewer,

it was gradually paved over, although the distinctive wave-patterned paving slabs were not added until after the Civil War.

From the Middle Ages to the Baroque era, many churches and convents were built along here, some of which have given their names to sections of the road. Descending from Plaça Catalunya, La Rambla is successively called Rambla de Canaletes, Rambla dels Estudis (or dels Ocells), Rambla de Sant Josep (or de les Flors), Rambla dels Caputxins and Rambla de Santa Mònica. For this reason, many people refer to it in the plural, as Les Rambles (Las Ramblas in Castilian).

La Rambla also served as the meeting ground for city and country dwellers in this era – on the far side of these church buildings lay the still scarcely built-up Raval, 'the city outside the walls', and rural Catalonia. At the fountain on the corner with C/Portaferrissa, colourful tiles depict the city gateway that once stood here (*porta ferrissa* means 'iron gate'). The space by the gates became a natural marketplace; from these humble beginnings sprang **La Boqueria** (*see p84*).

La Rambla took on its present form between approximately 1770 and 1860. The second city wall came down in 1775, and La Rambla was paved and turned into a boulevard. But the avenue only acquired its final shape after the closure of the monasteries in the 1830s, which made land available for new building. No longer on the city's edge, La Rambla became a wide path through the city's heart.

As well as having five names, La Rambla is divided into territories. The first part – at the top, by Plaça Catalunya – was long the territory of shoeshiners and groups of men who came to play chess and hold informal debates, although the sparse new single-seat benches have made it a markedly less sociable place to sit these days. The **Font de Canaletes** drinking fountain, which gives this section its name, is beside them, and is where Barça fans converge to celebrate their triumphs.

This part segues into the **Rambla dels Ocells**; it's named after the ranks of cacophonous bird (*ocell*) stalls that stood here until they were removed by the Ajuntament in an attempt to raise the tone of the boulevard. Next comes perhaps the best-loved section, known as **Rambla de**

> In the absence of any great buildings or museums, it's the people who provide the spectacle: from flower-sellers to living statues, operagoers to saucer-eyed clubbers, market shoppers to tango dancers, all human life is here

La Rambla de Santa Mònica

les Flors for its line of flower stalls. To the right is the Palau de la Virreina exhibition and cultural information centre (see p80), and the superb Boqueria market. A little further down is the Pla de l'Os (or Pla de la Boqueria), the centrepoint of La Rambla. On the left at no.82, where more streets run off into the Barri Gòtic, is the extraordinary Bruno Quadros building dating from 1883.

The lower half of La Rambla is initially a more restrained affair, flowing between the sober façade of the Gran Teatre del Liceu opera house (see p249) and the more fin-de-siècle (architecturally and atmospherically) Café de l'Opera (see p83). On the right is C/Nou de la Rambla (where you'll find Gaudí's neo-Gothic Palau Güell (seep113); the promenade then widens into the Rambla de Santa Mònica, an area that has long been a haunt of prostitutes. Clean-up efforts have reduced their visibility, and various renovations – including the 1980s addition of an arts centre, Arts Santa Mònica (see p76) –

have done much to dilute the seediness of the area, but single males walking at night can still expect to be approached.

Across the street is the unintentionally hilarious Museu de Cera (Wax Museum; see p78) and, at weekends, numerous stalls selling bric-a-brac and craftwork. Then it's a short hop to the port and the Columbus column.

❤ Don't miss

1 Font de Canaletes
If you drink from it, goes the legend, you'll return to Barcelona.

2 Joan Miró's mosaic
At the very centre, in the Pla de l'Os, is a pavement mosaic by Miró, dating to 1976.

3 Bruno Quadros building
A former umbrella shop, it is decorated with roundels of open parasols and a Chinese dragon carrying a Peking lantern.

South of the Plaça Sant Jaume

Back on the seaward side of the Barri Gòtic, if you walk from Plaça Sant Jaume up C/ Ciutat, to the left of the Ajuntament, and turn down the narrow alley of C/Hércules, you'll come to **Plaça Sant Just**. This fascinating old square holds a recently restored Gothic water fountain from 1367 and the church of **Sants Just i Pastor**, built in the 14th century on the site of a chapel founded by Charlemagne's son Louis the Pious, but now looking rather unloved inside.

The once-wealthy area between here and the port became more rundown throughout the 20th century. It has a different atmosphere from the northern part of the Barri Gòtic: shabbier and less prosperous. The city authorities made huge efforts to change this, particularly in the 1990s, when new squares were opened up: **Plaça George Orwell** on C/Escudellers, known as the 'Plaça del Tripi (Trippy)' by the youthful party crowd that hangs out there, and **Plaça Joaquim Xirau**, off La Rambla. Another tactic was the siting of parts of the Universitat Pompeu Fabra on the lower Rambla. Just above is the **Plaça Reial**, known for its bars, cheap backpacker hostels and rather scuzzy atmosphere at night. It's still a popular spot for a drink or an outdoor meal (provided you don't mind the odd drunk and are prepared to keep an eye on your bags).

The grand porticoes of a number of the buildings around the church of **La Mercè**, once merchants' mansions, stand as testament to the former wealth of the area before the building of the Eixample. The **Plaça de la Mercè** itself was only created in 1982, with the destruction of the houses that used to stand here; the 19th-century fountain was moved here from the port. There's also a dwindling number of lively *tascas* (small tapas bars) on C/Mercè. Beyond C/Ample and the Mercè, you emerge from narrow alleys or the pretty Plaça Duc de Medinaceli on to the Passeig de Colom, where a few shipping offices and ships' chandlers still recall the atmosphere of decades gone by. On Passeig de Colom stands the monolithic **Capitanía General**, the army headquarters. The façade has the dubious distinction of being the one construction in Barcelona that's directly attributable to the dictatorship of Primo de Rivera.

Sights & museums

Ajuntament (City Hall)
*Plaça Sant Jaume (93 402 73 64, www.bcn. cat). Metro Jaume I or Liceu. **Open** Office 8.30am-2.30pm Mon-Fri. Visits 10am-1.30pm Sun. **Admission** free. **Map** p71 H9.*

Around the left-hand corner of the City Hall's rather dull 18th-century neoclassical façade sits the old entrance, in a wonderfully flamboyant 15th-century Catalan Gothic façade. Inside, the building's centrepiece (and oldest part) is the famous Saló de Cent, where the Consell de Cent (Council of One Hundred) ruled the city between 1372 and 1714. The Saló de Cròniques is filled with Josep Maria Sert's immense black-and-gold mural (1928), depicting the early 14th-century Catalan campaign in Byzantium and Greece under the command of Roger de Flor. Full of art and sculptures by the great Catalan masters from Clarà to Subirachs, the interior of the City Hall is open on Sundays. The Ajuntament is also open from 11am to 8pm on certain holidays, such as Santa Eulàlia (12 February) and Sant Jordi (23 April), and Corpus Christi (11 days after Whitsunday).

Arts Santa Mònica
*La Rambla 7 (93 567 11 10, www. artssantamonica.net). Metro Drassanes. **Open** 11am-9pm Tue-Sat; 11am-5pm Sun. **Admission** free. **Map** p71 G10.*

This Generalitat-run contemporary art space calls itself a 'multidisciplinary centre for art, science, thought and communication'. Frequently changing temporary exhibitions cover a wide range of themes, from war correspondence to performance art.

Centre Cívic Pati d'en Llimona
*C/Regomir 3 (93 256 11 00, www.patillimona. org). Metro Jaume I. **Open** Exhibitions 9am-9.30pm Mon-Fri; 10am-2pm, 4-8pm Sat. Closed Aug. **Admission** free. **Map** p71 H10.*

From the street, peer through the glass paving slabs and windows to see the excavated foundations of a round defence tower dating from the earliest Roman settlement, along with the remains of a Roman bath and house that stood against one of the gates of the city wall. In the 15th century, a villa was built on the site; the courtyard still contains capitals from this period. The civic centre's cultural offerings include exhibitions, theatre shows and poetry readings.

In the know
Civic Gaudí

An addition from the 1840s, the Plaça Reial has the Tres Gràcies fountain in the centre, and lamp-posts designed by the young Gaudí. It's the only work he ever did for the city council.

💙 Catedral de Barcelona

Pla de la Seu (93 342 82 62, www.catedralbcn. org). Metro Jaume I. **Open** *Church, cloister & museum 1-5.30pm Mon-Fri; 1-5pm Sat; 2-5pm Sun. Worshippers only at other times.* **Admission** *Church, cloister & museum (combined ticket) €7. Lift to roof €3. Choir €3. Free to worshippers. No cards.* **Map** *p71 H9.*

The construction of Barcelona's Gothic cathedral began in 1298. However, thanks to civil wars and plagues, building dragged on at a pace that makes the Sagrada Família project look snappy: although the architects remained faithful to the vertical Nordic lines of the 15th-century plans, the façade and central spire were not finished until 1913. Indeed, the façade continues to cause problems, and in recent years has been painstakingly rebuilt with the same Montserrat stone that was used for the original. Inside, the cathedral is a cavernous and slightly forbidding place, but many paintings, sculptures and an intricately carved central choir (built in the 1390s) all shine through the gloom.

The cathedral is dedicated to Saint Eulàlia, an outspoken 13-year-old martyred by the Romans in AD 303. Her remains lie in the dramatically lit crypt, in an alabaster tomb carved with torture scenes from her martyrdom (being rolled in a nail-filled barrel down what is today the Baixada de Santa Eulàlia, for instance). To one side, there's a lift to the roof; take it for a magnificent view of the Old City.

The glorious, light-filled cloister is famous for its 13 fierce geese – one for each year of Eulàlia's life – and half-erased floor engravings, detailing which guild paid for which side chapel: scissors to represent the tailors, shoes for the cobblers and so on. The cathedral museum, housed in the 17th-century chapterhouse, includes paintings and sculptures by Gothic masters Jaume Huguet, Bernat Martorell and Bartolomé Bermejo.

A combined ticket (*visita especial*) has a timetable intended to keep tourists and worshippers from bothering and disturbing one another. From 1pm to 5pm, the entry fee is obligatory; however, ticket-holders have the run of the cloister, church, choir and lift; they can also enter the museum (otherwise closed) and some of the chapels, and take photos (normally prohibited).

Museu de l'Eròtica

Open *Mid July-mid Sept 10am-10pm daily. Mid Sept-mid July 10am-1.30pm, 4-8.30pm Mon-Fri; 11am-2pm, 4.30-7.30pm Sat, Sun.* **Admission** *€15; €9 reductions; free under-5s.* **Map** *p71 G10.*

Madame Tussauds it ain't, but the Wax Museum is an enjoyable enough way to pass a rainy afternoon, particularly if you have small children, who love the 'underwater' section (a submarine and creaky old ship). Be warned that the exhibits are very dated, and a curious mix of historical and 1980s (19th-century composers alongside ET, JR from *Dallas* and Lady Di). On Saturdays there are special 'night visits' (€20; Spanish only, at 9pm and 10pm) in the gloaming.

Museu Diocesà & Gaudí Exhibition Center

Avda de la Catedral 4 (93 315 22 13, www. cultura.arqbcn.cat). Metro Jaume I. **Open** *Apr-Oct 10am-8pm daily. Nov-Mar 10am-6pm daily.* **Admission** *€15; €12 reductions; €7.50 children; free under-7s. No cards.* **Map** *p71 H9.*

The building itself is something of a mishmash: it includes the Gothic Pia Almoina, an almshouse and soup kitchen founded in 1009, stuck on to a Renaissance canon's residence complete with Tuscan columns, which in turn was built inside an octagonal Roman defence tower. It houses both the Museu Diocesà – a hotchpotch of religious art, including 14th-century alabaster virgins, altarpieces by Bernat Martorell and wonderful Romanesque murals – and the new Gaudí Exhibition Center, an introduction to the architect's life and work that utilises the latest technology, such as virtual-reality glasses, to bring his world alive.

Museu de l'Eròtica

La Rambla 96 bis (93 318 98 65, www. erotica-museum.com). Metro Liceu. **Open** *10am-midnight daily.* **Admission** *€9; €8 reductions.* **Map** *p71 H9.*

Despite being a condom's toss from the red-light district, the Erotic Museum is a limp affair. Expect plenty of filler in the form of Kama Sutra illustrations and paintings of naked maidens, with the odd fascinating item such as studded chastity belts or a Victorian walking stick topped with an ivory vagina.

Museu Frederic Marès

Plaça Sant Iu 5-6 (93 256 35 00, www. museumares.bcn.cat). Metro Jaume I. **Open** *10am-7pm Tue-Sat; 11am-8pm Sun.* **Admission** *€4.20; €2.40 reductions; free under-16s. Free to all 3-8pm Sun & all day 1st Sun of mth.* **Map** *p71 J9.*

Domus de Sant Honorat

C/Fruita 2 (93 256 21 22, www.museuhistoria. bcn.cat). Metro Jaume I. **Open** *10am-2pm Sun; group visits available during the wk by appt.* **Admission** *€2; €1.50 reductions; free under-16s. No cards.* **Map** *p71 H9.*

The remains of a *domus* (townhouse) dating back to AD 4, situated at the heart of the former Roman town (known back then as Barcino). Also on show are medieval grain silos that were once part of Barcelona's Jewish quarter.

Hash Marihuana Cáñamo & Hemp Museum

C/Ample 35 (93 319 75 39, www. hempmuseumgallery.com) Metro Jaume I. **Open** *10am-10pm daily.* **Admission** *€9; free under-13s.* **Map** *p71 H10.*

An informative shrine to weed, set in a stunning Modernista mansion. The displays run from the botanic to the historical, with rooms devoted to prohibition, and to marijuana in art and popular culture. The Industrial Room looks at the uses of hemp through the ages, while the medicinal section contains moving testimony from those whose lives would be unbearable without it, creating, all told, an intelligent argument for decriminalisation.

Museu de Cera

Ptge de la Banca 7 (93 317 26 49, www. museocerabcn.com). Metro Drassanes.

❤ Museu d'Història de Barcelona (MUHBA)

Plaça del Rei 1 (93 256 21 00, www.
museuhistoria.bcn.cat). Metro Jaume I.
Open *10am-7pm Tue-Sat; 10am-8pm Sun.*
Admission *€7; €5 reductions; free under-16s.*
Free to all 3-8pm Sun & all day 1st Sun of mth.
No cards. **Map** *p71 J9.*

Stretching from the Plaça del Rei to the
cathedral are some 4,000sq m (43,000sq
ft) of subterranean Roman excavations
– streets, villas and storage vats for oil
and wine – all discovered by accident in
the late 1920s when a whole swathe of the
Gothic Quarter was dug up to make way
for the central avenue of Via Laietana. The
excavations continued until 1960.

Today, the labyrinth can be reached
via the Casa Padellàs, a merchant's
palace dating from 1498, which was
laboriously moved from its original
location in C/Mercaders to allow the
construction of Via Laietana.

Admission also allows access to the
Capella de Santa Àgata, with a 15th-
century altarpiece by Jaume Huguet, and
the **Saló del Tinell**, at least when there's
no temporary exhibition. This majestic
room began life in 1370 as the seat of the
Catalan parliament and was converted in
the 18th century into a Baroque church,
which was dismantled in 1934. The Rei
Martí watchtower is closed to the public.
Tickets for the museum are valid for
all seven MUHBA sites.

Kleptomaniac and general magpie Frederic
Marès (1893-1991) 'collected' everything he
could lay his hands on, from hairbrushes to
opera glasses and gargoyles. Unlike most
private 19th-century collectors, Marès didn't
come from a wealthy family, but spent
every penny he earned as a sculptor and art
professor on broadening his hoard. Even
when the Ajuntament gave him a palazzo in
which to display his collection (and house
himself), it wasn't enough; the overflow
eventually spread to two other Marès
museums in Montblanc and Arenys de Mar.

The exhibits here are divided into three
main sections. The basement, ground floor
and first floor are devoted to sculpture dating
from the Pre-Roman era to the 19th century,
including a vast array of polychromed
religious carvings, tombs, capitals and entire
church portals, exquisitely carved. On the
second floor sits the Collector's Cabinet,
with objects from everyday life; look out for
the Ladies' Room, filled with fans, sewing
scissors and perfume flasks, and a room
dedicated to smoking paraphernalia. Also
on the second floor is a room devoted to
photography, and Marès' study and library.
It's now filled with sculptures, many of them
his own. The second floor also houses the
Weapons Room, with collections from the
now defunct Military Museum on Montjuïc.
The Entertainment Room, with mechanical
toys and puppets, is found on the third floor.

Palau de la Generalitat

Plaça Sant Jaume (www.president.cat). Metro
Jaume I or Liceu. **Open** *guided tours (by appt,*
every 30-40mins) 2nd & 4th wknd of mth,
except Aug. **Admission** *free.* **Map** *p71 H9.*

Like the Ajuntament, the Palau de la
Generalitat has a Gothic side entrance, which

here opens out on to C/Bisbe, with a beautiful relief depicting St George (Sant Jordi), patron saint of Catalonia, made by Pere Johan in 1418. Inside the building, the finest features are the first-floor Pati de Tarongers (Orange Tree Patio), which was to become the model for many Barcelona patios, and the chapel of Sant Jordi (1432-34), the masterpiece of Catalan architect Marc Safont. The Generalitat is traditionally open to the public on Sant Jordi (St George's Day, 23 April), when its patios are spectacularly decorated with red roses, but queues are long. It normally also opens on 11 September (Catalan National Day) and 24 September (La Mercè). Tours need to be booked on the website, but the page is hard to find – put 'Palau' and *'visites'* into the search bar.

Palau de la Virreina
*La Rambla 99 (93 316 10 00, www.lavirreina. bcn.cat). Metro Liceu. **Open** noon-8pm Tue- Sun. **Admission** free. **Map** p71 G9.*

This classical palazzo, with Baroque features, takes its name from the widow of an unpopular viceroy of Peru – she commissioned it and lived in it after its completion in the 1770s. The Virreina now houses the city cultural department, and has information on events and shows as well as strong programming in its two gallery spaces. On the first floor, Espai 2 is devoted to exhibitions of contemporary art, while the free downstairs gallery is focused on photography and hosts Barcelona's prestigious annual photo competition, the FotoMercè, which takes place during the Mercè festival in September.

Sinagoga Shlomo Ben Adret
*C/Marlet 5 (93 317 07 90, www. calldebarcelona.org). Metro Jaume I or Liceu. **Open** June-Oct 10.30am-6.30pm Mon-Fri; 10.30am-2.30pm Sat, Sun. Nov-May 11am-3pm Sat, Sun. **Admission** €2.50; free under-11s. **Map** p71 H9.*

The main synagogue of the Call until the pogrom of 1391, this tiny basement building lay abandoned for many years, until its rediscovery and restoration in 1996. It's now a working synagogue once again. One of the two rooms is a place of worship with several interesting artefacts; the other houses the 14th-century dyeing vats used by the family that lived here until their status as crypto-Jews was discovered. The façade of the building, slightly skewing the street, fulfils religious requirements by which the synagogue has to face Jerusalem; the two windows constructed at knee height allow light to enter from that direction.

Temple d'August
*C/Paradís 10 (93 256 21 22, www. museuhistoria.bcn.cat). Metro Jaume I. **Open** 10am-2pm Mon; 10am-7pm Tue- Sat; 10am-8pm Sun. **Admission** free. **Map** p71 H9.*

Four stunning fluted Corinthian columns dating from the first century BC soar out of their podium in the most unlikely of places: a back patio of the Mountaineering Centre of Catalonia. Part of the rear corner of the temple devoted to the Roman emperor Augustus (who after his death was elevated to the pantheon), the columns were discovered and isolated from the structure of a medieval building in 1835. The current layout is actually a slight fudging of the original as the right-hand column resided separately in the Plaça del Rei until it was slotted next to the other three in 1956.

Restaurants

❤ Belmonte €€
*C/Mercè 29 (93 310 76 84). Metro Jaume I. **Open** 8-11.15pm Tue-Thur; 1-3.30pm, 8pm-midnight Sat, Sun. Closed 2wks Aug. **Map** p71 H10* ❶ *Catalan*

Cosy little Belmonte is one of the city's better-guarded secrets (or maybe just doesn't get the recognition it deserves). Its long and ever-changing list of daily specials is testament to the spontaneous approach in the kitchen and the freshness of the produce (much of it grown in the owners' garden). Try the quail, the pork with shallot confit, one of the ranges of home-made tortillas, or just order a bunch of tapas to share, along with a bottle of the good, cheap house red.

Cafè de l'Acadèmia €€
*C/Lledó 1 (93 319 82 53). Metro Jaume I. **Open** 1-3.30pm, 8-11pm Mon-Fri. Closed 2wks Aug. **Map** p71 J10* ❷ *Catalan*

An assured approach to the classics of Catalan cuisine, combined with sunny tables on the pretty Plaça Sant Just, make this one of the best-value restaurants around. The brick-walled dining room gets full and the tables are close together, so it doesn't really work for a date, but it's an animated spot for a power lunch among the suits from nearby City Hall. Eat à la carte for the likes of quail stuffed with duck's liver and *botifarra* with wild mushroom sauce.

Can Culleretes €
*C/Quintana 5 (93 317 30 22, www.culleretes. com). Metro Liceu. **Open** 1.30-4pm, 9-11pm Tue-Sat; 1.30-4pm Sun. Closed mid July-mid Aug. **Map** p71 H9* ❸ *Catalan*

The rambling dining rooms at the 'house of teaspoons' have been packing 'em in since 1786. The secret to this restaurant's longevity is a straightforward one: honest, hearty cooking and decent wine served at the lowest possible prices. Under huge oil paintings and a thousand signed black-and-white photos, diners munch sticky boar stew, tender pork with prunes and dates, goose with apples, partridge *escabeche* and superbly fresh seafood.

Chicken Shop €

Plaça del Duc de Medinaceli 2 (93 220 47 00, www.chickenshop.com/en/barcelona). Metro Drassanes. Open 1pm-midnight Mon-Thur, Sun; 1 pm-1am Fri, Sat. Map p71 H10 ❹ *American*

The name leaves few surprises, and the most complicated decision you'll need to make is whether to order a quarter, half or the whole beast, cooked on a spit. Sides are simple but generously portioned and the €8 cocktails make a great accompaniment. A bare-bricked space with a subtle sprinkling of Americana, the Chicken Shop attracts a fairly groovy crowd, thanks to its affiliation with the nearby Soho House Barcelona (*see p291*).

El Gran Café €€

C/Avinyó 9 (93 318 79 86, www.restaurantelgrancafe.com). Metro Liceu. Open 12.30-4pm, 7pm-midnight daily. Map p71 H9 ❺ *Mediterranean*

The fluted columns, bronze nymphs, suspended globe lamps and wood panelling help to replicate a classic Parisian vibe, and the cornerstones of brasserie cuisine – onion soup, duck magret, tarte tatin and even crêpe suzette – are all present and correct. The imaginative Catalan dishes spliced into the menu also work, but the distinctly non-Gallic attitude towards the hastily assembled set lunch is less convincing.

Matsuri €

Plaça Regomir 1 (93 268 15 35, matsuri-restaurante.com). Metro Jaume I. Open 8pm-midnight daily. Map p71 H10 ❻ *Asian*

Painted in tasteful shades of ochre and terracotta, with the obligatory trickling fountain, wooden carvings and wall-hung candles, Matsuri is saved from eastern cliché by some occidental jazz in the background. Reasonably priced tom yam soup and pad Thai feature, while less predictable choices include *pho bo* – a Vietnamese broth with meat and spices, and *sake niku*, a delicious beef dish with wok-fried broccoli and a lightly perfumed soy sauce. There is also an increasing number of Japanese options on the menu.
Other locations C/Avinyó 44.

Mercè Vins €

C/Amargós 1 (93 302 60 56). Metro Urquinaona. Open 8am-5pm Mon-Fri. Closed 2wks Aug. Map p71 H8 ❼ *Catalan*

Set in the heart of the Barri Gòtic, this cosy, daytime-only restaurant is aimed at office workers. Dishes on the *menú del día* change daily, but might include a pumpkin soup or inventive salad, followed by *botifarra* with sautéed garlic potatoes. Dessert regulars are flat, sweet coca bread with a glass of muscatel, chocolate flan or figgy pudding. In the morning, Mercè Vins opens for breakfast, which here tends to be *pa amb tomàquet* (bread rubbed with tomato) topped with cheese or ham.

Ocaña €€

Plaça Reial 13-15 (93 676 48 14, www.ocana. cat). Metro Liceu. Tapas 5pm-12.30am Mon-Thur, Sun; noon-12.30am Fri, Sat. Restaurant 8pm-12.30am Thur-Sun. Map p71 H10 ❽ *Spanish/Mexican*

A vast, multi-roomed space with a long terrace under the arcades of the Plaça Reial, Ocaña would be the coolest place in town if it weren't a victim of geography, trapped in the heart of touristville. It's impressively elegant, however, and combines a cosy basement cocktail bar with a couple of lively dining areas – one specialising in creative Mexican food and the other in Spanish and Catalan dishes and tapas. Check the website for details of its regular cultural events and exhibitions.

El Paraguayo €€

C/Parc 1 (93 302 14 41, www.elparaguayo. es). Metro Drassanes. Open noon-4pm, 8pm-midnight Tue-Sun. Map p71 H10 ❾ *Paraguayan*

The only way to go at El Paraguayo, and indeed at most South American restaurants, is to order a juicy steak, a bottle of good, cheap house Rioja and a bowl of piping hot yucca chips – the rest is so much menu filler. As to which steak, a helpful chart walks you through the various cuts, most of them unfamiliar to European butchers; a *bife de chorizo* should satisfy even the most ravenous. The place itself is warm and wood-panelled, brightened with Botero-esque oil paintings of buxom madams and their dapper admirers.

Peimong €

C/Templers 6-10 (93 318 28 73). Metro Jaume I. Open 1-4.30pm, 8-11.30pm Tue-Sat; 1-4pm Sun. Closed Aug. Map p71 H10 ❿ *Peruvian*

Els Quatre Gats

Not, perhaps, the fanciest-looking restaurant around (think Peruvian gimcracks, strip lighting and tapestries of Macchu Pichu) or indeed the fanciest-looking food, but it certainly is tasty. Start with a pisco sour and a dish of chunky yucca chips, or perhaps some spicy corn *tamales*. Next, move on to ceviche for an explosion of lime and coriander; or the satisfying *lomo saltado* – pork fried with onions, tomatoes and coriander. Service is friendly and there are two types of Peruvian beer, plus (for the very nostalgic or the hypoglycaemic) Inca Kola.

Els Quatre Gats €€
C/Montsió 3 (93 302 41 40, www.4gats.com). Metro Catalunya. **Restaurant** *noon-1am daily.* **Café** *9am-1am daily.* **Map** *p71 H8* ⑪ *Catalan*

Dazzling in its design, Els Quatre Gats, the 'Four Cats', is an unmissable stop for those interested in the architecture of the period. It was designed by Modernista heavyweight Puig i Cadafalch and patronised by the cultural glitterati of the era – most notably Picasso, who hung out here with Modernista painters Santiago Rusiñol and Ramon Casas. Nowadays, it chiefly caters to tourists, but makes an essential stop nonetheless. The restaurant is no crucible for Catalan gastronomy – nor is it cheap. There is, however, a more reasonably priced and generously portioned set lunch, and when it's all over you can buy the T-shirt. To appreciate the building without forking out for dinner, you can just have a drink in the café.

Les Quinze Nits €
Plaça Reial 6 (93 317 30 75, www. grupandilana.com). Metro Liceu. **Open** *1-3.45pm, 7.30-11.30pm Mon-Thur; 1-11.30pm Fri, Sat; 12.30-11pm Sun.* **Map** *p71 H9* ⑫ *Spanish*

The staggering success of the Quinze Nits enterprise (there are countless branches here in Barcelona and in Madrid, and a handful of hotels) is down to one concept: style on a budget. All the restaurants have a certain Manhattan chic, yet you'll struggle to spend much more than €20 a head. The food plays second fiddle and is a bit hit-or-miss, but order simple dishes and at these prices you can't go far wrong. The queues tend to be shorter at the other branches.
Other locations throughout the city.

Rasoterra €
C/Palau 5 (93 318 69 26, www.rasoterra.cat). Metro Liceu. **Open** *1-4pm, 7-11pm Tue-Sun.* **Map** *p71 H10* ⑬ *Spanish*

Putting aside the worthy manifesto about 'eating as dialogue', Rasoterra is a light, bright and chilled place, that cherishes locavore and healthy concepts but encourages the idea that no meal is complete without a glass of wine. A sprinkling of fusion enlivens a loosely Catalan-based menu, which includes dishes such as *trinxat* (a Catalan bubble-and-squeak) with chilli and seaweed mayonnaise, and cannelloni stuffed with radicchio, blue cheese and pears.

Shunka €€€

C/Sagristans 5 (93 412 49 91). Metro Jaume I.
Open *1.30-3.30pm, 8.30-11.30pm Tue-Sun.*
Closed Aug & 10 days during Christmas. ***Map***
p71 H9 ⓮ *Japanese*

The speciality here is prime-grade *toro*, fatty and deliciously creamy tuna belly. It's wildly expensive as a main, but you can sample it as *nigiri-zushi*. The house salad with raw fish also makes for a zingy starter, then you'll find all the usual staples of the sushi menu, along with heartier options such as the *udon kakiage*, a filling broth of langoustine tempura, vegetables and noodles. Its Michelin-starred branch, **Koy Shunka**, is round the corner at C/Copons 7 (93 412 79 39), and the same people now have a Japanese tapas bar, **Kak Koy**, at C/Ripoll 16 (93 302 84 14), and another upmarket *izakaya*-style tavern, **Majide**, at C/Tallers 48 (93 016 37 81).

Tokyo €€

C/Comtal 20 (93 317 61 80, tokiosushibcn. com). Metro Catalunya. ***Open*** *1.30-10.30pm Mon-Sat. Closed 3wks Aug.* ***Map*** *p71 H8* ⓯ *Japanese*

A small, simple space, where suspended beams, plastic plants and slatted partitions are used to clever effect and the walls are lined with photos and drawings from grateful clients. The speciality is *edomae* (hand-rolled *nigiri-zushi*), but the meat and vegetable *sukiyaki*, which is cooked at your table, is also good, while the *menú* of sushi and tempura is great value. The *daifuku* (red bean) and *midori* (green tea) *mochi* rolls to finish are something of an acquired taste.

Cafés

Ácoma

C/Boqueria 21 (93 301 75 97). Metro Liceu. ***Open*** *9.30am-11.30 pm daily.* ***Map*** *p71 H9* ❶

A regular enough looking bar from the street, Ácoma is almost unique in the Old City for its pleasant sheltered patio at the back. Here there are tables in the shade of an orange tree and the rear of the Santa Maria del Pi church, and a small pond from which bemused fish and turtles can observe singer-songwriters and small groups perform for a young and merry foreign crowd. A range of salads, burgers, burritos and the like are served from midday to 11.30pm.

❤ Cafè de l'Òpera

La Rambla 74 (93 317 75 85, www. cafeoperabcn.com). Metro Liceu. ***Open*** *8am-1am Mon-Thur, Sun; 8am-2am Fri, Sat.* ***Map*** *p71 G9* ❹

Cast-iron pillars, etched mirrors and bucolic murals create an air of fading grandeur at Cafè de l'Òpera, which now seems incongruous among the fast-food joints and tawdry souvenir shops on La Rambla. Coffee, hot chocolate, pastries and a handful of tapas are served by attentive bow-tied waiters to a largely tourist clientele, but given the atmosphere (and the competition), there's no better place to sit and enjoy a cup of coffee on the city's most celebrated boulevard.

Čaj Chai

C/Sant Domènec del Call 12 (93 301 95 92, www.cajchai.com). Metro Jaume I. ***Open*** *10.30am-10.30pm daily.* ***Map*** *p71 H9* ❺

A cosy tearoom, where first-flush Darjeeling is approached with the reverence afforded to a Château d'Yquem. A range of leaves comes with tasting notes not only describing the origins, but also giving suggestions for maximum enjoyment – Waternymph (an aromatic Oolong), for example, is apparently the ideal tea for those moments 'when your thoughts have been interrupted'.

❤ Federal

Passatge de la Pau 11 (93 280 81 71, www. federalcafe.es/barcelona-gotic). Metro Drassanes. ***Open*** *9am-midnight Mon-Thur; 9am-1am Fri, Sat; 9am-5.30pm Sun.* ***Map*** *p71 H10* ❻

One of the favoured haunts for the MacBook crowd, this relaxed Australian-run café is an easy place to spend some time, with a wide-ranging menu from fry-ups to veggie burgers, granola to Thai curry. Hidden down a sidestreet, it's spitting distance from La Rambla but you'll generally find a table, or at least space at a shared one.

La Granja 1872

C/Banys Nous 4 (mobile 617 370 290). Metro Liceu. ***Open*** *9am-9pm daily.* ***No cards.*** ***Map*** *p71 H9* ❽

La Granja is an old-fashioned café filled with yellowing photos and antiques, which has its very own section of Roman wall. You can stand your spoon in the tarry-thick hot chocolate, which won't be to all tastes, but the *xocolata amb café*, a mocha espresso, or the *xocolata picant*, chocolate with chilli, pack a mid-afternoon energy punch.

Milk

C/Gignàs 21 (93 268 09 22, www. milkbarcelona.com). Metro Jaume I. ***Open*** *9am-1am Mon-Thur, Sun; 9am-1.30am Fri, Sat.* ***Map*** *p71 H9* ❾

The first place in the Old City to provide a decent brunch, Milk's fry-ups, pancakes and smoothies are available every day, until 4pm.

❤ La Boqueria

*La Rambla 89 (93 318 25 84,
www.boqueria.info). Metro Liceu.*
Open *8am-8pm Mon-Sat.* **Map** *p71 G9.*

Thronged with tourists searching for a
little bit of Barcelona's gastro magic, but
all too often ending up with a pre-sliced
quarter of overpriced pineapple, Europe's
biggest food market is still an essential
stop for visitors. Admire the orderly
stacks of ridged Montserrat tomatoes,
the wet sacks of snails and the oozing
razor clams on the fish stalls. You can
also eat at one of the market tapas bars,
such as **Bar Pinotxo**.

If you visit in the morning, you'll see the
best produce, including the smallholders'
fruit and vegetable stalls in the little
square attached to the C/Carme side of the
market, where prices tend to be cheaper.
But if you come only to ogle, remember
that this is where locals come to shop.
Don't touch what you don't want to buy,
ask before taking photos and watch out for
vicious old ladies with ankle-destroying
wheeled shopping bags.

Try visiting earlier in the day, as some
stalls close at around 3pm. Fish-lovers
should bear in mind that the fish stalls
are closed on Mondays.

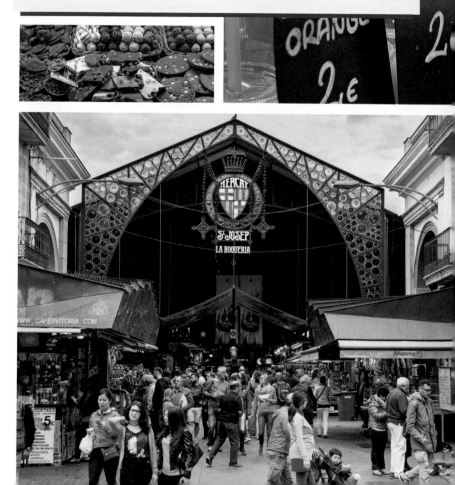

Its candlelit, low-key baroque look, charming service and cheap prices make it a good bet at any time, with home-made bistro grub ranging from Caesar salad to fish and chips.

Tapas

Bar Celta
C/Mercè 9 (93 315 00 06, www.barcelta.com). Metro Drassanes. **Open** *noon-midnight Tue-Sun.* **Map** *p71 H10* ❷

Celta's unapologetically '60s interior is fiercely lit, noisy and not recommended for anyone feeling a bit rough. It is, however, one of the more authentic experiences to be had in the Barri Gòtic. A Galician tapas bar, it specialises in food from the region, such as *lacón con grelos* (boiled gammon with turnip tops) and good seafood, accompanied by crisp Albariño wine served in traditional white ceramic bowls.

Bar Pinotxo
La Boqueria 466-467, La Rambla 89 (mobile 647 869 821). Metro Liceu. **Open** *6.30am-4pm Mon-Sat.* **No cards.** **Map** *p71 G9* ❸

Just inside the entrance of the Boqueria, on the right-hand side, is this essential market bar. It's run by Juanito, one of the city's best-loved figures. In the early morning the place is popular with ravenous night owls on their way home and, at lunchtime, foodies in the know. Various tapas are available, along with excellent daily specials such as tuna casserole or scrambled eggs with clams.

El Portalón
C/Banys Nous 20 (93 302 11 87). Metro Liceu. **Open** *9am-midnight Mon-Sat. Closed Jan & Aug.* **Map** *p71 H9* ⓫

A rare pocket of authenticity in the touristy Barri Gòtic neighbourhood, recent renovations notwithstanding, this traditional tapas bar is located in what were once medieval stables. The tapas list is long and the *torrades* are good: toasted bread topped with juicy red peppers and anchovies, cheese, ham or whatever takes your fancy. The house wine comes in terracotta jugs.

Taller de Tapas
Plaça Sant Josep Oriol 9 (93 301 80 20, www. tallerdetapas.com). Metro Liceu. **Open** *noon-midnight Mon-Thur; noon-1am Fri-Sun.* **Map** *p71 H9* ⓬

Taller de Tapas is an easy, multilingual environment, with plentiful outdoor seating and a good selection of tapas, from heavenly razor clams to local wild mushrooms, along with a well-priced wine list. At busy periods, however, the service can be a little hurried, so it pays to avoid the lunchtime and evening rush hours.

La Vinateria del Call

C/Sant Domènec del Call 9 (93 302 60 92, www.lavinateriadelcall.com). Metro Jaume I or Liceu. Open 7.30pm-1am daily. Map p71 H9 ⑬

An atmospheric little bar, with a real commitment to the sourcing of its wine, hams and cheeses, and excellent home-made dishes, including a delicious fig ice-cream. Despite the antique fittings and dusty bottles, the staff are – like the music they play – young and lively; some speak English.

Bars

♥ Ginger

C/Palma de Sant Just 1 (93 310 53 09, www.ginger.cat). Metro Jaume I. Open 8pm-2.30am Tue-Thur; 8pm-3am Fri, Sat. Map p71 H10 ⑦

Ginger manages to be all things to all punters: a swish art deco cocktail bar with comfortable buttercup yellow banquettes; purveyor of fine tapas and excellent wines; and, above all, a superbly relaxed place to chat and listen to music.

Polaroid

C/Còdols 29 (93 186 66 69, www.polaroidbar. es). Metro Jaume I. Open 7.30pm-2.30am daily. Map p71 H10 ⑩

With more '80s references than a *Stranger Things* mixtape, lively little Polaroid brings together film posters, fluorescent cocktails, superhero merch, VHS cassettes and the eponymous cameras, stirs in some retro pop and serves it all up with a jaunty cocktail parasol.

Shops & services

Almacenes del Pilar

C/Boqueria 43 (93 317 79 84, www. almacenesdelpilar.com). Metro Liceu. Open 10am-2pm, 4-8pm Mon-Sat. Closed 2wks Aug. Map p71 H9 ❶ *Fashion*

An array of fabrics and accessories for traditional Spanish costumes is on display in this colourful, shambolic interior, dating all the way back to 1886. Making your way through bolts of material, you'll find the richly hued brocades used for Valencian *fallera* outfits and other rudiments of folkloric dress from various parts of the country. Lace *mantillas*, and the high combs over which they are worn, are stocked, along with fringed, hand-embroidered pure silk

mantones de manila (shawls) and colourful wooden fans.

♥ Alonso

C/Santa Anna 27 (93 317 60 85, www. tiendacenter.com). Metro Liceu. Open 10am-8pm Mon-Sat. Closed 1wk Sept. Map p71 H8 ❷ *Fashion*

Elegant Catalan ladies have come to Alonso for those important finishing touches for their outfits for more than a century. Behind the Modernista façade lie soft gloves in leather and lace, intricate fans, both traditional and modern, and scarves made from mohair and silk.

Antiques Market

Plaça Nova (no phone). Metro Jaume I. Open 9am-7pm Thur. Closed 3wks Aug. No cards. Map p71 H9 ❸ *Antiques*

Thanks in part to its location in front of the cathedral, this market charges prices that are targeted at tourists – be prepared to haggle. The set-up dates from the Middle Ages, but antiques generally consist of smaller and more modern items: sepia postcards, manila shawls, pocket watches, typewriters, lace, cameras and jewellery, among bibelots and bric-a-brac. In the first week of August, and in the couple of weeks before Christmas, the market is held at Avda Portal de l'Àngel.

L'Arca

C/Banys Nous 20 (93 302 15 98, www.larca. es). Metro Liceu. Open 11am-2pm, 4.30-8.30pm Mon-Sat. Closed 1wk Aug. Map p71 H9 ❹ *Antiques*

Specialising in antique textiles, L'Arca smells wonderfully of cloves and freshly ironed linen and is bursting with both antique and reproduction curtains, bedlinen, tablecloths, clothes and a snowstorm of handmade lace. It specialises in vintage bridal wear, with a wide selection of original lace veils and dresses (there's a tailoring service). It is also the perfect place to go in search of a jaw-dropping lace *mantilla* (headdress) or lavishly embroidered *mantones* (fringed silk shawls).

Caelum

C/Palla 8 (93 302 69 93, www.caelum barcelona.com). Metro Liceu. Open 10.30am-8.30pm Mon-Thur; 10.30am-11pm Fri, Sat; 11.30am-9pm Sun. Closed 2wks Aug. Map p71 H9 ❺ *Food & Drink*

Spain's monks and nuns have a naughty sideline in sweets including 'pets de monja' (little chocolate biscuits known as 'nuns' farts'), candied saints' bones, and drinkable goodies such as eucalyptus and orange liqueur, all beautifully packaged. If you'd like to sample before committing to a whole box of Santa Teresa's sugared egg yolks, there's a café downstairs on the site of the medieval Jewish thermal baths.

Cereria Subirà

*Baixada de Llibreteria 7 (93 315 26 06). Metro Jaume I. **Open** 9.30am-1.30pm, 4.30-8pm Mon-Fri; 10am-2pm, 5-8pm Sat. **Map** p71 J9* ❻ *Gifts & Souvenirs*

With a staircase fit for a full swish from Scarlett O'Hara, this exquisite candle shop dates back to the pre-electric days of 1716, when candles were an everyday necessity at home and in church. These days, the votive candles sit next to novelties such as After Eight-scented candles and candles in the shape of the Sagrada Família, alongside related goods such as garden torches and oil burners.

Flora Albaicín

*C/Canuda 3 (93 302 10 35, www. tiendaflamenco.com). Metro Catalunya. **Open** 10.30am-1pm, 5-8pm Mon-Sat. **Map** p71 H8* ❼ *Fashion*

This tiny boutique is bursting at the seams with brightly coloured flamenco frocks, polka-dotted shoes, hair combs, bangles, shawls and everything else you need to dance the *sevillanas* in style.

Formatgeria La Seu

*C/Dagueria 16 (93 412 65 48, www. formatgerialaseu.com). Metro Jaume I. **Open** 10am-2pm, 5-8pm Tue-Sat. **No cards. Map** p71 H9* ❽ *Food & Drink*

Spain has long neglected its cheese heritage, to the point where this is the only shop in the country to specialise in Spanish-only farmhouse cheeses. Scottish owner Katherine McLaughlin hand-picks her wares, such as a manchego that knocks the socks off anything you'll find in the market, or the truly strange Catalan *tupí*. She also stocks six varieties of cheese ice-cream and some excellent-value olive oils. Her taster plate of three cheeses and a glass of wine for just a few euros is a great way to explore what's on offer.

Herboristeria del Rei

*C/Vidre 1 (93 318 05 12, www. herboristeriadelrei.com). Metro Liceu. **Open** 4-8pm Tue-Fri, 10am-8pm Sat. Closed 2wks Aug. **Map** p71 H9* ❾ *Health & Beauty*

Designed by a theatre set designer in the 1860s, this atmospheric shop hides myriad herbs, infusions, ointments and unguents for health and beauty. More up-to-date stock includes vegetarian foods, organic olive oils and organic mueslis; it's also a good place to buy saffron.

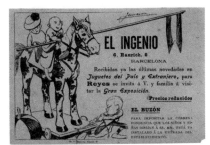

♥ El Ingenio

*C/Rauric 6 (93 317 71 38, elingenio.cat). Metro Liceu. **Open** 10am-1.30pm, 4.30-8pm Mon-Fri; 11am-2pm, 5-8.30pm Sat. **Map** p71 H9* ❿ *Children*

At once enchanting and disturbing, El Ingenio's handcrafted toys, tricks and costumes are reminders of a pre-digital world where people made their own entertainment. Its cabinets are full of practical jokes and curious toys; its fascinating workshop produces the oversized heads and garish costumes used in Barcelona's traditional festivities.

♥ La Manual Alpargatera

*C/Avinyó 7 (93 301 01 72, www. lamanualalpargatera.com). Metro Liceu. **Open** 9.30am-1.30pm, 4.30-8pm Mon-Fri, 10am-1.30pm, 4.30-8pm Sat. **Map** p71 H9* ⓫ *Shoes*

La Manual Alpargatera opened in 1910, stocking handmade espadrilles. The store has shod such luminaries as Pope John Paul II and Jack Nicholson during its years of service – be warned, however, that these names are good indications of the kind of styles you'll find on sale. Prices are fairly low (around €12) for basic models.

Sala Parés

*C/Petritxol 5 (93 318 70 20, www.salapares. com). Metro Liceu. **Open** July 10.30am-2pm, 4-8pm Mon-Fri; 10.30am-2pm, 4-8.30pm Sat. Oct-June 10.30am-2pm, 4-8pm Mon-Fri; 10.30am-2pm, 4-8.30pm Sat; 11.30am-2pm Sun. Closed Aug. **Map** p71 H9* ⓬ *Gallery*

The elegant Sala Parés, founded in 1840, is a grand, two-tier space that smells deliciously of wood varnish and oil paint. Conservative figurative and historical paintings are the mainstay. In September, Sala Parés hosts the Young Painters' Prize. A young Picasso held his very first solo show in the Sala Parés in 1905.

Born & Sant Pere

The area comprising the Born and Sant Pere is sometimes called La Ribera (the Waterfront), a name that recalls the time before permanent quays were built, when the shoreline reached much further inland and the area was contained within the 13th-century wall.

The most uptown area of downtown, the Born is a curious blend of the ecclesiastical, the elegant and the edgy, and now commands some of the highest property prices in the city. Label-happy coolhunters throng the primped pedestrian streets, where museums, restored 15th-century mansions and churches alternate with cafés, galleries and boutiques. Regeneration has come rather more slowly for the neighbouring area of Sant Pere, parts of which maintain a slightly grungier feel despite the municipal money-pumping, but it's home to the spectacularly reinvented Santa Caterina market.

♥ Don't miss

1 Palau de la Música Catalana *p98*
Possibly the world's most flamboyant concert hall.

2 Museu Picasso *p97*
An in-depth look at the artist's youthful works.

3 Parc de la Ciutadella *p94*
The Old City's elegant, landscaped green lung.

4 Santa Maria del Mar *p100*
The finest example of Catalan Gothic in the city.

In the know
Getting around

The Born is almost entirely pedestrianised, but only a five-minute walk from west to east. Jaume I metro station is the most convenient.

Palau de la Música Catalana

BORN & SANT PERE

Restaurants

1. Arcano
2. El Atril
3. Bacoa
4. Café Kafka
5. Cal Pep
6. Casa Delfín
7. En Aparté
8. Koku Kitchen Buns
9. Mosquito
10. Mundial Bar
11. Nakashita
12. La Paradeta
13. Picnic

Cafés, tapas & bars

1. Bar del Convent
2. Bar del Pla
3. La Báscula de la Cerería
4. El Bitxo
5. Bormuth
6. Casa Lolea
7. Casa Paco
8. Elsa y Fred
9. Euskal Etxea
10. Guzzo
11. Mudanzas
12. Paradiso
13. La Vinya del Senyor
14. El Xampanyet

Shops & services

1. Aire de Barcelona
2. Arlequí Màscares
3. La Campana
4. Capricho de Muñeca
5. Casa Antich
6. Casa Gispert
7. Custo Barcelona
8. Èstro
9. Helena Rohner
10. Loisada
11. Miriam Ponsa
12. On Land
13. El Rei de la Màgia
14. U-Casas
15. Vila Viniteca

— — — — Walking Tour
See *p94*

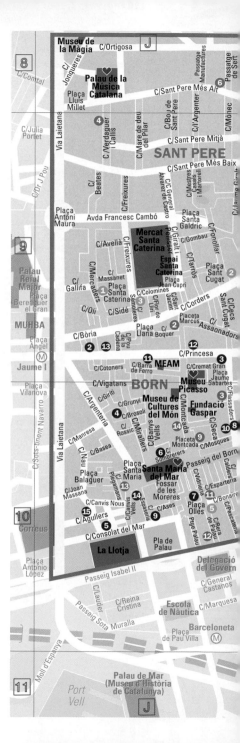

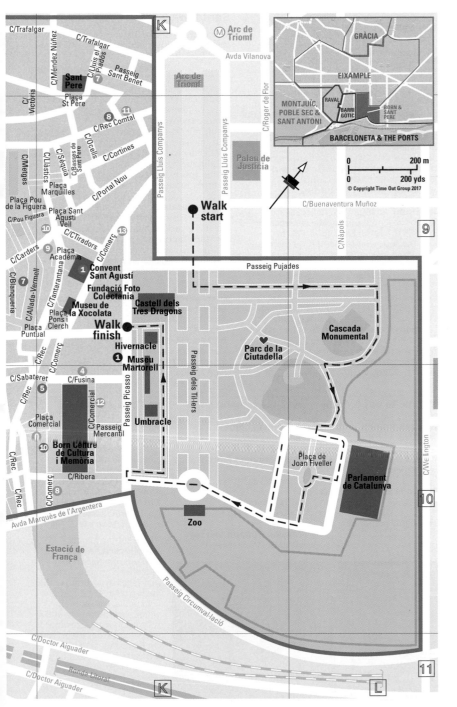

K

Ⓜ Arc de Triomf

C/Trafalgar

C/Méndez Nuñez

C/Trafalgar

C/Lluis el Piadós

Passeig Sant Benet

GRÀCIA

Arc de Triomf

Avda Vilanova

EIXAMPLE

Sant Pere ➐

C/Roger de Flor

Plaça St Père

➑ ⑪

C/Rec Comtal

C/Victòria

Passeig Lluís Companys

Passeig Lluís Companys

MONTJUÏC, POBLE SEC & SANT ANTONI

RAVAL

BARRI GÒTIC

BORN & SANT PERE

C/Metges

C/Llàstics

C/Sèquia

C/Basses de Sant Pere

C/Ocells

C/Cortines

C/Portal Nou

Palau de Justícia

BARCELONETA & THE PORTS

Plaça Marquilles

0   200 m
0   200 yds
© Copyright Time Out Group 2017

Plaça Pou de la Figuera

C/Pou Figuera

Plaça Sant Agustí Vell

⑩

C/Tiradors

C/Comerç

⑬

C/Buenaventura Muñoz

C/Nàpols

9

● Walk start

C/Carders

➒ Plaça Acadèmia

C/Tantarantana

1 Convent Sant Agustí

Passeig Pujades

C/Allada-Vermell

C/Blanqueria

➐

Fundació Foto Colectania

Museu de la Xocolata

Castell dels Tres Dragons

Cascada Monumental

Plaça Pons i Clerch

Plaça Puntual

Walk finish

Parc de la Ciutadella

C/Rec

C/Comerç

Hivernacle

Passeig dels Tillers

❶ Museu Martorell

C/Sabateret

④

C/Fusina

⑤

C/Rec

C/Comercial

⑫

Passeig Picasso

Umbracle

Plaça Comercial

Passeig Mercantil

C/We lington

C/Rec

⑩ Born Centre de Cultura i Memòria

Plaça de Joan Fiveller

Parlament de Catalunya

C/Comerç

C/Ribera

10

C/Rec

➑

Zoo

Avda Marquès de l'Argentera

Estació de França

Passeig Circumval·lació

C/Doctor Aiguader

Ronda Litoral

C/Doctor Aiguader

K   L

11

La Ribera is bounded to the east by **Parc de la Ciutadella** (*see p94*) and to the west by **Via Laietana**, both products of historic acts of urban vandalism. The first came after the 1714 siege, when the victors, acting on the orders of Philip V, destroyed around 1,000 houses, hospitals and monasteries to build a fortress: the Ciutadella (citadel). The second occurred when the Via Laietana was driven through the district in 1907, in line with the theory of 'ventilating' unsanitary city districts by creating wide avenues; it's now a traffic-choked canyon. Plans to turn over some of Via Laietana's car lanes to pedestrians continue to be postponed until an unspecified date in the future.

The grand gateway to the area is the **Arc de Triomf**, an imposing, red-brick arch built by Josep Vilaseca as the entrance for the 1888 Universal Exhibition. On the west side, the Josep Reynés sculptures adorning the arch represent Barcelona hosting the Exhibition, while the Josep Llimona ones on the east side depict prizes being awarded to the Exhibition's most outstanding contributors. Leading down to the park (and technically in the Eixample) is the grand palm-lined boulevard of **Passeig Lluís Companys**, adorned with street lamps and carved stone benches by Pere Falqués. Once inside the park, it's easy to while away a morning, particularly if combined with a trip to the **Zoo** (*see p99*).

Sant Pere

The area north of C/Princesa is centred on the tenth-century Benedictine convent of **Sant Pere de les Puelles** (open for Mass only), which still stands, if greatly altered, in Plaça de Sant Pere. For centuries, this area was Barcelona's main centre of textile production; to this day, C/Sant Pere Més Baix, C/Sant Pere Més Alt and the streets around them contain many textile wholesalers and retailers. Look out for the four low-slung Modernista warehouses of the Serra i Balet velvet manufacturers on neighbouring C/Ortigosa.

The area may be medieval in origin, but its finest monument is an extraordinary piece of Modernisme – the **Palau de la Música Catalana**, on C/Sant Pere Més Alt (*see p98*). Less often noticed on the same street is a curious feature, the **Passatge de les Manufactures**, a 19th-century arcade that passes inside a building between C/Sant Pere Més Alt and C/Ortigosa.

Sant Pere has been renovated with the gradual opening up of a continuation of

> **In the know**
> **Modernista drinking**
>
> By the main façade of Sant Pere de les Puelles sits a superb Modernista wrought-iron drinking fountain, designed by Pere Falqués.

♥ Time to eat & drink

Leisurely brunch
Casa Delfín *p101*

Market-fresh seafood
La Paradeta *p102*

Cocktails and rare groove
Guzzo *p103*

Late-night munchies
Paradiso *p102*

♥ Time to shop

Bohemian chic
Loisada *p105*

Hand-stitched leather bags
Capricho de Muñeca *p104*

Gifts for foodies
Casa Gispert *p104*

Masks, trinkets and toys
Arlequí Màscares *p103*

♥ Time well spent

Aire de Barcelona
Passeig Picasso 22 (93 295 5743, airedebarcelona. com). Metro Arc de Triomf or Jaume I. **Open** *9am-10.30pm Mon-Thur, Sun; 9am-midnight Fri, Sat.* **Baths** *(90mins) €36/€39; (incl 15min massage) €53/€56.* **Map** *p90 K9* ❶

These subterranean, bare-bricked Arab baths are superbly relaxing, and offer a range of extra massages in addition to the basic package of hot and cold pools, jacuzzi, salt-water pool, hammam and relaxation zone. Entrance is every hour from 10am (you get 90 minutes). If you've left your swimsuit at home, you can borrow one.

Aire de Barcelona

Avda Francesc Cambó, which now swings round to meet C/Allada-Vermell, a wide street that was formed when a block was demolished in 1994. Providing the area with some much-needed open space, the large square of **Pou de la Figuera**, between C/Sant Pere Més Baix and C/Carders, was completed in 2008 and houses gardens maintained by the residents themselves, playgrounds and a football pitch. The **Mercat de Santa Caterina** (Avda Francesc Cambó 16, 93 319 57 40, www.mercatsantacaterina.com), one of the city's oldest markets, was rebuilt to a Gaudí-esque design by Enric Miralles.

In the eastern corner of the market, by the recently created Plaça de Joan Capri, is the **Espai Santa Caterina** (open as market above; free), which houses a portion of the archaeological remains discovered during the market's remodelling. Visible through a glass floor are Bronze Age buildings, layered beneath a Christian necropolis, and the foundations of the medieval Convent of Santa Caterina, which became the headquarters of the Consell de Cent (an embryonic form of the democratic Barcelona government) and, later, the Inquisition.

Another nearby convent is the **Sant Agustí**, now a civic centre, on C/Comerç. The entrance contains *Deuce Coop*, a magical 'light sculpture' by James Turrell. Commissioned in the 1980s by the Ajuntament, it's turned on after dark. Almost next door is the **Museu de la Xocolata** (*see p99*).

Born

At one end of the neighbourhood's main artery, the Passeig del Born is the old **Born market**, a magnificent 1870s wrought-iron structure that used to be Barcelona's main wholesale food market; it closed in the 1970s and is now a cultural centre (*see p96*).

Off the Passeig del Born is **C/Montcada**, one of the unmissable streets of old Barcelona. A medieval Fifth Avenue, it's lined with a succession of merchants' mansions, five of which house the **Museu Picasso** (*see p97*). On a narrow street

Born Centre de Cultura i Memòria *p96*

EL BORN CCM

leading off this stretch is the **Museu Europeu d'Art Modern** (MEAM; *see p96*). At the far upper end of C/Montcada is the **Placeta d'en Marcús**, with the small 12th-century Capella d'en Marcús, built as part of an inn. It was founded by Bernat Marcús, and is said to have been the base for the *correus volants* ('flying runners'), Europe's first postal service by horse.

The streets nearby were once filled with workshops supplying products from candles to hemp; these trades are commemorated in street names such as Flassaders ('blanket makers'), Blanqueria ('bleaching') and Sombrerers ('milliners'). At the other end of the Passeig from the market stands the greatest of all Catalan Gothic buildings, the spectacular basilica of **Santa Maria del Mar** (*see p100*). Opposite the main doors is a 13th-century drinking fountain with gargoyles of an eagle and a dragon; on the east side is a funnel-shaped red-brick square, built in 1989 on the site where, it's believed, the last defenders of the city were executed after Barcelona fell to the Spanish army in 1714. Called the **Fossar de les Moreres** (Mulberry Graveyard), the square is inscribed with a patriotic

---

In the know
Street spectacle

'Born' originally meant 'joust' or 'list'. In the Middle Ages, and for many centuries thereafter, the Passeig del Born was the focal point of the city's festivals, processions, tournaments, carnivals and the burning of heretics by the Inquisition.

💙 Parc de la Ciutadella

Passeig Picasso (mobile 638 23 71 15). Metro Arc de Triomf or Barceloneta. **Open** *10am-sunset daily.* **Admission** *free.* **Map** *p90 K10.*

There's so much going on in this extensive park – the Zoo, Catalan parliament buildings, a school, a church, a boating lake, a bandstand – that it's sometimes hard to find a plain, old-fashioned patch of grass. On a sunny Sunday you'll have to fight with hordes of picnicking families, bongo players and dogs for a bit of the green stuff; even then it will be distinctly worn from serving as a back garden to the space-starved inhabitants of the Old City.

The park is named after the hated Bourbon citadel that occupied this site from 1716 to 1869, and came into being after the revolution of 1868, when General Prim announced the area could be reclaimed for public use. The garrison fort was gleefully pulled down by hundreds of volunteers. Later, pleasure gardens were built to host the 1888 Universal Exhibition, handsome reminders of which are scattered around the park.

Exploring the park

The entrance to the park is flanked by the first two of the four 'Statues of Progress' erected for the Exhibition: **Commerce** (**1**) is represented on the left, and **Industry** (**2**) on the right. Through the entrance is Domènech i Montaner's red-brick-and-tile **Castell de Tres Dragons** (**3**) on the right – this served as the exhibition café and later the zoology part of the Natural History Museum, which reopened elsewhere as the Museu Blau (*see p190*) in 2011. Stretching ahead is the wide, leafy **Passeig dels Til·lers** (Linden Tree Boulevard; **4**) and, to the left, Antoni Clavé's modern **Centenary Homage to the Universal Exhibition** (**5**).

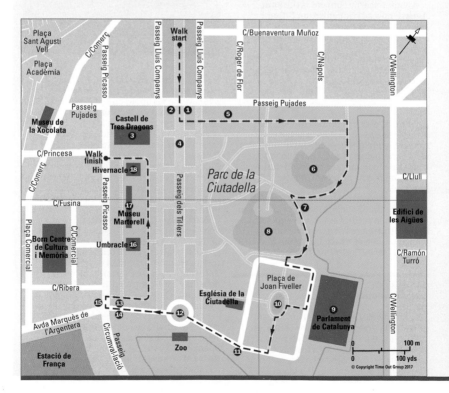

© Copyright Time Out Group 2017

Continue along this path to **La Cascada** (**6**), an extravagant waterfall. It was designed by Josep Fontseré, assisted by a young and – at the time – unknown Antoni Gaudí.

From here the path south leads past a scale model of a **mammoth** (**7**), on the left. The original plan was that the much-loved mammoth would be joined by 11 other scale models of prehistoric species, but the writer and geologist behind the idea, Norbert Font i Sagué, died before the plan could be realised. To the right is a pretty **boating lake** (**8**).

Continuing south on this path you will come to the **Catalan parliament** (**9**) buildings on the left, and the elegant Patio de Armes garden on the right, full of roses in spring. The garden was designed by JC Forestier in 1917, and its centrepoint is Josep Llimona's weeping woman, **Disconsolate** (**10**).

Turn right and soon you'll see the **Monument to the Catalan Volunteers** (**11**) on the left. The plaque reads 'To the Catalans killed in France and around the world in defence of freedom, 1914-1918/1939-1945'. During Franco's rule, the plaque was replaced with another,

mentioning only World War I, and the naked torso was adorned with a puritanical fig-leaf, which is there to this day. Beyond this is the entrance to the **Zoo** (*see p99*), in front of which stands an imposing equestrian **statue of General Prim** (**12**), the driving force behind the park.

Gracing the columns either side of the park entrance beyond Prim are the other two 'Progress' statues, **Agriculture** (**13**) and **Seamanship** (**14**). Just outside the entrance is one of the wrought-iron **Wallace Fountains** (**15**), donated to the city – along with another 12 – by English philanthropist Sir Richard Wallace in the 19th century, though only five remain.

Instead of leaving this way, turn right up the Passeig dels Til·lers where you'll see the **Umbracle** (Shade House; **16**). This elegant slatted wooden building, also by Fontseré, houses palms and tropical plants, though it has been closed for a while pending restoration. Beside it is the neoclassical former home of the geological section of the Natural History Museum, the **Museu Martorell** (**17**), now closed, and then, alongside the upper Passeig Picasso entrance, the iron-and-glass, Eiffel-inspired **Hivernacle** (Winter House; **18**).

Església de la Ciutadella

poem by Frederic Soler, and nationalist demonstrations converge here every 11 September for Catalan National Day. The red 'eternal flame' sculpture is a more recent, and less popular, addition.

From here, narrow streets lead to the **Plaça de les Olles**, or the grand **Pla del Palau** and another symbol of La Ribera, **La Llotja** (the Exchange, Passeig d'Isabel II). Its neo-classical outer shell was added in the 18th century, but its core is a superb 1380s Gothic hall, sadly closed to the public (open doors mean you can often peer inside). Until the exchange moved to Passeig de Gràcia in 1994, this was the oldest continuously functioning stock exchange in Europe.

In the know
Inside La Llotja

Upstairs at La Llotja is a gallery of mostly medieval paintings, open to the public from 10am to 2pm on weekdays. It forms part of the **Reial Acadèmia Catalana de Belles Arts de Sant Jordi** (mobile 670 46 62 60, www.racba.org) and is free to visit.

Sights & museums

Born Centre de Cultura i Memòria

Plaça Comercial 12 (93 256 68 51, www. elborncentrecultural.cat). Metro Jaume I or Barceloneta. **Open** *Mar-Oct 10am-8pm Tue-Sun. Nov-Feb 10am-7pm Tue-Sat; 10am-8pm Sun.* **Building** *free.* **Exhibitions** *€4.40; €3.08 reductions; free under-16s.* **Map** *p90 K10.*

Plans to turn the old Born market into a library were thwarted by the discovery of perfectly preserved medieval remains, the foundations of buildings razed by Philip V's troops in 1714. These were found to contain hundreds of objects, some domestic and some, like rusty bombs, suggesting the traumas of the period. It was then that the idea for the Born Centre came about – a vast, virtually open-air, space, open on four sides to the passing public, opened in time for the celebrations of the tricentenary of the Catalan defeat, in 2014. Even the naysayers (those who wanted a library, or those who resented public money being thrown at what they perceive as nationalist endeavour) were impressed. It's a glorious, lofty space, with the archaeological remains visible from above (or close up via a guided tour). There's a Catalan restaurant, a quirky gift shop, a permanent collection displaying some of the finds uncovered in the remains, and a handful of rooms used for cultural events.

Fundació Foto Colectania

Passeig Picasso 14 (93 217 16 26, www. fotocolectania.org). Metro Jaume I. **Open** *11am-8pm Tue-Sat; 11am-3pm Sun.* **Admission** *€4; €3 reductions; free under-14s. No cards.* **Map** *p90 K9.*

This private foundation is dedicated to the promotion of the photography of major Spanish and Portuguese photographers from the 1950s to the present. It also has an extensive library of Spanish and Portuguese photography books.

Fundació Gaspar

C/Montcada 25 (93 887 42 48, www. fundaciogaspar.com). Metro Jaume I. **Open** *10am-8pm Mon-Fri, Sun; 10am-9.30pm Sat.* **Admission** *€5; €3 reductions; free under-12s.* **Map** *p90 J10.*

Born from the ashes of the Sala Gaspar, which showcased the work of up-and-coming and, later, internationally renowned artists for the best part of a century, the Fundació Gaspar is still run by members of the Gaspar family. Now housed in the 14th-century Palau Cervelló, it endeavours to exhibit a multidisciplinary range of artists who have not previously held solo shows in Spain.

MEAM (Museu Europeu d'Art Modern)

C/Barra de Ferro 5 (93 319 56 93, www. meam.es). Metro Jaume I. **Open** *10am-8pm Tue-Sun.* **Admission** *€9; €7 reductions; free under-10s.* **Map** *p90 J9.*

The 'European Museum of Modern Art' has a slightly misleading name in that the collection is overwhelmingly Spanish, with only a handful of exceptions, and 'Modern', while accurate, turns out to mean 21st century only. It's a celebration of figurative art and sculpture, much of it verging on photorealism and mostly from young, little-known artists, which spreads over three floors of the splendid 18th-century Palau Gomis. There are some accomplished pieces, but the museum's philosophy – that art lost its way with the advent of abstraction and should return to the purely representational – will be off-putting to many.

Museu de Cultures del Món

C/Montcada 12 (93 256 23 00, museuculturesmon.bcn.cat). Metro Jaume I. **Open** *10am-7pm Tue-Sat; 10am-8pm Sun.* **Permanent exhibition** *€5; €3.50 reductions.* **Temporary exhibitions** *€2.20; €1.50 reductions. Free 3-8pm Sun & all day 1st Sun of mth.* **Map** *p90 J10.*

Occupying yet another 15th-century palazzo on the C/Montcada, the Museum of World Cultures takes a look at the ancient peoples

❤ Museu Picasso

*C/Montcada 15-23 (93 256 30 00, www. museupicasso.bcn.cat). Metro Jaume I. **Open** (last ticket 30mins before closing) 9am-7pm Tue, Wed, Fri-Sun; 9am-9.30pm Thur. **Admission** All exhibitions €11-€14; €7-€7.50 reductions. Annual pass €15. Temporary exhibition only €4.50-€6.50; €4.50 reductions; free under-18s. Free (permanent exhibition only) 3-7pm Sun & all day 1st Sun of mth. **Map** p90 J9.*

When it opened in 1963, the museum dedicated to Barcelona's favourite adopted son was housed in the Palau Aguilar. Five decades later, the permanent collection of some 3,500 pieces has now spread out across five adjoining palaces, two of which are devoted to temporary exhibitions.

By no means an overview of the artist's work, the Museu Picasso is a record of the vital formative years the young Picasso spent nearby at La Llotja art school (where his father taught), and later hanging out with Catalonia's fin-de-siècle avant-garde. Those looking for hits such as *Les Demoiselles d'Avignon* (1907) and the first Cubist paintings from the time (many of them done in Catalonia), as well as his collage and sculpture, will be disappointed. The founding of the museum is down to a key figure in Picasso's life, his friend and secretary Jaume Sabartés, who donated his own collection for the purpose. Tribute is paid with a room dedicated to Picasso's portraits of him (best known is the Blue Period painting of Sabartés wearing a white ruff), and Sabartés's own doodlings. The seamless presentation of Picasso's development from 1890 to 1904 – from deft pre-adolescent portraits and sketchy landscapes to the intense innovations of his Blue Period – is unbeatable, then it leaps to a gallery of mature Cubist paintings from 1917. The *pièce de résistance* is the complete series of 58 canvases based on Velázquez's famous *Las Meninas*, donated by Picasso himself after the death of Sabartés, and now stretching through the Great Hall. The display ends with linocuts, engravings and a wonderful collection of ceramics donated by Picasso's widow.

In the know
Skipping the line

Queues for the Museu Picasso can be punishingly long – visit at lunch or shortly before the last entry. Holders of the annual pass (which costs little more than a day pass) don't need to queue, which makes the extra €1 or so worth considering even for a single visit.

❤ Palau de la Música Catalana

C/Sant Francesc de Paula 2 (93 295 72 00, www.palaumusica.org). Metro Urquinaona. **Box office** *9.30am-9pm Mon-Sat; 10am-3pm Sun.* **Guided tours** *10am-3.30pm daily. Aug 9am-6pm daily.* **Admission** *€18; €11 reductions; free under-10s.* **Map** *p90 J8.*

Commissioned by the Orfeó Català choral society and opened in 1908, this jaw-dropping concert hall was intended as a paean to the Catalan *renaixença* and a showcase for the most outstanding Modernista workmanship available. Domènech i Montaner's façade is a frenzy of colour and detail, including a large allegorical mosaic representing the members of the Orfeó Català, and floral tiled columns topped with the busts of Bach, Beethoven and Palestrina on the main façade and Wagner on the side. Inside, a great deal of money has been spent improving the acoustics, but visitors don't really come to feast their ears: the eyes have it.

Decoration erupts everywhere. The ceiling is an inverted bell of stained glass on which the sun bursts out of a blue sky; 18 half-mosaic, half-relief muses appear out of the back of the stage; winged horses fly over the upper balcony. The carved arch over the stage represents folk and classical music: the left side has Catalan composer/conductor Anselm Clavé sitting over young girls singing 'Flors de Maig', a traditional Catalan song, while the right has Wagnerian Valkyries riding over a bust of Beethoven.

By the 1980s, the Palau was bursting under the pressure of the musical activity going on inside it, and a church next door was demolished to make space for Òscar Tusquet's extension, a project which, combined with the extensive renovations to the old building, spanned more than 20 years. Rather than try to compete with the existing façade, the new part has subtler organic motifs in ochre brick.

Guided tours are available in English every hour and start with a short film of the Palau's history. Be sure to ask questions: the guides are knowledgeable, but unless prompted, they tend to concentrate mainly on the triumphs of the renovation.

of Latin America, Asia, Oceania and sub-Saharan Africa through an impressive selection of artworks, sculpture, tools and weapons, from New Guinean fertility symbols to Ethiopian retablos. Many exhibits require background reading to be interesting, but the museum works hard on accessibility, with interactive gadgetry, a downloadable app and a series of suggested highlight tours aimed at children.

Museu de la Màgia

C/Jonqueres 15 (93 318 71 92, www. elreydelamagia.com). Metro Urquinaona. **Open** *11am-2pm, 4-8pm Tue-Sun.* **Admission** *€5; €3 reductions.* **Map** *p90 J8.*

This collector's gallery of 19th- and 20th-century tricks and posters from the magic shop El Rei de la Màgia will enchant any budding magicians. To see some live sleight of hand, book for the occasional shows (see website); places are limited. They're not in English, but they are very visual, so it doesn't matter too much.

Museu de la Xocolata

C/Comerç 36 (93 268 78 78, www. museudelaxocolata.cat). Metro Arc de Triomf or Jaume I. **Open** *mid June-mid Sept 10am-8pm Mon-Sat; 10am-3pm Sun. Mid Sept-mid June 10am-7pm Mon-Sat; 10am-3pm Sun.* **Admission** *€6; €5.10 reductions; free under-7s.* **Map** *p90 K9.*

The best-smelling museum in town draws chocoholics of all ages to its collection of chocolate sculptures made by Barcelona's master *pastissers* for the Easter competition; these range from multicoloured models of Gaudí's Casa Batlló to characters from the latest Pixar film. Audio-visual shows and touch-screen computers help children make their way through what would otherwise be the rather dry history of the cocoa bean.

Zoo

Parc de la Ciutadella (93 225 67 80, www. zoobarcelona.com). Metro Barceloneta or Ciutadella-Vila Olímpica. **Open** *Jan-mid Mar, Oct-Dec 10am-5pm daily. Mid Mar-mid May, mid Sept-end Oct 10am-6pm daily. Mid May-mid Sept 10am-7pm daily.* **Admission** *€19.90; €11.95 3-12s; free under-3s.* **Map** *p90 K10.*

A decently sized zoo with plenty of animals, all of which look happy enough in reasonably sized enclosures and the city's comfortable climate. The dolphin shows are no more, but other favourites include giant hippos, the prehistoric-looking rhino, sea lions, elephants, giraffes, lions and tigers. Child-friendly features include a farmyard zoo, pony rides, picnic areas and two excellent playgrounds. If all that walking is too much, there's a zoo 'train'. Bear in mind that on hot days many of the animals are sleeping and out of sight, whilst below 13°C many are kept inside.

Restaurants

▶ *For details of our restaurant price categories, see p36.*

Arcano €€

C/Mercaders 10 (93 295 64 67, arcanobcn. com). Metro Jaume I. **Open** *noon-midnight daily.* **Map** *p90 J9* ❶ *Argentinian*

Low ceilings, Gothic arches and subtle lighting make dining in this former stables a cosy affair. Formerly known as Diez, it is now under Argentinian management and the focus is on grilled steaks of various cuts, *empanadas* and other specialities of the region. It's not all hearty gaucho fare, however, and some less predictable options include *caprese* salad, Catalan *escalivada*, grilled octopus with lentils and cod with a garlic mousseline.

El Atril €€

C/Carders 23 (93 310 12 20, www. atrilbarcelona.com). Metro Jaume I. **Open** *11am-midnight daily.* **Map** *p90 J9* ❷ *Global*

El Atril's few tables require a reservation on most nights thanks to some reliably good cooking, traversing a range of cuisines. On the tapas menu, fried green plantains with coriander and lime mayonnaise sit alongside *botifarra* with caramelised onions, while a eclectic selection of main courses includes a bowl of Belgian-style mussels and chips and a kangaroo burger. There is occasional live music – normally jazz – midweek, and tables outside on the Plaça Sant Cugat.

Bacoa €

C/Colomines 2 (93 268 95 48). Metro Jaume I. **Open** *1-11pm Tue-Thur; 1pm-midnight Fri, Sat.* **No cards.** **Map** *p90 J9* ❸ *Burgers*

The best gourmet burger place around. Succulent chargrilled half-pounders are loaded up with manchego cheese, caramelised onions and a whole load of more outré toppings (try the Swiss, with rösti and gruyère, or the Japanese with teriyaki sauce). **Other locations** around the city.

Café Kafka €€

C/Fusina 7 (93 315 17 76, www.cafekafka.es). Metro Jaume I. **Open** *noon-4pm, 8pm-2am Tue-Sat; 1.30-4pm Sun.* **Map** *p90 K10* ❹ *Mediterranean*

This gleaming, high-ceilinged bar and restaurant is made characterful by some

♥ Santa Maria del Mar

Plaça de Santa Maria (93 310 23 90, www. santamariadelmarbarcelona.org). Metro Jaume I. **Open** *9am-1pm, 5-8 pm Mon-Sat; 10am-2pm, 5-8pm Sun.* **Admission** *free.* **Map** *p90 J10.*

One of the most perfect surviving examples of the Catalan Gothic style, this graceful basilica stands out for its horizontal lines, plain surfaces, square buttresses and flat-topped octagonal towers. Its superb unity of style is down to the fact that it was built relatively quickly, taking just 55 years (1329-1384). Named after Mary as patroness of sailors, it was built on the site of a small church known as Santa Maria d'Arenys (sand), for its position close to the sea. In the broad, single-nave interior, two rows of perfectly proportioned columns soar up to fan vaults, creating an atmosphere of space around the light-flooded altar. There's also superb stained glass, especially the great 15th-century rose window above the main door. The original window fell down during an earthquake, killing 25 people. The incongruous modern window at the other end was a 1997 addition, belatedly celebrating the Olympics.

It's perhaps thanks to the group of anti-clerical anarchists who set the church ablaze for 11 days in 1936 that its superb features can be appreciated – without the wooden Baroque furniture that clutters so many Spanish churches, the simplicity of its lines can emerge.

On Saturdays, the basilica is in great demand for weddings, and it's a traditional venue for concerts: look out for a Requiem Mass at Easter and Handel's *Messiah* at Christmas.

spruced-up flea market finds among the Scandi furniture and *objets d'art*. It's beloved of the beautiful people not only for its expertly made cocktails, but also for the menu of Mediterranean dishes catering for every diet, from a fat juicy sirloin to a super-healthy tortilla made with egg white.

Cal Pep €€

Plaça de les Olles 8 (93 310 79 61, www.calpep. com). Metro Barceloneta. Open 7.30-11.30pm Mon; 1-3.45pm, 7.30-11.30pm Tue-Fri; 1-3.45pm Sat. Closed 3wks Aug. Map p90 J10 ⑤ *Seafood*

As much tapas bar as restaurant, Cal Pep is always packed to the hilt: get here early to bag one of the coveted seats at the front. There is a cosy dining room at the back, but it's a shame to miss the show. The affable Pep will take the order, steering neophytes towards the *trifàsic* – a mélange of fried whitebait, squid rings and shrimp. Other favourites include the exquisite little *tallarines* (wedge clams), and *botifarra* sausage with beans. Then squeeze in four shot glasses of foam – coconut with rum, coffee, *crema catalana* and lemon – as a light and scrumptious pudding.

❤ Casa Delfín €€

Passeig del Born 36 (93 319 50 88, tallerdetapas.com/esp/casa-delfin). Metro Barceloneta or Jaume I. Open 8am-midnight Mon-Thur, Sun; 8am-1am Fri, Sat. Map p90 K10 ⑥ *Catalan*

Locals were heartbroken when the old, much-loved Casa Delfín served its last plate of fried sardines, but it has scrubbed up very nicely indeed in its new incarnation. Meticulous attention has been paid to respecting traditional Catalan recipes, with a rich and sticky *suquet* (fish stew) and excellent 'mountain' lamb with wild mushrooms. Brit owner Kate has left her imprint, however, and you'll also find the best Eton mess this side of Windsor.

En Aparté €

C/Lluís el Piadós 2 (93 269 13 35, www. enaparte.es). Metro Arc de Triomf. Open 10am-1.30am Mon-Thur, Sun; 10am-2am Fri, Sat. Map p90 K8 ⑦ *French*

The peaceful Plaça Sant Pere has never been well served with good places to eat or drink, so this relaxed, sunny and spacious café-restaurant has been joyfully received in the neighbourhood. French cheeses and charcuterie are the mainstays of the kitchen, served for the most part on toasted bread with a well-dressed salad. The all-French wine list makes for a refreshing change, and there is a good-value set lunch.

Koku Kitchen Buns €

C/Comerç 29 (93 269 65 36, kokukitchen.es). Metro Barceloneta. Open 1.30pm-1am Tue-Sun, 7.30pm–1am Mon. Map p90 K10 ⑧ *Asian*

Flush with the success of the Koku ramen bar (C/Carabassa 19, 93 315 64 11), a second, quieter branch has opened in the Born. The speciality upstairs is large steamed buns – choose from pork, chicken, beef or wild mushroom fillings – while downstairs they have added a gyoza dumpling and ramen bar.

Mosquito €

C/Carders 46 (93 268 75 69, www. mosquitotapas.com). Metro Arc de Triomf or Jaume I. Open 1pm-midnight Mon; 1-6pm, 7pm-midnight Tue-Sun. Map p90 K9 ⑨ *Asian*

Mosquito's speciality is Chinese dumplings in myriad forms, but its tapas comprise a grab bag from all over the continent. The *xiaolong bao* (steamed pork dumplings) and crispy duck are more than toothsome, and a steaming bowl of Vietnamese *pho* with noodles makes for a sturdy lunch on its own. Mosquito also has excellent beers, some of which are brewed for the restaurant; the *trigo* (wheat) beer is especially good. Under the same ownership and in a similar vein (but less crowded), is nearby Red Ant (C/Tiradors 3-5, 93 501 68 60). The latest addition to the group is Grasshopper (Plaça de la Llana 9, 93 017 84 84), which serves ramen and craft beer.

Mundial Bar €€

Plaça Sant Agustí Vell 1 (93 319 90 56). Metro Arc de Triomf or Jaume I. Open 1-3.30pm, 8pm-midnight daily. No cards. Map p90 K9 ⑩ *Seafood*

Since 1925, this family bar has been dishing up no-frills platters of seafood, cheeseboards and the odd slice of cured meat. Colourful tiles add charm to the rather basic decoration, but it's not as cheap as it looks. People come for the steaming piles of fresh razor clams, oysters, fiddler crabs and the like, but there's also plenty of tinned produce, so check the bar displays to see exactly which is which.

Nakashita €€

C/Rec Comtal 15 (93 295 53 78, www. nakashitabcn.com). Metro Arc del Triomf. Open 1-4.30pm, 8.30pm-midnight daily. Map p90 K9 ⑪ *Japanese*

A really superb sushi restaurant, with a handful of tables outside and in (though it's more fun to sit at the bar). High-end produce such as Wagyu beef, foie gras and *toro* tuna belly are used to great effect, but can of course cause the bill to rack up. If you're prepared to splash out, however, this is the place.

❤ La Paradeta €

C/Comercial 7 (93 268 19 39, www. laparadeta.com). Metro Arc de Triomf or Jaume I. **Open** *1-4pm, 8-11.30pm Tue-Thur; 1-4pm, 8pm-midnight Fri, Sat; 1-4pm Sun.* **No cards.** *Map* **p90 K10** ⑫ *Seafood*

Superb seafood, served in a refectory-style fashion. Choose from glistening mounds of clams, mussels, squid, spider crabs and other fresh treats, decide how you would like it cooked (grilled, steamed or *a la marinera*), pick a sauce (Marie Rose, spicy local romesco, allioli or onion), buy a drink and wait for your number to be called. A great – and cheap – experience for anyone who is not too grand to clear away their own plate. **Other locations** around the city.

Picnic €

C/Comerç 1 (93 511 66 61, www.picnic-restaurant.com). Metro Arc de Triomf or Jaume I. **Open** *1-4pm Mon; 1-4pm, 8pm-12.30am Tue-Fri; 10.30am-5pm, 8pm-12.30am Sat; 10.30am-5pm Sun.* *Map* **p90 K9** ⑬ *Chilean/American*

While the exterior is rather unlovely, Picnic is a welcoming space, with country-kitchen bar stools, dramatic flower arrangements and lounge music. The food is influenced by the US Deep South, with corn chowder, fried green tomatoes and some tasty little crab cakes with fennel salad and crème fraîche, all served in half-portions. If you come at the weekend, there's an excellent brunch: get there early for any chance of a table.

Cafés

Bar del Convent

Plaça de l'Acadèmia (93 256 50 17, www. bardelconvent.com). Metro Arc de Triomf or Jaume I. **Open** *10am-9pm Tue-Sat.* *Map* **p90 K9** ❶

The 14th-century Convent de Sant Agustí has had a new lease of life in recent years with James Turrell's fabulous 'light sculpture' surrounding the C/Comerç entrance, and a dynamic civic centre. This secluded little café is in the cloister. Croissants, pastries and light dishes are available all day, and bands, DJs, storytellers and other performers occasionally feature.

La Báscula de la Cerería

C/Flassaders 30 (93 319 98 66). Metro Jaume I. **Open** *1pm-11pm Wed-Sun.* **No cards.** *Map* **p90 J10** ❸

After a sustained campaign, the threat of demolition has been lifted from this former chocolate factory-turned-café. Just as well, since it's a real find, with good vegetarian food and a large dining room out back. An

impressive list of drinks runs from chai to glühwein, taking in cocktails, milkshakes, smoothies and iced tea; and the pasta and cakes are as good as you'll find anywhere.

Elsa y Fred

C/Rec Comtal 11 (93 501 66 11, www. elsayfred.es). Metro Arc de Triomf. **Open** *8.30am-1.30am Mon-Fri; 9am-1.30am Sat, Sun.* *Map* **p90 K9** ❽

Opened a few years ago, this friendly and vaguely Viennese-style café still needs to gather a little dust to go with its gleaming period fittings – fringed lampshades, wooden fireplace, oversized clocks, starburst light and hardwood floors – and then it will be unbeatable. It already has brunch on Saturday and Sunday mornings, a creative *menú del día* (€14.50) on weekdays and home-made cakes at any time to recommend it.

❤ Paradiso

C/Rera Palau 4 (93 360 72 22, paradiso.cat). Metro Arc de Triomf. **Open** *7pm-2am daily.* *Map* **p90 J10** ⑫

Speakeasy-style bars are all the rage these days, but no one does it better than Paradiso, a cavernous cocktail bar entered via the portal of an antique fridge. It's worth lingering in the antechamber, however, where a selection of smoked meats and pickles are served, with a pastrami sandwich second to none.

Tapas

Bar del Pla

C/Montcada 2 (93 268 30 03, www.bardelpla. cat). Metro Jaume I. **Open** *noon-11pm Tue-Thur; noon-midnight Fri, Sat.* *Map* **p90 J9** ❷

Positioned somewhere between a French bistro and a tapas bar, the bright Bar del Pla serves tapas or *raciones* (divine pig's trotters with foie gras, outstanding *pa amb tomàquet*). Drinks include Mahou on tap (a fine beer, often ignored here because it's from Madrid), plus some good wines by the glass.

El Bitxo

C/Verdaguer i Callis 9 (93 268 17 08). Metro Urquinaona. **Open** *7pm-midnight Mon; 1pm-1am Tue-Sun.* **No cards.** *Map* **p90 J9** ❹

This small, lively tapas bar specialises in excellent cheese and charcuterie from the small Catalan village of Oix, along with more outré fare such as salmon sashimi with a coffee reduction. The wine list is steadily increasing and now has around 30 suggestions, all of them good. Being so close to the Palau de la Música, the bar can get packed in the early evening before concerts.

Bormuth

C/Rec 31 (93 310 21 86). Metro Jaume I.
Open *12.30pm-1.30am Mon-Thur, Sun;*
12.30pm-2.30am Fri, Sat. **Map** *p90 K10* ❺

Bormuth fills a hole in the market with
good, honest tapas in an attractive setting,
at reasonable prices. All the usual tortillas,
patatas bravas and so on are present,
along with the highly recommended fried
aubergines drizzled with honey, tuna
belly with Raf tomatoes.

Casa Lolea

*C/Sant Pere mès Alt (93 624 10 16, casalolea.
com). Metro Urquinaona.* **Bar** *9am-1am
daily.* **Kitchen** *noon-midnight daily.*
Map *p90 J8*

Sangría gets a bad rap in northern Spain,
but Casa Lolea is chipping away at the stigma
with its craft version, in ceramic swing-
topped bottles with semi-ironic flamenco
polka dot patterns. The company has
now branched out with a tapas bar, where
you'll find the sangría complemented with
some top-class sharing plates, including
dry-cured tuna with orange and almonds,
salmon blinis with truffled honey and
smoked eel with ricotta.

Euskal Etxea

*Placeta Montcada 1 3 (93 343 54 10, www.
euskaletxetaberna.com) Metro Barceloneta
or Jaume I.* **Bar** *10am-12.30am Mon-Fri,
Sun; 10am-1am Sat.* **Restaurant** *1 4pm,
8pm-midnight daily.* **Map** *p90 J10* ❾

A Basque cultural centre and the best of the
city's many *pintxo* bars. Help yourself to
dainty *jamón serrano* croissants, chicken
tempura with saffron mayonnaise, melted
provolone with mango and crispy ham, or
a mini-brochette of pork. Hang on to the
toothpicks spearing each one: they'll be
counted up and charged for at the end. There
is also a dining room at the back.

Bars

Casa Paco

*C/Allada-Vermell 10 (93 295 51 18). Metro
Arc de Triomf or Jaume I.* **Open** *Apr-Sept
9am-1am Mon-Wed; 9am-2am Thur;
9am-3am Fri; 11pm-3am Sat; 11am-1am Sun.
Nov-Mar 5pm-1am Mon-Wed; 9am-2am
Thur; 9am-3am Fri; 11pm-3am Sat;
11am-1am Sun.* **Map** *p90 J9* ❼

Not much more than a hole in the wall with
a handful of zinc tables outside, Casa Paco
is the improbable nerve centre for a young
and thrusting scene that attracts DJs from
the higher echelons of cool. In the daytime,
mind you, it's simply a nice place for parents
to sit on the terrace and have a cheeky beer

in the sunshine while their children amuse
themselves in the playground in front.

♥ Guzzo

*Plaça Comercial 10 (93 667 00 36, www.
guzzoclub.es). Metro Barceloneta.* **Open**
*6pm-3am Mon-Thur; 6pm-3.30am Fri, Sat;
noon-3am Sun.* **Map** *p90 K10* ❿

One of Barcelona's best-loved DJs, Fred
Guzzo, finally opened his own bar, where he
can give full rein to his penchant for vintage
soul and funk, spiced up with some live
music acts at weekends. Cocktails are the
speciality, and there are snacks and light
dishes available during the day.

Mudanzas

*C/Vidrleria 15 (93 319 11 37). Metro
Barceloneta or Jaume I.* **Open** *10am-2.30am
Mon-Thur, Sun; 10am-3am Fri, Sat.* **Map**
p90 J10 ⓫

Eternally popular with all ages and
nationalities, Mudanzas has a beguiling, old-
fashioned look, with marble-topped tables, a
black-and-white chequered floor and a rack
of newspapers and magazines, many of them
in English. Its main drawback used to be that
it got very smoky in the winter months, but
this, of course, is now a thing of the past.

La Vinya del Senyor

*Plaça Santa Maria 5 (93 310 33 79). Metro
Barceloneta or Jaume I.* **Open** *noon-1am
Mon-Thur; noon-2am Fri, Sat; noon-
midnight Sun.* **Map** *p90 J10* ⓭

Though many pull up a chair simply to
appreciate the splendours of Santa Maria del
Mar's Gothic façade, it's a sin to take up the
tables of the 'Vineyard of the Lord' without
sampling a few of the excellent vintages on its
list, along with some top-quality tapas.

El Xampanyet

*C/Montcada 22 (93 319 70 03). Metro Jaume
I.* **Open** *noon-3.30pm, 7-11pm Tue-Sat; noon-
3.30pm Sun. Closed Aug.* **Map** *p90 J10* ⓮

The eponymous bubbly is actually a pretty
low-grade cava, but a drinkable enough
accompaniment to the house tapa – a
saucer of Cantabrian anchovies. Lined with
coloured tiles, barrels and antique curios,
the bar functions as a little slice of Barcelona
history and has been run by the same
family since the 1930s.

Shops & services

♥ Arlequí Màscares

*C/Princesa 7 (93 268 27 52, www.
arlequimask.com). Metro Jaume
10.30am-8.30pm Mon-Sat; 10.3*
Sun. **Map** *p90 J9* ❷ *Masks*

BORN & SANT PERE

La Campana

The walls in this lovely shop are dripping with masks, crafted from papier mâché and leather. Whether gilt-laden or in feathered *commedia dell'arte* style, simple Greek tragicomedy styles or traditional Japanese or Catalan varieties, they make striking fancy dress or decorative staples. Other trinkets and toys include finger puppets, mirrors and ornamental boxes.

La Campana
C/Princesa 36 (93 319 72 96). Metro Jaume
* . **Open** 10am-9pm daily. Map p90 J9* ❸
od & Drink

nded in 1922, this lovely shop in the Born
torrons, blocks of nougat traditionally
at Christmas. They come in two types:
'xona) or hard and brittle (*alacant*).
immer, there's *orxata*, an ice-cold
de from tiger nuts; there are also
es of ice-creams and pralines. The
nd the corner on C/Flassaders has
'uiet square.

ons C/Flassaders 15 (93 268

❤ Capricho de Muñeca
C/Brosolí 1 (93 319 58 91, www.
caprichodemuneca.com). Metro Jaume I.
***Open** 11.30am-3pm, 4.30-8.30pm Mon-Sat.*
***Map** p90 J10* ❹ *Luggage*

Soft leather handbags in cherry reds, parma violet and grass green made by hand just upstairs by designer Lisa Lempp. Sizes range from the cute and petite to the luxuriously large. Belts and wallets complement the handbags.

Casa Antich
C/Consolat del Mar 27-31 (93 310 43 91).
*Metro Jaume I. **Open** 9am-8.30pm Mon-Fri,*
*9.30am-8.30pm Sat. **Map** p90 J10* ❺
Luggage

A luggage shop that, in terms of levels of service and size of stock, recalls the golden age of travel. Here you can still purchase trunks for an Atlantic crossing and ladies' vanity cases that would be perfect for a sophisticated sojourn on the Orient Express. But you'll also find computer cases, backpacks and shoulder bags from the likes of Kipling and Mandarina Duck, as well as hardwearing numbers from Samsonite and so on.

❤ Casa Gispert
C/Sombrerers 23 (93 319 75 35, www.
*casagispert.com). Metro Jaume I. **Open***
*10am-8.30pm Mon-Sat. **Map** p90 J10* ❻
Food & Drink

Another Born favourite, Casa Gispert radiates a warmth generated by more than just its original wood-fired nut and coffee roaster. Like a stage-set version of a Dickensian shoppe, its wooden cabinets and shelves groan with the finest and most fragrant nuts, herbs, spices, preserves, sauces, oils and seasonings. The kits for making local specialities such as *panellets* (Halloween bonbons) make great gifts.

Custo Barcelona
Plaça de les Olles 7 (93 268 78 93, custo.com).
*Metro Jaume I. **Open** 10am-9pm Mon-Sat;*
*noon-8pm Sun. **Map** p90 J10* ❼ *Fashion*

The Custo look is synonymous with Barcelona style, and the loud, cut-and-paste print T-shirts have spawned a thousand imitations. Custodio Dalmau's signature prints can now be found on everything from coats to jeans to swimwear for both men and women, but a T-shirt is still the most highly prized (and highly priced) souvenir for visiting fashionistas. There's also a Custo Outlet (Plaça del Pi 2, Barri Gòtic, 93 304 27 53).
Other locations La Rambla 109, Barri Gòtic (93 481 39 30); C/València 245, Eixample (674 014 697).

Èstro

C/Flassaders 33 (93 310 40 77). Metro Jaume I. Open 5-9pm Mon; 11.30am-3pm, 5-9pm Tue-Sat. Map p90 J10 ❽ *Shoes*

This narrow street is full of original fashion boutiques, but Èstro stands out for its small but exquisite collection of Italian footwear for men and women. All beautifully made by hand from soft, supple leather, the range runs from high-heeled knee boots in rich berry shades for women to contemporary takes on the Oxford shoe for men. There is also a small selection of bags, belts and clothes.

Helena Rohner

C/Espaseria 13 (93 319 88 79, www. helenarohner.com). Metro Barceloneta. Open 11am-3pm, 4-8.30pm Mon-Sat. Map p90 J10 ❾ *Jewellery*

The style is Barbarella-at-the-boardroom in the boutique of one of Spain's most successful jewellery designers. Spare clean lines in gold or silver wrap around big, smooth chunks of ebony, coral, porcelain or even wood to create a look that's sleek but funky. Big rings are a speciality. There is also a small line of pretty things for the home (candle holders, teapots, vases and so on).

❤ Loisada

C/Flassaders 42 (93 295 54 92, www. loisadabcn.com). Metro Barceloneta. Open 10.30am-8.30pm Mon-Sat. Map p90 J10 ❿ *Fashion*

Housed in the cavernous former stables of the 18th-century Royal Mint building, Loisada sells a huge range of men's and women's clothing with a distinctly 'summer in the Hamptons' feel and a touch of retro bohemian chic. You'll also find beautifully packed toiletries, chocolates and a smattering of antiques.

Miriam Ponsa

C/Princesa 14 (93 295 55 62, www. miriamponsa.com). Metro Jaume I. Open 11am-8.30pm Mon-Sat. Map p90 J9 ⓫ *Fashion*

Miriam Ponsa's designs are squarely aimed at affluent young urbanites with a taste for stripped-down, quasi-Japanese style. The clothes are generally loose fitting and with a strong vertical silhouette, while materials can get pretty quirky; you might find yourself wondering how a T-shirt splattered in dripped latex and a hole-punched grey leather waistcoat could ever look so good.
Other locations C/València 29, Eixample (93 633 95 27).

On Land

C/Princesa 25 (93 310 02 11, www.on-land. com). Metro Jaume I. Open 1-8.30pm Mon; 11am-8.30pm Tue-Sat. Map p90 J9 ⓬ *Fashion*

This little oasis of urban cool has all you need to hold your head up high against the Barcelona hip squad: bags and wallets by Becksöndergaard and Can't Go Naked; cute skirts by y-dress; loose cotton trousers by IKKS; covetable T-shirts by Fresh from the Lab.

El Rei de la Màgia

C/Princesa 11 (93 319 39 20, www. elreydelamagia.com). Metro Jaume I. Open 10.30am-2pm, 4-7.30pm Mon-Sat. Map p90 J9 ⓭ *Magic tricks*

Cut someone in half, make a rabbit disappear or try out any number of other professional-quality stage illusions at the beautiful old 'King of Magic'. Less ambitious tricksters can practise their sleight of hand with the huge range of whoopee cushions, squirty flowers and itching powder.

The shop operates the city's only theatre dedicated exclusively to magic shows at C/ Jonqueres 15 (93 318 71 92).

U-Casas

C/Espaseria 4 (93 310 00 46, www.casasclub. com). Metro Jaume I. Open 10.30am-8.30pm Mon-Thur; 10.30am-9pm Fri, Sat. Map p90 J10 ⓮ *Shoes*

The pared-down, post-industrial decor so beloved of this neighbourhood provides the perfect backdrop for bright and quirky shoes. Strange heels and toes are still enjoying their moment in the sun, and after trying on all those snub-nosed winklepickers and rubber wedges from the likes of Helmut Lang, Fly, Fornarina and Irregular Choice, you can rest your weary pins on the giant, shoe-shaped chaise longue.

Vila Viniteca

C/Agullers 7 (902 32 77 77, www.vilaviniteca. es). Metro Jaume I. Open Sept-June 8.30am-8.30pm Mon-Sat. July, Aug 8.30am-8.30pm Mon-Fri; 8.30am-2pm Sat. Map p90 J10 ⓯ *Food & Drink*

Whether you want to blow €3,000 on a magnum of 2005 Clos Erasmus or just snag a €5 bottle of table wine, you'll find something to drink. The selection here is mostly Spanish and Catalan, but does cover international favourites. The food shop next door at no.9 stocks fine cheeses, cured meats and oils.
Other locations Vinacoteca, C/València 595, Eixample (93 232 58 35).

Raval

In the early 20th century, the Raval was notorious for its seedy theatres, brothels, anarchist groups and dosshouses. Despite decades of transformation – which, among other additions, saw the arrival of a huge modern art gallery (the MACBA) and a four-star hotel – the old red-light district still retains a busy crew of prostitutes and drug addicts. Many of these unshiftable locals could have stepped straight from the pages of Jean Genet's *The Thief's Journal*, a chronicle of the time he spent here as a teenage rent boy during the 1920s.

The area north of C/Hospital (here described as 'Upper Raval') has seen the most changes, and buzzes with art galleries and bars. The 'Lower Raval' still has a seedy port feel, but there are a couple of architectural gems: Gaudí's Palau Güell and the Romanesque Sant Pau del Camp church.

❤ Don't miss

1 MACBA *p111*
Barcelona's spanking white modern art gallery.

2 Palau Güell *p113*
Gaudí's first commission, a Gothic town house.

3 CCCB *p114*
An almshouse-turned-cultural centre, with quirky programming.

4 Sant Pau del Camp *p114*
A thousand-year-old church with a pretty cloister.

In the know
Getting around

The Raval is easily traversed on foot, and the closest metro stations are on La Rambla – from top to bottom, Catalunya, Liceu and Drassanes.

EXPLORING THE RAVAL

Ever on the margins, Raval (*arrabal* in Spanish) is a generic word adapted from the Arabic *ar-rabad*, meaning 'outside the walls'. When a defensive wall was built down the north side of La Rambla in the 13th century, the area now sandwiched between Avda Paral·lel and La Rambla was a sparsely populated green belt of garden plots. Over the centuries, the land absorbed the functional spill-over from the city in the form of monasteries, churches, religious hospitals, prisons and virtually any noxious industry that citizens didn't want on their doorstep. When industrialisation arrived in the 18th century, the area became Barcelona's working-class district.

This was also the part of town where most land was available; yet more was freed up after the government dissolved the monasteries in the Desamortización ('Disentailment') of 1836, and early industries, mainly the textile mills, took the space. Workers lived in crowded slums devoid of ventilation or running water, and malnutrition, TB, scrofula and typhus kept the average life expectancy to a mere 40 years. It's no coincidence that the city's sanatoriums, orphanages and hospitals were based here.

Widely known as the Quinto, or Fifth District, this was also where the underclass forged the centre of revolutionary Barcelona, and it became a breeding ground for anarchists and other radicals. Innumerable riots began here, and entire streets became no-go areas after dark. Heroin's arrival in the late 1970s caused extra problems; the semi-tolerated petty criminality became more and more threatening and affected tourism.

Since the 1980s, city planners have done their best to open up the Raval by turning the area into something of a cultural theme park, installing or rebuilding a slew of high-profile cultural institutions. Spurred on by the approaching 1992 Olympics, the authorities made a clean sweep of the Lower Raval. Whole blocks with links to prostitution or drugs were demolished, and many of the displaced families were transferred to housing estates on the edge of town, out of sight. A sports centre, a police station and office blocks were constructed, and some streets were pedestrianised.

However, the planners were caught by surprise by the sudden mass arrival of non-European immigrants into the area, starting in the 1990s. These new residents have perhaps done more to transform the Raval than any of the council's best laid plans. By the beginning of the 21st century, more than

RAVAL

Restaurants

1. Bar Cañete
2. Caravelle
3. Carlota Akaneya
4. Dos Trece
5. Elisabets
6. Las Fernández
7. Flax & Kale
8. Lúzia
9. Mam i Teca
10. Sésamo
11. Silenus
12. Suculent
13. Los Toreros

Cafés, Tapas & Bars

1. Bar Kasparo
2. Bar Lobo
3. Bar Mendizábal
4. Betty Ford's
5. Boadas
6. Buenas Migas
7. Cafè de les Delicies
8. Casa Almirall
9. El Colectivo
10. La Confitería
11. El Jardí
12. Granja M Viader
13. Marsella
14. Resolis
15. Els Tres Tombs

Shops & Services

1. Casa Beethoven
2. Discos Paradiso
3. Guitar Shop
4. Holala! Plaza + Gallery
5. Med Winds
6. Torres

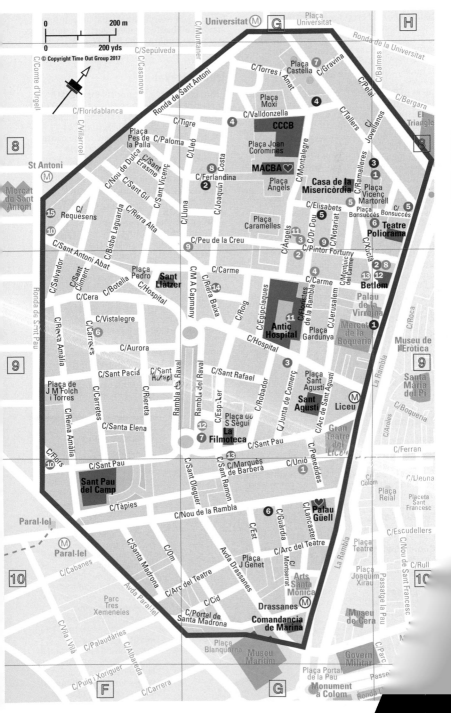

half the *barrio*'s residents were from outside Spain, the majority from Pakistan and Ecuador. The Raval is now one of the most ethnically diverse places in Europe, with more than 70 different nationalities calling it home. Shop signs appear in a babel of languages, plugging everything from halal meat to Bollywood films and cheap calls to South America.

Despite this immigration, the council continued with its ambitions to revive the area. The most dramatic plan was to create a *'Raval obert al cel'* ('Raval open to the sky'), the most tangible result of which is the sweeping, palm-lined **Rambla del Raval**, completed in 2000. Entire streets were knocked down to open up space – space now partly occupied by a luxury hotel, offices, housing, shops and the Filmoteca rep cinema (*see p228*).

The facelift has raised prices, however. Alongside the immigrants, a wealthier community of arty western expats and university students has begun to arrive, dotting the area with galleries, shops and cafés. In and around **C/Lluna** you'll find a good number of small, inviting boutiques stocking locally designed clothes; **C/Ferlandina** has its share of boho cafés; and old industrial spaces along **C/Riereta** now serve as studios to more than 40 artists.

Despite its gentrification, the Raval has not lost its associations with crime and sleaze. Take care, particularly after dark in the area down towards the port. That said, as long as you exercise the usual precautions – staying off badly lit sidestreets, not flaunting your new camera – the Raval can make for a fascinating wander.

Upper Raval

From La Rambla, signposts for the 'MACBA' carefully guide visitors along the gentrified 'tourist corridors' of C/Tallers, C/Elisabets and C/Bonsuccès to a playground of cafés, galleries and boutiques. The centre of the Upper Raval is the **Plaça dels Àngels**, where the 16th-century Convent dels Àngels houses both the FAD design institute and a gigantic almshouse, the **Casa de la Caritat**, converted into a cultural complex housing the **MACBA** and the **CCCB** (*see p114*).

When the clean, high-culture MACBA opened its doors in 1995, it seemed to embody everything the Raval was not, and was initially mocked as an isolated and isolating social experiment. Over the years, though, the square has become an unofficial home to the city's skateboarders, and the surrounding streets have filled with restaurants and boutiques. There are now university faculties of philosophy, geography and history across from the CCCB, and thousands of students are also changing the character of the place.

Below here, C/Hospital and C/Carme meet at the **Plaça Pedró**, where the tiny Romanesque chapel (and ex-lepers'

♥ Time to eat & drink

Coffee and a croissant
Café de les Delicies *p117*

A bargain set lunch
Bar Lobo *p117*, Silenus *p116*

Tea and cake
Granja M Viader *p118*

Cooking with soul
Caravelle *p115*, Mam i Teca *p116*

nightcap
*t*y Ford's *p118*, Almirall *p118*

♥ Time to shop

Elegant tailoring
Med Winds *p120*

A vintage Priorat
Torres *p120*

Cedarwood classical guitars
Guitar Shop *p120*

Vintage threads
Holala! Plaza + Gallery *p120*

In the know
Fortune's wheel

A circular wooden panel, a coat of arms and a slot for alms are all that remain on the façade of the **Casa de la Misericòrdia** at C/Ramalleres 17. Founded as a hospice in 1583, it later became the Casa Provincial de Maternitat i Expòsits (Maternity and Abandoned Children's Home), run by nuns. From 1853 to 1931, the foundling wheel behind the panel provided a means of leaving very young children in the nuns' care, anonymity intact. The infant would be placed on the revolving surface and a screen would close behind it. The nuns would hang a label round the baby's neck stating the date of entry.

💜 MACBA (Museu d'Art Contemporani de Barcelona)

Plaça dels Àngels 1 (93 412 08 10, www.macba. cat). Metro Catalunya. **Open** *24 June-24 Sept 11am-8pm Mon, Wed-Fri; 10am-9pm Sat; 10am-3pm Sun. 25 Sept-23 June 11am-7.30pm Mon, Wed-Fri; 10am-9pm Sat; 10am-3pm Sun.* **Admission** *allows unlimited entry to all exhibitions for 1 mth €10; €8 reductions; free under-14s.* **Map** *p109 G8.*

If you're used to being soft-soaped by eager-to-please art centres, you'll have to make a bit of a mental adjustment to accommodate the cryptic minimalism of the MACBA, where art is taken very seriously indeed. Yet if you can navigate the fridge-like interior of Richard Meier's enormous edifice, accept that much of the permanent collection is inaccessible to the uninitiated, tackle shows that flutter between the brilliant and the baffling, and, most importantly, are prepared to do your reading, a trip to the MACBA can be extremely rewarding.

Exhibitions flutter between the brilliant and the baffling in the fridge-like interior

RAVAL

Since its inauguration in 1995, the MACBA has become a power player on the contemporary arts scene. Its library and auditorium host an extensive programme that includes accessibly priced (or free) concerts, conferences and cinema, while two floors of exhibition rooms offer a showcase for large-scale installations and exhaustive, multidisciplinary shows. La Capella, a former medieval convent across the square, is free to enter, and provides a project space for specially commissioned works. The permanent collection sits on the ground floor of the main building, and is rooted in the second half of the 20th century. Media, sound and performance art experimentalists of the 1960s and '70s, including Bruce Nauman, Joan Jonas and John Cage, are well represented, as are Spanish and Catalan artists such as Antoni Muntadas, Antoni Tàpies and the Dau al Set group.

Sant Pau del Camp

hospital) of **Sant Llàtzer** sits. La Rambla is accessed along either street, or through **La Boqueria** market (*see p84*), itself the site of the Sant Josep monastery until the Desamortización. Behind the Boqueria is the **Antic Hospital de la Santa Creu** (*see p114*), which took in the city's sick from the 15th century until 1926. It now houses several cultural institutions, including **La Capella**, an attractive exhibition space.

C/Carme is capped at the Rambla end by the 18th-century **Església de Betlem**, with its serpentine pillars and geometrically patterned façade. Its name features on many shop signs nearby; older residents still refer to this part of the Raval as 'Betlem'.

Lower Raval

The lower half of the Raval, from C/Hospital down, is generally referred to as the **Barrio Chino** (or simply 'el Xino'). The nickname was coined in the 1920s by a journalist likening the neighbourhood to San Francisco's Chinatown, and referred to its underworld feel rather than to any Chinese population. In those days, drifters filled the bars and cheap hostels lined streets such as Nou de la Rambla, alongside high-class cabarets and brothels for the rich, and cheap porn pits for the poor. A glimpse of the old sleaze can still be found in bars such as **Bar Pastís** (*see p236*) and **Marsella** (also known as the 'absinthe bar'; *see p118*), while an appropriately seedy square is named after Jean Genet.

Just beneath C/Hospital in the Plaça Sant Agustí lies one of the Raval's more arresting pieces of architecture – the unfinished 18th-century church of **Sant Agustí** (no.2, no phone). The stone beams and jags protruding from its left flank on C/Arc de Sant Agustí and the undecorated sections of the Baroque façade show how suddenly work stopped when funding ran out.

C/Nou de la Rambla, the Lower Raval's main street, is home to Gaudí's first major project: the **Palau Güell**. Nearby, in C/Sant Pau, is a Modernista landmark, Domènech i Montaner's **Hotel España** (nos. 9-11), and at the end of the same street sits the Romanesque church of **Sant Pau del Camp** (*see p114*). Iberian remains dating to 200 BC have been found next to the building, marking it as one of the oldest parts of the city.

At the lower end of the Raval is the Gothic Drassanes (shipyards) building, now home to the **Museu Marítim** (*see p134*). Along the Avda Paral·lel side of it lies the largest remaining section of Barcelona's 14th-century city wall.

In the know
Unrequited roses

Inside **Sant Agustí**, the Capella de Santa Rita is packed on her feast day, 22 May; Rita is the patron saint of lost causes, and it is to her that the unhappy and unrequited bring their red roses to be blessed.

❤ Palau Güell

C/Nou de la Rambla 3-5 (93 472 57 75, www. palauguell.cat). Metro Drassanes or Liceu. **Open** *Apr-Oct 10am-8pm Tue-Sun. Nov-Mar 10am-5.30pm Tue-Sun.* **Admission** *€12; €9 reductions. Free under-10s & 1st Sun of mth.* **Map** *p109 G10.*

A fortress-like edifice shoehorned into a narrow six-storey sliver, the Palau Güell was Gaudí's first major commission, begun in 1886 for textile baron Eusebi Güell. After years of renovation, it is once again open to visitors, who can look around the subterranean stables, with their exotic canopy of stone palm fronds on the ceiling, and the vestibule with ornate *mudéjar* carved ceilings from which the Güells could snoop on their arriving guests through the jalousie trellis-work. At the heart of the house, the spectacular six-storey hall, complete with musicians' galleries and topped by a dome, is covered in cobalt honeycomb tiles. It's a somewhat gloomy place, but the antidote lies on its roof terrace, decorated with a rainbow forest of 20 mosaic-clad chimneys.

Sights & museums

Antic Hospital de la Santa Creu & La Capella

C/Carme 47-C/Hospital 56. Metro Liceu. **Open** *9am-11pm Mon-Sat.* **Admission** *free.* **Map** *p109 G9.*

This was one of Europe's earliest medical centres. There was a hospital on the site as early as 1024, but in the 15th century it expanded to centralise all the city's hospitals and sanatoriums (with the exception of the Santa Margarida leper colony, which remained outside the city walls). By the 1920s, it was hopelessly overstretched, and its medical facilities were moved uptown to the Hospital Sant Pau. One of the last patients was Gaudí, who died here in 1926; it was also where Picasso painted one of his first important pictures, *Dead Woman* (1903).

p112

The buildings combine a 15th-century Gothic core with Baroque and classical additions. They are now home to the Massana Arts School, and a small neighbourhood library, as well as the much larger Catalan National Library (the second largest in Spain), the headquarters of the Institute of Catalan Studies and the Royal Academy of Medicine, which hosts occasional concerts. Highlights include a neoclassical lecture theatre complete with revolving marble dissection table (open 10am-2pm Mon-Fri), and the entrance hall of the Casa de Convalescència, tiled with lovely Baroque ceramic murals telling the story of St Paul; one features an artery-squirting decapitation scene.

La Capella (93 442 71 71, lacapella.bcn.cat, open noon-8pm Tue-Sat, 11am-2pm Sun, free), the hospital chapel, was rescued from a sad fate as a warehouse and sensitively converted into an exhibition space for contemporary art. The courtyard is a popular spot for reading or eating lunch.

❤ CCCB (Centre de Cultura Contemporània de Barcelona)

C/Montalegre 5 (93 306 41 00, www.cccb.org). Metro Catalunya. **Open** *11am-8pm Tue-Sun.* **Admission** *1 exhibition €6; €4 reductions. 2 exhibitions €8; €6 reductions. Free under-12s. Free to all 3-8pm Sun.* **Map** *p109 G8.*

Spain's largest cultural centre forms part of the Casa de la Caritat, a former almshouse. The massive façade and part of the courtyard remain from the original building; the rest was rebuilt in dramatic contrast, all tilting glass and steel, by architects Piñón and Viaplana, known for the Maremagnum shopping centre (*see p135*). The CCCB's exhibitions can lean towards heavy-handed didacticism, but there are occasional gems.

❤ Sant Pau del Camp

C/Sant Pau 101 (93 441 00 01). Metro Paral·lel. **Open** *10am-1.30pm, 4-7.30pm Mon-Sat. Mass 8pm Sat (Spanish); noon Sun (Catalan).* **Admission** *€3; €2 reductions; free under-14s.* **Map** *p109 F10.*

The name St Paul in the Field reflects a time when the Raval was still countryside. In fact, this little Romanesque church is over 1,000 years old; the date carved on its most prestigious headstone – that of Count Guifré II Borrell, son of Wilfred 'the Hairy' and inheritor of all Barcelona and Girona – is AD 912. The church's impressive façade includes sculptures of fantastical flora and fauna along with human grotesques. The tiny cloister is another highlight, with its extraordinary Visigoth capitals, triple-lobed arches and central fountain.

Restaurants

▶ *For details of our restaurant price categories, see p36.*

Bar Cañete €€
C/Unió 17 (93 270 34 58, www.barcanete. com). Metro Universitat. **Open** *1-4pm, 8pm-midnight Tue-Sat.* **Map** *p109 G10* ❶ *Spanish*

Superb, upmarket tapas inspired by classic dishes from all over Spain but often given a twist: pork cheek with smoked herring; Santa Pau haricot bean stew with baby squid; beef sweetbreads with prawn and wild mushroom. The dining room is long but thin and it pays to book – get a seat up at the bar if you can.

❤ Caravelle €€
C/Pintor Fortuny 31 (93 317 98 92, www.caravelle.es). Metro Liceu. **Open** *9.30am-5pm Mon, Tue; 9.30pm-midnight Wed-Sat; 10am-5.30pm Sun.* **Map** *p109 G9* ❷ *Global*

A little slice of London's Shoreditch comes to the Raval in the shape of this bright and minimalist restaurant with its following of bearded and checkshirted hipsters. Don't be misled, however, for Caravelle's cooking is all heart and soul, whether it's a burger with gorgonzola and pickled cabbage or

southern fried rabbit with corn. It also serves one of the better brunch menus in town, from 10am to 4pm.

Carlota Akaneya €€€
C/Pintor Fortuny 32 (93 302 77 68, www. carlotaakaneya.com). Metro Liceu. **Open** *7-11pm daily.* **Map** *p109 G8* ❸ *Japanese*

Barcelona's first *sumiyaki* (with charcoal brasiers inset in every table) is a cosy wood-panelled place, hidden from the street and illuminated with backlit paper screens. Its speciality is kobe beef and three carefully crafted set menus – priced from €40 to €66 – offer tasters of various cuts (along with noodle dishes, gyoza dumplings and so on), or you can order à la carte. Chef Ferran Adrià is a fan, which tells you all you need to know.

Dos Trece €
C/Carme 40 (93 301 73 06, dostrece.net). Metro Liceu. **Restaurant** *10am-midnight daily.* **Bar** *10am-2am Mon-Thur, Sun; 10am-3am Fri, Sat.* **Map** *p109 G9* ❹ *Global*

A relaxation of local laws governing live music means that Dos Trece's cosy basement space once again jumps to DJs and jam sessions, but also functions as another dining room – this one with cushions and candles for post-prandial lounging. Apart from a little fusion confusion (ceviche with nachos, and

RAVAL

all manner of things served with yucca chips), the food is not half bad for the price.

Elisabets €
C/Elisabets 2-4 (93 317 58 26, www. elisabets1962.com). Metro Catalunya. **Open** *7.30am-11pm Mon-Thur, Sat; 7.30am-1am Fri. Closed Aug.* **No cards.** **Map** *p109 G8* ❺ *Catalan*

Open in the mornings for breakfast, and late night for drinking at the bar, Elisabets maintains a sociable local feel, despite the recent gentrification of its street. There is only a set lunch or, in the evenings, tapas and myriad bocadillos.The lunch deal (€10.85 Monday to Saturday) is terrific value, however, with osso buco, vegetable and chickpea stew, baked cod with garlic and parsley, and roast pork knuckle all making regular appearances on the menu.

Las Fernández €€
C/Carretes 11 (93 443 20 43, www. lasfernandez.com). Metro Paral·lel. **Open** *8.30pm-2am Tue-Sun. Closed 2wks Aug.* **Map** *p109 F9* ❻ *Spanish*

An inviting entrance, pillar-box red, is a beacon of cheer on one of Barcelona's less salubrious streets. Inside, the three Fernández sisters have created a bright and unpretentious bar/restaurant that specialises in wine and food from their native León. Alongside *cecina* (dried venison), gammon and sausages from the region are lighter, Mediterranean dishes and generous salads; smoked salmon with mustard and dill; pasta filled with wild mushrooms; and sardines with a citrus escabeche. When booking, be warned that there are two separate sittings – 9.15pm and 11.20pm.

Flax & Kale €€
C/Tallers 74B (93 317 56 64, www. teresacarles.com/fk). Metro Universitat. **Open** *9.30am-11.30pm Tue-Sun.* **Map** *p109 G8* ❼ *Vegetarian*

Describing itself as 'flexitarian', Flax & Kale is predominantly vegetarian, though it makes ·n allowance for fish. Its menu is long and ·ried, with nods to such cutting-edge food ·nds (cold-pressing, fermentation, active ·on) and so many on-point ingredients ·, chlorella, chia) that it contains a ·ry. The kitchen is open all day, but ·eed to book at lunch.

·€
·ortuny 3 (93 342 96 28, www. ·uz.com). Metro Catalunya. **Open** ·n-Thur, Sun; 1pm-12.30am Fri, · H9* ❽ *Global*

From the unstoppable Tragaluz group of restaurants comes this relaxed and sunny bistro just off La Rambla. It advertises what it does as 'street food', but seems to have an eye to the clients at Le Méridien hotel opposite, with a list of global standards beloved of room service menus – club sandwiches, dainty pizzas, chili con carne, chicken wings, burgers and so on. The tomato tartare with watercress is recommended, as is the tuna sashimi with chipotle mayo.

❤ Mam i Teca €€
C/Lluna 4 (93 441 33 35). Metro Sant Antoni. **Open** *1-3.30pm, 8-11.30pm Mon, Wed-Fri, Sun; 8-11.30pm Sat.* **No cards.** **Map** *p109 G8* ❾ *Catalan*

This bright little restaurant only has four tables, so it pays to reserve in advance. All the usual tapas, from anchovies to cured meats, are rigorously sourced, and complemented by superb daily specials such as organic lamb chops, pork confit and scrambled egg with asparagus and shrimp. Note that the restaurant is closed on Tuesdays.

Sésamo €€
C/Sant Antoni Abat 52 (93 441 64 11). Metro Sant Antoni. **Open** *8pm-midnight Tue-Sun.* **Map** *p109 F8* ❿ *Vegetarian*

Creative vegetarian and vegan dishes, served in a buzzing atmosphere. Options might include curry with dahl and wild rice or crunchy polenta with baked pumpkin, gorgonzola and radicchio. There is an excellent tasting menu for €25 and daily-changing specials. Leave space for the apple crumble, and try the organic wine and beer.

❤ Silenus €€
C/Àngels 8 (93 302 26 80, www. restaurantsilenus.com). Metro Liceu. **Café/ Bar** *9.30am-1am Mon-Sat.* **Restaurant** *1-11.30pm.* **Map** *p109 G8* ⓫ *Mediterranean*

Named after one of the drunken followers of Dionysus, Silenus is nonetheless all about restraint. Its quiet dining room has an air of scuffed elegance, with carefully chipped and stained walls whereon the ghost of a clock is projected and the faded leaves of a book float up on high. The food, too, is artistically presented. The set lunch (€14) is generally a good bet, offering dishes from Caesar salad to crunchy gnocchi with creamed spinach or spicy *botifarra* with puréed potatoes. There is also a set dinner (€18) and a tasting menu (€35).

Suculent €€
Rambla del Raval 43 (93 443 65 79, suculent. com). Metro Paral·lel. **Open** *12.30pm-1am Wed-Sun.* **Map** *p109 G9* ⓬ *Mediterranean*

Another from the stable of celebrity chef Carles Abellan, less fanciful than his Michelin-starred (but now closed) Comerç 24, but still upholding the highest standards in the kitchen. The dishes are mostly based on local specialities, but look out too for the steak tartare served on marrowbone and the skate with black butter, among other things. Leave room for the brie cheesecake with muscatel *gelée*.

Los Toreros €€
C/Xuclà 3-5 (93 318 23 25, www. restaurantelostoreros.com). Metro Catalunya or Liceu. **Open** *5pm-midnight Mon-Sat.* **No cards**. *Map p109 G9* ⑬ *Spanish*

For many diners, this will be the Spanish experience they were after: a warren of yellowing dining rooms, the walls lined with bullfighting posters and memorabilia, including a huge stuffed bull's head, a riotous atmosphere, delightfully friendly waiters, and carafes of cheap and decent house red. Most go for the set meals, which generally comprise old-school starters (melon with *ham*, *arroz cubano*) followed by grilled meats, but there's also a long list of tapas, paella and some generous salads.

Cafés

Bar Kasparo
Plaça Vicenç Martorell 4 (93 302 20 72, www.kasparo.es). Metro Catalunya. **Open** *9am-10.30pm Tue-Sat. Closed mid Dec-mid Jan. Map p109 H8* ①

Still the best of the various café terraces around the edges of the quiet, traffic-free Plaça Vicenç Martorell, Kasparo serves tapas, *bocadillos*, salads and a varying selection of more substantial dishes, available all day. There is no indoor seating, so this is more of a warm weather proposition.

♥ Bar Lobo
C/Pintor Fortuny 3 (93 481 53 46, www. grupotragaluz.com). Metro Catalunya. **Open** *9am-12.30pm Mon-Wed, Sun; 9am-1.30am Thur-Sat. Map p109 H9* ②

Bar Lobo is a friendly place, with excellent food that ranges from traditional tapas to fusion classics – guacamole, tuna tataki, decent burgers. There's a fußball table upstairs, and the terrace is a peaceful space for coffee or breakfast, despite the proximity to La Rambla, except at lunchtimes, when it can get packed.

Bar Mendizábal
C/Junta de Comerç 2 (93 566 70 52). Metro Liceu. **Open** *8am-midnight daily.* **No cards**. *Map p109 G9* ③

Considered something of a classic, Bar Mendizábal has been around for decades, its jolly multicoloured tiles and serving hatch a feature in thousands of holiday snaps. Until recently, it was little more than a hole in the wall – juices, sandwiches and soup were ordered and carried across to a terrace on the other side of the road, but its huge popularity means that it has recently expanded into a (small) dining room alongside the bar.

Buenas Migas
Plaça Bonsuccés 6 (93 318 37 08, www. buenasmigas.com). Metro Liceu. **Open** *8am-11pm Mon-Thur, Sun; 8am-midnight Fri-Sat. Map p109 H8* ⑥

A doggedly wholesome place, all gingham and pine and chewy spinach tart. The speciality is tasty focaccia with various toppings, along with the usual high-fibre, low-fun cakes you so often find in a vegetarian café. Its terrace sprawls across the wide pavement and continues across the street. **Other locations** around the city.

♥ Cafè de les Delicies
Rambla del Raval 47 (93 441 57 14). Metro Liceu. **Open** *9.30am-midnight Mon, Wed, Thur; 9.30am-4pm Tue; 9.30am-2am Fri; 11am-2.30am Sat, 11am-midnight Sun. Map p109 G9* ⑦

The delightful Cafè de les Delicies serves breakfast, along with tapas and light dishes, in its dining room at the back. Off the corridor there's a snug with armchairs, but otherwise the buzzing front bar is the place to be, with its theatre-set mezzanine, '70s jukebox and reams of club flyers. There's occasional live music at weekends.

El Colectivo
C/Pintor Fortuny 22 (93 318 63 80). Metro Catalunya. **Open** *9am-9pm Mon-Fri; 10am-9pm Sat; 10am-4pm Sun. Map p109 G8* ⑨

The love of a good home-made carrot cake knows no international boundaries, and El Colectivo welcomes a good mix of punters. Its other universally admired facets include hot ciabatta sandwiches (try avocado, brie and sun-dried tomato), great breakfasts, Magnífico coffee, fruit smoothies and a selection of vinyl on the stereo. On Th and Friday nights, tapas are also serv

El Jardí
C/Hospital 56 (93 329 15 50, www. eljardibarcelona.es). Metro Lice Nov 9pm-1am daily. Dec-Feb 9 Sat. Map p109 G9 ⑪

The courtyard of the Antic tranquil, tree-lined spot a

the hustle of C/Hospital. Terrace café El Jardí only has outdoor seating, warmed by heaters in winter. Breakfast pastries and all the usual tapas are present and correct, along with pasta dishes, quiches and salads.

♥ Granja M Viader

C/Xuclà 4-6 (93 318 34 86, www. granjaviader.cat). Metro Liceu. **Open** *9am-1.15pm, 5-9.15pm Mon-Sat.* **Map** *p109 H9* ⑫ ❺

The chocolate milk drink Cacaolat was invented in this old *granja* in 1931, and it's still on offer, along with strawberry and banana milkshakes, *orxata* (tiger nut milk) and hot chocolate. It's an evocative, charming place with century-old fittings and enamel adverts, but the waiters refuse to be hurried.

Tapas

Resolis

C/Riera Baixa 22 (93 441 29 48, www. facebook.com/barresolisbarcelona). Metro Liceu. **Open** *6pm-1am Mon-Sat.* **Map** *p109 G9* ⑭

A favourite with traders from along the C/ Riera Baixa, Resolis blends a trad look and run-of-the-mill tapas (tortilla, manchego cheese, prawns) with an immaculate selection of vinyl and some fanciful foodstuffs (salmon ceviche). In the summer months, its serving hatch to the alley alongside is thronged.

Els Tres Tombs

Ronda Sant Antoni 2 (93 443 41 11). Metro Sant Antoni. **Open** *6am-2.30am Mon-Thur, Sun; 6am-3am Fri, Sat.* **Map** *p109 F8* ⑮

Not, perhaps, the most inspired tapas bar in town, with its overcooked *patatas bravas*, sweaty manchego and sterile interior, but Els Tres Tombs is still a favourite for its pavement terrace and proximity to the Sunday morning book market. The *tres tombs* in question are nothing more ghoulish than the 'three turns' of the area performed by a procession of men on horseback during the Festa dels Tres Tombs in January (*see p223*).

˗ther options in the area, see Bar
˗36, and La Concha p237.

˗ord's

˗osta 56 (93 304 13 68). Metro
˗pen 1pm-2.30am daily. **Map**

˗u all you need to know
˗ this little Australian-
˗frequented by a mix of

locals and foreigners who check in for its cocktails, juicy burgers and chilled, good-time vibe. A tiny kitchen turns out superb daily specials: soups, curries and generously portioned bar snacks.

Boadas

C/Tallers 1 (93 318 95 92, boadascocktails. com). Metro Catalunya. **Open** *noon-2am Mon-Thur; noon-3am Fri, Sat.* **No cards.** **Map** *p109 H8* ❺

Set up in 1933 by Miguel Boadas, born to Catalan parents in Havana (where he became the first barman at the legendary La Floridita), this classic cocktail bar has changed little since Hemingway used to come here. In a move to deter the hordes of rubbernecking tourists, it has instituted a dress code.

♥ Casa Almirall

C/Joaquín Costa 33 (93 318 99 17, www. casaalmirall.com). Metro Universitat. **Open** *4.30pm-2am Mon-Wed; noon-2.30am Thur-Sun.* **Map** *p109 G8* ❽

Opened in 1860, the Casa Almirall is the second oldest bar in the city after Marsella (*see below*). The bar for all seasons, its swooping Modernista woodwork, soft lighting and deep sofas give it a cosy feel in winter, while its glass front opens up for the summer months.

La Confitería

C/Sant Pau 128 (93 140 54 35). Metro Paral·lel. **Open** *7pm-2.30am Mon-Thur; 6pm-3am Fri, Sat; 5pm-2.30am Sun.* **No cards.** **Map** *p109 F10* ❿

This former sweetshop (*confitería*), with its etched display windows, nowadays houses an art nouveau bar with dusty bottles, old chandeliers and extravagantly carved wooden panelling. Beyond is a cosy backroom, whose antique furniture is reproduction and only recently added under the new ownership, but tasteful and well done all the same. It's a favourite with concert-goers meeting before gigs at nearby BARTS or Sala Apolo.

Marsella

C/Sant Pau 65 (93 442 72 63). Metro Liceu. **Open** *10pm-2.30am Mon-Thur; 10pm-3am Fri, Sat.* **No cards.** **Map** *p109 G9* ⑬

This place was opened in 1820 by a native of Marseilles – who may just have changed the course of Barcelona's artistic history by introducing absinthe, still a mainstay of the bar's delights. Untapped 100-year-old bottles of the stuff sit in glass cabinets alongside old mirrors and William Morris curtains, probably covered in the same dust kicked up by Picasso and Gaudí.

Vermouth Sundays

And on the seventh day they danced

Leave the dirty cocktails, mead and single-origin double espresso to Hoxton and Williamsburg – the hipster tipple of choice in Barcelona is vermouth. Served with ice and a slice, along with a green olive and a quick squirt of soda, it is to brunch what the Bloody Mary once was.

Many bar owners and festival organisers have been quick to jump on the trend, but none with more aplomb than Esther and Patricia, the girls behind **Ven Tú!** (ventubcn. es; loosely translated as 'Why don't you come?'), the regular event that has made Sunday the new Saturday.

Its humble beginnings were in a modest square in the Raval a few years ago. Litres of *vermút* were aligned on a trestle table, a couple of local bands got up to play, children and dogs ran amok, and the general mood was a buoyant one. Since then, it has morphed into the hipster event par excellence, but has remained refreshingly inclusive and unpretentious for all that. The musical programming ranges from fun to excellent, and these days you can get a plate of paella when the deceptively drinkable *vermút* begins to hit. The venue changes almost every time

(see the website for details), and in the winter months the event takes place indoors. There's been a gradual shift from scruffy Raval bars to bigger, more established venues, such as **Sala Apolo** (*see p239*), **City Hall** (*see p239*) or concert hall **BARTS** (*see p238*). The party usually kicks off around midday. In theory, it's supposed to end at around 8pm. In reality, it carries on until the last punter drops (or leaves for work on Monday morning).

Ven Tú! has morphed into the hipster event par excellence, but has remained refreshingly unpretentious

There's rarely an entry fee, and food and drink goes for bargain prices – all you'll need are your Ray-Bans, a buttoned-to-the-neck shirt and some dancing shoes.

Shops & services

Casa Beethoven
*La Rambla 97 (93 301 48 26, www.
casabeethoven.com). Metro Liceu. **Open**
9am-8pm Mon, Tue, Thur, Fri; 9am-2pm,
4-8pm Wed; 9am-2pm, 5-8pm Sat. **Map**
p109 H9* ❶ *Music*

The sheet music and songbooks on sale in
this old shop in the Raval run the gamut
from Wagner to the White Stripes, with
a concentration on opera. Books cover
music history and theory, while CDs are
particularly strong on both modern and
classical Spanish music.

Discos Paradiso
*C/Ferlandina 39 (93 329 64 40, www.
discosparadiso.com). Metro Sant Antoni.
Open noon-8pm Mon-Sat. **Map** p109 G8*
❷ *Music*

Specialising in funk, dub, house and
electronica, Paradiso has a little bit of
everything in a number of formats, though
vinyl is the main event, and this is the place
local DJs come to stock their crates. There are
also T-shirts and other band merch.

♥ Guitar Shop
*C/Tallers 27 & 46 (93 412 19 19, 93 412 66
22, www.guitarshop.barcelona). Metro
Catalunya. **Open** 10am-2pm, 4.30-8pm
Mon-Sat. **Map** p109 H8* ❸ *Music*

A mecca for fretheads, these shops have all
the goodies: cedarwood Antonio Aparicio
classical guitars, Prudencio Saez flamenco
guitars and cheap Admiras. At no.27, there's a
whole host of vintage Fenders, '80s Marshall
amps and the like; bargain-hunters can
browse the second-hand gear.

♥ Holala! Plaza + Gallery
*Plaça Castella 2 (93 302 05 93, holala-ibiza.
com). Metro Universitat. **Open** 11am-9pm
Mon-Sat. **Map** p109 G8* ❹ *Fashion*

The upper swathe of the Raval remains
the grunge-tinged stomping ground of the
city's counterculture, and is dotted with
quirky vintage shops, particularly. Holala!
is the mothership, a vast cavern of a place
that incorporates a sizeable collection of
ice-cool retro furniture, a gallery and a
pop-up nail bar, as well as acres of preloved
threads from every decade.

♥ Med Winds
*C/Elisabets 7 (93 619 01 79, www.medwinds.
com). Metro Catalunya. **Open** 10am-8pm
Mon-Sat. **Map** p109 G8* ❺ *Fashion*

A small boutique that stands out for the
quality and detailing of a covetable range
of clothes and accessories for men and
women. Richly coloured patterns stand in
contrast to plain, elegant styling, and shoes
and bags, in particular, have a vintage feel.
Other locations Rambla de Catalunya 100,
Eixample (93 521 00 56).

♥ Torres
*C/Nou de la Rambla 25 (93 317 32 34, www.
vinosencasa.com). Metro Drassanes or Liceu.
Open 9am-2pm, 4-9pm Mon-Sat. **Map**
p109 G10* ❻ *Wine*

Torres's shiny shop seems a bit out of place
in the rundown end of the Raval, but it's
definitely worth a visit. There's a good
range of Spanish wines, along with plenty of
interesting beers and spirits from elsewhere,
including black Mallorcan absinthe.
Prices are competitive.

El Gat, Rambla del Raval p110

Sightseeing with Children

An awfully big adventure

The key to your children having a good time in Barcelona is your own flexibility; if you can adapt to later bedtimes and having them eat out without worrying about mess or noise, you'll all have a better time for it. You'd also do well to get used to complete strangers striking up conversations with your kids, because other people's children are considered public property round these parts.

In common with most Mediterranean countries, Spain tends to expect kids to rub along with whatever the adults are up to, so you won't find a dazzling range of child-orientated attractions. But Barcelona is a natural playground, and small children are as delighted by its spooky medieval alleys after dark as they are with its sandy beaches by day.

The two most child-friendly attractions are the excellent **Zoo** (*see p99*) and the marginally less exciting **Aquarium** (*see p133*). The **Magic Fountain** (Font Mágica; *see p142*) is also a huge hit; and a simple stroll down **La Rambla** (*see p74*), past the living statues, entertainers, artists and general hubbub, can be a good bet. Fun transport options include the two cable-car systems, the **Tramvia Blau** (*see p186*), and the rickshaws.

There isn't a multitude of museums aimed at children; one of the better ones is **CosmoCaixa**, the science museum (*see p184*). A must-see for junior footy fiends is the **Camp Nou Experience** (*see p180*), where kids can walk from the dressing rooms through the tunnel and take a few steps on the pitch. The fake Spanish village of **Poble Espanyol** (*see p146*) also has a certain appeal.

Magic Fountain

La Rambla

RAVAL

Barceloneta & the Ports

The 1992 Olympic Games were the catalyst for Barcelona's most notable transformation. The city had famously 'turned its back on the sea' until some sharp urban planners finally spotted the potential of its Mediterranean location. From industrial slum to leisure port, Barcelona's shoreline transformation is the result of two decades of development. The clean-up has extended to the whole seven kilometres of city seashore: this stretch is now a virtually continuous strip of modern construction, bristling with new docks, marinas, luxury hotels, cruise-ship terminals, ferry harbours and leisure areas. The seafront got a second blast of wind in its sails from the 2004 Fòrum, which spawned a huge swimming and watersports area.

♥ **Don't miss**

1 Beaches *p130*
Nine of 'em.

2 L'Aquàrium *p133*
Oceanic mysteries and hands-on fun.

3 Museu Marítim *p134*
Nautical treasures in a medieval building.

4 Monument a Colom *p133*
Take the lift to the top for a dizzying view.

In the know

Getting around

The shoreline is better reached by buses than the metro. Useful lines from Plaça Catalunya include no.45 (as far as the Vila Olímpica) and no.59 (as far as Platja de Bogatell).

BARCELONETA & THE PORTS

Restaurants

1 Agua
2 Bestial
3 Can Majó
4 Can Ramonet
5 Can Solé
6 Green Spot
7 Kaiku
8 Set Portes
9 El Suquet de l'Almirall

Cafés, tapas & bars

1 1881
2 Black Lab
3 Can Ganassa
4 Can Paixano
5 La Cova Fumada
6 Filferro
7 El Vaso de Oro

Shops & services

1 La Botiga del Barça
2 Maremagnum

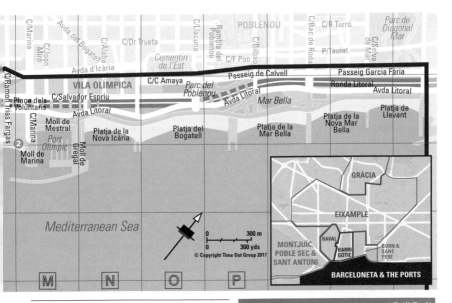

Estil Ferit

❤ Time to eat & drink

Breakfast with a view
1881 *p134*

Old-school tapas
La Cova Fumada *p131*,
El Vaso de Oro *p131*

Perfect paella
Can Majó *p128*, Kaiku *p129*

An afternoon tipple
Black Lab *p134*,
Can Paixano *p135*

Dinner by the sea
Agua *p128*, Bestial *p128*

❤ Time well spent

Estel Ferit
Rebecca Horn's tower of rusty iron boxes,
Estel Ferit (Wounded Shooting Star), pays
homage to the much-missed *xiringuitos*
(beach restaurants) that lined the
Barceloneta sands in pre-Olympic days. It
also references the dense geometric layout
of the *barrio*. Ten metres high, sitting on the
Platja de Sant Miquel, it's a popular meeting
place, known to local beach-goers as 'The
Cubes'. **Map** *p124 J11*.

BARCELONETA

Fishing tackle shops are moving out and cocktail bars are moving into the area. The tight-knit seaside community of **Barceloneta** ('Little Barcelona') is metamorphosing from a working-class neighbourhood dependent on fishing and heavy industry into a node of leisured bucket-and-spade tourism with ever greater numbers of bars, restaurants and homes converted into short-stay holiday flats. Millions of euros have been pumped in to improve buildings and sanitary conditions and open up the cramped interior to the main promenades, but many residents are suspicious of the motives behind this vision of a shiny new Barceloneta, fearful that it's simply a municipal push to transform a neglected slice of beachfront real estate into a tourist playground.

Controversy is not new to Barceloneta. When the old maritime *barrio* of La Ribera was demolished in 1714 to make way for the citadel, thousands were made homeless and forced to live in slums on the beach. The question of where to put them was solved by the broad tongue of silt that had built up after the construction of a breakwater in 1474; by the 18th century, it was solid enough to build on, and in 1753 the new district of Barceloneta was born. Military engineer Juan Martín Cermeño laid out narrow rows of cheap workers' housing set around a parade ground (now the market square). The two-storey houses became home to fishermen, sailors and dockers.

With the arrival of factories and shipbuilding yards in the 19th century, the area soon became so overcrowded with workers that the houses were split in half and later in quarters. These famous *quarts de casa* typically measured no more than 30 square metres (320 square feet), had no running water until the 1960s and often held families of ten or so. Most were later built up to six or more levels, but even today, many of the flats remain cramped and in bad condition despite their brightly painted façades.

Since the Olympic clean-up, Barceloneta has had a higher profile, and recent redevelopment includes university housing, Enric Miralles's glass-covered **Gas Natural headquarters** and, in the heart of the neighbourhood, the **market**, designed by Josep Miàs, a choppy composition of slats, undulating steel, solar panels and wrought iron recycled from the original 1884 structure. The market and large central square have acted as a catalyst for small businesses with new restaurants, food shops and boutiques.

The area has also been the beneficiary of a staggering amount of sculpture, particularly around the main promenade of **Passeig Joan de Borbó**. Lothar Baumgarten's *Rosa dels Vents* (Wind Rose) has the names of Catalan sea winds embedded in the pavement, and, at the other end of Passeig

Gas Natural headquarters

Boat Trips and Watersports

Activities for all abilities

If a boat trip is what you're after, there's a wealth of options.

Departing from the jetty just by the Monument a Colom, the 23m (75ft) sail **Catamaran Orsom** (93 221 82 83, www.barcelona-orsom.com) is the largest in Barcelona – it chugs up to 80 seafarers around to the Nova Bocana harbour area before unfurling its sails and peacefully gliding across the bay. There are three departures per day (noon, 3pm, 6pm) from May to October, and the trip takes about 1 hour 30 minutes in total. Tickets cost €15.50 (€13.50 reductions, free under-4s). There are also evening jazz/chill-out cruises at 6pm and 8pm on July and August weekends (€17.50, €14.50 reductions, free under-4s), and a 40-minute speedboat trip runs to the Fòrum and back (www.barcelonaspeedboat.com, €7.50, €4.50 reductions, free under-4s).

Since the 1888 World Exhibition, **Las Golondrinas** (Moll de Drassanes, 93 442 31 06, www.lasgolondrinas.com), the 'swallow boats', have chugged around the harbour, giving passengers a bosun's eye-view of Barcelona's rapidly changing seascape. The traditional double-decker pleasure boats serve the shorter port tour (approx 40mins, €7.40, €2.80 reductions), while the more powerful catamarans tour as far as the Port Fòrum (approx 1hr 30mins, €15, €5.50-€13.50 reductions, free under-4s). Sailings are hourly, from around 11.15am until sunset. Opening hours tend to be a bit erratic, so do check the website if possible.

For the willing and able, the **Base Nàutica de la Mar Bella** (93 221 04 32, www.basenautica.org) rents out kayaks, yachts, catamarans and windsurf gear to those with sufficient experience. It also offers lessons to individuals (including children aged six and above, €200/person for 8hrs) and groups of up to six participants (€50-€70/person for 2hrs). There is also a range of different options available for intensive or longer-term sailing proficiency courses. You'll find the Base Nàutica between Platja Bogatell and Platja de Mar Bella on Avda Litoral.

If you fancy a swim, the beachside **Club de Natació Atlètic Barceloneta** (Plaça del Mar, 93 221 00 10, www.cnab.cat) has an indoor pool and two outdoor pools, as well as a sauna and gym facilities. It's €12.01 for a non-member day pass, but you'll pay extra to use the sauna. There's also a *frontón* (Spanish ball-sports court) if you want to try your hand at the world's fastest sport: *jai alai*, a fierce Basque game that sits somewhere between squash and handball.

Joan de Borbó, is Juan Muñoz's disturbing sculpture of five caged figures, known as *Una habitació on sempre plou* (A Room Where It Always Rains). Monuments within the quarter include the 18th-century church of **Sant Miquel del Port**, with a muscular sculpture of the Archangel Michael on the façade, and, at the sea end of C/Sant Carles, the **Font de Carmen Amaya** – a fountain dedicated to the gypsy flamenco dancer born in 1913 in the Somorrostro, a long-gone beach slum.

Follow the yachts moored along the **Moll de la Barceloneta** down to the small remaining fishing area by the **clock tower** (previously a beacon to guide ships into port), which is the emblem of the neighbourhood. Further down, the road leads to the **Nova Bocana** complex, which combines high-end leisure facilities and offices and is dominated by Ricardo Bofill's **W Hotel**, a towering sail-shaped building. If you head left where Passeig Joan de Borbó passes the beach, you'll reach Rebecca Horn's *Estel Ferit* sculpture (*see p125*). The **Passeig Marítim** esplanade runs north from here, and is a popular hangout for skaters and strollers.

Clock tower

Restaurants

▶ *For details of restaurant price categories, see p36.*

♥ Agua €€

Passeig Marítim 30 (93 225 12 72, www. grupotragaluz.com). Bus 45, 59, 92. **Open** *9am-11.30pm Mon-Thur; noon-12.30am Fri, Sat.* **Map** *p124 L10* ❶ *Mediterranean*

Agua's main draw is its large terrace overlooking the beach, although the relaxed dining room is usually buzzing. The menu rarely changes, regardless of the time of year, but regulars never tire of the competently executed monkfish tail with *sofregit*, the risotto with partridge, and the fresh pasta with juicy prawns. Scrummy puddings are worth leaving space for and include marron glacé mousse and sour apple sorbet. It's advisable to book ahead, especially during the summer months and at weekends.

♥ Bestial €€

C/Ramón Trias Fargas 2-4 (93 224 04 07, www.grupotragaluz.com). Metro Barceloneta. **Open** *11am-11.30pm daily.* **Map** *p124 M10* ❷ *Italian*

A peerless spot for alfresco seaside dining, with tiered wooden decking and ancient olive trees framing a pleasant eating area. Bestial's dining room is also a stylish affair, with black-clad waiters sashaying along sleek runways, their trays held high. The food is of a modern Italian flavour: dainty mini-pizzas, rocket salad with parma ham and a lightly poached egg, tuna with black olive risotto and all the delicious puddings that you could ever hope to find – panna cotta, tiramisu and limoncello sorbet. At weekends, a DJ takes to the decks and drinks are served until 5am.

♥ Can Majó €€

C/Almirall Aixada 23 (93 221 54 55, www. canmajo.es). Metro Barceloneta. **Open** *1-4pm, 8-11.30pm Tue-Sat; 1-4pm Sun.* **Map** *p124 K11* ❸ *Seafood*

This place is famous for its fresh-from-the-nets selection of oysters, scallops, Galician clams, whelks and just about any other mollusc that you might care to mention. Even though the menu reads much as you would expect of a Barceloneta seafood restaurant, with plates of shellfish or (exemplary) fish soup as starters, followed by rich paellas and exquisitely tasty *fideuà*, the quality is a cut above the norm. Sit inside the dapper white and cornflower dining room, or across the road on the terrace, gazing out at the beautiful view of the sea.

Can Ramonet €€

C/Maquinista 17 (93 319 30 64, grupramonet. com). Metro Barceloneta. **Open** *noon-midnight daily.* **Map** *p124 K10* ❹ *Seafood*

Tucked away in the heart of Barceloneta, this quaint space with two quiet terraces is mostly overlooked by tourists, and consequently suffers none of the drop in standards of some of the paella joints on the seafront. Spectacular displays of fresh seafood show what's on offer that day, but it's also worth sampling the velvety fish soup and the generous paellas.
Other locations around the city.

Can Solé €€€

C/Sant Carles 4 (93 221 50 12, restaurantcansole.com). Metro Barceloneta. **Open** *1-4pm, 8-11pm Mon-Thur; 1-4pm, 8.30-11pm Fri, Sat; 1-4pm Sun.* **Map** *p124 J11* ❺ *Seafood*

Portly, jovial waiters have been charming moneyed regulars for more than a hundred years at Can Solé. Over the course of time, many of these diners have added to the framed photos, sketches and paintings that line the sky-blue walls. What continues to lure them is the freshest shellfish (share a plate of *chipirones* in onion and garlic, Cantabrian anchovies or red shrimp to start) and fillets of wild turbot, lobster stews and sticky paellas. Beware the steeply priced extras (coffee, cover).

♥ Kaiku €€

Plaça del Mar 1 (93 221 90 82, www. restaurantkaiku.cat). Metro Barceloneta. **Open** *mid Sep-mid May 1-4pm Tue-Sun; mid May-mid Sept 1-3.30pm, 7-10.30pm Tue-Sun.* **Map** *p124 J11* ❼ *Seafood*

With its simple look, missable façade and paper tablecloths, Kaiku looks a world apart from the upmarket seafood restaurants that pepper this *barrio*, but its dishes are sophisticated takes on the seaside classics. At Kaiku, a salad starter comes with shavings of foie or red fruit vinaigrette, and paella is given a rich and earthy spin with wild mushrooms. Book ahead, particularly for any chance of reserving one of the terrace tables that look out across the lovely beach.

El Suquet de l'Almirall €€€

Passeig Joan de Borbó 65 (93 221 62 33, suquetdelalmirall.com). Metro Barceloneta. **Open** *1-4pm, 8-11pm Tue-Sat; 1-4pm Sun.* **Map** *p124 J11* ❾ *Seafood*

One of the famous beachfront *xiringuitos* that was moved and refurbished in preparation for the 1992 Olympic Games in the city, El Suquet de l'Almirall remains a friendly and family-run concern despite the smart decor and mid-scale business lunchers. The fishy favourites on offer range from *xató* salad to *arròs negre* and include a variety of set menus, such as the 'blind' selection of tapas, a gargantuan taster menu and, most popular of all, the *pica-pica*, which includes roasted red peppers with anchovies, a bowl of steamed cockles and clams, and a heap of *fideuà* accompanied by lobster.

💙 Beaches

Barcelona never had much of a beach culture until the 1992 Olympics opened the city's eyes to the commercial potential of its location. What little sand there was before then was grey and clogged with private swimming baths and *xiringuitos* (beach-side eateries) that served seafood on trestle tables set up on the sand; the remainder was given over to heavy industry and waste dumps, cut off from the rest of the city by a strip of rail track, warehouses and factories.

For the grand Olympic makeover, the beaches were swiftly cleared and filled with tons of golden sand, imported palm trees and landscaped promenades. Visitors flocked, but the city beaches have become a victim of their own popularity, and keeping them clean is something of a Sisyphean task for the city council. Dubbed the 'Bay of Pigs' by the papers, the most central area has been subjected to a massive clean-up campaign with more beachfront toilets, extra bins and endless posters and loudspeaker announcements reminding people to pick up their rubbish.

Of the nine city beaches, the most southerly is **Platja de Sant Sebastià**, running from the W Hotel and popular with nudists. Next is **Platja de Sant Miquel**, which gets crowded in the summer months; it's popular with a gay crowd. **Platja de la Barceloneta** and **Platja del Somorrostro** next to it provide a sandy porch for restaurants and nightclubs. The covered walkway is home to tables where old men play dominoes with all the aggressiveness of a contact sport; it also

houses the beach centre, which has a small beach library (*see p135* In the know).

After the Port Olímpic and just down from the Ciutadella-Vila Olímpica metro station, **Platja de Nova Icària** is much broader, with plenty of space for volleyball and beach tennis, while **Platja de Bogatell** boasts the hippest *xiringuito*, with torches and loungers out at night from May to October. Further north, **Platja de Mar Bella** is all about sport, with the sailing club Base Nàutica, basketball nets, volleyball courts, table-tennis tables and a half-pipe for BMXers and skaters.

The most remote beaches are quiet **Platja Nova Mar Bella**, which is mostly used by local families, and the newer **Platja Llevant**, which opened to the public in 2006 when the Prim jetty was removed.

Cafés

Filferro

C/Sant Carles 29 (93 221 98 36). Metro Barceloneta. **Open** *July-Oct 10am-1am daily. Nov, Dec, Apr-June 10am-1am Tue-Sun. Jan-Mar 10am-11pm Tue-Sun.* **Map** *p124 K11* **6**

Simply but edgily decorated with cascades of red 1950s lampshades and rusted iron balustrades, this Italian-owned café is a restful, sunny spot for breakfast, lunch or tapas, with tables outside on a quiet square. As well as a decent range of fresh juices, there are pastries, toasted sandwiches, pasta and salads.

Tapas

Can Ganassa

Plaça de la Barceloneta 6 (93 221 75 86, canganassa.es). Metro Barceloneta. **Open** *8am-midnight Tue-Sun.* **Map** *p124 J10* **3**

Chaotic, noisy Can Ganassa has had a facelift, and lost a lot of its charm in the process, but still relies on its sizeable terrace on a quiet square. Good tapas are nearly all on display, so you don't need to worry about flexing your Catalan, just point. Try the *bomba Ganassa*; a huge potato and bacon croquette served with *allioli* and a fiery chilli sauce.

❤ La Cova Fumada

C/Baluard 56 (93 221 40 61). Metro Barceloneta. **Open** *9am-3.15pm Mon-Wed; 9am-3.15pm, 6-8.15pm Thur, Fri; 9am-1.15pm Sat. Closed 1wk July, 3wks Aug, 1 wk Feb.* **No cards. Map** *p124 K10* **5**

An authentic family-run *bodega*, hugely popular with local workers, where you'll need to arrive early for a cramped and possibly shared table. Said to be the birthplace of the spicy potato *bomba*, La Cova Fumada also turns out a great tomato and onion salad, delicious chickpeas with *morcilla* (black pudding) and unbeatable marinated sardines.

❤ El Vaso de Oro

C/Balboa 6 (93 319 30 98, vasodeoro.com). Metro Barceloneta. **Open** *10pm-midnight Mon-Fri; noon-midnight Sat, Sun. Closed Sept.* **No cards. Map** *p124 K10* **7**

The enormous popularity of this long, narrow cruise ship-style bar tells you everything you need to know about the tapas, but it also means that he who hesitates is lost when it comes to ordering. Elbow yourself a space and demand, loudly, *choricitos*, patatas bravas, *solomillo* (cubed steak) or *atún* (tuna, which here comes spicy). The beer (its storage, handling and pouring) is also a point of great pride.

PORT VELL

The initial focus of the Olympic makeover was the area rechristened **Port Vell** (Old Port), sandwiched between the Barri Gòtic and the spit of land that became Barceloneta. Tearing out the railroad, warehouses and waste dumps that cut the city off from the sea, developers carved out a palm-lined promenade ringing a luxury yacht marina in what was Barcelona's main port in medieval times. In those days the city was the dominant naval power in western Mediterranean trade; the nearby **Drassanes Reials** (Royal Shipyards), now home to the **Museu Marítim** (*see p134*), are among the finest pieces of civilian Gothic architecture in Spain.

Barcelona's power was dealt a blow when Christopher Columbus sailed westwards and found what he thought was the East. Soon, the Atlantic became the important trade route and Barcelona went into recession. Still, the city commemorates Columbus with the **Monument a Colom**. Prosperity returned in the 19th century, when the city became the base for the Spanish industrial revolution. Trade continues to boom at the **Moll d'Espanya**, an artificial island linked to the bottom of La Rambla by the undulating wooden **Rambla de Mar** footbridge designed by Viaplana and Piñón. The island is home to the **Maremagnum** mall (*see p135*) and **L'Aquàrium**.

At Columbus's feet, both the **Golondrinas** and the **Catamaran Orsom** pleasure boats begin their excursions out to sea (*see p127* Boat trips and watersports). To the south-west, beyond the busy ferry and cruise ports, is the grandly named **Porta d'Europa**, the longest drawbridge in Europe, which curtains off the vast container port. Big as it already is, plans are in place to enlarge the container port by diverting the mouth of the River Llobregat a mile or so to the south, which will double the size of the port area by 2050. Andreu Alfaro's enormous sculpture *Onas* (Waves) greatly cheers up the gridlocked roundabout of **Plaça de les Drassanes**, where a grim basin of coal marks the spot where steamboats once refuelled.

Parallel with the Passeig de Colom, the **Moll de la Fusta** wharf was built after the city sea walls were demolished in 1878. The wooden pergolas, one of which is topped by Javier Mariscal's popular fibreglass *Gamba* (Shrimp), are all that remain of some ill-fated restaurants and clubs. Traffic noise and congestion have been greatly reduced by passing the coastal motorway underneath the boulevard.

Just across the grassy slopes stands the *Ictineo II*; it's a replica of the world's first combustion-powered submarine, which was created by Narcis Monturiol and launched from Barcelona port in 1862. Roy Lichtenstein's pop art *Barcelona Head* signposts the marina, which is home to more than 450 moorings for leisure boats and the **Palau de Mar**, the only remaining warehouse from the area's industrial past, now converted into offices, restaurants and the **Museu d'Història de Catalunya**. The adjoining Moll del Dipòsit is crammed

Monument a Colom

In the know
Columbus' finger

Despite putting the city out of business, Columbus was commemorated with this monument in 1888. Consistent with the great discoverer's errant sense of direction, he's pointing not west to the Americas, but eastwards to Mallorca.

at the weekends with a craft market and immigrants flogging all manner of knock-off goods from sheets on the ground.

Sights & museums

❤ L'Aquàrium
Moll d'Espanya (93 221 74 74, www. aquariumbcn.com). Metro Barceloneta or Drassanes. Open (last entry 1hr before closing) Nov-Mar 10am-7.30pm Mon-Fri; 10am-8pm Sat, Sun. Apr, May, Oct 10am-8pm Mon-Fri; 10am-8.30pm Sat, Sun. June, Sept 10am-9pm daily. July, Aug 10am-9.30pm daily. Admission €20; €7-€15 reductions; free under-3s. Map p124 H10

The main draw here is the Oceanari, a giant shark-infested tank traversed via a glass tunnel on a slow-moving conveyor belt. Other tanks house shoals of kaleidoscopic fish where kids can play 'hunt Nemo'. The upstairs section is devoted to children. For pre-schoolers, Explora! has 50 activities, such as climbing inside a mini-submarine. Older children should head to Planet Aqua – an extraordinary, split-level circular space with Humboldt penguins.

❤ Monument a Colom
Plaça Portal de la Pau (93 285 38 34). Metro Drassanes. Open Mar-Sept 8.30am-8.30pm daily. Oct-Feb 8.30am-7.30pm daily. Tickets €6, €4 reductions; free under-4s. Map p124 G10

Inspired by Nelson's Column in London, and complete with eight majestic lions, the Christopher Columbus monument was designed for the Universal Exhibition of 1888. Positioned at the base of La Rambla, the monument allegedly marks the spot where Columbus docked in 1493 after his discovery of the Americas, and the carvings illustrate key moments in his voyages. Take the lift to the top for a fantastic view.

Museu d'Història de Catalunya
Plaça Pau Vila 3 (93 225 47 00, www. mhcat.net). Metro Barceloneta. Open 10am-7pm Tue, Thur-Sat; 10am-8pm Wed; 10am-2.30pm Sun. Admission All exhibitions €6.50; €4.50 reductions; free under-8s; free to all last Tue of mth Oct-June. Permanent exhibition €4.50; €3.50 reductions. Temporary exhibitions €4; €3 reductions. Map p124 J10

With exhibits spanning from the Lower Paleolithic era up to Jordi Pujol's proclamation as President of the Generalitat in 1980, the Catalan History Museum offers a virtual chronology of the region's past. There are two floors of text, film, animated models and stage-set reproductions, from a medieval shoemaker's shop to a 1960s bar. Hands-on activities, such as irrigating lettuces with a Moorish water wheel, add a little pizzazz to the rather dry early history, and to exit the exhibition, visitors walk over a huge 3D map of Catalonia. Every section has a decent introduction in English; the reception

Museu Marítim p134

desk can offer in-depth English-language museum guides free of charge. Excellent temporary exhibitions typically examine recent aspects of regional politics and history, while the huge rooftop café terrace, dating from 1881, has unbeatable views over the city and marina (*see p134*).

❤ Museu Marítim
Avda Drassanes (93 342 99 20, www. mmb.cat). Metro Drassanes. Open 10am-8pm daily. Tickets €5, €2.50 reduction; free under-17s, free to all Sun from 3pm. Map p124 G10

Even if you can't tell a caravel from a catamaran, the excellent Maritime Museum is worth a visit, as the soaring arches and vaults of the vast former *drassanes* (shipyards) represent one of the most perfectly preserved examples of civil Gothic architecture in Spain. In medieval times, the shipyards sat right on the water's edge and were used to dry-dock, repair and build vessels for the royal fleets. The finest of these was Don Juan de Austria's galley, from which he commanded the fleet that defeated the Ottoman navy in 1571: a full-scale replica is the mainstay of the collection. Several years of renovations end in mid 2017.

With the aid of an audio guide, the maps, mastheads, nautical instruments, multimedia displays and models show you how shipbuilding and navigation techniques have developed over the years. The admission fee also covers the beautiful 1917 *Santa Eulàlia* schooner, docked nearby in the Moll de la Fusta, and the Marítim often has some interesting temporary exhibitions. *Photo p133.*

Teleféric del Port
Torre de Sant Sebastià (93 441 48 20, www.telefericodebarcelona.com). Metro Barceloneta. Open June-mid Sept 10.30am-8pm daily. Nov-Feb 11am-5.30pm daily. Mar-May, Sept, Oct 10.30am-7pm daily. Tickets €11 single; €16.50 return; free under-7s. Map p124 H11

These rather battered cable cars do not appear to have been touched – except for the installation of lifts – since they were built for the 1929 Expo. They provide sky-high views over Barcelona on their grinding, squeaking path from the Sant Sebastià tower at the very far end of Passeig Joan de Borbó to the Jaume I tower in front of the World Trade Center; the final leg ends at the Miramar lookout point on Montjuïc. Make sure you go late in the day to avoid long queues.

Restaurants

Green Spot €€
C/Reina Cristina 12 (93 802 55 65, www. encompaniadelobos.com/the-green-spot). Metro Barceloneta. Open 12.30pm-midnight Mon-Fri; 1pm-midnight Sat, Sun. Map p124 J9 ⑥ Vegetarian

It's been a long time in coming, but it's finally here – a truly stylish vegetarian restaurant. Enter through a corridor of slatted oak panels to a huge, light-filled dining room with Scandi furniture, gracious curves and an interior garden. The menu combines new trends (including a short list of black pizzas) with fresh, local produce in unexpected ways.

Set Portes €€€
Passeig Isabel II 14 (93 319 30 33, www.7portes.com). Metro Barceloneta. Open 1pm-1am daily. Map p124 J9 ⑧ Seafood

The eponymous seven doors open on to as many dining salons, all kitted out in elegant 19th-century decor. Long-aproned waiters bring regional dishes, served in vast portions, including a stewy fish *zarzuela* with half a lobster, a different paella daily (shellfish, for example, or rabbit and snails), a wide array of fresh seafood, heavier dishes such as herbed black-bean stew with pork sausage and *orujo* sorbet to finish. Reservations are available only for certain tables; otherwise, make sure that you get there early for dinner.

Cafés

❤ 1881
Plaça Pau Vila 3 (93 221 00 50, www.sagardi. com). Metro Barceloneta. Open 10am-1am daily. Map p124 J10 ❶

There's no need to buy a ticket to the Museu d'Història de Catalunya to make the most of this little-known rooftop museum café with fabulous views. The set lunches don't break any ground gastronomically speaking, but are reasonable enough; or you can take coffee and a croissant to the vast terrace and watch the boats bobbing in the harbour.

Bars

❤ Black Lab
Palau de Mar, Plaça Pau Vila (93 221 83 60, www.blacklab.es). Metro Barceloneta. Open noon-1.30am daily. Map p124 J10 ❷

Barcelona's first tap room is a lively place, with a huge terrace. Dozens of beers are brewed on site (tours are given on Sundays). Five of these are available year round (try El Predicador, a superb IPA), but others change with the seasons and owner James is constantly experimenting with new flavours and methods. Decent pub grub is also available.

♥ Can Paixano

*C/Reina Cristina 7 (93 310 08 39, www. canpaixano.com). Metro Barceloneta. **Open** 9am-10.30pm Mon-Sat. Closed 2wks Jan. **No cards.** Map p124 J9* ❹

The 'Champagne Bar', as it's invariably known, has a huge following among young Catalans and the legion of foreigners who think they discovered it first. It can be impossible to talk, get your order heard or move your elbows, yet it's always mobbed due to its age-old look and atmosphere, dirt-cheap bottles of house cava and (literally) obligatory sausage butties.

Shops & services

La Botiga del Barça

*Maremagnum, Moll d'Espanya (93 225 80 45). Metro Drassanes. **Open** 10am-10pm daily. Map p124 H10* ❶ *Sport*

Everything for the well-dressed Barça fan, from the standard blue and burgundy strips to scarves, hats, crested ties and even underpants, plus calendars, shirts printed with your name, shield-embossed ashtrays, beach towels and so on.
Other locations around the city.

Maremagnum

*Moll d'Espanya 5 (93 225 81 00, www. maremagnum.es). Metro Drassanes. **Open** Shops 10am-10pm daily. Food court & entertainment 11am-3am daily. Map p124 H10* ❷ *Mall*

When Viaplana and Piñon's black-mirrored shopping and leisure centre opened in 1995, it was the place to hang out, but after years of declining popularity, it has ditched most of the bars and nightclubs. All the high-street staples are present (Mango, H&M, Women's Secret) and the ground floor focuses on the family market, with sweets, children's clothes and a Barça shop. The upper floor is dominated by food halls, with terraces running around the outside.

VILA OLÍMPICA

At the far end of the Passeig Marítim, the gateway to the Port Olímpic is heralded by the twin skyscrapers of the huge **Hotel Arts** and the **Torre Mapfre**, and Frank Gehry's shimmering copper *Fish* sculpture.

The large square of land behind these three was once an area of industry, but by the 1980s it had fallen into disuse and presented the perfect blank slate for the

Vila Olímpica

model neighbourhood of the Olympic Village for the Games in 1992. Based on Cerdà's Eixample grid, it provided parks, a cinema, four beaches, a leisure marina and accommodation for 15,000 athletes.

The lack of cafés and shops, however, leaves it void of distinctive Mediterranean charm. Most social activity takes place in the Port Olímpic. The empty boulevards do, however, lend themselves to sculpture, including a jagged pergola on Avda Icària by Enric Miralles and Carme Pinós.

Bars

The loud, tacky bars lining the Port Olímpic draw a mixture of drunken stag parties staring at the go-go girls and curious locals staring at the drunken stag parties. Avoid.

> **In the know**
> **Borrowing books and balls**
> The city council has established two *biblioplatges* (beach libraries) for the use of tourists, stocking around 200 novels, a wide selection of kids' books and comics, magazines and newspapers from around the world. You merely need to provide valid ID. Running alongside these services are the *ludoplatja*, which lends out buckets and spades, and the *esportplatja, for* volleyballs, boules and frisbees.
> The services are open daily at the Centre de la Platja (July, Aug 11am-7pm daily) underneath the boardwalk below the Hospital del Mar, and at the Bac de Roda breakwater (July-Sept 11am-7pm daily). For more information, visit www.bcn.cat/platges.

Montjuïc, Poble Sec & Sant Antoni

The mists of time obscure the etymology of the name 'Montjuïc'. 'Mont' means hill, and one widely accepted theory is that 'juïc' comes from the old Catalan word meaning Jewish. It was here that the medieval Jewish community buried their dead; some of the excavated headstones are to be found in the Castell de Montjuïc. Today, the Cementiri de Montjuïc still stands on the sea-facing side of the hill, but Montjuïc nowadays is thought of as a huge playground, with parks, cable cars, museums and a Greek-style amphitheatre.

Poble Sec, the area that sits on the hill's northern flank, is undergoing something of a transformation from sleepy residential zone, as it links up with newly cool Sant Antoni on the other side of Avda Paral·lel to form the latest hipster neighbourhood, bristling with new bars and cafés.

❤ **Don't miss**

1 Fundació Miró *p143*
Huge splashy artworks and superb views.

2 CaixaForum *p141*
Reliably good exhibitions in a Modernista factory.

3 Font Màgica *p142*
A gloriously kitsch celebration of light, water and music.

4 MNAC *p144*
Stunning collections of Romanesque and Gothic Catalan art.

5 Jardí Botànic *p142*
Plants from all over the world, and a view that's second to none.

In the know
Getting around

The easiest way to get up the hill is the funicular railway, integrated with the city's metro system and leaving from Paral·lel station. This will take you to the upper funicular station – from there you can walk up to the castle or get on the (expensive) cable car that runs to the top (see *p146*). Alternatively, bus no.150 runs from Plaça Espanya all the way up to the castle.

Poble Sec is between Avda Paral·lel and the hill and is easily accessible by metro. Sant Antoni (technically in the Eixample) borders the Raval; the nearest metro stations are Poble Sec or Sant Antoni.

View of Barcelona from Montjuic

MONTJUÏC

If Montjuïc sees relatively few visitors, it's largely because the city's constantly remodelled infrastructure has passed it by. The hillside is relatively inaccessible; to the uninitiated, the only way up seems to be from Plaça d'Espanya and the grandiose **Avda Reina Maria Cristina** or the vertigo-inducing cable car from Barceloneta, although the funicular from Paral·lel is easy and convenient. Plans to convert Montjuïc into the Central Park of Barcelona involve opening up access from Poble Sec, with broad boulevards and escalators leading up to Avda Miramar.

Castell de Montjuïc (*see p141*) occupies a prime defensive position, with a commanding view of both the sea and the city. In reality, however, its vantage point has been used to attack the city, not to defend it. Catalan mythology has it that it was built by Philip V, after Barcelona fell to his forces in 1714, in order to keep an eye on his unwilling and rebellious subjects. In fact, it was built 43 years before Philip was born and, although it has become a symbol of Spanish oppression, in 1706 the people rallied to its defence and that of its Austrian garrison against attacks from Bourbon forces. The most violent attack launched from the fortress was not the work of fascists or their precursors, but was ordered by the progressive Catalan general Joan Prim i Prats, who to this day has an entire Barcelona *rambla* named in his honour. Some 460 houses were damaged or destroyed in the bombardment Prim launched on 7 September 1843. The Franco years cemented the role of the fortress as a symbol of oppression, particularly after the Republican president Lluís Companys was executed by firing squad there in 1940. Earlier in the Civil War, however, the Republicans themselves executed some 58 people in the castle.

The 1929 Exhibition was the first attempt to turn the hill into a leisure area. Then, in the 1940s, thousands of immigrant workers from the rest of Spain settled on the hill. Some squatted in precarious shacks, while others rented brick and plaster sheds laid out along improvised streets. These *barraques* thrived until the last few stragglers moved out in the 1970s, although the area still attracts intermittent waves of illegal tent and hut dwellers. Energetic visitors can follow the same steep routes these residents once took home, straight up C/Nou de la Rambla or C/Margarit in Poble Sec; the stairway at the top leaves you just a short distance from the **Fundació Joan Miró** (*see p143*) and the Olympic stadium area.

The long axis from **Plaça d'Espanya** is still the most popular access to the park, with the climb now eased by a sequence of open-air escalators. In the centre of Plaça d'Espanya is a monument designed by Josep Maria Jujol (who created the wrought-iron balconies on La Pedrera), with representations of the rivers Ebre, Tagus and Guadalquivir. On the north of the Plaça is what used to be the **Las Arenas** bullring. The last bull met its fate here in the 1970s; until 2003, the arena lay derelict, but Richard Rogers oversaw a huge regeneration project that has turned the ring into a leisure complex, while restoring the neo-Mudéjar façade. The concept encompasses a 'piazza in the sky' – a giant roof terrace that allows for alfresco events and panoramic views over Barcelona. In a city already well endowed with shopping centres, this has the makings of a white elephant, and a museum dedicated to rock 'n' roll on the fourth floor closed within 11 months of opening.

On the other side of the square, a pair of Venetian-style towers announces the start of the **Fira**, the trade show area, with pavilions from 1929 and newer buildings used for conventions. Off it to the right, Josep Puig i Cadafalch's Modernista factory has been converted into the excellent **CaixaForum** cultural centre (*see p141*). Opposite, the rebuilt **Pavelló Mies van der Rohe** (*see p145*) contrasts sharply with the

---

💚 **Time to eat & drink**

Eggs over easy
Federal *p149*

Lunch with a view
Martinez *p146*

Tapas and a glass of wine
Quimet i Quimet *p149*,
Lando *p149*

Ceviche and a pisco sour
Lascar 74 *p148*

A stiff gin and tonic
Xixbar *p149*

In the know
Summer showings

In summer, Montjuïc comes alive with events, including **Montjuic de Nit** (concerts, films and the late opening of the CaixaForum, see *p218*) and **Sala Montjuïc**, a festival of independent films shown outdoors in the castle moat.

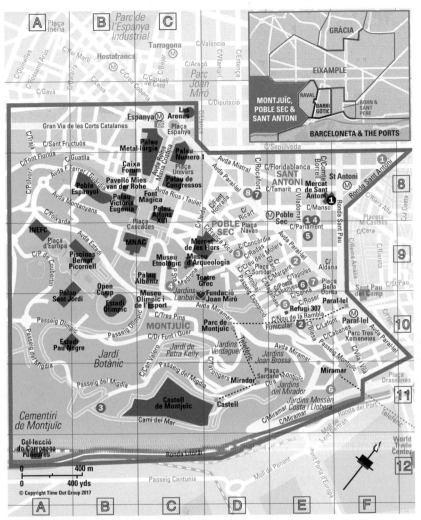

MONTJÜIC, POBLE SEC & SANT ANTONI

Restaurants

1. Alkimia
2. La Bella Napoli
3. Casa Xica
4. La Font del Gat
5. Lascar 74
6. Martinez
7. Tatami Room
8. Tickets

Cafés, tapas & bars

1. Bar Calders
2. Bar Seco
3. La Caseta del Migdia
4. Federal
5. Lando
6. Quimet i Quimet
7. Xix Bar

Shops & services

1. Book & Coin Market

On Your Bike

Two wheels good

You'll need the legs of Miguel Indurain to get up to Montjuïc's higher slopes, but you can take your bike on the funicular (from the Paral·lel metro station). Once at the top, take the right-hand exit and you'll come out on the **Avda del Miramar**. Turn right and follow the signs to the **Jardins de Joan Brossa**. Once inside the gate, follow the path that snakes through a delightful array of interactive sculptures and gadgetry. Once on the other side, turn right on to the **Ctra Montjuïc**. At this point you might need to wheel your bike a short way up to the **Plaça de la Sardana** – the location of the monument to Catalonia's national dance.

Just beyond this, take the **C/Tarongers** downhill and turn left at the bottom, whooshing past the **Jardí de Petra Kelly** to the **Passeig Olímpic**. Here are the **Estadi Olímpic**, the **Palau de Sant Jordi** and Santiago Calatrava's **telecommunications tower**. Swing left and round the stadium to the **Avda de l'Estadi**. Soon you'll arrive at the rear of the **MNAC** (*see p144*). Here, you can cut through gardens and lift your bike down an escalator to the front entrance. Continue to the other side and follow the curving **Passeig de Santa Madrona** to the entrance of the **Grec amphitheatre**. Any downhill road will lead you back to Avda Paral·lel, where you can ride back to the Paral·lel metro stop on a bike lane.

▶ *For details of bike hire, see p298.*

Bicycle hire at Montjuïc

neo-classical structures nearby. Further up the hill to the left is the **Poble Espanyol** (*see p146*), a model village designed in 1929 to showcase Spanish crafts and architecture.

Presiding over it all is the bombastic Palau Nacional, originally built as a temporary exhibition space for the Expo, and now home to the **MNAC** (Museu Nacional d'Art de Catalunya, *see p144*), housing Catalan art from the last millennium. At night, the scene is illuminated by a water-and-light spectacular, the **Font Màgica** (*see p142*), still operating with its complex original mechanisms. Other nearby buildings erected for the 1929 Expo have been

converted into the **Museu d'Arqueologia de Catalunya** (*see p144*) and the Ciutat del Teatre (Theatre City) complex, which houses the **Mercat de les Flors** (*see p253*). From the same period are the nearby **Teatre Grec** (Greek theatre), used for summer concerts during the **Grec Festival** (*see p218*), and the beautifully restored **Jardins Laribal**.

Montjuïc's **Anella Olímpica** (Olympic Ring) is a convergence of diverse constructions laid out for the 1992 Olympic Games. The **Estadi Olímpic**, although entirely new, was built within the façade of a 1929 stadium by a design team led by Federico Correa and Alfonso Milà. The horse sculptures are copies of originals by Pau Gargallo. Next to it is the most attractive of the Olympic facilities, Arata Isozaki's **Palau Sant Jordi** indoor arena. Its undulating façade evokes Gaudí, and its high-tech interior features a transparent roof. In the stark, white *plaça* in front rises Santiago Calatrava's remarkable, Brancusi-inspired communications tower.

Across the square is the city's best pool, the **Piscines Bernat Picornell**, while further down is the INEFC physical education institute, by architect Ricardo Bofill. Walk across the road and you look down a steep drop on to a rugby pitch and an equestrian area offering pony rides; the rock face itself is a favourite with climbers.

The many parks and gardens include the **Jardins Mossèn Costa i Llobera** (*see p144*), which abound in tropical plants, but particularly cacti, and are set just below Miramar on the steep flank nearest the port. Not far above are the **Jardins del Mirador**, which afford a spectacular view over the harbour. These gardens are also the starting point for a path that runs below the castle and leads to an outdoor café, **La Caseta del Migdia** (*see p146*). Nearby are the **Jardins de Joan Brossa** (*see p144*), featuring humorous, hands-on contraptions where children can experiment with sounds by bouncing on musical rubber pads or talking through wooden speakers. Walk down towards the funicular station and you'll reach the enchanting **Jardins Cinto Verdaguer**, with ponds filled with lotus flowers and water lilies. All these gardens play an adjunct role to the creative biospheres of the **Jardí Botànic** (*see p142*), just above the Olympic stadium, sharply designed and finally maturing into an important scientific collection.

Sights & museums

♥ CaixaForum
Casaramona, Avda Francesc Ferrer i Guàrdia 6-8 (93 476 86 00, www.obrasociallacaixa. org). Metro Espanya. **Open** *Sept-June 10am-8pm daily. July, Aug 10am-8pm Mon, Tue, Thur-Sun; 10am-11pm Wed.* **Admission** *€4.* **Map** *p139 B8*

One of the masterpieces of industrial Modernisme, this former yarn and textile factory was designed by Puig i Cadafalch and celebrated its centenary in 2011. It spent most of the last century in a sorry state, briefly acting as a police barracks before falling into disuse. Fundació La Caixa, the charitable arm of Catalonia's largest savings bank, bought it and set about rebuilding. The original brick structure was supported, while the ground below was excavated to house a strikingly

modern entrance plaza by Arata Isozaki, a Sol LeWitt mural, an auditorium, a bookshop and a library. In addition to the permanent contemporary art collection, there are three impressive spaces for temporary exhibitions – often among the most interesting shows to be found in the city.

Castell de Montjuïc
Ctra de Montjuïc 66 (93 256 44 40, www. bcn.cat/castelldemontjuic). Metro Paral·lel then funicular & cable car. **Open** *Apr-Oct 10am-8pm daily. Nov-Mar 10am-6pm daily.* **Admission** *€5, €3 reduction; free under-16s.* **Map** *p139 C11.*

The Military Museum that was once located here closed down in 2009 and its contents were moved to Figueres, but visitors can still stroll through the castle grounds, climb the battlements for fabulous views, or picnic in the wide moat. Exhibitions explain a little about the history of the castle, but the real attraction here is the view.

Cementiri de Montjuïc
C/Mare de Déu de Port 56-58 (93 484 19 69). Bus 21. **Open** *8am-6pm daily.* **Admission** *free.* **Map** *p139 A11.*

Designed by Leandro Albareda in 1880, this enormous necropolis sits at the side of the motorway and acts as a daily reminder to commuters of their own mortality. The cemetery was originally divided up into four sections: one for Catholics, one for Protestants, one for non-Christians and a fourth for stillborn babies. It now stretches over the south-west corner of the mountain, with family tombs stacked five or six storeys high. Many, especially those belonging to the *gitano* (Roma) community, are a riot of colour and flowers. The Fossar de la Pedrera memorial park remembers the fallen of the International Brigades and the Catalan martyrs from the Civil War. There is also a Holocaust memorial and a mausoleum to the former president of the Generalitat, Lluís Companys.

The cemetery is much visited, particularly on All Saints' Day, when the roads become clogged with cars. It now also

In the know
The long way up

A more circuitous ascent up the hill is to take the **Teléferic del Port** cable car built for the 1929 Expo. Leave from the Sant Sebastià tower at the very far end of Passeig Joan de Borbó in Barceloneta, across the harbour to Miramar, a peaceful spot with unrivalled views across the city – though the tranquillity has been somewhat disturbed by the construction of the swish Hotel Miramar.

Jardí Botànic

provides a home for the city's collection of funeral carriages.

Col·lecció de Carrosses Fúnebres

C/Mare de Déu de Port 56-58 (93 484 19 99, www.cbsa.cat). Bus 21. **Open** *10am-2pm Sat, Sun.* **Admission** *free.* **Map** *p139 A12.*

Moved in 2012 from a funeral parlour in the Eixample to the Montjuïc cemetery, this is the world's largest collection of funeral carriages and hearses, dating from the 18th century to the 1950s. There are ornate Baroque carriages, more functional Berlins and Landaus, and a wonderful '50s silver Buick. The white carriages were designed for children and virgins; there's a windowless black-velour mourning carriage for the mistress, ensuring her anonymity. The vehicles are manned by ghoulish mannequins, whose eyes follow you around the spaces.

❤ Font Màgica de Montjuïc

Plaça Carles Buïgas 1 (www.bcn.es/ fontmagica). Metro Espanya. **Shows** *(every 30mins) Apr, May, Oct 9-10.30pm Fri, Sat. June-Sept 9.30-11pm Thur-Sun. Nov-Mar 7-8.30pm Fri, Sat.* **Map** *p139 C8.*

Still in possession of its original plumbing, the 'magic fountain' works its wonders with 3,600 pieces of tubing and more than 4,500 light bulbs. The multiple founts swell and dance to anything from the *1812 Overture* to Freddie Mercury and Montserrat Caballé's 'Barcelona', showing off a kaleidoscope of pastel colours.

❤ Jardí Botànic

C/Doctor Font i Quer (93 426 49 35, www. museuciencies.cat). Metro Paral·lel then Funicular de Montjuïc or 150, 13 bus. **Open** *Oct-Mar 10am-5pm daily. Apr-Sept 10.30am-7pm Tue-Sun.* **Admission** *€3.50; €1.70 reductions; free under-16s. Free after 3pm Sun & all day 1st Sun of mth.* **Map** *p139 B10.*

After the original 1930s botanical garden was disturbed by the construction for the Olympics, the only solution was to build an entirely new replacement. This opened in 1999, housing plants derived from seven global regions with a climate similar to that of the western Mediterranean. Everything about the futuristic design, from the angular concrete pathways to the raw sheet steel banking (and even the design of the bins), is the complete antithesis of the more naturalistic, Gertrude Jekyll-inspired gardens of England. It is meticulously kept, with plants tagged with Latin, Catalan, Spanish and English names, along with the date of planting, and has the added advantage of

---

In the know
Cemetery tours

If your Spanish is up to it, there are guided tours of the **Cementiri de Montjuïc** at 11.15am on the second and fourth Sundays of the month, visiting 37 graves and tombs of artistic and historic interest.

💙 Fundació Joan Miró

Parc de Montjuïc s/n (93 443 94 70, www. fmirobcn.org). Metro Paral·lel then Funicular de Montjuïc or no.150, 55 bus. **Open** *Apr-Oct 10am-8pm Tue, Wed, Fri, Sat; 10am-9pm Thur; 10am-3pm Sun. Nov-Mar 10am-6pm Tue, Wed, Fri; 10am-9pm Thur; 10am-8pm Sat; 10am-3pm Sun.* **Admission** *All exhibitions €12; €7 reductions. Temporary exhibitions €7; €5 reductions; free under-15s.* **Map** *p139 C10.*

Josep Lluís Sert, who spent the years of the Franco dictatorship as dean of the School of Design at Harvard University, designed one of the world's greatest museum buildings on his return. Approachable, light and airy,

Primary colours and organic forms symbolise stars, the moon, birds and women

these white walls and arches house a hugely impressive collection of more than 225 paintings, 150 sculptures and all of Miró's graphic work, plus some 5,000 drawings. The permanent collection, highlighting Miró's trademark use of primary colours and simplified organic forms symbolising stars, the moon, birds and women, occupies half of the space.

In other works, Miró is shown as a cubist (*Street in Pedralbes*, 1917), naive (*Portrait of a Young Girl*, 1919) and surrealist (*Man and Woman in Front of a Pile of Excrement*, 1935). In the upper galleries, large, black-outlined paintings from Miró's final years precede a room of works with political themes.

In the know
Fountain from Paris

On the way to the museum's sculpture gallery lies Alexander Calder's rebuilt Mercury Fountain, which was originally seen at the Spanish Republic's Pavilion at the 1937 Paris Fair.

MONTJUÏC, POBLE SEC & SANT ANTONI

wonderful views across the city. A small space plays host to occasional exhibitions, and useful, free audio guides lead visitors through the gardens.

Jardins de Joan Brossa

Plaça Dante (010, ajuntament.barcelona. cat/ecologiaurbana). Metro Paral·lel then Funicular de Montjuïc or 150, 55 bus. **Open** *10am-sunset daily.* **Admission** *free.* **Map** *p139 E10.*

Set in 5.2 hectares of the former fairground, Montjuïc's latest park is part forest, with 40 species of tree, and part urban playground. As well as a climbing frame, there are various oversized wooden instruments and creations designed for children, allowing them to play tunes and pump water.

Jardins Mossèn Costa i Llobera

Ctra de Miramar 38 (010, ajuntament. barcelona.cat/ecologiaurbana). Metro Paral·lel then Funicular de Montjuïc or 150, 55 bus. **Open** *10am-sunset daily.* **Admission** *free.* **Map** *p139 E11.*

The port side of Montjuïc is protected from the cold north wind, creating a microclimate that is 2°C warmer than the rest of the city – allowing some 800 species of the world's cacti to flourish here.

♥ MNAC (Museu Nacional d'Art de Catalunya)

Palau Nacional, Parc de Montjuïc (93 622 03 60, www.museunacional.cat). Metro Espanya. **Open** *May-Sept 10am-8pm Mon-Sat; 10am-3pm Sun. Oct-Apr 10am-6pm Tue-Sat; 10am-3pm Sun.* **Admission** *Permanent & temporary exhibitions (valid 2 days) €12; €8.40 reductions. Combined ticket with Poble Espanyol €19. Free under-16s & over-65s. Free to all after 3pm Sat & all day 1st Sun of mth.* **Map** *p139 B9.*

'One museum, a thousand years of art' is the slogan of the National Museum, and the collection provides a dizzying overview of Catalan art from the 12th to the 20th centuries. In recent years, the museum has added an extra floor to absorb the section of the Thyssen-Bornemisza collection that was previously kept in the convent in Pedralbes, along with the mainly Modernista holdings from the former Museum of Modern Art in Ciutadella park, a fine photography section, coins and the bequest of Francesc Cambó, founder of the autonomist Lliga Regionalista, a regionalist conservative party.

The highlight, however, is the Romanesque collection. As art historians realised that scores of solitary tenth-century churches in the Pyrenees were falling into ruin – and with them, extraordinary Romanesque murals that had served to

instruct villagers in the basics of the faith – the laborious task was begun of removing the murals from church apses. The display here features 21 mural sections arranged in loose chronological order. A highlight is the tremendous *Crist de Taüll*, originally from the 12th-century church of Sant Climent de Taüll. Even 'graffiti' scratchings (probably by monks) of animals, crosses and labyrinths have been preserved. The museum also contains a major 13th-century Romanesque mural from the cathedral at La Seu d'Urgell.

The excellent Gothic collection starts with some late 13th-century frescoes that were discovered in 1961 and 1997, when two palaces in the city were undergoing renovation. There are carvings and paintings from local churches, including works by the indisputable Catalan masters of the Golden Age, Bernat Martorell and Jaume Huguet. The highlight of the Thyssen collection is Fra Angelico's *Madonna of Humility* (c1430), while the Cambó bequest contains some wonderful Old Masters. Also unmissable is the Modernista collection, which includes Ramon Casas' mural of himself and Pere Romeu on a tandem, which decorated the famous Els Quatre Gats café. The rich collection of decorative arts includes original furniture from Modernista houses.

Museu d'Arqueologia de Catalunya

Passeig de Santa Madrona 39-41 (93 423 21 49, www.mac.cat). Metro Poble Sec. **Open** *9.30am-7pm Tue-Sat; 10am-2.30pm Sun.* **Admission** *€4.50; €3.50 reductions; free under-8s. No cards.* **Map** *p139 C9.*

The time frame for this archaeology collection starts with the Palaeolithic period, and there are relics of Greek, Punic, Roman and Visigothic colonisers, with artefacts from up to the early Middle Ages. A massive Roman sarcophagus is carved with scenes of the rape of Persephone, and an immense statue of Aesculapius, the god of medicine, towers over one room. A few galleries are dedicated to the Mallorcan Talayotic cave culture, and there is an exemplary display on the Iberians – the pre-Hellenic, pre-Roman inhabitants of south-eastern Spain. An Iberian skull with a nail driven through it effectively demonstrates a typical method of execution from that time. The display ends with the marvellous, jewel-studded headpiece of a Visigoth king. One of the best-loved pieces, inevitably, is an alarmingly erect Priapus, found during building work in Sants in 1848 and kept under wraps 'for moral reasons' until 1986.

Museu Etnològic

Passeig de Santa Madrona 16-22 (93 424 68 07, ajuntament.barcelona.cat/ museuetnologic). Metro Poble Sec.

***Open** 10am-7pm Tue-Sat; 10am-8pm Sun.*
***Admission** €5, €3.50 reduction. Free under-16s; free to all after 4pm Sun & all day 1st Sun of mth. **Map** p139 C9.*

With the opening of the Museu de Cultures del Mòn (*see p96*) in the Born, much of the vast collection of items, from Australian Aboriginal boomerangs to rugs and jewellery from Afghanistan, moved over there, and the Ethnology Museum now focuses mainly on Catalan history. Along with archaeological finds, farming implements and so on, is a selection of items recognisable from neighbourhood *festes* – papier-mâchéd';?: giants, dragons and typical costumes used for various celebrations.

Museu Olímpic i de l'Esport

Avda Estadí 60 (93 292 53 79, www.museuolimpicbcn.cat). Metro Paral·lel then Funicular de Montjuïc or 150, 55 bus. ***Open** Apr-Sept 10am-8pm Tue-Sat; 10am-2.30pm Sun. Oct-Mar 10am-6pm Tue-Sat; 10am-2.30pm Sun.* ***Admission** €5.80; €3.60 reductions; free under-7s & over-65s.* ***Map** p139 C10.*

Opened in 2007 in a new building across from the stadium, the Olympic and Sports Museum gives an overview of the Games (and, indeed, all games), from Ancient Greece to the present day. As well as photographs and film footage of great sporting moments and heroes, there's an array of related objects (Ronaldinho's boots, Mika Häkkinen's Mercedes), along with a collection of opening ceremony costumes and Olympic torches on show. Perhaps more entertaining are the interactive displays, including one that compares your effort at the long jump with those of the pros.

Open Camp

Estadi Olímpic Lluís Companys, Passeig Olímpic 17-19 (902 070 753, www.opencamp.com). Metro Paral·lel, then 10-minute walk or bus 150, 13. ***Open** Apr, Sept 10am-6pm daily; June, Aug 10am-7pm daily; Nov 10am-5pm Thur-Sun; Dec 10am-5pm Fri-Sun, public hols.* ***Admission** €20, €15 reductions, free under-5s.* ***Map** p139 B10.*

A huge hit with kids, this sports park offers more than 25 experiences, including state-of-the-art simulators for football training, boxing and motorbike racing. Out in the main stadium, visitors can sprint, hurdle, high-jump and long-jump to a rousing soundtrack of applause blasting through the speakers, as well as practise goal-scoring on the football pitch. Inside, you can try your hand at everything from archery to basketball. Guided bike rides around the whole Olympic Ring and entrance to the Olympic Museum are also included.

Pavelló Mies van der Rohe

Avda Francesc Ferrer i Guàrdia 17 (93 423 40 16, www.miesbcn.com). Metro Espanya. ***Open** Mar-Oct 10am-8pm daily. Nov-Feb 10am-6pm daily.* ***Admission** €5; €2.60 reductions; free under-16s. No cards.* ***Map** p139 B8.*

Mies van der Rohe built the Pavelló Alemany (German Pavilion) for the 1929 World Exhibition not as a gallery but as a simple reception space, which was sparsely furnished with his trademark steel-framed 'Barcelona Chair'. The pavilion was a founding monument of modern rationalist architecture, with its flowing floor plan and revolutionary use of materials. Even though the original pavilion was demolished

Telefèric de Montjuïc

following the exhibition, a fine replica was built on the same site in 1986, the simplicity of its design setting off the warm tones of the marble, and the expressive Georg Kolbe sculpture in the pond.

Poble Espanyol
Avda Francesc Ferrer i Guàrdia 13 (93 508 63 00, www.poble-espanyol.com). Metro Espanya. **Village & restaurants** *9am-8pm Mon; 9am-midnight Tue-Thur, Sun; 9am-4am Fri, Sat.* **Shops** *Dec-May 10am-6pm daily. June-Aug 10am-8pm daily. Sept-Nov 10am-7pm daily.* **Admission** *€13; €7-€10 reductions; €35 family ticket; free under-4s. Night ticket €7. Combined ticket with MNAC €19.* **Map** *p139 B8.*

Built for the 1929 World Exhibition and designed by the Modernista architect Josep Puig i Cadafalch, this composite Spanish village may appear charming or kitsch, depending on your personal tastes, and features reproductions of traditional buildings and squares from every region in Spain. The cylindrical towers at the entrance are copied from the walled city of Ávila and lead on to a typical Castilian main square; from here, visitors can explore a tiny whitewashed street from Arcos de la Frontera in Andalucía, then head to the 16th-century House of Chains from Toledo. There are numerous bars and restaurants along the way, including a flamenco *tablao* and more than 60 shops selling Spanish crafts. Outside, street performers recreate snippets of Catalan and Spanish folklore.

Telefèric de Montjuïc (cable car)
Estació Funicular, Avda Miramar (93 465 53 13,www.telefericdemontjuic.cat). Metro Paral·lel then Funicular de Montjuïc or 150, 55 bus. **Open** *Oct-Feb 10am-6pm daily. Mar-May 10am-7pm daily. June-Sept 10am-9pm daily.* **Tickets** *One way €8.20; €6 reductions. Return €12.50; €9 reductions; free under-4s.* **Map** *p139 D10.*

The rebuilt system features eight-person cable cars that soar from the funicular up to the castle.

Restaurants
La Font del Gat €€
Passeig Santa Madrona 28 (93 289 04 04, www.lafontdelgat.com). Funicular de Montjuïc or bus 55. **Open** *10am-6pm Tue-Sun. Closed 2wks Christmas.* **Map** *p139 C9* ❹ *Catalan*

La Font del Gat is a welcome watering hole located high on Montjuïc, between the Miró and ethnological museums. The small, informal-looking restaurant has a surprisingly sophisticated menu (à la carte served only at weekends): ravioli with truffles and wild mushrooms, for example, or foie with Modena caramel. However, most punters head up to this restaurant for the set lunch: try starting with the scrambled egg with Catalan sausage and peppers or a salad; follow it with baked cod or chicken with pine nuts and basil, and finish with fruit or a simple dessert. If you want to reserve a table outside, you'll have to pay a surcharge.

❤ Martinez €€€
Ctra Miramar 38 (93 106 60 52, martinezbarcelona.com). Funicular de Montjuïc or bus 150. **Open** *1pm-1.30am daily.* **Map** *p139 E11* ❻ *Spanish*

Martinez is loosely based on a *xiringuito* (open-air beach restaurant), but sits in a stunning location high on Montjuïc, next to the Miramar hotel and the cactus gardens. The specialities are paellas and other rice dishes, along with classic tapas, but – while the food is perfectly good – know that the elevated prices are really all about the spectacular views across the port, and city. It is especially romantic at night.

Cafés
La Caseta del Migdia
Mirador del Migdia, Passeig del Migdia (mobile 617 956 572, www.lacaseta.org). Funicular de Montjuïc or 150 bus, then 15min walk. Follow signs to Mirador de Montjuïc. **Open** *June-Sept 9pm-midnight Wed (only with reservation); 8pm-1am Thur;*

New Block on the Block

Hipsters have taken over an unlikely residential zone

In 2006, with characteristic foresight, Albert Adrià, brother of superchef Ferran, opened a tapas bar on C/Tamarit in the unexciting neighbourhood of Sant Antoni. Heads were scratched. Sant Antoni has at its heart a handsome old market, beloved for its Sunday morning book fair, but aside from that it's a fairly drab residential sub-neighbourhood of the Eixample. The city council had made much of plans to tart up the area, particularly the traditional theatre district of Avda Paral·lel, but few people were listening – except for a handful of entrepreneurial bar and restaurant owners.

Since then, the area has taken off with breathtaking speed, and the streets around one block, particularly, have become the place where men with ironic lion-tamer moustaches and women with KD Lang haircuts and clear Ray-Bans in acid colours come to meet their peers. C/Parlament is the epicentre, arguably thanks to the opening of **Federal** (*see p149*), a breezily cool café that nails its colours to the mast by stocking the *New Yorker* and *Vogue* and serving its eggs in a skillet. Cocktails in a shoe can't be far away.

Next to open was **Bar Calders** (*see p149*). Other wine bars followed, as did cutesy cupcake shops, until the overspill of cool was forced around the block to C/Viladomat and C/Aldana. Here you'll find – among others – **Jonny Aldana** (C/Aldana 9, 93 174 20 83, www.jonnyaldana.com), a tiny bar with a big following, and next to it the youthful **Bar Olimpia** (C/Aldana 11, mobile 606 200 800). Both have tables on the pavement, where you can snack al fresco on tapas and all-day brunch.

8pm-1.30am Fri; noon-1.30am Sat; noon-midnight Sun. Oct-May noon-sunset Sat, Sun. **No cards. Map p139 B11** ❸

Completely alfresco, high up in a clearing among the pines, this is a magical space, scattered with deckchairs, hammocks and candlelit tables. Rather surreally, DJs spinning funk, rare groove and lounge alternate with a faltering string quartet; food is grilled sausages and salad, plus a few rice dishes. To find it, cut through the Brossa gardens from the funicular and follow the Camí del Mar footpath south around the castle. Be aware it's a lot cooler up here than in town.

POBLE SEC & SANT ANTONI

Poble Sec, the name of the neighbourhood between Montjuïc and the Avda Paral·lel, means 'dry village'; it was 1894 before the thousands of impoverished workers who lived on the flanks of the hill celebrated the installation of the area's first water fountain (which is still standing today in C/Margarit).

These days, Poble Sec is a friendly, working-class area of quiet streets and leafy squares, with an increasingly Latin American flavour, reflecting the large immigrant population that comes from Ecuador and elsewhere. Around a quarter of the 40,000 people in Poble Sec are from outside Spain.

On the stretch of the Paral·lel opposite the city walls, three tall chimneys stand amid modern office blocks. They are all that remains of the Anglo-Canadian-owned power station known locally as **La Canadença** ('The Canadian'), the centre of the city's largest general strike in 1919. Beside the chimneys, an open space has been created and dubbed the **Parc de les Tres Xemeneies** (Park of the Three Chimneys).

Towards the Avda Paral·lel are some distinguished Modernista buildings, which local legend maintains were built for artistes from the nude cabarets by their sugar daddies. At C/Tapioles 12 is a beautiful, narrow, wooden Modernista door with particularly lovely writhing ironwork, while at C/Elkano 4 is **La Casa de les Rajoles**, known for its mosaic façade.

The name **Paral·lel** derives from the fact that the avenue coincides exactly with 41º 44' latitude north, one of Ildefons Cerdà's more eccentric conceits. This was the centre of Barcelona nightlife in the early 20th century, full of theatres, nightclubs and music halls. A statue on the corner with C/Nou de la Rambla commemorates Raquel Meller, a legendary star of the street who went on to big-screen success. She now stands outside Barcelona's notorious live-porn venue, the Bagdad. There are grand plans to revive this as a theatre district.

To the other side of Paral·lel is the triangle that forms **Sant Antoni**, which centres on the market of the same name. Strictly speaking, this is part of the Eixample, but its recent promotion to desirable hipster-'hood means it now shares more characteristics with Poble Sec than with the rest of the Eixample, from which it is also separated by geography. Beyond its century-old iron and brick market – under endless renovation, with a temporary building housing stalls nearby – it has no real sights of interest except for the **Refugi 307**, but it does have some of the city's liveliest bars and restaurants.

Sights & museums

Refugi 307

C/Nou de la Rambla 175 (93 256 21 22, www. museuhistoria.bcn.cat). Metro Paral·lel. ***Open*** *(guided tour & by appt only) 10.30am (English), 11.30am (Spanish) Sun.* ***Admission*** *€3.40; free under-7s. No cards.* ***Map*** *p139 E10.*

Around 1,500 Barcelona civilians were killed during the Civil War air raids, a fact that the government has long silenced. Poble Sec was hit particularly hard, and a large air-raid shelter was built partially into the mountain at the top of C/Nou de la Rambla; this is one of some 1,200 in the city. Now converted into a museum, it's worth a visit; the tour takes about 45 minutes.

Restaurants

Alkimia €€€€

Ronda Sant Antoni 41 (93 207 61 15, www. alkimia.cat). Metro Sant Antoni. ***Open*** *1.30-3.30pm, 8-11pm Mon-Fri.* ***Map*** *p139 F8* ❶ *Catalan*

Chef Jordi Vilà is hugely respected, and turns out complex dishes that play with Spanish classics – for instance, liquid *pa amb tomàquet* with fuet sausage, or wild rice with crayfish and strips of tuna on a bed of foamed mustard. There is also an enviably stocked wine cellar. A recent move across town from its former home near the Sagrada Família to the Fàbrica Moritz, a gastronomic centre, has meant a more welcoming dining room – with pretty tiled floors and only six tables – and a new space, 'Alkimia Unplugged', for simpler dishes at a lower price.

La Bella Napoli €€

C/Margarit 12 (93 442 50 56). Metro Paral·lel. ***Open*** *1.30-4pm, 8.30pm-midnight daily.* ***Map*** *p139 E9* ❷ *Italian*

La Bella Napoli's welcoming Neapolitan waiters can talk you through the long, long list of antipasti and pasta dishes, and you certainly can't go wrong by opting for one of the crispy baked pizzas. These include the Sofia Loren, complete with provolone, basil, bresaola, cherry tomatoes, rocket and parmesan. The speciality beers and wine list are a strictly all-Italian affair; in fact, the only thing that lacks authenticity is the

catalogue of pre-made ice-cream desserts. There is home-made tiramisu available, but you have to ask for it.

Casa Xica €€€

C/França Xica 20 (93 600 58 58, www. facebook.com/casaxicabarcelona). Metro Poble Sec. ***Open*** *8.30pm-midnight Mon; 1.30-3.30pm, 8.30pm-midnight Tue-Sat.* ***Map*** *p139 D9* ❸ *Catalan/Asian*

A wonderfully cosy little space of bare-brick walls and marble tables, with an unlikely blend of Asian and Catalan, often within the same dish. This means, for example, that you can have steamed buns with lamb; Thai *suquet* (Catalan fish stew), or local oysters with ginger. Much is made of the wine list, which features 'natural' and organic wines, but they are not quite on a par with the cooking.

❤ Lascar 74 €€

C/Roser 74 (93 017 98 72, lascar.es). Metro Paral·lel. ***Open*** *8-11.45pm Mon-Wed, 1-4pm, 8pm-11.45pm Thur, Fri; 1-11.45pm Sat, Sun.* *p139 E10* ❺ *Ceviche*

The latest vogue to hit Barcelona is the 'cevichería', but nowhere does it better or with a more reasonable price than Lascar. Run by a Scot and an Englishman, it's a welcoming little space with good music, great cocktails (the pisco sours are the best in the city) and an unpretentious vibe. As well as classic versions of the dish, there are 'ceviches of the world', such as the tropical, the Japanese and the laksa.

Tatami Room €€

C/Poeta Cabanyes 22 (93 329 67 40, thetatatamiroombcn.com). Metro Paral·lel. ***Open*** *1.30-3.30pm, 8-11pm Mon-Thur; 1.30-3.30pm, 8pm-midnight Fri, Sat.* ***Map*** *p139 E9* ❼ *Japanese*

Opened by a trio of Japanophile Brits, the Tatami Room is based on the concept of *izakayas* – which nearly equate to the idea of tapas bars, only with rather more comfortable seating areas. Downstairs, in a cosy basement bar, there are sunken tables and tatami mats to sit on (your footwear stacks away in a neat space underneath), at which you can chow down on shared plates of grilled *yakitori* brochettes, sashimi, tempura, noodle and rice dishes.

Tickets €€€€

Avda Paral·lel 164 (no phone, www. ticketsbar.es). Metro Poble Sec. ***Open*** *7-11.30pm Tue-Fri; 1-3.30pm, 7-11.30pm Sat.* ***Map*** *p139 D8* ❽ *Modern Spanish*

This venture comes from superchef Ferran Adrià and his brother Albert and, in the wake of El Bulli's closure, is preternaturally popular. You'll need to book (online – there is deliberately no phone). Expect a parade of avant-garde and fanciful dishes at appropriately highfalutin prices.

Cafés

Bar Seco
Passeig Montjuïc 74 (93 329 63 74, www.bar-seco.com). Metro Paral·lel. **Open** *10am-5pm Tue, Wed; 10am-5pm, 8pm-midnight Thur-Sat; 10am-5pm Sun.* **Map** *p139 E10* ②

The 'Dry Bar' is, in fact, anything but, and its ethically friendly choices range from local beers and organic wines to fair-trade Brazilian *cachaça* and veggie burgers. Despite a quiet location it has rapidly gathered a following for the quality of its Italian-Spanish vegetarian dishes and tapas, its fresh milkshakes and a heavenly home-made chocolate and almond cake. Those who run it are keen advocates of the Slow Food Movement.

♥ Federal
C/Parlament 39 (93 187 36 07, www.federalcafe.es). Metro Sant Antoni. **Open** *8am-11pm Mon-Thur; 8am-12.30am Fri; 9am-12.30 Sat; 9am-5.30pm Sun.* **Map** *p139 E9* ④

Australian-run Federal exudes a breezy oceanside chic and is often credited with kickstarting the hipsterisation of Sant Antoni – previously a *barrio* of old-timers and market-goers. Spacious, open to the street and crowned with a pretty little roof garden, it offers own-made cupcakes, excellent brunch (try the skillet of eggs, pancetta, caramelised onion and crème fraîche) and copies of the *New Yorker* to leaf through.

Tapas

♥ Lando
C/Poeta Cabanyes 25 (93 348 55 30, lando.es). Metro Paral·lel. **Open** *7pm-midnight Mon-Thur; 7pm-2am Fri; noon-2am Sat; noon-1am Sun.* **Map** *p139 E9* ⑤

Lando's magpie approach to the menu means that you will find mussels with coconut, lemongrass and ginger next to smoked pastrami, taramasalata and pulled pork with gnocchis. It's a hip and spacious joint in the heart of happening Sant Antoni, with tables outside on a pedestrianised side street.

♥ Quimet i Quimet
C/Poeta Cabanyes 25 (93 442 31 42). Metro Paral·lel. **Open** *noon-4pm, 7-10.30pm Mon-Fri; noon-4pm Sat. Closed Aug.* **Map** *p139 E6* ⑥

Packed to the rafters with dusty bottles of wine, this classic but minuscule bar makes up in tapas what it lacks in space. The specialities are *conservas* (shellfish preserved in tins), which aren't always to non-Spanish tastes, but the *montaditos*, sculpted tapas served on bread, are spectacular. Try salmon sashimi with cream cheese, honey and soy, or cod, passata and black olive pâté. Get there early for any chance of a surface on which to put your drink.

Bars

Bar Calders
C/Parlament 25 (93 329 93 49). Metro Sant Antoni. **Open** *5pm-1.30am Mon-Thur; 5pm-2.30am Fri; 11am-2.30am Sat; 11am-midnight Sun.* **Map** *p139 E9* ①

Bar Calders was one of the places that kickstarted the regeneration of the Sant Antoni neighbourhood – a hybrid café, tapas and wine bar with an adjoining terrace, it's hugely popular among the hip young families of the *barrio*. Occasional events include live music, craft-beer tastings and guest chefs.

♥ Xixbar
C/Rocafort 19 (93 423 43 14, www.xixbar.com). Metro Poble Sec. **Open** *6.30pm-2.30am Mon; 6pm-2.30am Tue, Wed; 5pm-2.30am Thur; 5pm-3am Fri, Sat.* **Map** *p139 D8* ⑦

Xix (pronounced 'chicks', and a play on the street number, among other things) is an unconventional cocktail bar in the candlelit surroundings of a prettily tiled former *granja* (milk bar). It's exceedingly cosy and the list of almost 300 brands of gin – the house speciality – is impressive.

Shops & services

Book & Coin Market
C/Comte Borrell with C/Tamarit, Eixample (www.dominicaldesantantoni.com). Metro Sant Antoni. **Open** *9am-2.30pm (approx) Sun.* **No cards.** **Map** *p139 E8* ① *Books*

The Sunday book market continues to trade in temporary digs throughout the refurbishment of the main Sant Antoni market (due to open in late 2017). It houses tables packed with every manner of reading material, ranging from arcane old tomes to well-pawed bodice-rippers and yellowing comics. There are also stacks of coins and more contemporary merchandise such as music, software and posters. Arrive early to beat the crowds.

Eixample

From an aerial perspective, it is the Eixample (pronounced esh-*am*-pluh) that gives Barcelona its distinctive appearance: the middle section of the city looks as if it has been stamped with a sizzling waffle iron. This extraordinary city plan, the Expansion (*eixample* in Catalan, or *ensanche* in Spanish) of Barcelona into an orthogonal grid of identical blocks, was designed as an extendable matrix for future growth, gradually developing to connect the city with the outlying villages of Gràcia, Sarrià, Les Corts, Sant Gervasi and Sant Martí de Provençals. In essence, it unifies the city as we know it today. Tourists tend to focus on the Old City and its medieval quarter, but fans of architecture and, in particular, Modernisme – the Catalan answer to art nouveau – will do well to spend a day strolling along the elegant boulevards of the Eixample.

❤ Don't miss

1 Sagrada Família *p158*
Gaudí's unfinished cathedral and Barna's best-loved attraction.

2 Casa Batlló *p156*
Another of Gaudí's masterworks, with a shimmering tiled façade.

3 Recinte Modernista de Sant Pau *p163*
The gardens and pavilion wards of the former Hospital de Sant Pau.

4 La Pedrera *p160*
An undulating apartment block that is unmistakably Gaudí.

5 Lasarte *p162*
Barcelona's first three-Michelin-star restaurant, a blow-out that's worth every penny.

In the know
Getting around

The grid-like Eixample is divided into two areas, either side of C/Balmes: the Esquerra (left) and Dreta (right). It is criss-crossed by various bus and metro lines, most of which conjoin at Plaça Catalunya. To walk from one end of Passeig de Gràcia to the other takes around 15 minutes.

It can be hard to get your bearings, but locals will often indicate directions using a handy code – 'mar' (sea) or 'muntanya' (mountain) refer to the bottom or top of the area, while 'Besos' and 'Llobregat' are the rivers to the right and left of the city, indicating which side of an Eixample street something falls on.

Sagrada Família

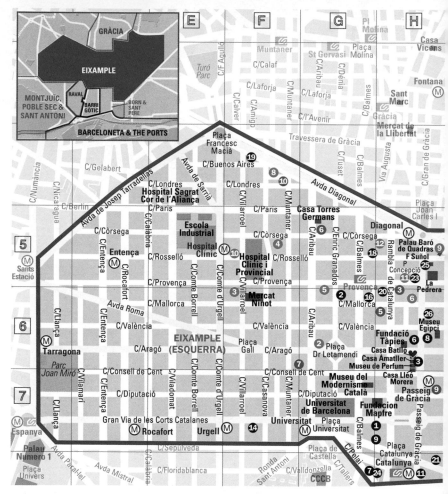

EIXAMPLE

Restaurants

1 Casa Calvet
2 Cinc Sentits
3 Disfrutar
4 Gaig
5 Gresca
6 Lasarte
7 Manairó
8 Le P'ty Mon
9 Roca Moo
10 La Taverna del Clínic
11 Tragaluz
12 Windsor

Cafés, tapas & bars

1 Bar Mut
2 Bauma
3 La Bodegueta
4 Cafè del Centre
5 Cervesería Catalana
6 Dry Martini
7 Garage Beer Co
8 Granja Petitbó
9 Tapas 24
10 Velódromo

Shops & services

1 Altaïr
2 Antonio Miró
3 Bagués-Masriera
4 Barcelona Glòries
5 BCN Books
6 Bulevard dels Antiquaris
7 Camper
8 Casa del Libro
9 Casanova Fotografía
10 Chicco
11 El Corte Inglés
12 Dos i Una
13 Els Encants
14 Escribà
15 Flors Navarro
16 Galeria Estrany · De La Mota
17 Instituto Francis
18 Janina
19 Jean-Pierre Bua
20 Du Pareil au Même
21 Prénatal
22 Queviures Múrria
23 Santa Eulàlia
24 Sephora
25 Stella McCartney
26 Twenty One by Esther Llongueras

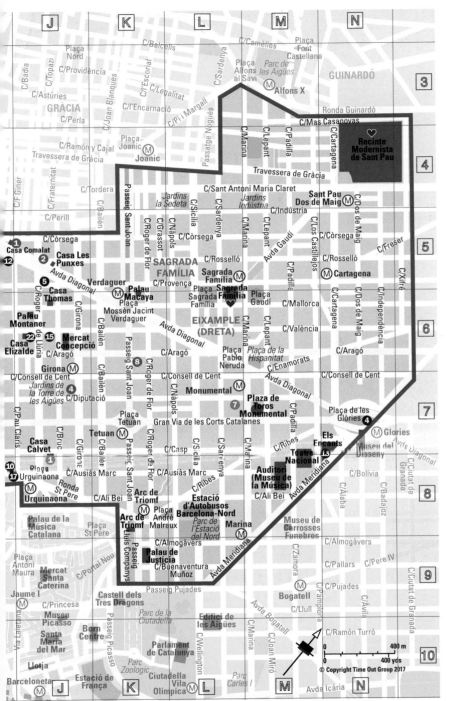

EIXAMPLE

Balcons de Barcelona

💜 Time to eat & drink

Eggs over easy
Granja Petitbó *p165*

A mid-morning vermouth
La Bodegueta *p164*

Affordable haute cuisine
Gresca *p169*

A smooth IPA
Garage Beer Co *p170*

Inspired neo-trad tapas
Tapas 24 *p165*

The perfect martini
Dry Martini *p170*

💜 Time to shop

Satisfy your wanderlust
Altaïr *p165*

Designer threads
Santa Eulàlia *p168*

Patisserie pleasures
Escribà *p170*

The 24/7 flower market
Flors Navarro *p166*

Rummage for treasure
Els Encants *p166*

💜 Time well spent

Platja de l'Eixample
Jardins de la Torre de les Aïgues, C/Roger de Llúria 56 interior (mobile 637 402 866). Metro Girona. **Open** *End June-early Sept 10am-8.30pm daily. Admission €1.55; free under-1s & over-65s. No cards.* **Map** *p152 J7.*

In the summer, this leafy inner patio becomes the 'Eixample Beach', an oasis for small kids. There's a knee-high wading pool, plenty of sand with buckets and spades provided, trees for shade and a water tower in the centre, along with outdoor showers, changing tents and toilets.

The Eixample was Europe's first expansive work of urban planning, necessitated by the chronic overcrowding of old Barcelona – which, by the 1850s, had become rife with cholera and crime, tightly corseted by its much-hated city walls. It was eventually decided the walls must come down, whereupon the Ajuntament held a competition to build an ambitious urban zone on the sloping fields outside the city's ramparts. The competition was won by municipal architect Antoni Rovira i Trias, whose popular fan-shaped design can be seen at the foot of his statue in the Gràcia *plaça* that bears his name. The government in Madrid, however, vetoed the plan, choosing instead the work of social idealist Ildefons Cerdà, a military engineer.

Cerdà's plan, reflecting the rationalist mindset of the era, was for a grid of uniform blocks with chamfered corners (known as *illes* in Catalan, *manzanas* in Spanish). It would stretch from Montjuïc to the Besòs river, criss-crossed by the diagonal highways of Avda Diagonal and Avda Meridiana – meeting at **Plaça de les Glòries**, which was to become the hub of the modernised city. The ideas were utopian: each block was to be built on only two sides and be no more than two or three storeys high; the remainder of the space was to contain gardens, their leafy extremes joining in the crossroads and forming a quarter of a bigger park. Predictably, however, developers made a travesty of Cerdà's plans, and a concrete orchard of gardenless, fortress-like, six- or seven-storey blocks grew up instead.

Fortunately, the period of construction coincided with Barcelona's golden age of architecture: the city's bourgeoisie employed Gaudí, Puig i Cadafalch, Domènech i Montaner and the like to build them ever more daring townhouses in an orgy of avant-garde one-upmanship. The result is extraordinary but can be tricky to negotiate on foot: the lack of open spaces and the similarity of many streets can cause confusion. The city council, meanwhile, is attempting to make the area more approachable by reclaiming pavement space for pedestrians, repaving roads with noise-absorbent materials and reducing traffic.

The overland railway that ran down C/Balmes was the dividing line of the neighbourhood. The fashionable **Dreta** ('Right') side contains the most distinguished Modernista architecture, the main museums and the shopping avenues. The **Esquerra** ('Left') was built slightly later; it contains some less well-known Modernista sights. Other subdivisions of the Eixample include the wealthy Sagrada Família area, and the scrappier residential neighbourhoods of Sant Antoni, near the Raval, and Fort Pienc, to the south of Glòries.

In its entirety, the Eixample covers about nine square kilometres. However, most of the sights of interest are within a few blocks of the grand central boulevard of **Passeig de Gràcia**, which ascends directly from the city's central square of Plaça Catalunya. Incorporating some of Barcelona's finest Modernista buildings, it is the showpiece of the **Quadrat d'Or** (Golden District) – a vast open-air museum between C/Muntaner and C/Roger de Flor that contains 150 protected buildings, many of them Modernista gems.

DRETA

The central boulevard of **Passeig de Gràcia** has always been the Eixample's most desirable address, and it's where you'll find Modernisme's most flamboyant townhouses. The three most famous sit on the block known as the **Manzana de la Discòrdia**. It's a Catalan appropriation of the Spanish word *manzana* (rather than the usual Catalan word for block, *illa*), which puns on the double meaning of 'block' and 'apple', and alludes to the fatal choice of Trojan mortal Paris when judging which of a bevy of divine Greek beauties would win the golden Apple of Discord.

If the volume of camera-toting admirers is anything to go by, the fairest on the Manzana de la Discòrdia is surely Gaudí's **Casa Batlló** (no.43, *see p156*). Runners up are Puig i Cadafalch's **Casa Àmatller** (no.41, *see p157*) and Domènech i Montaner's **Casa Lleó Morera**, a decadently melting wedding cake of a building (partially defaced during the architecturally delinquent Franco era) on the corner of C/Consell de Cent at no.35. Further up, on the other side of the Passeig, is the Gaudí-designed apartment block, **La Pedrera** (*see p160*).

In the know
Balconies of Barcelona

As part of the Ajuntament's campaign to beautify Barcelona in preparation for the '92 Olympics, it was decided to camouflage some of its unsightly party walls. One of the most spectacular projects is **Balcons de Barcelona**, on the corner of Plaça de la Hispanitat with C/Enamorats, a stunning 450sq m (19,380sq ft) trompe l'oeil painting of balconies spread over six floors, from which a galaxy of Catalan luminaries and former residents – including Gaudí, Miró and anarchist educator Francesc Ferrer – look out.

❤ Casa Batlló

Passeig de Gràcia 43 (93 216 03 06, www. casabatllo.cat). Metro Passeig de Gràcia. **Open** *9am-9pm daily; last entrance 8pm.* **Admission** *€23.50; €20.50 reductions; free under-7s.* **Map** *p152 H6.*

In one of the most extreme architectural makeovers ever seen, Gaudí and his long-time collaborator Josep Maria Jujol took an ordinary apartment block and remodelled it inside and out for textile tycoon Josep Batlló between 1902 and 1906. The result was one of the most impressive and admired of all Gaudí's creations.

Opinions differ as to what the building's remarkable façade represents, particularly its polychrome shimmering walls, its sinister skeletal balconies and its humpbacked scaly roof. Some say it's the spirit of carnival, others a Costa Brava cove. However, the most popular theory, which takes into account the architect's deeply patriotic feelings, is that the façade depicts Sant Jordi and the dragon – the idea being that the cross on top is the knight's lance, the roof represents the back of the beast, and the balconies below are the skulls and bones of its hapless victims.

The chance to explore the interior (at a cost) offers the best opportunity of understanding how Gaudí, sometimes considered the lord of the bombastic and overblown, was really the master of tiny details – from the ingenious ventilation in the doors to the amazing natural light reflecting off the inner courtyard's azure walls – and the way the brass window handles are curved so as to fit the shape of a hand. An apartment is open to the public, and access has been granted to the attic: the whitewashed arched rooms of the top floor, originally used for laundering and hanging clothes, are among the master's most atmospheric spaces.

The façade may depict Sant Jordi and the dragon – the cross, the knight's lance; the roof, the back of the beast; the balconies below, the skulls and bones of its hapless victims

As the area surrounding Passeig de Gràcia is one of the wealthiest parts of the city, it's not surprising that it's also extraordinarily rich in privately owned art collections and museums; these include **Fundació Suñol** (*see p161*), the **Museu Egipci de Barcelona** (*see p161*), the **Fundación Mapfre** (*see p161*), the **Fundació Antoni Tàpies** and the **Espai VolART** (C/Ausiàs Marc 22, 93 481 79 85), which hosts final-year art shows and the like. The area is equally well provided with shops, with a mix of boutiques, international designers and high-street brands jostling for space along the golden retail belts of Passeig de Gràcia, the parallel Rambla de Catalunya and the central section of the Avinguda Diagonal.

For most visitors, however, the crowning glory of the Eixample experience is the darkly beautiful **Sagrada Família** (*see p158*). Whether you love it or hate it (George Orwell called it 'one of the most hideous buildings in the world'), it has become the city's emblem and a *sine qua non* of Barcelona tourist itineraries. A less famous masterpiece, in the shape of Domènech i Montaner's **Hospital de la Santa Creu i Sant Pau**, bookends the northerly extreme of the Avda Gaudí, and has in recent years been enclosed as a tourist attraction, now known as the **Recinte Modernista de Sant Pau** (*see p163*). A few blocks south, there's more welcome green space in the **Parc de l'Estació del Nord** (*see p162*).

The streets above the Diagonal boast some striking Modernista buildings, such as Puig i Cadafalch's 1901 **Palau Macaya** (Passeig de Sant Joan 108). Other buildings of interest include the tiled **Mercat de la Concepció** (C/Aragó 311), designed by Rovira i Trias, and the turret-topped **Casa de les Punxes**, the work of the prolific Puig i Cadafalch, combining elements of Nordic Gothic with Spanish plateresque. Moving down C/Roger de Llúria, you pass the **Palau Montaner** on the corner with C/Mallorca, and **Casa Thomas** just off to the left at C/Mallorca 293, both designed by Lluís Domènech i Montaner. On reaching C/Casp, you arrive at one of Gaudí's lesser-known works, the **Casa Calvet** (*see p162*). Also over on this side of the Eixample is the egg-topped **Plaça de Braus Monumental**: this was the city's last active bullring until the ban on bullfighting.

It is now used for occasional concerts, and out of season hosts tatty travelling circuses. Not far from the bullring, at C/Lepant 150, is the ultra-modern concert hall of **L'Auditori de Barcelona**, which also houses the newly reopened **Museu de la Música** (*see p161*).

Sights & museums

Casa Àmatller

Passeig de Gràcia 41 (93 461 7460, www. amatller.com). Metro Passeig de Gràcia. ***Open** 10am-6pm daily. **Admission** €14; guided tour €17; free under-7s. **Map** p152 H6.*

Built for chocolate baron Antoni Àmatller, this playful building is one of Puig i Cadafalch's finest creations. Inspired by 17th-century Dutch townhouses, its distinctive stepped Flemish pediment is covered in shiny ceramics, while the lower façade and the doorway are decorated with lively sculptures by Eusebi Arnau. These sculptures include chocolatiers at work, almond trees and blossoms (which is a reference to the family name), and Sant Jordi slaying the dragon.

Besides chocolate, Àmatller's other great love was photography. His daughter later converted the family home into an art institute and archive for her father's vast collections, from which excellent selections are on display in the ground floor exhibition space. The guided tour of the house lasts around an hour and includes the ornate entrance hall, Antoni Àmatller's period photography studio and a tasting of Àmatller chocolate in the original kitchen.

Casa de les Punxes

Avda Diagonal 420 (93 018 5242, www. casadelespunxes.com). Metro Diagonal. ***Open** 9am-8pm daily; last entrance 7pm. **Admission** €12.50; €11.25 reductions; free under-5s; audio guide included. **Map** p152 J5.*

Also known as the Casa Terradas, the Casa de les Punxes ('House of Spikes', named for its pointed turrets) is a magnificently medieval-looking creation designed by Puig i Cadafalch and built in 1905. Though neo-Gothic was all the rage among the architects of the time, Puig i Cadafalch was first and foremost a Modernista, and the sombre look of the façade contrasts with the colour and light of the interiors, its stained glass and tiling.

Fundació Antoni Tàpies

C/Aragó 255 (93 487 03 15, www. fundaciotapies.org). Metro Passeig de Gràcia. ***Open** 10am-7pm Tue-Sun. **Admission** €7; €5.60 reductions; free under-16s. **Map** p152 H6.*

♥ Sagrada Família

C/Mallorca 401 (93 207 30 31, www. sagradafamilia.org). Metro Sagrada Família. **Open** *Apr-Sept 9am-8pm daily. Oct, Mar 9am-7pm daily; Nov-Feb 9am-6pm daily.* **Admission** *€15; €11-€13 reductions; free under-11s. Guided tour €24, €8-€22 reductions (admission & audio guide included). Towers €29, €22-€27 reductions (admission & audio guide included).* **Map** *p152 L6.*

'Send Gaudí and the Sagrada Família to hell,' wrote Picasso – and while it is easy to see how some of the religious clichés of the building and the devotional fervour of its creator might annoy an angry young Cubist, Barcelona's iconic temple still manages to inspire delight.

Gaudí dedicated more than 40 years (the last 14 of them exclusively) to the project, and is buried beneath the nave. Many consider the crypt and the Nativity façade, which were completed in his lifetime, to be the most beautiful elements of the church. The latter, on C/Marina, looks at first glance as though some careless giant has poured candle wax over a Gothic cathedral, but

closer inspection shows every protuberance to be an intricate sculpture of flora, fauna or a human figure, combining to form an astonishingly moving stone tapestry depicting scenes from Christ's early years.

Providing a grim counterpoint to the excesses of the Nativity façade is the Passion façade on C/Sardenya, where there are bone-shaped columns and haunting, angular sculptures by Josep Maria Subirachs that show the 12 Stations of the Cross. The vast metal doors, which are set behind the sculpture of the flagellation of Jesus, are particularly arresting, covered in quotations from the Bible in various languages.

The Glory façade on C/Mallorca, the final side to be built and the eventual main entrance, is currently shooting up behind the scaffolding and is devoted to the Resurrection, a mass of stone clouds and trumpets emblazoned with quotations from the Apostles' Creed.

The most amazing thing about the Sagrada Família project, however, is that it is happening at all. Begun in 1882, setbacks have ranged from 1930s anarchists blowing up Gaudí's detailed plans and models, to

EIXAMPLE

lack of funds. The ongoing work is a matter of conjecture and controversy, with the finishing date expected to be somewhere within the region of 25 to 30 years; it was hoped the masterpiece would be completed in 2026 to coincide with the 100th anniversary of Gaudí's death, although this now seems unlikely. It's still something of an improvement on the prognosis in the 1900s, when construction was expected to last several hundred years; advanced computer technology is now being used to shape each intricately designed block of stone offsite to speed up the process. The latest tribulation for the architects to overcome is the municipal approval of plans to build the AVE bullet train tunnel just a few feet away from the temple's foundations.

Passion façade

The Nativity façade looks at first glance as though some careless giant has poured candle wax over a Gothic cathedral, but closer inspection shows intricate sculptures of flora, fauna or a human figure

Around five million tourists visit the Sagrada Família each year, with more than half of them entering the building. The admission fee allows you to wander through the interior of the church, a marvellous forest of columns laid out in the style of the great Gothic cathedrals, with a multi-aisled central nave crossed by a transept. The central columns are fashioned of porphyry – perhaps the only natural element capable of supporting the church's projected great dome, which is destined to rise 170m (558ft).

A ticket also gives visitors access to the museum in the basement, with displays on the history of the construction, original models for sculptural work and the chance to watch sculptors working at plaster-cast models through a large window.

Nativity façade

💙 La Pedrera (Casa Milà)

C/Provença 261-265 (93 484 59 00, www.
lapedrera.com). Metro Diagonal. **Open**
Nov-Feb 9am-6.30pm daily. Mar-Oct 9am-
8pm daily. **Admission** €22; €11-€16.50
reductions; free under-7s. **Map** p152 H5.

Described variously as rising dough,
molten lava and a stone lung, the last
secular building designed by Antoni
Gaudí, the Casa Milà (popularly known
as La Pedrera, 'the stone quarry') has no
straight lines. It is a stupendous and daring
feat of architecture, and the culmination
of the architect's experimental attempts
to re-create natural forms with bricks and
mortar (not to mention ceramics and even
smashed-up cava bottles). Now a UNESCO
World Heritage Site, it appears to have been
washed up on shore, with a marine feel
complemented by collaborator Josep Maria
Jujol's tangled balconies, doors of twisted
kelp ribbon, sea-foamy ceilings and interior
patios as blue as a mermaid's cave.

La Pedrera appears to have been washed up on shore, with tangled balconies, doors of twisted kelp ribbon, sea-foamy ceilings and interior patios as blue as a mermaid's cave

When it was completed in 1912, it was
so far ahead of its time that the woman
who financed it as her dream home, Roser
Segimon, became the laughing stock of
the city – hence the 'stone quarry' tag. Its
rippling façade led local painter Santiago
Rusiñol to quip that a snake would be a
better pet than a dog for the inhabitants. But
La Pedrera has become one of Barcelona's
best-loved buildings, and is adored by
architects for its extraordinary structure:
it is supported entirely by pillars, without
a single master wall, allowing the vast,
asymmetrical windows of the façade to
invite in great swathes of natural light.

There are three exhibition spaces at
Casa Milà. The first-floor art gallery hosts

free shows of work by a variety of eminent
artists, while the upstairs space is dedicated
to giving visitors a finer appreciation of
Gaudí: accompanied by an audio guide
(included in the admission price), you can
visit a reconstructed Modernista flat on the
fourth floor, with a sumptuous bedroom
suite by Gaspar Homar, while the attic,
framed by parabolic arches worthy of a
Gothic cathedral, holds a museum offering
an insightful overview of Gaudí's career.
Best of all is the chance to stroll on the roof
of the building amid its *trencadís*-covered
ventilation shafts: their heads are shaped
like the helmets of medieval knights, which
led the poet Pere Gimferrer to dub the spot
'the garden of warriors'.

EIXAMPLE

Antoni Tàpies exploded on to the art scene in the 1950s, when he began to incorporate waste paper, mud and rags into his paintings, eventually moving on to the point where his works included whole pieces of furniture, running water and girders. Today, he's Barcelona's most celebrated living artist, and his trademark scribbled and paint-daubed pieces are sought after to illustrate items from wine bottle labels to theatre posters.

The artist set up the Tàpies Foundation in this, the former Montaner i Simon publishing house, in 1984, dedicating it to the study and appreciation of contemporary art. In a typically contentious act, Tàpies crowned the building with a glorious tangle of aluminium piping and ragged metal netting (*Núvol i Cadira*, or 'Cloud and Chair'). The building remains one of the earliest examples of Modernisme to combine exposed brick and iron, and is now a cultural centre and museum dedicated to the work and life of the man himself, with exhibitions, lectures and films.

Fundación Mapfre

*C/Diputació 250 (93 272 31 80, www. fundacionmapfre.org). Metro Passeig de Gràcia. **Open** 2-8pm Mon; 10am-8pm Tue-Sat; 11am-7pm Sun. **Admission** €3; €2 reductions; free under-16s; free to all Mon 2-8pm. **Map** p152 H7.*

Since 2015, the Modernista masterpiece Casa Garriga i Nogués –, has housed exhibitions put on by the charitable arm of the Mapfre insurance company. The opening exhibition was a blockbuster of impressionist artworks loaned from the Musée d'Orsay in Paris, but subsequent exhibitions have focused on bringing attention to lesser known artists and photographers.

Fundació Suñol

*Passeig de Gràcia 98 (93 496 10 32, www. fundaciosunol.org). Metro Diagonal. **Open** 11am-2pm, 4-8pm Mon-Fri; 4-8pm Sat. **Admission** €4; €3 reductions; free under-12s. No cards. **Map** p152 H5.*

Opened in 2007, the foundation's two floors house the contemporary art collection of businessman Josep Suñol. There are 100 works on show at a time, including painting, sculpture and photography, shuffled every six months (in January and July) from an archive of 1,200 pieces amassed over 35 years. The collection includes historic – and predominantly Catalan and Spanish – artists of the avant-garde: Picasso, Miró and Pablo Gargallo, with international input from Giacometti, Man Ray and Warhol.

With superfluities removed (including labels), and chronology abandoned, works are arranged in careful, coherent compositions, by style, colour or even mood, in interlinking rooms. English-speaking staff and a pamphlet aid visitors; an additional booklet costs €2. Nivell Zero is a large exhibition space available to younger avant-garde artists, with shorter-term installations, poetry cycles and multimedia projects.

Museu de la Música

*L'Auditori, C/Lepant 150 (93 256 36 50, www. bcn.cat/museumusica). Metro Marina. **Open** 10am-6pm Tue, Wed, Fri; 10am-9pm Thur; 10am-7pm Sat, Sun. **Admission** €6; €4.50 reductions; free under-16s; free to all every Sun from 3pm and all day first Sun of mth. **Map** p152 M8.*

Housed in the Auditori concert hall complex (*see p248*), the Music Museum's collections comprise over 1,600 instruments, displayed like precious jewels in red velvet and glass cases, along with multimedia displays, interactive exhibits and musical paraphernalia. With pieces spanning the ancient world to the modern day, and including instruments from all corners of the world, the museum's high note is the world-class collection of 17th-century guitars.

Museu del Modernisme Català

*C/Balmes 48 (93 272 28 96, www.mmbcn.cat). Metro Passeig de Gràcia. **Open** 10.30am-8pm Tue-Sat; 10.30am-2pm Sun. **Admission** €10; €5-€8 reductions; free under-5s. **Map** p152 G7.*

Inaugurated in 2010, this private collection includes work by all the heavyweights of the Modernisme movement. There is a Gaudí-designed kissing chair, some extravagant ecclesiastical pieces by Puig i Cadafalch, tiled bedheads by Gaspar Homar, marble sculptures by Josep Llimona and paintings by Santiago Rusiñol, Joaquim Mir and Ramon Casas. The furniture created by lesser-known craftsmen also includes some stunning pieces, with a collection of marquetry escritoires.

Museu del Perfum

*Passeig de Gràcia 39 (93 216 01 21, www. museudelperfum.com). Metro Passeig de Gràcia. **Open** 10.30am-8pm Mon-Fri; 11am-2pm Sat. **Admission** €5; €3 reductions; free under-5s. No cards. **Map** p152 H6.*

In the back room of the Regia perfumery sit some 5,000 scent bottles, cosmetic flasks and related objects. The collection is divided in two. One displays all manner of unguent vases and essence jars in chronological order, from a tube of black eye make-up from pre-dynastic Egypt to Edwardian atomisers and a prized double-flask pouch that belonged to Marie Antoinette. The second section exhibits perfumes from brands such as Guerlain and

Dior; some are in rare bottles, among them a garish Dalí creation for Schiaparelli and a set of golliwog flasks by Vigny Paris. The museum's most recent additions include a collection of 19th-century perfumed powder bottles and boxes.

Museu Egipci de Barcelona
C/València 284 (93 488 01 88, www. museuegipci.com). Metro Passeig de Gràcia. Open Jan-mid June, mid Sept-Nov 10am-2pm, 4-8pm Mon-Fri; 10am-8pm Sat; 10am-2pm Sun. Dec, mid June-mid Sept 10am-8pm Mon-Sat; 10am-2pm Sun. Admission €11; €8 reductions; free under-6s. Map p152 H6.

This is one of the finest museums of Ancient Egyptian artefacts in Europe. The collection is owned by prominent Egyptologist Jordi Clos and spans 3,000 years of Nile-drenched culture. Exhibits include religious statuary, such as the massive baboon heads used to decorate temples, everyday copper mirrors and alabaster headrests, and some rather moving infant sarcophagi. Outstanding pieces include some painstakingly matched fragments from the Sixth Dynasty Tomb of Iny, a bronze statuette of the goddess Isis breastfeeding her son Horus, and mummified cats, baby crocodiles and falcons. Another highlight is a 5,000-year-old bed, which still looks comfortable enough to sleep in. On Friday and Saturday nights there are dramatic reconstructions on popular themes, such as the mummification ritual or the life of Cleopatra, for which reservations are essential.

Parc de l'Estació del Nord
C/Almogávers 27-61 (no phone). Metro Arc de Triomf. Open 10am-sunset daily. Admission free. Map p152 L8.

Otherwise known as Parc Sol i Ombra (meaning 'Sun and Shadow'), this small but well-used park is perked up by three pieces of landscape art in glazed blue and white ceramic by New York sculptor Beverly Pepper. Along with a pair of white stone entrance walls, *Espiral Arbrat* (Tree Spiral) is a spiral bench set under the cool shade of lime flower trees, while *Cel Caigut* (Fallen Sky) is a seven metre (23 ft) ridge rising from the grass. The colourful tiles recall Gaudí's *trencadís* smashed-tile technique.

Restaurants
Casa Calvet €€€
C/Casp 48 (93 412 40 12, www.casacalvet.es). Metro Urquinaona. Open 1-3.30pm, 8.30-11pm Mon-Sat. Map p152 J7 ❶ *Catalan*

Casa Calvet allows the time-strapped visitor to sample some excellent cooking and appreciate the master of Modernisme at the same time. One of Gaudí's more understated buildings from the outside, Casa Calvet has an interior full of glorious detail in the carpentry, stained glass and tiles. The food is up to par, with surprising combinations almost always hitting the mark: sole with pistachio sauce and sautéed aubergine; scallops with black olive tapenade and wild mushroom croquettes; and roast beef with apple sauce and truffled potatoes. The puddings are superb – try the chestnut parfait with figs in brandy and a mandarin coulis, or the mango and banana tatin.

❤ Lasarte €€€€
C/Mallorca 259 (93 445 32 42, www. restaurantlasarte.com). Metro Passeig de Gràcia. Open 1.30-3.30pm, 8.30-11pm Tue-Sat. Map p152 H6 ❻ *Mediterranean*

Located in what is now the Monument Hotel, Lasarte has undergone a huge revamp and now has a spacious and gloriously designed dining room, a fleet of charming waiters and the best food in town. It's not cheap, but is unforgettable, and combines all the latest haute techniques with the finest Mediterranean produce. In 2016, Lasarte became the first restaurant in Barcelona to be awarded three Michelin stars.

Manairó €€€€
C/Diputació 424 (93 231 00 57, www. manairo.com). Metro Monumental. Open 1.30-3.30pm, 8.30-11pm Mon-Sat. Map p152 L7 ❼ *Catalan*

If you're curious to try some of the more extreme experiences in postmodern haute cuisine (we're talking tripe and brains rather than the latest flights of fancy from the Blumenthal school), Manairó is the place to start. Its divine tasting menus (€77 or €90) take in small portions of Catalan specialities such as *cap i pota* (a stew of calves' head and feet) and langoustine with *botifarra* sausage and cod tripe, and renders them so delicately that even the most squeamish diner will be seduced. Other star turns include a 'false' anchovy – actually a long strip of marinated tuna dotted prettily with pearls of red vermouth. There is a simpler lunch menu for €40.

♥ Recinte Modernista de Sant Pau

C/Sant Antoni Maria Claret 167 (93 553 78 01, www.santpaubarcelona.org). Metro Sant Pau Dos de Maig. **Open** *Apr-Oct 10am-6.30pm Mon-Sat; 10am-2.30pm Sun. Nov-Mar 10am-4.30pm Mon-Sat; 10am-2.30pm Sun.* **Admission** *€13; €9.10 reductions; free under-12s & over-65s.* **Map** *p152 N4.*

When part of the roof of the gynaecology department collapsed in 2004, it was clear that restoration work was needed on the century-old Modernista 'garden city' hospital, a UNESCO World Heritage Site. In 2009, the last of the departments was transferred to the modern Nou Sant Pau building to the north, and the complex was fenced off and spruced up in order to turn what had been a hidden Modernista treasure into a major tourist attraction. Given its proximity to the Sagrada Familia, it still sees relatively few visitors, and offers a peaceful way to contemplate some of the finest architecture of the period.

The former hospital is entered through a fairytale hypostyle hall of elegant pillars, polychromatic mosaics, stained glass and Gothic iron lamps. This leads out to the 20 pavilions that once served as wards. These are abundantly adorned with the colourful Byzantine, Gothic and Moorish flourishes that characterise Domènech i Montaner's style and set in peaceful gardens that spread over nine blocks in the north-east corner of the Eixample. It's set at a 45° angle from the rest of Ildefons Cerdà's grid system, so that it catches more sun: Domènech i Montaner built the hospital very much with its patients in mind, convinced that aesthetic harmony and pleasant surroundings were good for the health. Guided tours in English are held daily at 11am.

Sant Pau offers a peaceful way to contemplate some of the finest architecture of the period

EIXAMPLE

Roca Moo €€€

C/Rosselló 265 (93 445 40 00, www. hotelomm.es). Metro Diagonal. **Open** *1.30-3.30pm, 8-10.30pm Mon-Sat. Closed 3wks Aug.* **Map** *p152 H5* **9** *Catalan*

The tables at Moo are as desirable as the rooms in its parent, Hotel Omm. The cooking, overseen by the celebrated Roca brothers, is some of the most exciting in the city, presenting classics such as a chocolatey hare royale with as much aplomb as more fanciful numbers such as a gold-plated quail's egg yolk on a bed of puréed, truffled potato. There are various tasting menus, at different prices, and particular wines (from a list of 500) are suggested to go with every course.

Tragaluz €€€

Ptge de la Concepció 5 (93 487 01 96, www. grupotragaluz.com). Metro Diagonal. **Open** *1.30-4pm, 8-11.30pm daily.* **Map** *p152 H5* **11** *Mediterranean*

The stylish flagship for this extraordinarily successful restaurant group has weathered the city's culinary revolution exceptionally well over recent years, and is still covering fresh ground on the Mediterranean creative scene. Although the food certainly doesn't come cheap, and the wine mark-up is particularly hard to swallow, there is no faulting the tuna *tataki* served with a cardamom wafer and a dollop of ratatouille-like *pisto*; monkfish tail in a sweet tomato *sofregit* with black olive oil; or juicy braised oxtail with cabbage.

Windsor €€€

C/Còrsega 286 (93 237 7588, www. restaurantwindsor.com). Metro Diagonal. **Open** *1.15-3.45pm, 8.30-11pm Mon-Thur, 1.15-3.45pm, 8.30-11pm Fri, Sat.* **Map** *p152 H5* **12** *Catalan*

Although it is let down slightly by a smart but drab dining room, and a clientele formed, in great part, by English-speaking business executives, Windsor nevertheless serves some of the most creative and uplifting food around. Most dishes riff on the cornerstones of Catalan cuisine – pigs' trotters stuffed with *cap i pota*, squab risotto and so on – whereas others have a lighter, Mediterranean feel: turbot with orange risotto and citrus powder, or salt cod with stewed tomatoes and olives. There is a set lunch for €29.90, available Monday to Friday.

Cafés

Bauma

C/Roger de Llúria 124 (93 207 54 31). Metro Diagonal. **Open** *8am-midnight Mon-Fri, Sun.* **Map** *p152 J5* **2**

An old-style café-bar that's good for lazy Sunday mornings, with its battered leather seats, ceiling fans and shady tables outside, although staff can sometimes be less than friendly. There's a decent list of *bocadillos* and tapas, along with well-priced, substantial dishes such as baked cod and wild boar stew served from the adjoining restaurant.

Cafè del Centre

C/Girona 69 (93 488 11 10). Metro Girona. **Open** *9am-midnight Mon-Sat. Closed 2wks Aug.* **Map** *p152 J7* **4**

The oldest café in the Eixample, and possibly the only one of its type left in the city, with a delightfully dusty air, Modernista wooden banquettes, walls stained with the nicotine of ages and marble tables sitting on a chipped chequered floor that almost certainly dates back to the bar's opening in 1873. It is still in the hands of the same family, whose youngest members' attempts to instigate change include a list of over 50 types of craft beer.

Tapas

Bar Mut

C/Pau Claris 192 (93 217 43 38). Metro Diagonal. **Open** *1-11.30pm daily.* **Map** *p152 J5* **1**

Bar Mut has an ineffably Gallic feel, with its etched glass, bronze fittings, *chanteuses* on the sound system, and (whisper it) Paris prices. The tapas are undeniably superior, however, running from a carpaccio of sea urchin to fried eggs with foie gras. Other sophisticated food for the soul to look out for includes haricot beans with wild mushrooms and *morcilla* or poached egg with chips and chorizo sauce. *Formidable*.

♥ La Bodegueta

Rambla de Catalunya 100 (93 215 48 94, www.labodegueta.cat). Metro Diagonal. **Open** *7am-1.45am Mon-Sat; 6.30pm-1.45am Sun.* **Map** *p152 H6* **3**

This delightful old bodega, with a pretty tiled floor and terrace on the Rambla, is dusty and welcoming, supplying students, businessmen and pretty much everyone in between with reasonably priced wine, vermouth on tap and good-quality tapas. The emphasis is placed on locally sourced products (try Montserrat tomatoes with tuna), among old favourites such as *patatas bravas*. **Other locations** C/Provença 233, (93 215 17 25).

Cerveseria Catalana

C/Mallorca 236 (93 216 03 68). Metro Passeig de Gràcia. Open 8am-1.30am Mon-Fri; 9am-1.30am Sat, Sun. Map p152 H6 **❺**

The 'Catalan Beerhouse' lives up to its name with a winning selection of brews from around the world, but the real reason to come is the tapas. A vast array is yours for the pointing; only hot *montaditos*, such as bacon, cheese and dates, have to be ordered from the kitchen. Arrive early for a seat at the bar, and even earlier for a pavement table.

♥ Granja Petitbó

Passeig de Sant Joan 82 (93 265 6503, www.granjapetibo.com). Metro Tetuan or Verdaguer. Open 9am-11pm Mon-Wed, 9am-11.30pm Thur-Fri; 10am-11.30pm Sat, 10am-5pm Sun. Map p152 K6 **❽**

Granja Petitbó was at the vanguard of the hipsterfication of the Passeig de Sant Joan, and though it has since been joined by a dozen other cafés and bars, it is still packed at peak times. It's a sunny place, amiably scruffy, with deep, battered leather sofas and a creaky wooden floor. As well as all the usual brunch dishes – eggs Benedict, pancakes, porridge – there are burgers, salads and pasta, along with huge bricks of cake.

♥ Tapas 24

C/Diputació 269 (93 488 09 77, www. carlesabellan.com). Metro Passeig de Gràcia. Open 9am-midnight Mon-Sat. Map p152 H7 **❾**

Another nu-trad tapas bar focusing on excellent quality produce. Among the oxtail stews, fried prawns and cod croquettes, however, fans of chef Carles Abellan will also find playful snacks more in keeping with his signature style. The McFoie Burguer is an exercise in fast-food heaven, as is the Bikini, a small version of his take on the ham and cheese toastie; his comes with truffle.

Shops & services

♥ Altaïr

Gran Via de les Corts Catalanes 616 (93 342 71 71, www.altair.es). Metro Universitat. Open 10am-8.30pm Mon-Sat. Map p152 H7 **❶** *Books*

Every aspect of travel is covered in this, the largest travel bookshop in Europe. You can pick up guides to free eating in Barcelona, academic tomes on geolinguistics, handbooks on successful outdoor sex and CDs of tribal and world music. Of course, all the less arcane publications are also here: maps for hikers, travel guidebooks, multilingual dictionaries, travel diaries, atlases and equipment such as mosquito nets.

Bagués-Masriera

Passeig de Gràcia 41 (93 216 01 74, bagues-masriera.com). Metro Passeig de Gràcia. Open 10am-8.30pm Mon-Fri; 11am-8pm Sat. Map p152 H6 **❸** *Jewellery*

Lluis Masriera, the original master jeweller of the house, created revolutionary pieces using a 'translucid enamel' technique at the start of the 20th century. His signature motifs, the art nouveau favourites of flowers, insects and birds, are reflected in today's designs.

Barcelona Glòries

Avda Diagonal 208 (93 486 04 04, www. lesglories.com). Metro Glòries. Open Shops 10am-10pm Mon-Sat. Food court & entertainment 10am-1am daily. Map p152 N7 **❹** *Mall*

Since opening its doors in 1995, this mall and leisure centre has become a focus of local life. There's a seven-screen cinema (foreign films are mostly dubbed into Spanish) and more than 220 shops, including a Carrefour supermarket, H&M, Mango and Disney Store, facing on to a large café-filled square and small children's playground. Useful family-friendly attractions include a free pram-lending service and entertainment such as bouncy castles and trampolines.

BCN Books

C/Roger de Llúria 118 (93 457 76 92, www. bcnbooks.com). Metro Diagonal. Open July, Aug 9am-8pm Mon-Fri. Sept-June 9am-8pm Mon-Fri; 9am-2pm Sat. Map p152 J5 **❺** *Books*

This well-stocked English-language bookstore has a wide range of learning and teaching materials for all ages. There's also a decent selection of contemporary and classic fiction, a good kids' section, some travel guides and plenty of dictionaries.

Other locations C/Amigó 81 (93 200 79 53).

Bulevard dels Antiquaris

Passeig de Gràcia 55 (93 215 44 99, www. bulevarddelsantiquaris.com). Metro Passeig de Gràcia. Open 10am-2pm, 5-8.30pm Mon-Sat. Map p152 H6 **❻** *Antiques*

This small antiques 'mall' is one of the most convenient and safest places to shop for antiques in Barcelona (experts inspect every object for authenticity). Check out the style of ethnic art that influenced the likes of Miró at Guilhem Montagut (nos.11-22), where you can pick up a Nigerian funeral urn. Collectors will love the antique playthings at Cañas (nos.35-36) and D'Art (no.70), and the vintage textiles and shawls at Antigüedades Pilar (no.65).

Camper

C/Pelai 13-37 (93 302 41 24, www.camper. com). Metro Catalunya. **Open** *10am-10pm Mon-Sat.* **Map** *p152 G8* ❼ *Shoes*

Mallorca-based eco shoe company Camper has sexed up its ladies' line in recent years. Each year, the label seems to flirt more with high heels (albeit rubbery wedgy ones) and girly straps. Of course, it still has its classic round-toed and clod-heeled classics, but Camper is definitely worth another look if you've previously dismissed it.
Other locations Passeig de Gràcia 100 (93 467 41 48); Plaça del Àngels 4, Raval (93 342 41 41); and throughout the city.

Casa del Libro

C/Passeig de Gràcia 62 (93 272 34 80, www. casadellibro.com). Metro Passeig de Gràcia. **Open** *9.30am-9.30pm Mon-Sat.* **Map** *p152 H6* ❽ *Books*

Part of a well-established Spanish chain, the Casa del Libro bookstore offers a diverse assortment of titles that includes some English-language fiction. Glossy, Barcelona-themed coffee-table tomes with good gift potential are located by the front right-hand entrance.

Casanova Fotografía

Ronda Universitat 35 (902 10 04 05, www. casanovafoto.com). Metro Universitat. **Open** *10am-2pm, 4-8.30pm Mon-Sat.* **Map** *p152 H7* ❾ *Electronics*

An extensive stock of new and second-hand digital and film equipment: camera bodies, lenses, tripods, darkroom gear, bags and more. There's also a slow but thorough repair lab, and a full range of processing services for film and digital photos.

Chicco

Ronda Sant Pere 13 (93 301 49 76, www.chicco. es). Metro Catalunya. **Open** *10am-8.30pm Mon-Sat.* **Map** *p152 H8* ❿ *Children*

The market leader in Spain, this colourful store has every conceivable babycare item, from dummies and high chairs to bottle-warmers and travel cots. Its clothes and shoes are practical and well designed, and made for children up to eight years old.
Other locations Diagonal Mar, Avda Diagonal 3, Poblenou (93 356 03 74).

♥ El Corte Inglés

Plaça Catalunya 14 (93 306 38 00, www.elcorteingles.es). Metro Catalunya. **Open** *9.30am-9.30pm Mon-Sat.* **Map** *p152 H8* ⓫ *Department store*

This monolith sits on Plaça Catalunya and stocks all the major international brand names, along with plenty of Spanish labels. This branch is the place for toiletries, cosmetics, clothes and homewares. It also houses a well-stocked but pricey supermarket and a gourmet food store, plus services ranging from key-cutting to currency exchange. On the top floor, there's a restaurant with great views (but service station-style food). The Portal de l'Àngel branch stocks CDs, DVDs, books, electronic equipment, stationery and sports gear. There are fashion and accessories geared to a younger market on the ground floor.
Other locations Avda Portal de l'Àngel 19-21, Barri Gòtic (93 306 38 00) and around the city.

Dos i Una

C/Rosselló 275 (93 217 70 32). Metro Diagonal. **Open** *11am-2.30pm, 4.30-8pm Mon-Sat.* **Map** *p152 H5* ⓬ *Gifts*

The first ever design shop in Barcelona (est. 1977) and an early patron of celebrated designer Javier Mariscal, Dos i Una stocks good-quality designer frippery such as retro, round-cornered postcards in glorious technicolour, cheese graters in the shape of flamenco dancers, flower-shaped teacups, chrome cuckoo clocks, colourful prints and jewellery.

♥ Els Encants

C/Dos de Maig 177-187, Plaça de les Glòries (93 245 22 99, www.encantsbcn.com). Metro Glòries. **Open** *9am-8pm Mon, Wed, Fri, Sat. Auctions 7.30-8.30am Mon, Wed, Fri.* **Map** *p152 N7* ⓭ *Flea market*

Now in a spiffy new home on the other side of the monster intersection at Glòries, this vast and rambling flea market is still a stew of shouts, musty smells and teetering piles of everything from old horseshoes and Barça memorabilia to cheap electrical gadgets, religious relics and ancient Spanish schoolbooks.

If you want to buy furniture at a decent price, join the commercial buyers at the auctions from 7am, or arrive at noon, when unsold stuff drops in price. Avoid Saturdays, when prices shoot up and the crowds move in, and be on your guard for pickpockets and short-changing.

♥ Flors Navarro

C/València 320 (93 457 40 99, floristeriasnavarro.com). Metro Verdaguer. **Open** *24hrs daily.* **Map** *p152 J6* ⓯ *Flowers*

At Flors Navarro, fresh-cut blooms, pretty house plants and stunning bouquets are available to buy 24 hours a day. A dozen red roses can be delivered anywhere in town, until 10pm, for €36.

Els Encants

Galeria Estrany · De La Mota

Ptge Mercader 18 (93 215 70 51, www. estranydelamota.com). FGC Provença. **Open** *10.30am-7pm Tue-Fri. Closed Aug.* **No cards.** **Map** *p152 G6* ⓰ *Gallery*

This cavernous basement is one of the most intriguing art spaces in the city. It hosts outstanding contemporary exhibitions, particularly in photography and film, from the likes of Finnish artist Esko Männikkö and Scottish film buff Douglas Gordon.

Instituto Francis

Ronda de Sant Pere 18 (93 317 78 08, institutofrancis.com). Metro Catalunya. **Open** *9.30am-8pm Mon-Sat.* **Map** *p152 H8* ⓱ *Spa*

Europe's largest beauty centre has seven floors and more than 50 staff all dedicated to making you beautiful – inside and out. As well as offering all the usual facials, massages, anti-cellulite treatments and manicures, the institute specialises in depilation, homeopathic therapies and non-surgical procedures such as teeth whitening and micropigmentation.

Janina

C/Rosselló 233 (93 215 04 84, www. janinalenceria.com). Metro Diagonal/FGC Provença. **Open** *Sept-July 10am-8.30pm Mon-Fri; 10.30am-8pm Sat. Aug 10am-2pm, 5-8.30pm Mon-Sat.* **Map** *p152 G5* ⓲ *Lingerie*

Janina offers women's underwear and nightwear by Calvin Klein, Christian Dior, La Perla and others. Some larger sizes are stocked; alternatively, bras can be sent to a seamstress to be altered overnight.
Other locations Avda Pau Casals 8 (93 202 06 93).

Du Pareil au Même

Rambla Catalunya 95 (93 487 14 49, www. dpam.com). Metro Diagonal/FGC Provença. **Open** *9.30am-8.30pm Mon-Sat.* **Map** *p152 H6* ⓴ *Children*

This French chain stocks everything a pint-sized fashionista might need, though the girls do a bit better than the boys, and babies do best of all, with fabulously colourful babygros. Newborns to 14-year-olds are served with a covetable range of funky, bright and well-designed clothes.

Prénatal

Ronda de Sant Pere 5 (93 318 03 57, www. prenatal.es). Metro Catalunya. **Open** *10am-9pm Mon-Sat.* **Map** *p152 H8* ㉑ *Children*

This ubiquitous but pricey chain has maternity wear, clothes for under-eights, buggies, car seats, cots, feeding bottles and toys.
Other locations Diagonal Mar, Avda Diagonal 3, Poblenou (93 356 25 71); La Illa, Avda Diagonal 617 (93 366 71 00).

Queviures Múrria

*C/Roger de Llúria 85 (93 215 57 89). Metro Passeig de Gràcia. **Open** 9am-2pm, 5-9pm Tue-Sat. Closed Aug. **Map** p152 J6* ㉒ *Food*

Queviures Múrria's shopfront is a veritable art gallery, featuring original hand-painted adverts for local booze Anis del Mono by Modernista artist Ramon Casas. Head inside for a wonderful selection of cheeses, sausages and wines from Catalonia and further afield.

♥ Santa Eulàlia

*Passeig de Gràcia 93 (93 215 06 74, www.santaeulalia.com). Metro Diagonal. **Open** 10am-8.30pm Mon-Sat. **Map** p152 H5* ㉓ *Fashion*

Barcelona's oldest design house and a pioneer in the local catwalk scene, Santa Eulàlia was founded in 1843 and remains a seriously upmarket proposition. The prêt-à-porter selection at the shop is fresh and up-to-the-minute, and includes labels such as Balenciaga, Jimmy Choo, Stella McCartney and Ann Demeulemeester. Services include bespoke tailoring and wedding wear for grooms, and there is a bistro and champagne bar.
Other locations C/Pau Casals 8 (93 201 70 51).

Sephora

*El Triangle, C/Pelai 13-37 (93 306 39 00, www.sephora.es). Metro Catalunya. **Open** 10am-10pm Mon-Sat. **Map** p152 H8* ㉔ *Beauty*

Of all Barcelona's beauty options, Sephora is your best bet for unfettered playing around with scents and make-up. Products include most of the usual mid- to high-end brands; there are also handy beauty tools, such as eyebrow tweezers and sharpeners.
Other locations throughout the city.

Stella McCartney

*Passeig de Gràcia 102 (93 487 71 36, www.stellamccartney.com). Metro Diagonal. **Open** 10.30am-8.30pm Mon-Sat. **Map** p152 H5* ㉕ *Fashion*

Stella McCartney's first store in Spain occupies a fiercely modern space within an elegant Modernista building. Sharp tailoring meets flashes of neon in her 1980s revivalist style, and is complemented by lingerie, childrenswear and accessories. Do not expect leather shoes or bags, however – Stella is a product of her parents.

Twenty One by Esther Llongueras

*Passeig de Gràcia 78 (93 215 41 75, www.twenty-one-21.com). Metro Passeig de Gràcia. **Open** 9am-6.30pm Mon-Fri; 9am-1.30pm Sat. **Map** p152 H6* ㉖ *Hairdresser*

A safe bet for all ages, this pricey Catalan chain has well-trained stylists who take the time to give a proper consultation, wash and massage. The cuts are up-to-the-minute but as natural as possible.

ESQUERRA

When Cerdà designed the Eixample, he consciously tried to avoid creating any upper- or lower-class side of town, imagining each of his homogeneous blocks as a cross-section of society. This vision of equality did not come to pass, however, and the left (west) side of the tracks was immediately less fashionable than the right; eventually it was to become the repository for the sort of city services the bourgeoisie didn't want ruining the upmarket tone of their new neighbourhood.

A huge slaughterhouse was built at the western edge of the area and was only knocked down in 1979, when it was replaced by the **Parc Joan Miró**. Also here is the busy **Hospital Clínic**, an ugly, functional building that covers two blocks between C/Corsega and C/Provença; to visit a market frequented by locals rather than tourists, try the **Ninot**, by the Clínic. On C/Entença, a little further out, was the grim, star-shaped La Model prison. It has since been relocated out of town and replaced by subsidised houses and offices. The vast **Escola Industrial** on C/Comte d'Urgell, formerly a Can Batlló textile factory, was redesigned in 1909 as a centre to teach workers the methods used in the textile industry. Another building worth seeing is the central **Universitat de Barcelona** building on Plaça Universitat, completed in 1872. It is an elegant construction with a pleasant, cloister-like garden.

The Esquerra also contains a number of Modernista jewels, such as the **Casa Boada** (C/Enric Granados 106) and the **Casa Golferichs** (Gran Via 191), built in 1901 by Joan Rubio i Bellver, one of Gaudí's main collaborators, and now a civic centre. Beyond the hospital, the Esquerra leads

---

In the know
Breathing space

The **ProEixample** was set up in 1985 to reclaim some 50 of the courtyards that were proposed in Ildefons Cerdà's original plans, so that everybody living in the area should be able to find an open space within 300m of their home. Two of the nicest examples are the fake beach around the Torre de les Aigües water tower (C/Llúria 56) and the patio at Passatge Permanyer (C/Pau Claris 120).

to **Plaça Francesc Macià**, centre of the business district and a gateway to the Zona Alta. In recent years, **ProEixample** has restored many of its interior patios and reduced the traffic lanes in several streets. In a turnaround of fortunes, the lower left side of the Eixample has also become home to the 'Gaixample', an affluent gay neighbourhood where the rainbow flag flies proudly from many a restaurant, bar and hairdresser's.

Sights & museums

Parc Joan Miró (Parc de l'Escorxador)

C/Tarragona & C/Aragó 2. Metro Espanya. Open 10am-sunset daily. Map p152 C6.

Covering an area the size of four city blocks, the old slaughterhouse (*escorxador*) was demolished in 1979 to provide some much-needed parkland, although there's little greenery. The rows of palms and pines are dwarfed by Miró's sculpture *Dona i Ocell* (Woman and Bird) getting its feet wet in a cement lake; there's also a good playground for small kids.

Restaurants

Cinc Sentits €€€€

C/Aribau 58 (93 323 94 90, www.cincsentits. com). Metro Passeig de Gràcia or Universitat. Open 1.30-3pm, 8.30-9.30pm Tue-Sat. Map p152 G6 ② *Catalan*

Talented Canadian-Catalan chef Jordi Artal shows respect for local classics, while adding his own unique touch in dishes such as Pyrenees beef, slow-roasted for 24 hours and served with potato gratin, chargrilled onion and shaved Catalan truffle, or a fire-roasted sweet potato with quail's egg, spice-bread wafer and oak smoke. There are set tasting menus only, for €55, €100 or €120. Service is formal but friendly, and Cinc Sentits is a great place to sample some top-end Catalan wines.

Disfrutar €€€€

C/Villaroel 163 (93 348 6896, en.disfrutarbarcelona.com). Metro Hospital Clínic. Open 1-2.30pm, 8-9.30pm Tue-Sat. Map p152 F6 ③ *Catalan*

Disfrutar is run by three of Ferran Adrià's former chefs at El Bulli, and anyone who missed that particularly dining experience will find something close here. There are two tasting menus, which may sound expensive at €105 and €145, but every dish – from the 'spherified' olives to luxury pork scratchings with corn ice-cream – is so dazzling that it's hard to imagine anyone feeling short-changed.

Gaig €€€€

C/Còrsega 200 (93 453 20 20, www. restaurantgaig.com). Metro Hospital-Clinic. Open 1.30-3.30pm, 8.30-11pm Tue-Sat; 1.30-3.30pm Sun. Map p152 F5 ④ *Catalan*

The eponymous chef Carles Gaig's cooking never fails to thrill the visitor. From his signature cannelloni with truffle cream to a shot glass holding layers of tangy lemon syrup, crema catalana mousse and caramel ice-cream, topped with burned sugar (to be eaten by plunging the spoon all the way down), every dish is as surprising and perfectly composed as the last.

♥ Gresca €€€

C/Provença 230 (93 451 61 93, www.gresca. net). Metro Diagonal or Passeig de Gràcia. Open Restaurant 1.30-3.30pm, 8.30-10.30pm Mon-Fri. Bar 1.30-3.30pm, 8.30-10.30pm Mon, Tue, Thur-Sun. Restaurant closed 2wks Aug. Map p152 G6 ⑤ *Modern European*

After extensive remodelling and expansion into an adjacent building, Gresca's chef, Rafa Peña, has been able to slot in a wine bar and considerably expand his kitchen – perhaps this will win him a merited Michelin star, finally. There is a suitably classy wine list, but the real highlights are dishes such as foamed egg on a bed of *jamón ibérico*, fennel and courgette, or puddings like the coca bread with Roquefort, and lychee and apple sorbet.

Le P'ty Mon €

Ptge Lluis Pellicer 13 (93 410 90 02, www. leptymon.com). Metro Hospital Clínic. Open 1.30-3.30pm Mon; 1.30-3.30pm, 8.30-11.30pm Tue-Fri; 8.30-11.30pm Sat. Map p152 F4 ⑧ *French*

A small restaurant and centre for all things Breton, with live music on Wednesday evenings. There is a blend of specialities from across the region, with Spanish produce in starters such as *andouille* sausage and *membrillo* (quince jelly), but from there onwards, it's French cuisine all the way. Gallic specialities include a range of sweet and savoury galettes (crêpes made with buckwheat flour), some scrumptious little blinis (try them smothered with strawberry jam and cream) or crêpes suzettes served in a pool of flaming Grand Marnier. The Petite menu will take care of *les enfants*, while a bowl or two of Breton cider will take care of the grown-ups.

La Taverna del Clínic €€

C/Rosselló 155 (93 410 42 21, www. latavernadelclinic.com). Metro Hospital Clínic or Diagonal. Open 1-3.45pm, 8-11.30pm Mon-Sat. Map p152 F5 ⑩ *Spanish*

La Taverna del Clínic sums up much that is good about the Spanish sense of priorities. The lighting is hideous, the decor is cheap and crappy, the television is permanently on, the walls and floor are tiled in the ugliest terrazzo imaginable, and yet the loving care that goes into the food is the match of many a luxury dining room. The menu concept lies somewhere between tapas and restaurant, so you will probably need to order a stack of dishes to share among friends. Try the creamy morels with foie; a sticky oxtail stew made with Priorat wine; or a tiny skillet of chips, fried egg and crispy *jamón*. The octopus 'igloo' is also superb.

Cafés

Velódromo

C/Muntaner 213 (93 430 60 22). Metro Hospital Clínic. Open 6am-2.30am Mon-Thur, Sun; 6am-3am Fri, Sat. Map p152 F4 ❿

For most of the 20th century, this was a favoured meeting place of the Catalan intelligentsia, underground political groups and – in the 1960s – an artistic group known as La Gauche Divine. It lay fallow during the noughties, but its elegant art deco interior was dusted off and gussied up thanks to a collaboration between chef Jordi Vilà and Moritz beer. There's a long list of tapas and larger dishes, along with excellent coffee and bathrooms that pay technicolour homage to Paul Smith.

Bars

♥ Dry Martini

C/Aribau 162-166 (93 217 50 72, www. javierdelasmuelas.com). FGC Provença. Open 1pm-2.30am Mon-Thur; 1pm-3am Fri; 6.30pm-3am Sat; 6.30pm-2.30am Sun. Map p152 G5 ❻

A shrine to the famous cocktail, which is honoured in Martini-related artwork and served in a hundred forms. All the trappings of a traditional cocktail bar are here (bow-tied staff, leather banquettes, antiques and wooden cabinets displaying a century's worth of bottles) but there's a notable lack of stuffiness, and the musical selection owes more to trip hop than middle-aged crowd-pleasers.

♥ Garage Beer Co

C/Consell de Cent 261 (93 528 59 89, garagebeer.co). Metro Universitat. Open 5pm-midnight Mon-Thur; 5pm-2.30am Fri; noon-3am Sat; 2pm-midnight Sun. Map p152 G6 ❼

Of the rash of tap rooms to open in recent years, Garage is the least pretentious and has some of the best beer. It started with a couple of pals making beer in a garage, and even this space has an industrial feel to it, despite the small size and the jumble of leather sofas in the back room. At any one time, they have around ten kegs of their own beer, in a range of styles, and the occasional cask of guest beer.

Shops & services

Antonio Miró

C/Enric Granados 46 (93 113 26 97, www.antoniomiro.es). FGC Provença. Open 10.30am-8.30pm Mon-Sat. Map p152 G6 ❷ *Fashion*

Miró famously likes to cause a stir on the catwalk, using illegal immigrants and even local prisoners to model his wares. His clothes, however, for men and women, couldn't be less controversial, with sober, almost uniform-like designs in muted tones. His diffusion line, Miró jeans, is more relaxed and playful.

♥ Escribà

Gran Via de les Corts Catalanes 546 (93 454 75 35, www.escriba.es). Metro Urgell. Open 8am-3pm, 5-8.30pm Mon-Fri; 8am-8.30pm Sat, Sun. Map p152 F7 ⓮ *Food*

Antoni Escribà, the 'Mozart of Chocolate', died in 2004, but his legacy lives on. His team produces jaw-dropping creations for Easter, from a chocolate Grand Canyon to a life-size model of Michelangelo's *David*, some of which are later displayed in the Museu de la Xocolata (*see p99*). The smaller miracles include cherry liqueur encased in red chocolate lips. The Rambla branch is situated in a pretty Modernista building. **Other locations** La Rambla 83, Raval (93 301 60 27).

Jean-Pierre Bua

Avda Diagonal 469 (93 439 71 00, www. jeanpierrebua.com). Metro Hospital Clínic. Open 10am-8.30pm Mon-Sat. Map p152 F4 ⓲ *Fashion*

The clothes are the highest of high-end fashion, the assistants are model-beautiful, and the shop itself has the air of a runway at a Paris catwalk show. No inferiority complexes are allowed: if you have the money, the figure and the label knowledge (and only if), come to worship at the altar of Miu Miu, Dries van Noten and many more. Next door at no.467 is Jean-Pierre Symbol, with three floors of what they term 'alternative' clothing.

Passeig de Gràcia

Gràcia & Other Districts

The inexorable expansion that began when Barcelona's walls were demolished in the 19th century ate away at the fields that once separated Gràcia from its neighbour. By 1897, the conurbation of Barcelona had all but swallowed up this fiercely independent town, and, amid howls of protest from its populace, Gràcia was annexed. Still, it retains its character and continues to draw visitors – as do neighbourhoods such as Les Corts (where football pilgrims head to the Camp Nou); Tibidabo, with its funfair and fantastic views; the upmarket Zona Alta, home of monster science museum, the CosmoCaixa; and Poblenou, scene of the most energetic attempts at urban regeneration.

❤ Don't miss

1 Park Güell *p177*
Gaudí's fairytale garden city.

2 Camp Nou Experience *p180*
The hallowed ground of Barça FC.

3 CosmoCaixa *p184*
Europe's biggest science museum.

4 Monestir de Pedralbes *p185*
A peaceful convent with a stunning cloister.

5 Museu del Disseny *p190*
Fashion, graphic and industrial design through the ages.

❤ Time to eat & drink

Crêpes and coffee
La Nena *p178*

A slap-up lunch
Pepa Tomate *p178*,
La Panxa del Bisbe *p176*

A sundowner
Balius *p191*,
El Maravillas *p181*,
Bodega Quimet *p178*

Top-flight Thai
Bangkok Café *p181*

Tapas with a twist
El 58 *p191*

❤ Time well spent

Gelateria Caffetteria Italiana
Plaça de la Revolució 2, Gràcia (93 210 23 39). Metro Fontana or Joanic. **Open** *Apr-Oct noon-1am Mon-Thur, Sun; noon-2am Fri, Sat. Nov-Mar 9am-9pm Mon-Thur, Sun; 9am-11pm Fri, Sat.* **No cards. Map** *p175 J4* ❸

Barcelona's favourite ice-cream parlour is run by an Italian mother and daughter, and famous for its own-recipe dark chocolate ice-cream – which invariably sells out every night. Other freshly made, additive-free flavours include fig, strawberry and peach: basically, whatever fruit happens to be in season. There are tables outside on the square, if you're lucky enough to get one – be prepared to queue, especially on balmy summer evenings.

GRÀCIA & PARK GÜELL

Gràcia's reputation as a breeding ground for political insurgency came from the effects of industrial expansion. Centred on the 17th-century convent of **Santa Maria de Gràcia**, it was a village in 1821, with 2,600 residents. But by the time it was annexed 78 years later, its population had risen to 61,935; it had become the ninth largest town in Spain, and a hotbed of Catalanism, republicanism and anarchism.

Dissent has been a recurring feature in Gràcia's history. Streets boast names such as Llibertat, Revolució and Fraternitat, and for the 64 years preceding the Civil War, there was a satirical political magazine called *La Campana de Gràcia*, named after the bell in **Plaça Rius i Taulet** (now known as **Plaça Vila de Gràcia**). However, few vestiges of radicalism remain. Sure, the *okupa* squatter movement inhabits a relatively high number of buildings in the area, but the middle-class population has been waging an increasingly successful campaign to dislodge them.

Gràcia is both 'alternative' and upmarket, and anything bigger than a shoebox costs a fortune to rent or buy. For many, though, it's the only place to be in Barcelona. As a result it radiates a youthful chic, with buzzy bars, yoga centres and practitioners of shiatsu, acupuncture and every form of holistic medicine, as well as piercing and tattoo parlours, dotted among the antique shops and *jamonerías*. The *barrio* is a favourite hangout of the city's bohemians: there are numerous workshops and studios, and the many small, unpretentious bars are often frequented by artists, designers and students.

The neighbourhood really comes into its own for a few days in mid August, when its famous *festa major* grips the entire city and all Barcelona converges here to party (*see p219*). Residents spend months preparing startlingly original home-made street decorations, and there is fierce competition for the accolade of best-decorated street. Open-air meals are laid on for the residents, bands are dotted on every street and films are screened in *plaças* and bars, while old-timers sing along to *habaneros* (shanties) and resident squatters pogo to punk bands.

Much of Gràcia was built in the heyday of Modernisme, including the district's splendid main street, **C/Gran de Gràcia**. Many of the buildings are rich in nature-inspired curves and fancy façades, but the finest example of architecture is Lluís Domènech i Montaner's **Casa Fuster** at no.2, now a luxury hotel. Gaudí's disciple Francesc Berenguer was responsible for much of the civic architecture, most notably the **Mercat de la Llibertat** (Barcelona's oldest covered market, still proudly adorned with Gràcia's old coat of arms) and the old **Casa de la Vila** (Town Hall).

However, the district's most overwhelming Modernista gem is one of Gaudí's earliest and most fascinating works: the **Casa Vicens** (www.casavicens.org), built in 1883-88, which is hidden away in C/Carolines. The building is a private residence but due to open to visitors in late 2017. In the meantime, the castellated red brickwork and colourful tiled exterior inspired by Indian and Mudéjar influences should not be missed; notice, too, the spiky wrought-iron leaves on the gates.

One of Gaudí's last works, the extraordinary **Park Güell** (*see p177*) is a short walk away, across the busy Travessera de Dalt and up the hill. This is worth the effort (there are escalators at certain points), not only for the architecture but also for the magnificent view of Barcelona and the sea.

Sights & museums

Gaudí Experiència

C/Larrard 41 (93 285 44 40, www.gaudiexperiencia.com). Bus 24, 31, 32. **Open** *Apr-Sept 10.30am-7pm daily. Oct-Mar 10.30am-5pm daily.* **Admission** *€9; €7.50 reductions.* **Map** *p175 K1.*

The core attraction of the Gaudí Experiència is a ten-minute film in 4D – a three-dimensional film with a physical element. You might fly through a rain cloud and feel damp, for example, or zoom through a flock of birds and feel their wings against your legs. It's an intense and thoroughly entertaining affair, although best enjoyed as a fantasy rather than something educational. Those with a reasonable knowledge of Gaudí will understand the many hidden allusions; those without will not.

If you fall into the latter category, check out the futuristic touchscreens in the entrance lobby. Swipe, click, enlarge, shrink and play with images and text to learn more about Gaudí's buildings. There are also screens specially designed for children, who can create their own 'Gaudí building' or simply colour in a mosaic.

In the know
Getting around Gràcia

Gràcia is just north of the Eixample, accessed easily by metro, either L3 to Fontana or L4 to Joanic. The *barrio* is mostly pedestrianised, and it's a ten-minute walk from one side to the other.

GRÀCIA

Restaurants

1. Botafumeiro
2. Café Godot
3. Cantina Machito
4. Envalira
5. Himali
6. La Panxa del Bisbe
7. San Kil
8. La Singular
9. Somodó
10. Les Tres a la Cuina

Cafés, tapas & bars

1. Bodega Quimet
2. Châtelet
3. Gelateria Caffetteria Italiana
4. La Nena
5. Pepa Tomate

Shops & s

1. A Casa
2. Hiber
3. Lad

▶ *Although they are beyond '
map, many of the areas dis
shown on the fold-out ma'*

Restaurants

▶ *For details of our restaurant price categories, see p36.*

Botafumeiro €€€
C/Gran de Gràcia 81 (93 218 42 30, www. botafumeiro.es). Metro Fontana. **Open** *noon-1am daily.* **Map** *p175 H4* ❶ *Seafood*

The speciality at this vast Galician restaurant is seafood in every shape and form, served with military precision by a fleet of nautically clad waiters. The sole cooked in cava with prawns is superb, as are more humble dishes such as a cabbage and pork broth, typical of the region. The platter of seafood (for two) is an excellent introduction to the various molluscs of the Spanish coastline. It can be hard to get a table at peak times, but the kitchen is open throughout the day.

Café Godot €€
C/Sant Domènec 19 (93 368 20 36, www. cafegodot.com). Metro Fontana. **Open** *10am-1am Mon-Fri; 11am-2am Sat, Sun.* **Map** *p175 J4* ❷ *Global*

Café Godot is an easygoing bistro, with a little terrace at the back and a play area for kids (along with plenty on the menu that will appeal to them, too) – the perfect spot for a lazy Sunday brunch (featuring eggs Benedict, banana pancakes, french toast and so on). The sandwich menu is particularly inspired, with roast beef, club sandwiches and Vietnamese *banh mi*, among others, while more substantial dishes include duck magret and steak frites.

Cantina Machito €€
C/Torrijos 47 (93 217 34 14, www. cantinamachito.com). Metro Joanic. **Open** *11am-1am daily.* **Map** *p175 J3* ❸ *Mexican*

…e red and blue colour scheme, tissue paper
…ring and chaotic hubbub make this a little
…f old Mexico. The minuscule writing
…enu and low lighting make for some
…k when placing your order (the
…io at the back is brighter), but the
…andard enough – quesadillas,
…chiladas – with a couple of
…s the tasting platter of insects.
…eshing on summer nights –
…and honey or pineapple
…be slow and the kitchen
…th the sauces, but
…es decent.

…ww.
…Fontana.
…ue-Sat;
…stmas,

Most regions of Spain are represented at this deeply traditional restaurant. There is a particular emphasis on Galicia (*caldeirada gallega* is a hearty fish stew, *lacón con grelos* is gammon with turnip tops and *tarta de Santiago* is an almond cake), but the Basque oxtail stew is also a tasty dish. The dining room could use a lick of paint and some subtlety in its lighting; arrive early for the more comfortable leather banquettes at the front of the restaurant, and book ahead at weekends.

Himali €
C/Milà i Fontanals 60-68 (93 285 15 68). Metro Joanic. **Open** *noon-4.30pm, 8pm-midnight Tue-Sun.* **Map** *p175 K4* ❺ *Nepalese*

A comic metaphor for modern-day Barcelona, Himali moved into what was a local boozer, but has retained the silhouettes of famous Catalans – Dalí and Montserrat Caballé among them – on the windows; inside, meanwhile, there are Nepalese prayer flags and tourist posters of the Himalayas. The alien and impenetrable menu looks a little daunting at first glance, but the waiters are helpful with their recommendations. Alternatively, you could start your meal with *momo* dumplings or Nepalese soup, followed by *mugliaco kukhura* (barbecued butter chicken in creamy tomato sauce) or *khasi masala tarkari* (baked spicy lamb). All dishes include rice and naan bread as accompaniments.

❤ La Panxa del Bisbe €€
C/Torrent de les Flors 158 (93 213 70 49). Metro Joanic. **Open** *1.30-3.30pm, 8.30-midnight Tue-Sat.* **Map** *p175 K2* ❻ *Mediterranean*

Not long after opening, the 'Bishop's Belly' had to move to bigger premises thanks to the popularity of its exquisitely presented cooking. It's not all about looks, however, and there is real soul to beef cheeks with beetroot gnocchi, courgette flowers in tempura with sea anemones and langoustines, or a wonderful take on the Catalan favourite of bread with olive oil, salt and chocolate.

San Kil €€
C/Legalitat 22 (93 284 41 79). Metro Joanic. **Open** *1-3.30pm, 8.30-10.30pm Mon-Thur; 1.30-3.30pm, 8.30-10.30pm Fri, Sat. Closed 3wks Aug.* **Map** *p175 K3* ❼ *Korean*

If you've never eaten Korean food before, it would probably pay to gen up before you head to this jolly but no-frills restaurant. *Panch'an* (on the house) is served first: four dishes containing vegetable appetisers, one of which will be tangy *kimch'i* (fermented cabbage with chilli). Or you could try the *empanadas*

❤ Park Güell

C/Olot (www.parkguell.cat). Metro Lesseps or Vallcarca (for top entrance) or bus 24, 32, 92. **Open** *10am-sunset daily.* **Monumental zone** *€8, €5.60 reduction, free under-7s.* **Park** *free. No cards.* **Map** *p175 K1.*

Gaudí's brief for the design of what became Park Güell was to emulate the English garden cities so admired by his patron, Eusebi Güell: to lay out a self-contained suburb for the wealthy, but also to design the public areas. (This English influence explains the anglicised spelling of 'Park'.) The original plan called for the plots to be sold and the properties designed by other architects. But the idea never took off – perhaps because it was too far from the city, or because it was too radical – and the Güell family gave the park to the city in 1922. It is now a UNESCO World Heritage Site.

The fantastical exuberance of Gaudí's imagination remains breathtaking. Visitors were once welcomed by two life-size mechanical gazelles, a typically bizarre religious reference by Gaudí to medieval Hebrew love poetry, although these were unfortunately destroyed in the Civil War. The two gatehouses that remain were based on designs the architect made for the opera *Hänsel and Gretel*, one of them featuring a red and white mushroom for a roof. From here you enter the 'monumental zone', and

walk up a splendid staircase flanked by multicoloured battlements, past the iconic mosaic lizard sculpture, to what would have been the main marketplace. Here, 100 palm-shaped pillars hold up a roof, reminiscent of the hypostyle hall at Luxor. On top of this structure is the esplanade, a circular concourse surrounded by benches in the form of a sea-serpent decorated with shattered tiles – a technique called *trencadís*, perfected by Gaudí's talented assistant Josep Maria Jujol. Nearby, twisted stone columns support curving colonnades or merge with the natural structure of the hillside.

The park surrounding the fenced-off monumental zone has at its peak a large cross, and offers an amazing panorama of Barcelona and the sea stretching out beyond.

In the know
Casa-Museu Gaudí

Designed by his student Francesc Berenguer, Gaudí's former residence, the pink Torre Rosa, is now the Casa-Museu Gaudí (93 219 38 11, www.casamuseugaudi.com), restored to look as it was in his day and featuring furniture that he designed. Tours of the building, some in English, are available

(fried dumplings, strictly speaking Chinese, but tasty). Then try *pulgogi* (beef served sizzling at the table and eaten rolled into lettuce leaves) and maybe the mouthwatering seafood omelette. Finish up with a shot of *soju* rice wine for the full experience.

La Singular €

C/Francisco Giner 50 (93 237 50 98, www. lasingular-barcelona.com). Metro Diagonal. **Open** *1-4pm, 8.30-11.30pm Mon-Thur; 1-4pm, 8.30pm-12.30am Fri, Sat. Closed last wk Aug & 1st wk Sept.* **Map** *p175 J4* **8** *Mediterranean*

While this is often described as a lesbian-friendly restaurant, in fact that's the least noteworthy thing about it, and all are made welcome. Most come here for the good-value set lunch (salads and light pasta dishes to start, followed by dishes such as roast beef carpaccio with red cabbage and onion; €10.50, available Monday to Friday) in snug surroundings of red walls with pale green woodwork and a tiny, leafy patio. It can get noisy when full, so come early and beat the rush. Reservations are necessary for a table on Friday and Saturday nights.

Somodó €€

C/Ros de Olano 11 (93 415 65 48, www.somodo. es). Metro Fontana. **Open** *1.30-3.15pm, 9-11.30pm Tue-Sat. Closed Aug & 1wk Easter.* **Map** *p175 H3* **9** *Japanese*

A surprisingly successful mix of Catalan and Japanese applies to the decor as much as the food at Somodó, with mosaic flooring and dark-green paintwork setting off a feng-shuied look. It only serves set meals (water, wine, coffee and tax are included in the €22 lunch, available Tuesday to Friday). So, after an amuse-bouche, there may be foie steamed with *umeshu* (plum wine), mackerel cooked with miso and white aubergine, followed ∿ venison with wild mushrooms and black ⌐il. Two puddings are included in the price ⌐nner (from €32, food only).

⌐s a la Cuina €

⌐uís 35 (93 105 49 47, www. ⌐ina.com). Metro Joanic. **Open** *⌐ Mon-Fri; 12.30-4pm Sat. Closed ⌐ K3* **10** *Mediterranean*

⌐s

sted to visit one of
⌐ny commercial
was here,
⌐s was

If there's a better lunch deal in town (€10 Monday to Friday, €11.50 Saturday), we've yet to find it. Baffling licensing laws mean you'll be eating off a plastic plate, but who cares when it holds chicken baked with Pernod, fennel and clementine; a delicious baked garlic tart with goat's cheese; or the much-requested pork and beef lasagne? Outside lunch hours Les Tres offers coffee and home-made cakes and, on Saturday, a scrumptious brunch.

Cafés

❤ La Nena

C/Ramón y Cajal 36 (93 285 14 76). Metro Fontana or Joanic. **Open** *9am-2pm, 4-10pm Mon-Wed; 10am-10.30pm Thur-Sun. Closed Aug.* **No cards. Map** *p175 J4* **4**

With whitewashed stone walls, piles of books and games, and a gaily painted table-and-chair set for children, La Nena is wonderfully cosy – or would be if the staff would only lighten up. The speciality is sugar and spice and all things nice, waffles, crêpes, hot chocolate, fresh juices and ice-cream. Savoury delights include sandwiches and toasted bread with various toppings. Note there is no alcohol and that, rather infuriatingly, it's closed at lunchtime from Monday to Wednesday.

Tapas

❤ Pepa Tomate

Plaça de la Revolució 17 (93 213 75 56, www. pepatomate.com). Metro Fontana or Joanic. **Open** *8am-1am Tue-Fri; 10am-1am Sat, Sun.* **Map** *p175 J4* **5**

A funky new addition to Gràcia's favourite square, with two lively dining rooms where you can get sandwiches, salads, *montaditos* (tapas served on slices of bread) and more substantial dishes. Try the *croquetas* with prawn and wild mushrooms or 'el Pepitu' – a toasted sandwich of pork and melted cheese. From Tuesday to Friday there is a set lunch for €12.50.
Other locations C/Mandri 58, Sant Gervasi (93 254 17 97).

Bars

❤ Bodega Quimet

C/Vic 23 (93 218 41 89). FGC Gràcia or Metro Fontana. **Open** *2-11.30pm Mon-Fri; 1-11.30pm Sat, Sun.* **Map** *p175 H4* **1**

A classic of the *barrio*, Bodega Quimet has been around since 1954 and has hardly changed since, either in decor or in what's on offer. A handful of local wines are still available from the barrels (which adorn the walls), as is dirt-cheap *vermut*, and there is a list of simple but good tapas.

Châtelet

C/Torrijos 54 (93 284 95 90). Metro Fontana. **Open** *6pm-2.30am Mon-Thur, Sun; 6pm-3am Fri, Sat.* **Map** *p175 J3* ❷

Crammed with funkily mismatched flea market finds, old movie posters and chandeliers, the Châtelet is part of a small chain of bars with a Parisian flavour. It has the edge over the others thanks to its corner location just a block from the Verdi art cinema, with huge windows that open up completely in summer. Comfy sofas and armchairs plus occasional film screenings make this a favourite with an arty, studenty crowd.

Shops & services

A Casa Portuguesa

C/Or 8 (93 368 35 28, www.facebook.com/ acasaportuguesa). Metro Fontana. **Open** *10.30am-9pm daily.* **Map** *p175 J3* ❶ *Food & Drink*

Fado provides the soundtrack at this mellow little bakery/deli, which is dedicated to all things nice from Portugal. Sit down with a coffee and a freshly made *pastéis de Belém* (little custard tarts with a dusting of cinnamon), choose from a great selection of wines, preserves, pâtés, jams and cheeses. Check the Facebook page for wine tastings and other special events.

Hibernian Books

C/Montseny 17 (93 217 47 96, www.hibernian-books.com). Metro Fontana. **Open** *4-8.30pm Mon; 11am-8.30pm Tue-Sat.* **No cards.** **Map** *p175 J3* ❷ *Books*

With its air of pleasantly dusty intellectualism, Hibernian feels like a proper British second-hand bookshop. There are books for all tastes, from beautifully bound early editions to classic Penguin paperbacks, biographies, cookbooks and so on, more than 30,000 titles in all. Part-exchange is possible.

Ladyloquita

C/Travessera de Gràcia 126 (93 217 82 92, www.ladyloquita.com). Metro Fontana. **Open** *5-8.30pm Mon; 11am-2pm, 5-8.30pm Tue-Sat.* **Map** *p175 H4* ❸ *Fashion*

Meeta and Laura's charming, quirky Gràcia boutique stocks a host of labels such as Pepa Loves, YUMI and Meeta's own label, Tiralahilacha, along with accessories galore, from earrings to bags. Cool interior design, chill-out area and reasonable price tags complete the pretty picture.

SANTS & LES CORTS

Sants – or at least the immediate environs of **Estació de Sants**, which is all that most visitors see of the area – stands as a monument to the worst of 1970s urban design. To coincide with the arrival of the overdue high-speed AVE train connection with Madrid, the station has undergone a makeover. The place is no longer shabby, but it's not one that you would want to hang around, and few people do. When they step outside, most take one look at the **Plaça dels Països Catalans**, a snarl of traffic around a roundabout whose centrepiece looks like a post-Miró bus shelter, and make a hasty exit.

However, for those with time to spare, Sants merits investigation for historic, if not aesthetic, reasons. Mid August is one of the better times to visit: following the Festa Major de Gràcia, Sants launches its own, lower-key version (*see p219*), and the *barri* sheds its drab industrial coat in favour of street parties, decorations and music.

Sants was originally built to serve those who arrived after the town gates had shut at 9pm, with inns and blacksmiths to cater for latecomers. In the 19th century, though, it became the industrial motor of the city. Giant textile factories such as **Vapor Vell** (which is now a library), **L'Espanya Industrial** (now the **Parc de l'Espanya Industrial**) and **Can Batlló** (still a workplace) helped to create the wealth that the likes of Eusebi Güell spent on the Modernista dream homes that still grace the more salubrious areas of the city. The inequality did not go unnoticed. The *barri* was a hotbed of industrial action; the first general strike in Catalonia broke out here in 1856, only to be violently put down by the infamous General Zapatero (known as the 'Tiger of Catalonia').

Most routes of interest start and finish at the **Plaça de Sants**, which lies halfway up the high street of C/Sants and is where Jorge Castillo's *Ciclista* statue is to b... Also worth a look are the showy M... buildings at nos.12, 130, 145 and... designed by local architect Mo...

Returning to the Plaça de S... taking C/Olzinelles, you'll f... **Plaça Bonet i Muixí** and... **de Santa Maria del Sa**... which it is believed th... This is the focal poi... Easter, when Sem... grips Spain.

Following C/... Montjuïc, the... Coberta, an... known as... to Spain... you'll...

❤ Camp Nou Experience

Camp Nou, Avda Arístides Maillol, access 14, Les Corts (902 189 900, www.fcbarcelona. cat). Metro Collblanc, Les Corts or Maria Cristina. **Open** *Apr-mid Oct 9.30am-7pm daily. Mid Oct-Mar 10am-6.30pm Mon-Sat; 10am-2.30pm Sun.* **Admission** *€25; €20 reductions; free under-6s.* **Map** *Fold-out A3.*

Camp Nou, where FC Barcelona has played since 1957, is one of football's great stadiums – a vast cauldron of a ground that holds 99,000 spectators. That's a lot of noise when the team is doing well, and an awful lot of silence when it isn't. For football fanatics, a trip to Barcelona would not be complete without visiting the hallowed turf.

Even if you can't get there on match day, it's worth visiting the club museum. The excellent audio-guided tour of the stadium takes you through the players' tunnel to the dugouts and then, via the away team's changing room, on to the President's box, where there is a replica of the UEFA Champions League Cup, which the team has won five times.

The club museum makes much of the 'Dream Team' days when the likes of Kubala, Cruyff, Maradona, Koeman and Lineker trod the hallowed turf, ⸴ith pictures, video clips and souvenirs ⸴nning the century that has passed since ⸴wiss businessman Johan Gamper and ⸴glishman Arthur Witty founded the ⸴899. The last tour begins an hour ⸴sing time.

⸴ Barça match can be a
⸴re's a good ticketing
⸴ailability is ever
⸴olders can give
⸴not attending, and
⸴on the website
⸴f these seats
⸴re a game. So,
⸴ys before,
⸴larly right
⸴has

Mercat d'Hostafrancs, where there's also a stop for the tourist bus. Further along still is C/Sant Roc and the Modernista-inspired church of **Sant Angel Custodi**. North of Sants lies the *barri* of **Les Corts** (meaning 'cowsheds' or 'pigsties'), another village engulfed by the expanding city in the 19th century. Les Corts remains one of the most Catalan of the city's *barris*. Rows and rows of unlovely apartment blocks have stamped out almost any trace of its bucolic past, although the **Plaça de la Concòrdia**, a quiet square dominated by a 40m (131ft) bell tower, remains. This is an anachronistic oasis housing the civic centre **Can Deu**, formerly a farmhouse and now home to a great bar hosting regular jazz acts). The area is much better known, though, for what happens every other weekend, when tens of thousands pour in to watch FC Barcelona, whose **Camp Nou** takes up much of the west of the neighbourhood. Note that at night the area is the haunt of transvestite prostitutes and their kerb-crawling clients.

Sights & museums

Parc de l'Espanya Industrial
C/Muntadas 1-37, Sants (no phone). Metro Sants Estació. **Open** *9am-sunset daily.* **Admission** *free.* **Map** *Fold-out I/6.*

During the 1970s, the owners of the old textile factory announced their intention to use the land to build blocks of apartments. The neighbourhood's residents, though, put their collective foot down and insisted on a park, which was eventually laid out in 1985. The result is a puzzling space, designed by Basque Luis Peña Ganchegui, with little in the way of greenery. Ten watchtowers overlook a boating lake with a statue of Neptune in the middle, which is flanked by a stretch of mud used mainly by dog walkers; by the entrance, children can climb over Andrés Nagel's *Drac*, a massive and sinister black dragon sculpture.

Restaurants

♥ Bangkok Café €€
C/Evarist Arnús 65, Les Corts (93 339 32 69). Metro Plaça del Centre. **Open** *8-11.30pm Mon-Thur; 1-4pm, 8-11.30pm Fri-Sun. Thai*

Without a doubt, the best Thai restaurant in Barcelona, and not ridiculously expensive either. Entered via a pretty little mews street, it's a squeezed and fairly noisy little place, with an open kitchen and a handful of tables (reserve if you can). All the Thai standards are present and beautifully executed with a good amount of heat. Leave room for mango and rice pudding.

La Parra €€
C/Joanot Martorell 3, Sants (93 332 51 34). Metro Hostafrancs. **Open** *8pm-midnight Tue-Fri; 1.30-4.30pm, 8.30pm-12.30am Sat; 1.30-4.30pm Sun. Closed Aug. Catalan*

A charming converted 19th-century coaching inn with a shady, vine-covered terrace. The open wood grill sizzles with various parts of goat, pig, rabbit and cow, as well as deer and even foal. Huge, oozing steaks are slapped on to wooden boards and accompanied by baked potatoes, *calçots* (large spring onions), grilled vegetables and *allioli*, with jugs of local wine from the giant barrels.

Tapas

Fragments Café
Plaça de la Concòrdia 12, Les Corts (93 419 96 13, www.fragmentscafe.com). Metro Les Corts or Maria Cristina. **Open** *1pm-1am Tue, Wed; 1pm-1.30am Thur; 1pm-2.30am Fri; noon-2.30am Sat; noon-12.30am Sun.*

A tapas bar with a smart, classy look in the one remaining pocket of charm left in Les Corts. Sit at the tables in the square or the bar's garden at the back (candlelit at night), and order some *vermut* and *gildas* (anchovies with chilli) before you so much as begin to peruse the menu. There are scrambled eggs with foie gras, juicy steaks, home-made pasta and cherry crumble to finish. Prices can be a bit steep for what are quite small portions.

Bars

♥ El Maravillos
Plaça de la Concòrdia 15, Les Corts (93 360 73 78). Metro Les Corts. **Open** *noon-12.30am daily.*

Should you find yourself in need of a drink, head for Les Corts' most relaxed square and pull up a chair on the terrace of pretty little El Maravillas. There are some superior tapas on offer, but the real highlight is the ever-changing list of cocktails, most dreamt up by the barman. Try, for example, the Frida Kahlo, with vodka, vermouth, maraschino, fig confit and lime.

In the know
The view from the top

For the best view of the city from of Tibidabo (see p182), either lift up Norman Foster's tower **de Collserola**, or walk up (viewpoint) at the feet of Sagrat Cor.

TIBIDABO & COLLSEROLA

Before car pollution blurred the horizon, it was said that you could see Mallorca from **Tibidabo**. The mountain takes its name from the Devil's temptation of Christ, when he took Jesus to the top of a mountain and offered him all before him, with the words '*tibi dabo*' (Latin for 'To thee I will give'). Tibidabo is the dominant peak of the **Collserola** massif, with its sweeping views of, if not Mallorca, at least the whole of the Barcelona conurbation stretching to the sea: a tempting offer, given the present-day price of the city's real estate.

Crowning the peak, the neo-Gothic **Sagrat Cor** church has become one of the city's most recognisable landmarks, visible for miles. At weekends, thousands of people head to the top of the hill in order to whoop and scream at the **funfair**. Now the only one in the city, it's been running since 1921 and has changed little since: the rides are creaky and old-fashioned, but very quaint. The marionette show is also a survivor from the early days; a more recent addition is Spain's first freefall ride, where visitors are dropped 38 metres (125 feet) in 2.8 seconds. Within the funfair, the **Museu d'Autòmats** showcases a fine collection of fairground coin-operated machines from the early 1900s.

The vast **Parc de Collserola** is more a series of forested hills than a park, its shady paths through holm oak and pine opening out to spectacular views. A ten-minute walk from Baixador de Vallvidrera station (there's an information board just outside) up into the woods will take you to the **Vil·la Joana**, an old *masia* covered in bougainvillea and containing the **Museu Verdaguer** (93 256 21 00, www.museuhistoria.bcn.cat), dedicated to 19th-century Catalan poet Jacint Verdaguer, who used this as his summer home. Just beyond the Vil·la Joana is the park's information centre (93 280 35 52, open 9.30am-3pm daily), which has free basic maps and more detailed maps for sale. Most of the information is in Catalan, but staff are helpful. There's also a snack bar.

Sights & museums

Funicular de Tibidabo

Plaça Doctor Andreu to Plaça Tibidabo (93 211 79 42). FGC Avda Tibidabo then Tramvia Blau. **Open** *as funfair, but from 15mins earlier, until 15mins later.* **Tickets** *€7.70; €2-€4.10 reductions; free under-3s.*

This art deco vehicle offers occasional glimpses of the city below as it winds through the pine forests up to the summit. The service has been operating since 1901, but

In the know
Getting around Tibidabo & Collserola

To get to the top of Tibidabo, take the **Tramvia Blau** (Blue Tram, *see p186*) from Avda Tibidabo FGC station and then the **funicular railway**; between the two is **Plaça Doctor Andreu**, a great place for an alfresco drink.

If the Tibidabo funicular isn't running, take the FGC line from Plaça de Catalunya to Peu del Funicular, get this funicular up to Vallvidrera Superior, and then catch the 111 bus to Tibidabo (a process not half as complicated as it sounds).

Alternatively, it's nearly an hour's (mostly pleasant) hike up from Plaça Doctor Andreu for those who are feeling energetic.

To access the **Parc de Collserola**, take the FGC train on the Terrassa-Sabadell line from Plaça Catalunya or Passeig de Gràcia and get off at Baixador de Vallvidrera station.

only according to a complicated timetable. Holders of tickets for the funfair are entitled to a discount.

Torre de Collserola
Ctra de Vallvidrera al Tibidabo (93 211 79 42, www.torredecollserola.com). FGC Peu del Funicular then funicular. **Open** *as funfair.* **Admission** *€5.60; €3.30 reductions; free under-4s.*

Just five minutes' walk from the Sagrat Cor is its main rival, and Barcelona's most visible landmark. Norman Foster's communications tower was built in 1992 to transmit images of the Olympics around the world. Those who don't suffer from vertigo attest to the wonderful views of Barcelona and the Mediterranean from the top.

Tibidabo Funfair
Plaça del Tibidabo 3-4 (93 211 79 42, www. tibidabo.cat). FGC Avda Tibidabo & funicular. **Open** *check website. Closed Jan, Feb.* **Tickets** *Camí del Cel Mar-Dec €12.70; €7.80 under 120cm; free under 90cm. Parc d'Atraccions (unlimited rides) €28.50; €10.30 under 120cm; free under 90cm.*

This hilltop fairground, dating from 1889, is investing millions in getting itself bang up to date, with the freefall Pendulum and a hot-air balloon-style ride for smaller children. Adrenalin freaks are delighted with the new 80km/h rollercoaster, and the many other attractions include a house of horrors, bumper cars and the emblematic Avió, the world's first popular flight simulator when it was built in 1928. Don't miss the antique mechanical puppets and contraptions at the Museu d'Autòmats, and there are scheduled puppet shows at the Marionetàrium. At the weekends, there are circus parades at the end of the day and, in summer, *correfocs* (parades where participants let off fireworks) and street theatre.

The opening hours are fiendishly complex and vary from week to week (check the website), but roughly speaking what's now known as the Camí del Cel (this includes the more traditional rides, such as the carousel, the Avió, and so on) is open daily, while the Parc d'Atraccions (including the rollercoaster) is open at weekends.

Restaurants

La Venta €€
Plaça Doctor Andreu, Tibidabo (93 212 64 55, www.restaurantelaventa.com). FGC Avda Tibidabo, then Tramvia Blau or bus 196. **Open** *1.30-3.30pm, 8.30-11pm Mon-Sat; 1.30-3.30pm Sun. Mediterranean*

Tibidabo Funfair

La Venta's pretty Moorish-influenced interior plays second fiddle to the terrace during every season: shaded by day and uncovered by night in summer, sealed and warmed with a wood-burning stove in winter. Complex starters include lentil and spider crab salad, sea urchins au gratin (a must), and langoustine ravioli, filled with leek and foie mousse. Simpler but high-quality mains run from rack of lamb to delicate monkfish in filo pastry.

ZONA ALTA

Zona Alta (the 'upper zone', or 'uptown') is the name given collectively to the series of smart neighbourhoods – including **Sant Gervasi**, **Sarrià**, **Pedralbes**, **Vallcarca** and **Putxet** – that stretches out across the lower reaches of the Collserola hills. Here, you'll find a handful of tourist sights, including the **Palau Reial de Pedralbes** (not to be confused with the Palau Reial

Major in the Barri Gòtic). Gaudí fans are rewarded by a trip up to its gatehouse, the **Pavellons de la Finca Güell** at Avda Pedralbes 7; its extraordinary wrought-iron gate features a dragon into whose gaping mouth the foolhardy can fit their heads. Once inside the gardens, via the main gate on Avda Diagonal, look out for a delightful fountain designed by the master himself. Other attractions up here include the **CosmoCaixa** science museum and the **Monestir de Pedralbes** convent. The convent is still worth a visit, even though the religious paintings from the Thyssen-Bornemisza collection have been moved to the revamped Museu Nacional d'Art de Catalunya (MNAC; *see p144*). The centre of Sarrià and the streets of old Pedralbes around the monastery retain a flavour of the sleepy country towns these once were.

For many downtown residents, the Zona Alta is a favourite place to relax in the parks and gardens that wind into the hills. At the end of Avda Diagonal, next to the functional Zona Universitària (university district), is the **Jardins de Cervantes**, with its 11,000 rose bushes, the striking *Rombes Bessons* (Twin Rhombuses) sculpture by Andreu Alfaro and, during the week, legions of picnicking students, continuing in the scholastic traditions of the founder of Catalan literature, Ramon Llull.

From the park, a turn back along the Diagonal towards Plaça Maria Cristina and Plaça Francesc Macià will take you to the city's main business and shopping district. Here, the small **Turó Parc** is a semi-formal garden, good for writing postcards amid inspirational plaques of poetry. The **Jardins de la Tamarita** park, which lies at the foot of Avda Tibidabo, is a pleasant dog-free oasis with a playground, while further up at the top of the tramline is the little-known **Parc de la Font de Racó**, full of shady pine and eucalyptus trees. A fair walk to the north-east, an old quarry has been converted into a swimming pool, the **Parc de la Creueta del Coll**.

Across near Putxet is Gaudí's relatively sober **Col·legi de les Teresianes** (C/ Ganduxer 85-105), while up towards Tibidabo, just off Plaça Bonanova, rises his Gothic-influenced **Torre Figueres** (or Torre Bellesguard).

In the know
Getting around the Zona Alta

FCG trains run from Plaça Catalunya to Sarrià and El Putxet, or various stations for Sant Gervasi. The best stop for Pedralbes is Reina Elisenda.

Sights & museums

❤ CosmoCaixa

C/Isaac Newton 26, Sant Gervasi (93 212 60 50, www.cosmocaixa.com). FGC Avda Tibidabo. **Open** *10am-8pm Tue-Sun.* **Admission** *€3; €2 reductions; free under-6s & over-65s. Free to all 1st Sun of mth. Planetarium €4; €3 reductions. Toca Toca! €2; €1.50 reductions; free under-3s.*

Said to be the biggest science museum in Europe, CosmoCaixa doesn't, perhaps, make the best use of its space. A glass-enclosed spiral ramp runs down an impressive six floors, but represents a long walk to reach the main collection five floors down. Here you'll find the Flooded Forest, a reproduction of a flora- and fauna-filled corner of Amazonia, and the Geological Wall, along with temporary exhibitions.

From here, it's on to the Matter Room, which covers 'inert', 'living', 'intelligent'

One of the real highlights, for both young and old, is the hugely entertaining sound telescope outside on the Plaça de la Ciència.

💙 Monestir de Pedralbes

*Baixada del Monestir 9, Pedralbes (93 256 3434). FGC Reina Elisenda. **Open** Apr-Sept 10am-5pm Tue-Fri; 10am-7pm Sat; 10am-8pm Sun. Oct-Mar 10am-2pm Mon-Fri; 10am-5pm Sat, Sun. **Admission** €5; €3.50 reductions; free under-16s. Free 1st Sun of mth and Sun 3-8pm. No cards.*

In 1326, the widowed Queen Elisenda of Montcada used her inheritance to buy this land and construct a convent for the Poor Clare order of nuns, which she soon joined. The result is a jewel of Gothic architecture; an understated single-nave church with fine stained-glass windows and a beautiful three-storey 14th-century cloister. The place remained out of bounds to the general public until 1983, when the nuns, a closed order, opened it up as a museum (they moved to a nearby annexe). The site offers a fascinating insight into life in a medieval convent, taking you through the kitchens, pharmacy and refectory, with its huge vaulted ceiling. To one side is the tiny chapel of Sant Miquel, with murals dating from 1343 by Ferrer Bassa, a Catalan painter and student of Giotto. In the former dormitory next to the cloister is a selection of illuminated books, furniture and items reflecting the artistic and religious life of the community. The admission charge includes an audio guide.

Parc de la Creueta del Coll

*C/Mare de Déu del Coll 77, Vallcarca (no phone). Metro Penitents. **Open** 10am-sunset daily. **Admission** free.*

Created from a quarry north of Park Güell in 1987 by Josep Martorell and David Mackay the team that went on to design the Vila Olímpica, this park boasts a large swimming pool complete with a 'desert island' and a charming sculpture by Eduardo Chillida: a 50-ton lump of curly granite suspended on cables, called *In Praise of Water*.

Pavellons de la Finca Güell

*Avda Pedralbes 7, Pedralbes (93 317 76 52. www.rutadelmodernisme.com). Metro P Reial. **Open** 10am-4pm daily. Tours in English 10.15am, 11.15am, 3pm. **Admi** €5; €2.50 reductions; free under-11s. cards. **Map** Fold-out B1.*

Industrial textile businessman Eu bought what is now Palau Reial i as a summer home, contracting remodel the entrance lodges a for the estate. In 1883, they be what would be one of Gaudí' in Barcelona for the Güell fa

CosmoCaixa

and then 'civilised' matter: in other words, natural history. However, for all the fanfare that is made by the museum about taking exhibits out of glass cases and making scientific theories accessible, many of the displays still look very dated. Written explanations often tend towards the impenetrable, containing phrases such as 'time is macroscopically irreversible', and making complex those concepts that previously seemed simple.

On the plus side, the installations for children are excellent: the Bubble Planetarium (a digital 3D simulation of the universe); the Toca Toca! space, where mini explorers can get up close and personal with tarantulas and snakes; and the candy-bright Javier Mariscal-designed spaces of Clik (for three- to six-year-olds) and Flash (for seven- to nine-year-olds), where children learn how to generate electricity and how a kaleidoscope works.

also the first project on which Gaudí used his signature *trencadís* (mosaic motif).

The huge gardens were accessed by three entrances, of which only two remain. The Porta del Drac (Dragon's Gate), the most impressive, used to be the private entrance for the Güell family. It was connected to the Güell home in Barcelona by a private, walled road exclusively for their use when the family travelled between the city and the country. Nowadays, the gatehouses belong to the University of Barcelona. The family of Güell's original groundsman still lives in the same small house on the site. The Pavellons must be visited with a guide, and tours are offered in Spanish and English. Really, though, it isn't much of a tour, lasting for about 25 minutes with a look at nothing more than the gate and the stables.

Torre Bellesguard

C/Bellesguard 16 (93 250 4093, www. bellesguardgaudi.com) FGC Avda Tibidabo. Open 10am-3pm daily. Admission €9, €7.20 reduction, free under-8s.

The medievalist lines of this privately owned house are Gaudí's reference to the castle that stood here in the Middle Ages, and acted as country home for King Martí 'the Humane'. It is unmistakeably the work of the master, however, with his trademark sinuous forms, four-sided cross, colourful stained glass and *trencadís* (smashed-tile) benches.

Owned since the 1940s by the Guilera family, members of whom still live here, it has recently been opened to the public. Guided tours (€16) are given in English on Saturdays and Sundays at 11am.

Tramvia Blau

Avda Tibidabo (Plaça Kennedy) to Plaça del Funicular (902 075 027, www.tmb.cat). FGC Avda Tibidabo. Open Nov-Mar 10am-6.15pm Sat, Sun. Apr, Aug, Sept 10am-7.30pm daily. May, June, Oct 10am-7.30pm Sat, Sun. Every 20mins. Tickets €5.50 single. No cards.

Barcelonins and tourists have been clanking ˮ,225m (4,000ft) up Avda Tibidabo in ᵉe 'blue trams' since 1902. When the ᵐ isn't running, a rather more prosaic ᵈ(no.195) takes you up – or you can ᵗit in 15 minutes.

ᵘrants

ᵇre €€

ᵐea 18, Sant Gervasi (93 ᵉtro Diagonal/FGC Gràcia. ᵐ, 8.30-11.30pm Mon-Thur; ᵗSat. Catalan

in this quiet little spot, with ʰioned decor, swathes of

lace and brown table linen. Time often stands still, in fact, between placing an order and receiving any food, but this is all part of 18 Octubre's sleepy charm. Also contributing to its appeal is a roll-call of reasonably priced, mainly Catalan dishes: squid stuffed with meatballs on a bed of *samfaina*; pig's trotter with fried cabbage and potato; and cod with a nut crust and pumpkin purée.

Hisop €€€€

Passatge Marimon 9, Sant Gervasi (93 241 32 33, www.hisop.com). Metro Diagonal or Hospital Clínic. Open 1.30-3.30pm, 8.30-11pm Mon-Fri; 8.30-11pm Sat. Mediterranean

Run by two young, enthusiastic and talented chefs, Hisop aims to bring serious dining to the non-expense-account masses by keeping its prices low and its service approachable – here's hoping its shiny new Michelin star doesn't change all that. The €63 tasting menu (€92 with wine pairing) is a popular choice; dishes vary according to the season, but often include rich 'monkfish royale' (which is served with its liver, a cocoa-based sauce and tiny pearls of saffron) or a pistachio soufflé with kaffir lime ice-cream and rocket 'soup'.

El Petit Bangkok €€

C/Vallirana 26, Sant Gervasi (mobile 640 847 254). Metro Lesseps/FGC Plaça Molina. Open 1-3.30pm, 8-11.30pm Tue-Sat. Closed 1wk Xmas & all Aug. Map Fold-out H2 Thai

Unlike most Thai restaurants in Barcelona, with their trickling fountains and garlanded Buddhas, El Petit Bangkok is bright, simply decorated and a pain to get to. Also unlike most Thai restaurants in Barcelona, Petit Bangkok serves really excellent food – authentic, hot and fantastically cheap dishes, ranging from aromatic tom yam soup to spicy duck rolls.

Other locations C/Balmes 106, Eixample (mobile 616 185 196).

Cafés

Café Berlin

C/Muntaner 240-242, Sant Gervasi (93 200 65 42). Metro Diagonal. Open 9.30am-1am Mon; 9.30am-1.30am Tue; 9.30am-2am Wed; 9.30am-2.30am Thur; 9.30am-3am Fri, Sat.

Downstairs in the basement, the low sofas fill up with amorous couples, while upstairs everything is sleek and light, with brushed steel, dark leather and a Klimt-like mural. A rack of newspapers and plentiful sunlight make Berlin popular for coffee or snacks all day; as well as tapas, there are pasta dishes, *bocadillos* and cheesecake. Note the 20 per cent surcharge for pavement tables.

Flash Flash

*C/Granada del Penedès 25, Sant Gervasi (93 237 09 90, www.flashflashtortilleria.com). FGC Gràcia. **Open** 1pm-1.30am daily.*

Opened back in 1970, this bar was a design sensation in its day, with its white leatherette banquettes and walls imprinted with silhouettes of a life-size, frolicking, Twiggy-like model. The owners describe it as a *tortilleria*, with 60 or so tortilla variations available, alongside a list of child-friendly dishes and adult-friendly cocktails.

Shops & services

L'Illa

*Avda Diagonal 545-557, Sant Gervasi (93 444 00 00, www.lilla.com). Metro Maria Cristina. **Shops** 10am-9.30pm Mon-Sat. **Supermarket & food court** 9.30am-9.30pm Mon-Sat. Mall*

This monolithic mall is designed to look like the Rockefeller Center fallen on its side, stretching 334m (1,100ft) along Avda Diagonal. It features all the usual fashion favourites but also has a good collection of renowned Catalan brands such as Camper, Custo and Antonio Miró. L'Illa has been gaining a good reputation for its food, with specialist gourmet food stalls and interesting eateries such as sushi and oyster bars.

Pedralbes Centre

*Avda Diagonal 609-615, Pedralbes (93 410 68 21, www.pedralbescentre.com). Metro Maria Cristina. **Shops** 10am-9pm Mon-Sat. **Food court** 9.30am-9pm Mon-Sat. Mall*

When this black Rubik's Cube of a building opened in the early '90s, it caused such excitement that it even inspired a short-lived TV soap of the same name. The mall's focus is on upmarket clothes, accessories and homewares, with plenty of local names such as Majoral jewellers and Ingrid Munt in among the likes of Tous and Timberland. The cafés and restaurants appeal to ladies who lunch, with salad buffets, gourmet tapas and a Bubó pâtisserie, along with a crèche, regular catwalk shows and art exhibitions. In winter, the mall's plaza is transformed into an ice rink.

HORTA & AROUND

North of Gràcia are the *barrios* of Horta and Guinardó, the neighbourhoods sprawling uphill into the Collserola hills.

Once a picturesque little village, Horta still remains aloof from the city that swallowed it in 1904. Originally a collection of farms (its name means 'market garden'),

the *barrio* is peppered with old farmhouses, such as **Can Mariner** on C/Horta, dating back to 1050, and the medieval **Can Cortada** at the end of C/Campoamor, which is now a huge restaurant set in beautiful grounds. An abundant water supply also made Horta the place where much of the city's laundry was done: a whole community of *bugaderes* (washerwomen) lived and worked in lovely C/Aiguafreda, where you can still see their wells and open-air stone washtubs.

To the south, joined to Gràcia by Avda Mare de Déu de Montserrat, the steep-sided neighbourhood of **Guinardó**, with its steps and escalators, consists mainly of two big parks. **Parc del Guinardó**, a huge space designed in 1917 (making it Barcelona's third oldest park), is full of eucalyptus and cypress trees, and a relaxing place to escape.

The **Vall d'Hebron** is a leafy area located just above Horta in the Collserola foothills. Here, formerly private estates have been put to public use; among them are the chateau-like **Palauet de les Heures**, now a university building. The area was one of the city's four major venues for the Olympic Games and consequently is rich in sporting facilities, including public football pitches and tennis courts, as well as cycling and archery facilities at the Velòdrom. It's also the home to one of Barcelona's major concert venues. Around these environs there are several striking examples of street sculpture, including Claes Oldenburg's *Matches* and Joan Brossa's *Visual Poem* (in the shape of the letter 'A').

The area also conceals the **Pavelló de la República**, built in 1992 as a facsimile of the emblematic rationalist pavilion of the Spanish Republic designed by Josep

Lluís Sert for the Paris Exhibition in 1937, and later to hold Picasso's *Guernica*. Here, too, is the **Parc del Laberint**, dating back to 1791 and surrounded by a modern park. More modern still is the **Ciutat Sanitària**, Catalonia's largest hospital; a good proportion of *barcelonins* first saw the light of day here.

Sights & museums
Parc del Laberint
Passeig dels Castanyers 1, Horta (010, ajuntament.barcelona.cat/ecologiaurbana). Metro Mundet. **Open** *10am-sunset daily.* **Admission** *€2.23; €1.42 reductions; free under-5s, over-65s; free Wed, Sun. No cards.*

In 1791, the Desvalls family, owners of this marvellously leafy estate, hired Italian architect Domenico Bagutti to design scenic gardens set around a cypress maze, with a romantic stream and a waterfall. The mansion may be gone (replaced with a 19th-century Arabic-influenced building), but the gardens are remarkably intact, shaded in the summer by oaks, laurels and an ancient sequoia. Best of all, the maze, an ingenious puzzle that intrigues those brave enough to try it, is also still in use. Nearby, stone tables provide a handy picnic site. On paying days, last entry is one hour before sunset.

Restaurants
Can Travi Nou €€€
C/Jorge Manrique s/n, Parc de la Vall de Hebron, Horta (93 428 03 01, www.gruptravi.com). Metro Horta or Montbau. **Open** *1-4pm, 8-11pm daily. Catalan*

An ancient rambling farmhouse clad in bougainvillea, perched high above the city, Can Travi Nou offers wonderfully rustic dining rooms with roaring log fires in the winter, whereas in the summer the action moves out to a covered terrace in a candlelit garden. The food is hearty, traditional Catalan cuisine, even though it's a little expensive for what it is, and suffers from the sheer volume being churned out of the kitchen. Puddings are better and served with a *porrón* (a glass jug with a drinking spout) of muscatel. But CTN is really all about location.

Tapas
L'Esquinica
Passeig Fabra i Puig 296, Horta (93 358 25 19). Metro Virrei Amat or Vilapicina. **Open** *8am-midnight Tue-Fri; 8am-4pm, 6.30pm-midnight Sat; 8am-5pm Sun.*

Think of it not as a trek, but as a quest; queues outside are testament to the great value of the tapas. On especially busy nights you'll be asked to take a number, supermarket-style. Waiters will advise first-timers to start with *chocos* (creamy squid rings), *patatas bravas* with allioli, *llonganissa* sausage and *tigres* (stuffed mussels). After which the world is your oyster, cockle or clam.

Quimet d'Horta
Plaça Eivissa 10, Horta (93 358 19 16, www.quimethorta.com). Metro Horta. **Open** *9am-midnight Mon, Tue, Thur, Sun; 9am-1am Fri, Sat. Closed Aug.*

Sadly, Juanito the house parrot has gone to the great perch in the sky (though his image remains on the menu), but the same regulars have been coming to Quimet d'Horta for decades, to chew the fat over a beer in the sunshine. Ciabatta sandwiches are a speciality, and come loaded with every filling imaginable.

POBLENOU & BEYOND

Bordered by the Born and the Eixample, Poblenou stretches north along the coastline, linking up with the area of Diagonal Mar and the Fòrum area.

In its industrial heyday, Poblenou was known as 'little Manchester' due to its concentration of cotton mills. Now, the old mills and other factories are being bulldozed or remodelled as the district is rebranded as a technology and business district, snappily tagged 22@, which will exist side by side with the innumerable garages, exhaust fitters, wheel balancers and car washes that are a feature of the *barrio*.

The main drag, the pedestrianised **Rambla de Poblenou**, dating from 1886, is a much better place for a relaxing stroll than its busy central counterpart, and gives the area a heart. Meanwhile, a bone's throw away, the city's oldest and most atmospheric cemetery, the **Cementiri de Poblenou**, shows that most *barcelonins* spend their death as they did their life: cooped up in large, high-rise blocks. Some were able to afford roomier tombs, many of which were built at the height of the romantic-Gothic craze at the end of the 19th century. A leaflet or larger guide (€15) sold at the entrance suggests a route around 30 of the more interesting monuments.

A few blocks away, at the edge of the Eixample, **Plaça de les Glòries** finally seems ready to fulfil its destiny. The creator of the Eixample, Ildefons Cerdà, hoped that the square would become the new centre of the city, believing his grid-pattern blocks would spread much further north than they did and shift the emphasis of the city from west to east. Instead, it became little more than a glorified roundabout on the way out of town. The ambitious plan is to make this a sizeable 'green zone', and take the traffic underground.

Until recent years, it was best known for its huge commercial shopping complex and the bustling market **Mercat Els Encants** (*see p166*), which has everything from kitchen sinks to dodgy DVDs, now in a new designer home in a purpose-built building to the south of the *plaça*.

Now, however, the *plaça* is home to the long-awaited design museum, the **Museu del Disseny** (*see p190*), known as '*el martell*' (the hammer), for its top-heavy, protruding shape. Next to it is the hugely phallic **Torre Agbar**, designed by French architect Jean Nouvel and owned by the Catalan water board, which has been a bold and controversial project. A concrete skyscraper with a domed head and a glass façade, it's not unlike London's famed Gherkin. Nouvel says its design reflects the Catalan mentality: the concrete represents stability and severity; the glass, openness and transparency. At 144 metres (472 feet), it's Barcelona's third highest building (behind the two Olympic towers) and contains 4,400 multiform windows. Remarkably, it has no air conditioning: the windows let the breeze do the job. Nouvel claims Gaudí is the inspiration for the multicoloured skin – it has 4,000 LED lights that change colour at night – of a building that has already polarised opinion and come to dominate the district. Ask any taxi driver to take you to *el supositori* (the suppository) and they'll know you mean the Torre Agbar.

The walled **Parc Central del Poblenou**, also designed by Nouvel, is one of a number of high-design gardens in Barcelona and features giant plants, an island, a cratered lunar landscape and a perfumed garden. It's only a few years old, and while it might be aesthetically pleasing, only time will tell if the park takes on a life of its own and if the hundreds of weeping willows can survive the rigours of the Mediterranean climate.

Another breath of fresh air is the **Parc del Clot**. Just beyond it is the **Plaça de Valentí Almirall**, with the old town hall of **Sant Martí** and the 17th-century former **Hospital de Sant Joan de Malta** somewhat at odds with the buildings that have mushroomed around them. Further north, up C/Sagrera, the entrance to an old truck factory now leads to the charming **Parc de la Pegaso**. The area also has a fine piece of recent architecture, the supremely elegant **Pont de Calatrava**. Designed by Santiago Calatrava, it links to Poblenou via C/Bac de Roda.

Diagonal Mar & the Fòrum

To many people, the Diagonal Mar development represents the worst hypocrisy of the Barcelona authorities: pure venality dressed up as philanthropy. The stalking horse for the five-star hotels and luxury apartments that were to come was the **Fòrum**, a six-month cultural symposium held in 2004. Its tangible legacy is the enormous conference halls and hotels that draw many wealthy business clients into the city, together with a scarcely believable increase in real-estate values. More recently, the Parc del Fòrum has benefited the city's youth, with its open spaces providing an excellent venue for one of Barcelona's biggest music festivals, **Primavera Sound** (*see p213*).

Coming from the city, the first sign of this resurgent *barri* is **Parc de Diagonal Mar**, containing an angular lake decorated with scores of curling aluminium tubes and vast Gaudían flowerpots. Designed by the late Enric Miralles (of Scottish Parliament fame), the park may not be to most *barcelonins'* taste, but flocks of seagulls have found it an excellent roosting spot. Just over the road from here is the **Diagonal Mar** shopping centre, a three-storey mall of high-street chains, cinemas and the grand **Hotel Princesa**, a triangular skyscraper designed by architect, designer, artist and local hero Oscar Tusquets.

The **Edifici Fòrum**, a striking blue triangular construction by architects Herzog and de Meuron (responsible for London's Tate Modern), is the centrepiece of the €3 billion redevelopment. The remainder of the money was spent on the solar panels, marina, new beach and Illa Pangea, an island 60 metres (197 feet) from the shore, accessible only by swimming. The building itself now houses the **Museu Blau** (Blue Museum), which comprises the main collections of the Natural History Museum, transplanted here from the Born.

It's all in striking contrast to the local residential neighbourhood, **Sant Adrià de Besòs**, a poor district of tower blocks that includes La Mina, an area rife with drug-related crime. It's hoped that the new development will help to regenerate the area, best known for its **Feria de Abril** celebrations in April (*see p215*) – the Andalucían community's version of the more famous annual celebrations in Seville.

Sights & museums

Can Framis
C/Roc Boronat 116-126 (93 320 87 36, www. fundaciovilacasas.com). Metro Glòries. **Open** *11am-6pm Tue-Sat; 11am-2pm Sun.* **Admission** *€5; €2 reductions.*

Set in a stunningly restored 19th-century cotton mill, Can Framis is owned by the Fundació Vila Casas, whose vast collection of artworks is rotated between the three museums they run in Catalonia. The work displayed is from Catalan artists, sculptors and photographers from the last 50 years or so, both unknown and internationally successful. Arguably, however, the star of the show is the building itself, a startling revamp that showcases the building's original features but adds a new element of sharp angles and poured concrete, with sunlight pouring through plate glass to illuminate the displays in a refreshingly natural way.

Museu Blau
Plaça Leonardo da Vinci 4-5, Parc del Fòrum (93 256 60 02, www.museuciencies.cat). Metro El Maresme-Forum. **Open** *Oct-Feb 10am-6pm Tue-Fri; 10am-7pm Sat; 10am-8pm Sun. Mar-Sept 10am-7pm Tue-Sat; 10am-8pm Sun.* **Admission** *€6; €2.70 reductions; free under-16s. Free to all 1st Sun of mth.*

The Universal Forum of Cultures in 2004 was a vastly ambitious, wildly expensive attempt to put Barcelona back on the world map after years basking in the afterglow of the 1992 Olympic Games. It was pretty much an unmitigated flop, but it did leave one positive legacy in the form of some architecturally striking buildings. One such building was Herzog and de Meuron's Edifici Fòrum, a glittering creation, painted deep blue and crisscrossed with mirrored strips that give it a marine effect. Since 2011 it has been the new home of the Museum of Natural History, now also known as the Museu Blau (Blue Museum), after the building that houses it.

The museum combines the two collections of the former zoology and geology museums in Parc de la Ciutadella, whose buildings will now be given over to archiving and studying the materials.

The museum is said to be structured around James Lovelock's Gaia hypothesis, which views the earth as a self-regulating organism, though – so far, at least – this isn't obvious from the collection. Despite the breathlessly modern architecture that surrounds it, this is a strictly old-school affair of glass cases and formaldehyde jars, enlivened by some dramatic lighting and the odd touchscreen.

It begins with the geology section, which includes meteorites, gems, crystals, radioactive minerals and rocks from the earth's lithosphere. There's an extensive collection of fossils and funghi, and the zoology section features dozens of stuffed animals, preserved insects and molluscs, though not much attempt is made to contextualise them.

Several animals from the collections have enjoyed a moment of fame being lent out for TV and theatre shows, and the horned Mouflon skull was the direct inspiration for the Oscar-winning faun make-up in the film *Pan's Labyrinth*.

♥ Museu del Disseny
Plaça de les Glòries 37 (93 256 68 00, www. ajuntament.barcelona.cat/museudeldisseny) Metro Glòries. **Open** *10am-8pm Tue-Sun.* **Admission** *Permanent exhibition €6, €4 reduction. Temporary exhibition €4.40, €3 reduction. Combined ticket €8, €5.50 reduction.* **Map** *Fold-out N7.*

This huge monolith, squatting at the side of Plaça de les Glòries, houses the collections from the former museums of clothing, decorative arts and ceramics. The collection from the old Textile and Clothing Museum provides a chronological tour of fashion, from a man's Coptic tunic from a seventh-century tomb through to Karl Lagerfeld's creations. There are many curiosities, such as an 18th-century bridal gown in black figured silk and the world's largest collection of kidskin gloves, but the real highlight is the haute couture collection.

The Museum of Decorative Arts' collection is informative and fun, and looks at the different styles informing the design of artefacts in Europe since the Middle Ages. A second section is devoted to post-war Catalan design of objects as diverse as urinals and man-sized inflatable pens.The collections from the erstwhile Ceramics Museum are equally fascinating, showing how 13th-century Moorish ceramic techniques were developed after the Reconquista with the addition of colours (especially blue and yellow) in centres such as Manises, in Valencia, and Barcelona. There is also a section on 20th-century ceramics, including many by Miró and Picasso.

MONTSERRAT

It's unsurprising that Montserrat is seen as the spiritual heart of Catalonia. The vast bulbous-peaked sandstone mass dominates the landscape to the west of Barcelona, its appearance creating a mystical aura that's made this rocky range a centre of worship and veneration for centuries. These days, Montserrat (meaning jagged mountain') is something of a tourist trap and gets unbearably crowded in the summer. But an excursion is still worthwhile, if only for the views.

In the Middle Ages, Montserrat was an important pilgrimage destination, as **Santa Maria de Montserrat** (www. montserratvisita.com), the Benedictine monastery that sits near the top, became the jewel in the crown of a politically independent fiefdom. Surrounded by a number of tiny chapels and hermitages, the monastery is still venerated by locals, who queue in the 16th-century basilica to say a prayer while kissing the orb held by **La Moreneta** (the Black Virgin). Open 7am to 7.30pm daily, the basilica is at its most crowded around 1pm Monday to Friday, when the celebrated boys' choir sings mass. Elsewhere in the monastery, there's a museum stocked with fine art by the likes of Picasso, Dalí, El Greco, Monet and Caravaggio, as well as collections of liturgical gold and silverware, archaeological finds and gifts for the Virgin.

If all this piety isn't to your taste, it's still worth the trip up the mountain by road, cable car or rack railway. The tourist office gives details of walks to the various caves; among them is **Santa Cova** where the statue of the Black Virgin was discovered, reachable via funicular or a 20-minute hike from the monastery. The most accessible hermitage is **Sant Joan**, also 20 minutes or a funicular ride away. But the most rewarding trek is the lengthy one to the peak of **Sant Jeroni**, which offers 360-degree views from a vertigo-inducing platform.

In the know
Walking in Catalonia

Catalonia's hills and low mountain ranges are great for hiking and biking. In many places, it's made easier by GR (*gran recorregut*) long-distance footpaths, marked with red-and-white signs. Good places for walking within reach of the city include **Parc de Collserola** (see *p182*) and **Montserrat**. Another useful website with good walk information is www.catalunya. com. To purchase maps, try **Altaïr** (see *p165*) or **Llibreria Quera** (C/Petritxol 2, 93 318 07 43).

Santa Maria de Montserrat

Museu del Disseny & Torre Agbar

Finally, there is a floor devoted to graphic design, as interesting historically as it is visually, showing the progression of book covers, posters and packaging design from the end of the Civil War to the 1980s.

Restaurants

♥ El 58 €€

*Rambla Poblenou 58 (93 601 39 03, www. facebook.com/el58poblenou). Metro Poblenou. **Open** 1-4pm, 7-11pm Tue-Sat; 1-4pm Sun. French/Spanish*

El 58 (pronounced '*cinquante huit*' thanks to its partly French ownership) is something of an oasis in an area bafflingly short on good eating options, for all the hoo-ha about Poblenou as the latest cool 'hood in which to live. Recommended dishes include the superb *patatas bravas* (the home-made sauce is a cut above the usual) to share, followed by a warming *tartiflette* in winter, or maybe razor clams with pomegranate.

Els Pescadors €€€

*Plaça Prim 1 (93 225 20 18, www.elspescadors. com). Metro Poblenou. **Open** 1-3.45pm, 8-11pm daily. Closed 1wk Christmas. Seafood*

In a forgotten, almost rustic, square of Poblenou lies this first-rate fish restaurant, with tables under the canopy formed by two huge and ancient *ombú* trees. Start with crunchy sardine skeletons as an aperitif (trust us, they are delicious), and move on to tasty fried *chipirones*, followed by cod and pepper paella or creamy rice with prawns and smoked cheese. Creative desserts include the likes of strawberry gelatine 'spaghetti' in a citric soup. The waiters are masters of their art.

Bars

♥ Balius

*C/Pujades 196 (93 315 86 50, www.baliusbar. com). Metro Poblenou. **Open** 5pm-1am Tue-Thur; 4pm-3am Fri, Sat; 4pm-1am Sun.*

Until a couple of years ago, Balius was an old-time drugstore, its windows stacked high with shampoo and bleach. The name and fabulously retro façade have stayed intact, but its interior has been transformed into a glamorous cocktail bar, filled with sunlight by day and romantically lit by night.

Shops & services

Diagonal Mar

*Avda Diagonal 3 (93 567 76 37, www. diagonalmarcentre.es). Metro El Maresme-Fòrum. **Shops** 10am-10pm Mon-Sat. **Food court & entertainment** 10am-midnight Mon-Thur; 10am-1am Fri, Sat; noon-midnight Sun. Mall*

This three-level mall at the sea end of Avda Diagonal has an airy marine theme and a sea-facing roof terrace filled with cafés and restaurants of the fast-food variety. As well as major anchors, such as an Alcampo supermarket, Zara, Primark and FNAC, there's a particular emphasis on children's clothes and toy shops, plus plenty of smaller global brands (Superdry to Swarovski). Extras include a wheelchair-lending service and golf carts in which to drive your purchases to your car; for the kids, there's a crèche, a play area and miniature cars for hourly rental. The centre provides free Wi-Fi.

Day Trips

Just two hours separate sand from snow in this part of the world. But that's not all: a gastronomic heritage, pretty villages, fine wines and amazing festivals all add to the appeal of Catalonia. Just a short ride from Barcelona, a very different atmosphere awaits – a world of monasteries, vineyards and market towns. You'll also find attractive and manageable cities such as Girona and Tarragona, better beaches such as those at Sitges or Castelldefels and, at Colònia Güell, more of Gaudí's fantastical creations. Hire a car and you'll have even more freedom to explore some of Catalonia's honey-coloured villages. But in many cases, the transport is part of the fun – take the cog-wheel train or cable car that ascends the mountain of Montserrat to its famous abbey.

❤ Don't miss

1 Girona *p198*
Medieval buildings and futuristic food.

2 Penedès *p206*
Grape expectations.

3 Sitges *p203*
Picture-perfect seaside town.

4 Tarragona *p204*
A wealth of Roman remains.

5 Tossa de Mar *p197*
Head straight to its ancient core.

Roman column in Tarragona

194

In the know
Essential information

The **Palau Robert** tourist centre in Passeig de Gràcia (*see p308*) is a hub of useful information about the region. **Catalunya Turisme** (www.catalunya.com) is another thorough guide.

The **Estació d'Autobusos Barcelona-Nord** (C/Alí Bei 80, 902 260 606, www.barcelonanord.cat, fold-out map L8) is the principal bus station for services in Catalonia.

RENFE trains (902 320 320, www.renfe.es) serve much of the region, and stop at **Sants** station, and some at **Passeig de Gràcia**, **Estació de França** or **Plaça Catalunya**. RENFE's local and suburban trains (*rodalies/cercanías*) are integrated into the metro and bus fares system (*see p295* Arriving & Leaving).

For more information on public transport, visit the Generalitat's website, www.mobilitat.org, and see Gettting Around *pp295-299*.

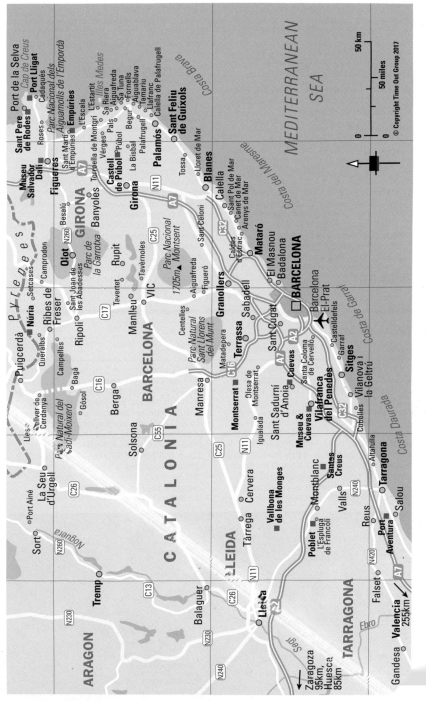

ARAGON

CATALONIA

LLEIDA

TARRAGONA

GIRONA

BARCELONA

BARCELONA

MEDITERRANEAN SEA

Pyrenees

Costa Brava

Costa del Maresme

Costa de Garraf

Costa Daurada

Noguera

 Segre

Ebro

N230
N240
C13
C26
N260
N420
A7
A2
N11
C55
C16
C17
C25
C32
C37
AP7

Port Aïné
Sort
Tremp
Balaguer
Lleida
Falset
Gandesa
Valencia 255km
Zaragoza 95km, Huesca 85km
Reus
Salou
Port Aventura
Valls
Tarragona
Altafulla
Cubelles
Cunit
Vilanova i la Geltrú
Sitges
Castelldefels
Garraf
Santa Coloma de Cervelló
Vilafranca del Penedès
Museu & Cuevas
Sant Sadurní d'Anoia
Igualada
Olesa de Montserrat
Montserrat
Manresa
Solsona
Berga
Gósol
Bagà
Campelles
Queralbs
Bellver de Cerdanya
Lles
La Seu d'Urgell
Puigcerdà
Núria
Ribes de Freser
Setcases
Camprodon
Sant Joan de les Abadesses
Ripoll
Campdevànol
Taverte
Tavertet
Manlleu
VIC
Centelles
Aiguafreda
Figueró
Granollers
Sabadell
Terrassa
Sant Cugat
Matadepera
Parc Natural Sant Llorenç del Munt
Cervera
Tàrrega
Vallbona de les Monges
Poblet
L'Espluga de Francolí
Montblanc
Santes Creus

Parc Natural del Cadí-Moixeró

Parc de la Garrotxa

Parc Nacional 1705m Montsent

Museu Salvador Dalí
Figueres
Besalú
Banyoles
GIRONA
Girona
Olot
Rupit
Tavèrnoles

Sant Pere de Rodes
Port de la Selva
Cap de Creus
Port Lligat
Cadaqués
Roses
Parc Nacional dels Aiguamolls de l'Empordà
Sant Martí d'Empúries
Empúries
L'Escala
L'Estartit
Illes Medes
Torroella de Montgrí
Verges
Sa Riera
Pals
Castell de Púbol
Púbol
La Bisbal
Begur
Sa Tuna
Aiguafreda
Aiguablava
Fornells
Tamariu
Llafranc
Palafrugell
Calella de Palafrugell
Sant Feliu de Guíxols
Palamós
Tossa
Lloret de Mar
Blanes
Calella
Sant Pol de Mar
Canet de Mar
Arenys de Mar
Sant Celoni
Caldes d'Estrac
Mataró
El Masnou
Badalona
BARCELONA
Barcelona El-Prat
Cuevas

0   50 miles
0   50 km

© Copyright Time Out Group 2017

It's a good idea to eat before you leave or bring something with you: the characterless, pricey restaurants on Montserrat are best avoided.

Essential information

Montserrat Tourist Office *Plaça de la Creu (93 877 77 77, www.montserratvisita.com).* **Open** *9am-6.45pm daily.*

Getting there
A Julià bus (93 402 69 00, www. autocaresjulia.es) leaves at 9.15am from Sants bus station and returns at 5pm (6pm July-Sept); journey time 80mins.

FGC trains (93 205 15 15, www.fgc.net) from Plaça d'Espanya run roughly every half-hour from 6.17am to Aeri de Montserrat (journey time 1hr) for the cable car (€10.30 return, departs every 15mins, last car 5.45pm in winter, 7pm in summer); or to Monistrol de Montserrat (4mins later) for the rack train (which leaves at 48mins past the hour) to the monastery. The last cable car/rack train is at 6.15pm (8.35pm July-mid Sept). FGC offers all-inclusive packs which include train ticket, cable car, rack railway, and admission to museum and exhibitions.

THE COSTA BRAVA

In its heyday, the Costa Brava was the most exclusive resort area in Spain, attracting film stars, artists and writers to its sandy beaches. By the 1970s, though, things had changed. Encouraged by the local authorities, package tours from the UK descended on the area, and all manner of tacky restaurants and ugly apartment blocks soon followed. The area, which covers the stretch of coast between Blanes and the French border, is blighted by its reputation as the playground of unimaginative British holidaymakers. However, there's plenty to enjoy if you know where to stop.

Most of the good stuff is further north. Ruined by holiday-home high-rises, the towns of **Blanes** and **Lloret del Mar** boast enviable locations but are really

Colònia Güell
Gaudí's unfinished yet fascinating church

Just near Barcelona, on the western outskirts of Santa Coloma de Cervelló, stands the unusual Colònia Güell (C/Claudi Güell 6, 93 630 58 07, www.gaudicoloniaguell.org). Textile baron Eusebi Güell commissioned Antoni Gaudí to build a garden city for the textile workers around the factory where they worked. Like so many of Gaudí's projects, it was never completed – in this case because Güell's funding ran dry. But Gaudí did finish the crypt of the church, an extraordinary achievement, with a ribbed ceiling, twisted pillars and textbook examples of Gaudí's use of the 'catenary' arch – so named after the form a chain takes when you let it hang. (You can see this most clearly in the model for the church in the Sagrada Família.)

Note that the Colònia Güell is sometimes closed for private events (weddings, funerals, communion), so call ahead before making a special trip. Mass is at 8pm on Saturdays, 11am and 1pm on Sundays. To get there, take a 20-minute train from Plaça d'Espanya (2-4 per hour) to Colònia Güell station and follow the blue steps along the floor to the visitors' centre.

t avoided. Continue, instead, to **Tossa Mar**, the southern entry to the Costa Brava proper and by far the loveliest town on this stretch. The painter Marc Chagall once described it as a 'blue paradise'; Ava Gardner spent so much time here with lover Frank Sinatra that they erected a statue in her honour. The new town has been constructed with little thought, but Tossa has retained one of Spain's most handsome medieval quarters.

The twisting 20-kilometre (12-mile) drive through coastal pine forests from here to **Sant Feliu de Guíxols** offers brief but unforgettable views of the sea. And when you arrive, Sant Feliu itself has superb Modernista buildings along the Passeig Marítim. Other sights include the free-to-enter Benedictine monastery, **Monestir de Sant Feliu de Guíxols** (Plaça Monestir, 972 82 15 75, www.guixols.cat/museu), which incorporates the celebrated Porta Ferrada, a tenth-century portico, and the town museum, which houses part of the Carmen Thyssen-Bornemisza Catalan art collection. Sant Feliu also pulls in big names for an excellent music festival every summer (www.festivalportaferrada.cat). **Sant Pol** beach is three kilometres north of the crowded town sands, and offers more towel room.

A scenic ten-kilometre walk begins at the northern end of Sant Pol beach. The GR92 path, or **'Camino de Ronda'**, starts out from below the Hostal de la Gavina in S'Agaró, where Ava and Frank spent much of their time, and continues on along many secluded coves and rocky outlets for swimming. The sandy bay of **Sa Conca**, considered to be one of the most beautiful beaches on the Costa Brava, has a couple of good *xiringuitos* for a sardine lunch. From here, there's a tedious stretch through the ugly **Platja d'Aro** that then picks up and takes you all the way to **Torre Valentina**,

from where you can catch a bus back to Sant Pol.

Palamós has never really recovered from an attack by the infamous pirate Barba Roja (Redbeard) in 1543; the most exciting thing about the town is its famous and terrifyingly expensive giant red prawns. Continue, instead, to the area around **Palafrugell**, which has pretty villages built into its rocky coves. All of them make great bases for a little leisurely beach-hopping. The **Fundació Vila Casas** (Plaça Can Mario 7, 972 30 62 46, www.fundaciovilacasas.com) in Palafrugell itself houses a good collection of works by local artists and sculptors, and gives an idea of the kind of creativity the environment inspires.

Calella de Palafrugell, not to be confused with its ugly near-namesake down the coast, is a lively and attractive town sitting around a clear water bay. The cliff-top botanical gardens at **Cap Roig** (972 61 45 82, obrasociallacaixa.org/en/centros/jardines-de-cap-roig) host a music and arts festival every July and August, attracting names such as Status Quo and Rod Stewart (www.caproigfestival.com). Nearby **Llafranc** is not quite as pretty but has a long curved beach where you can swim between fishing boats in the bay.

Tamariu, known for its good seafood, is the perfect base for scuba-diving and fishing. **Giro Náutic** (www.gironautic.com) is a useful portal for all things aquatic in the area. Next up is **Aiguablava**, with its modern parador and white sandy beach, and **Fornells** – the town that inspired Norman Lewis's *Voices of the Old Sea*, now much changed. Both are accessible from **Begur**, as is the small **Aiguafreda**, a cove that's sheltered by pines.

Beyond the Ter estuary and the Montgri hills, which divide the Baix and Alt Empordà, is **L'Estartit**. This small resort town caters for tourists interested in exploring the **Illes Medes**, a group of rocky

DAY TRIPS

Ava Gardner statue in Tossa de Mar

Girona

limestone outcrops. The biggest housed a British prison in the 19th century, but Les Illes are now home only to a unique ecosystem, an underwater paradise where divers can contemplate colourful coral and hundreds of different species of sea life. For a view of the islands, it's worth the climb up to the 12th-century **Castell de Montgrí**.

Essential information

L'Estartit Tourist Office *Passeig Marítim (972 75 19 10, www.visitestartit.com).* **Open** *June, Sept 9.30am-2pm, 4-8pm daily. July, Aug 9am-9pm daily. Oct-Apr 9am-1pm, 3-6pm Mon-Fri; 10am-2pm Sat, Sun. May 9am-1pm, 4-7pm daily.*

Palafrugell Tourist Office *Avda Generalitat 33 (972 300 228, www. visitpalafrugell.cat).* **Open** *Sept-June 10am-5pm Mon-Fri; 10am-1pm, 4-7pm Sat; 9.30am-1.30pm Sun. July, Aug 9am-8pm daily.*

Sant Feliu de Guíxols Tourist Office *Plaça Monestir (972 82 00 51, www.guixols.cat).* **Open** *Mid June-mid Sept 10am-9.15pm daily. Mid Sept-mid June 10am-6pm Mon-Sat; 10am-5pm Sun.*

Getting there
Sarfa (902 30 20 25, www.sarfa.com) runs six buses daily to Tossa de Mar (journey time 1hr 20mins), seven buses daily to Sant Feliu (1hr 25mins), and seven to Palafrugell (2hrs 15mins); some continue to Begur and Torroella. All leave from Estació del Nord. Change at Torroella for L'Estartit (10mins, www.ampsa.org) or get the train to Girona and then a bus (1hr).

GIRONA

For travellers in search of big-city facilities without big-city stress, Girona is a classy compromise. The city combines a healthy dose of culture with more hedonistic pursuits: within its beautifully restored medieval heart sits an imposing cathedral and some interesting museums. In addition, some of the region's best restaurants can be found here, along with a handful of smart bars.

The **River Onyar** divides the Old City from the new, and connects one to the other by the impressive Eiffel-designed bridge, the **Pont de les Peixateries**. A walk up the lively riverside **Rambla de la Llibertat** takes you towards the city's core and its one major landmark, the magnificent **Catedral de Girona** (Plaça del Catedral, 972 42 71 89, www.catedraldegirona.org). The building's 1680 Baroque façade conceals a graceful Romanesque cloister and understated Gothic interior, which boasts the widest nave in Christendom. In the cathedral treasury is the stunning 12th-century **Tapestry of Creation** and the **Beatus**, an illuminated set of tenth-century manuscripts. Note that during mass, you can only visit the cathedral's treasury and cloister.

Before their expulsion in 1492, the city's many Jews had their own district: the **Call**, whose labyrinthine streets running off and around the C/Força are among the most beautifully preserved in Europe. The story of the community is told in the Jewish museum in the **Centre Bonastruc ça Porta** (C/Força 8, 972 21 67 61, www.girona.cat/call), built on the site of a 15th-century synagogue.

Heading north from here, the **Mudéjar Banys Àrabs** (C/Ferran el Catòlic, 972 19 07 97, www.banysarabs.cat) is actually a Christian creation, a 12th-century bathhouse blending Romanesque and Moorish architecture. The nearby monastery of

DAY TRIPS

Pablo be damned. Sure, the artist has his admirers; and, in Barcelona, he's celebrated by a fine museum. But north-east of the city, close to the French border, another very different artist dominates: Salvador Dalí, who lived and worked in this corner of Catalonia. Several Dalí-related landmarks remain open to the public today; see www.salvador-dali.org.

Start just east of Girona at the 12th-century **Castell Gala-Dalí** (Plaça Gala Dalí, Púbol, 972 48 86 55) bought by Dalí to house his wife-muse Gala (who's buried here) in her later years. Relations were strained by the time she moved in: Dalí had to book appointments to see her, and the tomb that he prepared for himself lies empty (he changed his mind), guarded by a stuffed giraffe and two oversized chess knights.

Due north lies Figueres, the capital of the Alt Empordà region and Dalí's birthplace. The artist donated many of his works to the **Teatre-Museu Dalí** (Plaça Gala-Salvador Dalí 5, 972 67 75 00), housed in the town's old theatre, and also redesigned the place, putting thousands of yellow loaves on the external walls and huge eggs on its towers. The highlight is the three-dimensional room-sized Mae West face, a collection of furniture arranged to look like the star when viewed

from a certain angle; a plump red sofa takes the place of her famous pout. And if you're wondering what happened to Dalí's body after seeing the empty tomb at the Castell de Gala-Dalí, wonder no more: he's buried here.

The tomb that Dalí prepared for himself lies empty, guarded by a stuffed giraffe and two oversized chess knights

East of here, on the coast, lies relatively isolated Cadaqués, another former Dalí haunt. The artist spent his childhood summers here, then brought his surrealist circle along and eventually built his home – now a museum – in nearby Port Lligat. The **Casa-Museu de Port Lligat** (972 25 10 15) is filled with zany furniture, peculiar fittings and stuffed animals, offering an extraordinary insight into the genius's lifestyle. Early booking is required – only eight people are allowed in at a time.

Teatre-Museu Dalí

DAY TRIPS

Sant Pere de Galligants is a fine example of Romanesque architecture, its 12th-century cloister rich with intricate carvings. It also houses the **Museu Arqueològic** (C/Santa Llúcia 8, 972 20 26 32, www.mac.cat), which shows objects from the Paleolithic to the Visigothic periods. Continuing from here, the **Passeig Arqueològic** runs along what's left of the old city walls, intact until 1892. One of the main draws of Girona, however, is the **Celler de Can Roca** (C/Can Sunyer 48, 972 22 21 57, www.cellercanroca.com, €€€€). Located in a quiet suburb, it has twice been awarded the top slot in the World's 50 Best Restaurants list. Booking is essential, although you may get lucky with a last-minute cancellation. The restaurant's tasting menu starts at €180 and it is closed Mondays and Sundays, plus three weeks at Christmas.

Essential information

Girona Tourist Office *Rambla de la Llibertat 1 (972 226 575, www.girona.cat/ turisme).* **Open** *Apr-Sept 9am-8pm Mon-Fri; 9am-2pm, 4-8pm Sat; 9am-2pm Sun; Nov-Mar 9am-7pm Mon-Sat, 9am-2pm Sun.*

Getting there
Empresa Sagalés (902 13 00 14, www. sagales.com) runs approximately five buses daily (three on Sun) from Estació del Nord (journey time approx 1hr 40mins).

RENFE trains from Sants or Passeig de Gràcia (approx 1hr 20mins) leave hourly, 6am-9.45pm daily. You can also get the pricey (but popular) **AVE** high-speed train to Girona – from Sants, the journey takes 38 mins.

VIC & AROUND

Just 45 minutes away by train from the centre of Barcelona, Vic provides a handy taste of Catalan rural life. The beech forests, medieval villages, steep gorges and Romanesque hermitages make this area rewarding to explore by car, on foot or by bicycle, but it's also a centre of both paragliding and hot air ballooning.

At the town's heart is the impressive arcaded **Plaça Major**, home to a famous market on Tuesday and Saturday mornings that's nearly as old as the town itself. It's good for picking up local basketware, terracotta pots and, of course, the town's famous *embotits* (cured sausages), which are among the best in Spain. The **Museu Episcopal** (Plaça del Bisbe Oliba 3, 93 886 93 60, www.museuepiscopalvic.com) is worth a visit for its magnificent 12th-century murals and a superb collection of Romanesque and Gothic art.

There are also other architectural gems. In one corner of the market square is the Modernista **Casa Comella**; graffiti depicts the four seasons and was designed by Gaietà Buïgas, who was also responsible for the Monument a Colom in Barcelona. Vic also has many interesting churches, and the **Catedral de Sant Pere** (Plaza de la Catedral,

In the know
From the air

For hot air balloon rides, see **Osona Globus** (93 889 33 36, www.aircat.cat), which offers experiences from €130 per person (€80 under-12s, free under-4s).

Ski for a Day

An easy one-day visit to the slopes

The best bet for a skiing day trip is the resort of **La Molina** (972 89 20 31, www.lamolina. cat), which you can reach on a train or bus package called **Ski Tren** (€41 adult, €31 child, includes train and ski pass) or **Ski Bus** (€39 Wed, €54 Sat, includes bus, ski pass and insurance). A RENFE train from Plaça Catalunya at 6.08am, 7am or 9.36am takes you to La Molina train station, from where you catch a bus up to the resort. Trains return at 5.58pm and 7.17pm (check the timetable in the station or www.renfe.com). The ski bus service, run by **Sagalés** (www.sagales. com, 902 13 00 14), departs on Mondays, Wednesdays, Fridays and Saturdays at 6.45am and returns at 4pm. There are ski runs to suit all standards.

La Molina

www.bisbatvic.com/catedral.htm) contains Romanesque, Gothic and neo-classical elements, along with a set of dramatic 20th-century murals by Josep María Sert, who is buried here. The **Temple Romà** (C/ Pare Xifré 2), rediscovered in 1882 when the 12th-century walls that surrounded it were knocked down, now houses a municipal gallery (www.patronatestudisosonencs.cat).

There's more of note outside the town. Following the C153 road towards Olot, **Rupit** is an ancient village built on the side of a medieval castle, its fairytale air enhanced by a hanging bridge across the Ter gorge. Later building has been done so sympathetically that it's difficult to tell the old from the new. Almost as lovely, and not quite as touristy, is nearby **Tavertet**.

Essential information

Vic Tourist Office *Plaça Pes (93 886 20 91, www.victurisme.cat). Open 10am-2pm, 4-8pm Mon-Fri; 10am-2pm, 4-7pm Sat; 11am-2pm Sun.*

Getting there

Empresa Sagalés (902 13 00 14, 93 889 25 77) runs buses throughout the day from Estació del Nord and/or C/Casp 30 (journey time 1hr 10mins) to Vic. For Rupit, take a local bus from Vic.

RENFE from Sants or Plaça Catalunya to Vic. Trains leave about every hour (journey time 1hr 20mins).

DOWN THE COAST TO SITGES

The sands in Barcelona have become cleaner in recent years, but they can still seem grubby in comparison to those found a short train ride away. Either side of the city, up and down the coast, lie a number of beautiful beaches that make a welcome and relatively isolated break from the hurly-burly of the city itself. Add the cluster of small, handsome towns that adjoin the beaches, and you have plenty of reasons to make your escape for an afternoon or more.

About half an hour south from Passeig de Gràcia station, the **Castelldefels** is a broad strand of sand. The backdrop of urban sprawl is particularly unlovely, but there's plenty of towel space to compensate. The beach is also something of a mecca for kite-surfers, as well as other watersports. Try **Escola Náutica Garbi** (Passeig Marítim 271-275, mobile 609 752 175, www.escolagarbi. com) for equipment.

Two stops beyond the Castelldefels lies the tiny and relatively undiscovered port of **Garraf**. Its small curved beach is backed by green-and-white striped bathing huts, and the steep-sided mountains that surround it mean that development is not a worry. At the northern tip of the bay sits the **Celler de Garraf**, a magical Modernista creation built by Gaudí for the Güell family in 1895 but now home to a restaurant. Behind the village stretches the **Parc del Garraf**

Catalonia's Gay Mecca

Elegant little Sitges is also the region's most flamboyant party town

To the surprise of many, Sitges is charmingly pretty and family-orientated during the day. But its Jekyll and Hyde character is revealed during hot summer nights, when the town is bustling with gay partygoers. The **Platja dels Balmins** beach to the north of the centre is where to preen and be seen, preferably in your birthday suit. If you would rather not have to stare directly into your neighbour's armpit, hit the seafront and walk right for an hour or so until you reach the **Platja de l'Home Mort** nudist beach (with corresponding cruising ground behind).

Bars & nightclubs

Sitges has a definite circuit, which begins around midnight with an early drink at one of the many pavement cafés on **C/Primer de Maig**, aka Sin Street. Most other bars start filling up around 1.30am. For those who want to dance, **Privilege** (C/Bonaire 24, www.privilegesitges.com) fits the bill, and those who want to cruise will like **Bunker** (C/Bonaire 15, www.parrots-sitges.com). For other night-time activities, just head for the beach.

Accommodation

Carnival week in February, the Pride festival in June and the whole of August can be a nightmare, so booking three months in advance is advisable if you want to get anything decent. This goes in particular for **El Xalet** (C/Illa de Cuba 35, 93 811 00 70, €) and its sister **Hotel Noucentista** (C/Illa de Cuba 21, 93 810 26 66, www.hotelnoucentista.com, €), both of which occupy Modernista palaces and are furnished with period furniture.

Almost next door is **Hotel Liberty** (C/Illa de Cuba 45, 93 676 69 50, www.libertyhotelsitges.com, €), which has spacious rooms, a lush garden and, if you feel like splashing out, a luxury penthouse with two terraces overlooking the town. The owners also have 41 apartments for rent in town; for more details, see www.staysitges.com.

The romantics' choice, naturally, is **Hotel Medium Romàntic**, a beautifully restored 19th-century house with a secluded palm-filled garden (C/Sant Isidre 33, 93 894 83 75, www.mediumhoteles.com, €). In a quieter residential area is the welcoming, French-run **Hotel Los Globos** (Avda Nuestra Señora de Montserrat 43, 93 894 93 74, www.hotellosglobos.com, €), recently renovated with new bathrooms and with a balcony or private garden for each room.

nature reserve, with hiking and biking trails (marked out on maps available from the tourist office in Sitges).

Further south along the coast, the pretty, whitewashed streets of **Sitges** do double-duty. In summer, they're packed with party-goers – since the 1960s, this has been Spain's principal gay resort, served by a hotchpotch of bars and nightclubs. In winter, though, it's a different story: the scene is far more relaxed, and it's a mellow place for a getaway.

In the 19th century, the town was a fashionable retirement spot for local merchants who had made their fortunes in the Caribbean. More than a hundred of the palaces owned by '*los americanos*', as they were known, are dotted around the centre of town. To find out more, pick up an excellent booklet from the tourist office.

Sitges's highest building, topping a rocky promontory, is the pretty 17th-century church of **Sant Bartomeu i Santa Tecla** (Plaça de l'Ajuntament 20), offering wonderful views of the sea. Behind the church is the extraordinary **Museu Cau Ferrat** (museusdesitges.cat), a collection of ancient and modern art founded in 1893 by the artist Santiago Rusiñol and described by some as a 'temple of Modernisme'. Nearby is the **Palau Maricel** (C/Fonollar, 93 894 03 64, www.museusdesitges.cat), an old hospital that's been converted into a Modernista palace and is now used as a concert hall in summer. The building contains medieval and Baroque paintings and sensuous marble sculptures. Also worth a look is the **Museu Romàntic** in the handsome **Casa Llopis** (C/Sant Gaudenci 1, 93 894 29 69, museusdesitges.cat), which portrays the lifestyle of the 19th-century family that once lived there.

Those who prefer messing about in boats are served well at the **Port Esportiu Aiguadolç**. The **Centro Náutico Aiguadolç-Vela** (93 811 31 05, www.advela. net) rents out sailing boats and organises sailing excursions. To escape the crowds on Platja de Sant Sebastià or those south of the town centre, head just beyond the Port of Aiguadolç to **Platja de Balmins**, a hidden oasis with an excellent restaurant, **La Caleta** (Platja del Balmins, 93 811 20 38, lacaletadesitges.es, €€).

▶ *For details of our accommodation price categories, see p288.*

Essential information

Castelldefels Tourist Office *C/Pintor Serrasanta 4 (93 635 27 27, www. castelldefelsturismo.info). Open 10am-2pm, 4-7pm Mon-Fri.*

Sitges Tourist Office *Plaça Eduard Maristany 2 (93 894 42 51, www.sitgestur. com). Open mid June-mid Oct 10am-2pm, 4-8pm Mon-Sat; 10am-2pm Sun. Mid Oct-mid June 10am-2pm, 4-6.30pm Mon-Fri; 10am-2pm, 4-7pm Sat; 10am-2pm Sun.*

Getting there

Mon-Bus (93 893 70 60, www. monbus.cat) runs a frequent service – 7am-11.20pm Mon-Fri, 7.20am-10.20pm Sat, 9.20am-11.20pm Sun – from Ronda Universitat 33 to Sitges (journey time 45mins), and an hourly night service Mon-Thur, Sun between 12.13am and 3.13am back to Barcelona.

Frequent **trains** leave from Passeig de Gràcia for Platja de Castelldefels (20mins) and Sitges (35mins), though not all stop at Castelldefels and Garraf.

TARRAGONA

Tárraco, as the Romans knew Tarragona, was once Catalonia's biggest powerhouse. Dating back to 218 BC, it was one of the first Roman cities to be built outside Italy; it was constructed with a flourish that ticked all the Roman boxes for hedonism, while also serving as a more sensible centre for commerce. The town is gradually being restored: modern-day Tarragona rather nattily integrates its crumbling ruins with modern town planning and an increasingly hip dining and wining scene. It's all far more appealing than the area's other main attraction: the ghastly but immensely popular **Port Aventura** theme park, a short drive from the town.

The **Passeig Arqueològic** (Avda Catalunya, 977 24 57 96), the path along the Roman walls that once ringed the city, has its entrance at **Portal del Roser**, one of three remaining towers. In the old part of town, Roman remains include the ancient Pretori – a praetorium, used as both palace and government office, and reputed to have been the birthplace of Pontius Pilate (Plaça del Rei, 977 23 01 71). Nearby, the ruined **Circ Romans** (Rambla Vella 2, 977 23 01 71) was where the chariot races were held, while the **Museu Nacional Arqueològic** (Plaça del Rei 5, 977 23 62 09, www.mnat.cat) is home to an important collection of Roman artefacts and mosaics.

To see all of the **Catedral de Santa Maria**, not to mention an impressive collection of religious art and archaeological finds, you'll need to visit the **Museu Diocesà**

(C/Claustre 5, 977 22 36 71, museu.dio. arquebisbattarragona.cat). The cathed. was built on the site of a Roman temple to Jupiter, and is Catalonia's largest. The glorious cloister was built in the 12th and 13th centuries; the carvings alone are worth the trip.

Leading from the Old Town towards the sea, the **Passeig de las Palmeres** runs to the **Balcó del Mediterrani** and overlooks the **Roman amphitheatre** (Parc de l'Amfiteatre Romà, 977 24 22 20). The same street also leads to the shop-packed, pedestrianised **Rambla Nova**, from where you can follow C/Canyelles to the **Fòrum de la Colònia** (C/Lleida, 977 24 25 01) and the remains of the juridical basilica and Roman houses.

But while the town's history remains dominant, the biggest news in Tarragona in recent years has been the recent gentrification of **El Serrallo**. This old port area now boasts fountains and slick promenades, upmarket fish restaurants and, in one of the old warehouses, the **Museu del Port** (Refugi 2, Moll de Costa, 977 25 94 00, www.porttarragona.cat), displaying the usual maritime accoutrements.

In the know
Tarragona tickets

An all-in ticket for sites belonging to the **Museu d'Història de Tarragona** (MHT, museuhistoria.tarragona.cat) is €7.40 (€3.65 reductions, free under-16s). This includes: the Pretori, Circ Romans, Roman amphitheatre and Fòrum. Entry to a single venue is €3.30.

ort Aventura

Splashing good fun

Port Aventura (977 77 90 90, www. portaventura.es), is a highly popular theme park with some 90 rides spread across five internationally themed areas (Mexico, the Wild West, China, Polynesia and the Mediterranean). The truly stomach-curdling Dragon Khan rollercoaster is one of the park's highlights for older kids; for the little ones, there's the usual slew of carousels and spinning teacups. There are also 100 daily live shows and a spectacular lakeside Fiesta Aventura with lights, music and fireworks. Trains from Passeig de Gràcia take approximately 1 hour 30 minutes. Tickets are €45 (€39 reductions, free under-4s) and there's also the option of a night ticket (7pm-midnight, €26, €21 reductions). Check the website for opening times.

Roman aqueduct outside Tarragona

Essential information

Tarragona Tourist Office *C/Major 39 (977 25 07 95, www.tarragonaturisme.cat).*
Open *Oct-June 10am-2pm, 3-5pm Mon-Fri; 10am-2pm, 3-7pm Sat; 10am-2pm Sun. July-Sept 10am-8pm Mon-Sat; 10am-2pm Sun.*

Getting there
Alsa (902 42 22 42, www.alsa.es) runs six buses daily from Barcelona Nord station, and one from Barcelona Sants station (journey time 1hr 30mins).

RENFE trains run from Sants or Passeig de Gràcia to Tarragona. Trains depart half-hourly (journey time 1hr 18mins).

Catedral de Santa Maria, Tarragona *p204*

WINE COUNTRY

An easy day trip south-west from Barcelona lie Catalonia's best-known wine regions, with a range of *denominaciones de origen* (DOs) from the workaday **Penedès** to the prestigious **Priorat**. With numerous companies offering guided tours, and the wineries themselves now opening their doors to visitors, Spain is becoming a serious destination for oenophiles.

The Penedès comprises gently undulating hills and ancient Roman routes. It's the most accessible destination if you're limited to public transport – you can reach it in about an hour by train. At its heart is **Vilafranca**, a handsome medieval town with a lively Saturday market and the elegant 14th-century **Basílica de Santa Maria**. The town's wine museum, **Vinseum** (Plaça Jaume I 1-5, 93 890 05 82, www. vinseum.cat), has displays covering ancient winemaking tools, as well as a train for taking visitors out to the vineyards. It's closed on Mondays and free the first Sunday of the month.

The two main wineries in the area are both owned by the Torres family and offer entertaining tours, but you'll need your own transport, or a taxi, to take you there. **Torres** (Finca El Maset, Pacs del Penedès, www. torres.es) is Penedès' largest winemaker; but for serious wine-lovers, the more cutting-edge **Jean León** (Pago Jean León, 93 817 76 90, www.jeanleon.com) has a sleek tasting room that looks on to a sea of vines (tours from €10.50). Nearby **Albet i Noya** (Can Vendrell de la Codina, Sant Pau d'Ordal, 93 899 48 12, www.albetinoya.cat) was Spain's first organic winery and now leads the way in restoring traditional, pre-phylloxera varietals to the area. Its €10 tour includes tasting the produce too. There's also **Can Ràfols dels Caus** (Avinyonet del Penedès, 93 897 00 13, www.canrafolsdelscaus.com), which produces superb pinot noir and delightful pink bubbles and has a cool designer *bodega*. Tours here are a shade steeper at €20.

North of here is **Sant Sadurní d'Anoia**, the capital of the Penedès cava industry: 90 per cent of Spain's cava is made here, a fact celebrated during Cava Week (www. turismesantsadurni.com/cavatast) every October. It's not a pretty town, but its wine producers are at least easily accessible on public transport. **Codorníu** (Avda Codorníu, 93 891 33 42, www.codorniu.com), one of the largest producers, offers a theme park-style tour of its Modernista headquarters, designed by Puig i Cadafalch – your €12 admission ticket includes taking a train through parts of the 26 kilometres (16 miles) of underground cellars, and finishes, of course, with a tasting. Elsewhere, **Freixenet**

Codorníu winery

(C/Joan Sala 2, 93 891 70 00, www.freixenet. es) is opposite Sant Sadurní station.

The Priorat area is renowned for its full-bodied (and full-priced) red wines. Monks were producing wine here as long ago as the 11th century, but the area had been all but abandoned as a centre of viticulture when young winemaker **Álvaro Palacios** set up a tiny vineyard here in the late 1980s. He battled steep hills and a rather sceptical wine industry, but within a few years he won global acclaim; the region is now one of Spain's most exclusive.

The small **Alella** district, east of Barcelona, is best known for light, dry whites, but more important is **Terra Alta**; near the Priorat in Tarragona, with Gandesa as its capital, the area is famous for its heavy reds. **Montsant**, another local DO, is also growing in popularity.

▶ See p38 Catalonia Uncorked for more on choosing your regional tipple.

In the know
Wine tours

Touring wineries can be a great way of exploring the area. Booking is nearly always necessary, so do plan ahead. You can combine a few of the wineries through **El Molí Tours** (www.elmolitours.com), which offers boozy sip-and-cycle day trips of the area.

Essential information

Sant Sadurní d'Anoia Tourist Office
*C/Hospital 21 (93 891 31 88, www. turismesantsadurni.com). **Open** 9.15am-2.45pm, 4-6.30pm Tue-Fri; 10am-2pm, 4.30-7pm Sat; 10am-2pm Sun.*

Vilafranca del Penedès Tourist Office
*C/Hermenegild Clascar 2 (93 818 12 54, www.turismevilafranca.com). **Open** 3-6pm Mon; 9.30am-1.30pm, 3-6pm Tue-Sat; 10am-1pm Sun.*

Getting there
Hispano Igualadina (93 890 11 51, 902 29 29 00, www.igualadina.com) provides 8-12 buses daily to Vilafranca del Penedès from Sants (journey time 55mins). **Hillsa** (93 091 25 61, www.hillsabus.com) runs about 12 services daily (fewer at weekends) to Sant Sadurní d'Anoia from the corner of C/ Urgell and C/París (journey time 45mins). **Hispano Igualadina** (93 804 44 51) runs two buses daily from Sants to Gandesa.

RENFE trains go from Sants or Plaça Catalunya; hourly 5.30am-11pm (journey time 50mins), then taxi for Torres, Jean León and Codorníu. Also six trains daily (2hrs 20 mins) from Sants or Passeig de Gràcia to Mora la Nova. From here, catch a bus to Gandesa.

Experience

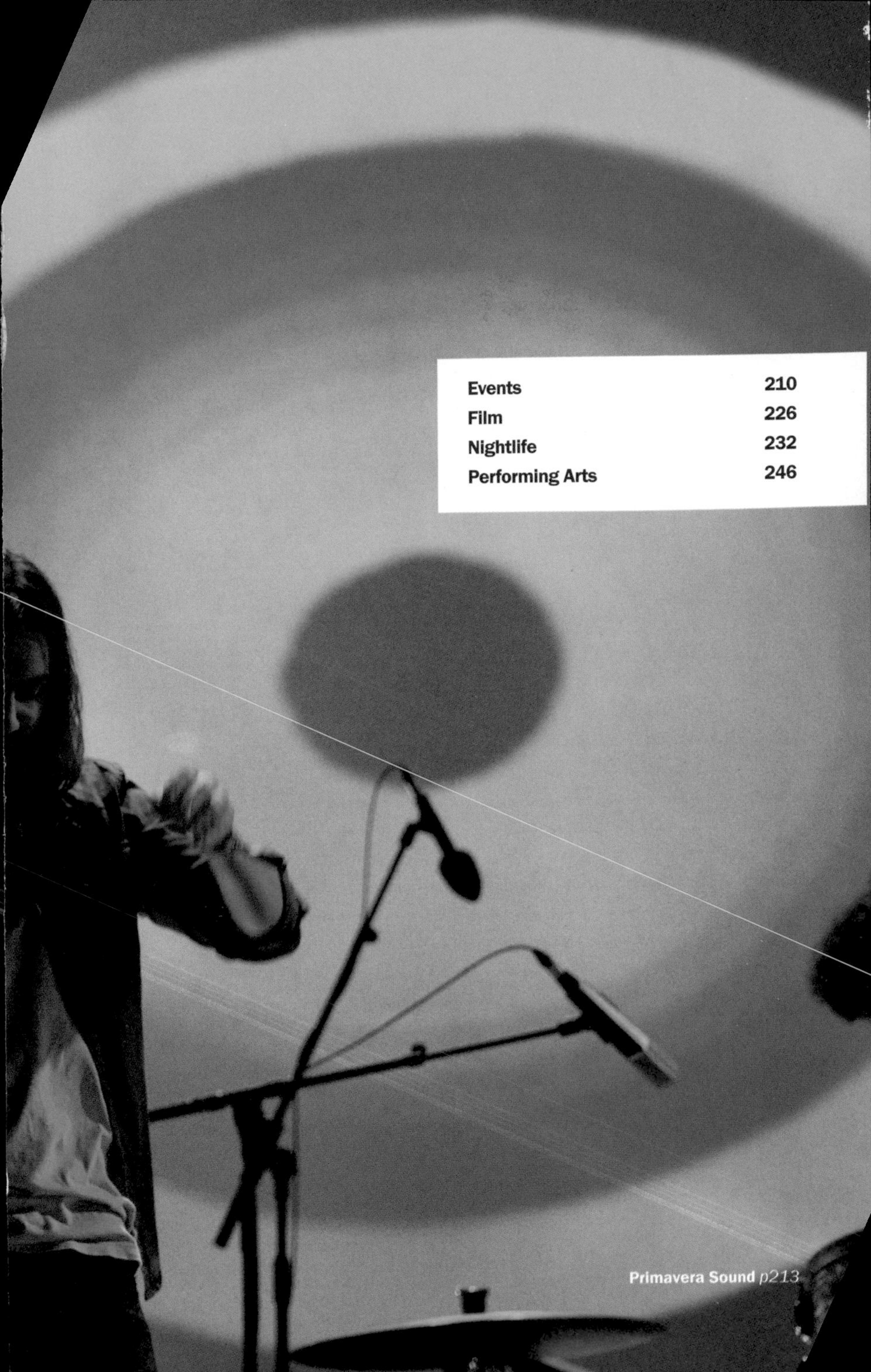

Events

A rundown of Barcelona's packed calendar

The Catalans' seemingly endless enthusiasm for festivals and parties means that there's scarcely a week in the year that doesn't include at least a couple of events. These range from the full-on traditional knees-up, with giants, dwarfs and dragons wheeling through fireworks, to gentle street fairs selling artisanal honey and sausages, and perhaps laying on a bouncy castle.

The array of religious events and old-fashioned pageants, all of which spotlight what makes Catalonia unique, are supplemented by a wide variety of more modern celebrations. You're just as likely to stumble across a festival of rock documentaries, graffiti art, hip hop or cyber sculpture as you are to see a traditional parade: renowned music and technology festival Sónar attracts some 80,000 people each year.

▶ *Many events take place on or around public holidays, when most of the city's shops, bars and restaurants close; these are marked★*

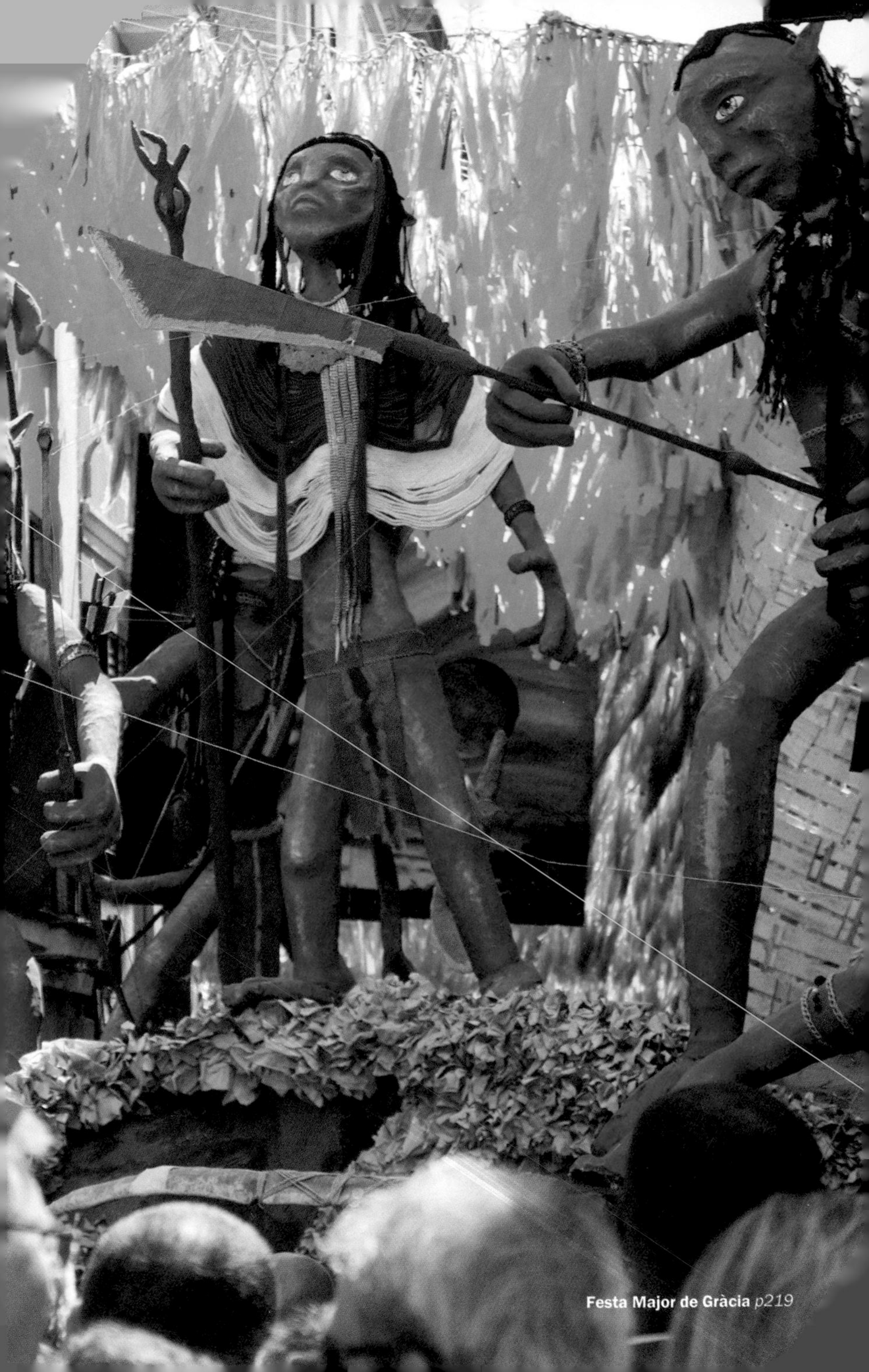

Spring

Guitar BCN

Various venues (www.theproject.es).
Date Feb-June.

This prestigious festival of guitars has the ability to attract world-class players. Previous guests have included Pat Metheny and Paco de Lucía. Styles span everything from flamenco to Latin sounds, classical guitar and gypsy jazz.

Festes de Sant Medir de Gràcia

Gràcia to Sant Cugat (www.santmedir.org).
Starting point Metro Fontana. Date 3 Mar.

On or around the feast day of St Emeterius (Sant Medir in Catalan), for almost 200 years colourfully decorated horse-drawn carts have gathered around the Plaça Trilla to ride up to his hermitage in the Collserola hills. The most popular element is the carts, which circle the streets of Gràcia and shower the crowd with 100 tons of blessed boiled sweets.

Setmana Santa

Kosmopolis

CCCB, Raval (see 114, www.cccb.org/kosmopolis). Metro Universitat. Date held in odd-numbered years. Map p109 G8.

Subtitled the 'International Literature Festival', Kosmopolis runs every other year and explores every aspect of the written word (and indeed the oral tradition), with conferences, workshops and readings, though the roster of international authors has become more modest of late.

Marató Barcelona

Around the city (93 431 55 33, www. zurichmaratobarcelona.es). Starting point Plaça Espanya. Date mid Mar.

Barcelona's hugely popular annual marathon starts and ends at Plaça Espanya.

Setmana Santa ★ (Holy Week)

Barri Gòtic & throughout the city.
Date wk leading up to Easter.

Easter for Catalans is a relatively sober affair, with none of the pageantry embraced by their southern cousins. The main event is the blessing of the palms on *diumenge de rams* (Palm Sunday). Crowds surge into the cathedral clutching bleached palm fronds bought from stalls around the city; these are then used to bring luck to households. On Good Friday, a series of small processions and blessings takes place in front of the cathedral. On Easter Sunday, godparents dole out the *mones*: handsome chocolate confections that are more elaborate than humble Easter eggs.

Open Tennis

Real Club de Tennis Barcelona-1899, C/Bosch i Gimpera 5, Les Corts (96 580 76 36, www. barcelonaopenbancosabadell.com). Metro María Cristina, FGC Reina Elisenda, bus 63 or 78. Date Apr.

The annual Open Comte de Godó tournament in Pedrables is considered one of the ATP circuit's most important clay-court tournaments.

La Cursa del Corte Inglés

Around the city (www.cursaelcorteingles. net). Starting point Passeig de Gràcia. Date Apr.

Barcelona's 11km (seven-mile) fun run starts at Passeig de Gràcia and is free to enter, attracting more than 80,000 participants.

Fira de la Terra

Parc de la Ciutadella & Passeig Lluís Companys, Born (p94, www.diadelaterra. org). Metro Arc de Triomf. Date 2 days mid Apr. Map p90 K10.

Primavera Sound

Parc del Fòrum (see p189, www.primavera sound.com). Metro El Maresme/Fòrum. **Date** *May.*

For a long time, this four-day Maytime music festival was seen as Sónar's poor relation, an indie playground where bed-headed boys and girls wearing twee hair clips and crocheted scarves could work up to an appreciative shimmy to Belle and Sebastian. Then it exploded. Suddenly Primavera was pulling in 200,000 people and was attracting the kind of names that monster festival Benicàssim, a couple of hours' drive south, could only dream of.

Though it gets better year after year, it's hard to imagine that any line-up could top that of 2016, whose bigger names included Radiohead, PJ Harvey, Sigur Rós, LCD Soundsystem, Air, Tame Impala and Richard Hawley, along with superb world music acts such as Orchestra Baobab; the obligatory dinosaur headliner, in this case

Brian Wilson; and some beautifully offbeat invitees, such as legendary film composer/ director John Carpenter.

The festival is held at the Parc del Fòrum, which overlooks the sea and is great by day, but some chilly nights have been known. Wear comfortable shoes, too – there is very little grass and distances between stages are not short. After a massive effort in 2016 to improve the facilities, there are now plentiful Portaloos and catering options, as well as itinerant beer sellers (beware of fake euro notes, however – not easy to spot in the dark).

Tickets sell out quickly and are not cheap, but the first day is free to all (and in 2017 featured Saint Etienne, Kate Tempest and the Wedding Present), and the organisers put on free concerts around the city over the same period. Most of these take place on outdoor stages in the Raval or the Parc de la Ciutadella, though there are (ticketed) concerts at Sala Apolo (*see p239*) and BARTS (*see p238*).

Castellers at Festes de la Mercè

The Fira de la Terra is a two-day eco-festival held around Earth Day (22 April). There are child-friendly handicrafts, food stalls and performances, along with talks on environmental issues.

Sant Jordi
La Rambla (see p74) & throughout the city. **Date** *23 Apr.*

On the feast day of Sant Jordi (St George), the patron saint of Catalonia, nearly every building bears the red and gold Catalan flag, while bakeries sell Sant Jordi bread streaked with red *sobrassada* pâté. Red roses decorate the Palau de la Generalitat and the city's many statues and paintings of George in all his dragon-slaying glory.

It's said that as the drops of the dragon's blood fell, they turned into red flowers – and for more than five centuries, this has been the Catalan version of St Valentine's Day. Men traditionally gave women a rose tied to an ear of wheat, and women reciprocated with a book; this is also the 'Day of the Book'. It accounts for an amazing 10% of Catalonia's annual book sales, and street stalls and bookshops give good discounts.

Feria de Abril de Catalunya
Fòrum (www.fecac.com). Metro El Maresme-Fòrum. **Date** *1 wk Apr/May.*

A pale imitation of Seville's grand Feria de Abril, this week-long, sprawling and joyously tacky event is still a whole heap of fun, especially for fans of fried squid and candyfloss. The rows of decorated marquees are a sea of polka dots, as young and old twirl on and off the stages, and onlookers glug sherry and scoff some of the greasiest food imaginable. It's great for children, and there's a funfair.

Dia del Treball★ (May Day)
Various venues. **Date** *1 May.*

A day of demonstrations and marches led by trade unionists representing various left-wing organisations. The main routes cover Plaça da la Universitat, Via Laietana, Passeig de Gràcia, Passeig Sant Joan and Plaça Sant Jaume.

Fira de Sant Ponç
C/Hospital, Raval. Metro Liceu. **Date** *11 May.* **Map** *p109 G9.*

A street market held in honour of the patron saint of beekeepers and herbalists, and ablaze with candied fruit, fresh herbs, natural infusions, honey and honeycomb, most of it straight off the farmer's cart.

Festival Traditions
Castellers, correfoc and sardana

From September's spectacular Festes de la Mercè to the other 30 or so neighbourhood *festes* – some very low key – you'll find a wild variety of events in Barcelona. The city's festivals share many traditional ingredients: dwarfs, *castellers* (human castles), and *gegants* (huge papier-mâché/fibreglass giants dressed as princesses, fishermen, sultans and even topless chorus girls). There are also two unique not-to-be-missed exercises: the *correfoc* and the *sardana*.

The *correfoc* ('fire run') is a frenzy of pyromania. Groups of horned devils dance through the streets, brandishing tridents that spout fireworks and generally flouting every safety rule in the book. Protected by cotton caps and long sleeves, the more daring onlookers try to stop the devils and touch the fire-breathing dragons being dragged along in their wake.

The orderly antidote to this pandemonium is the *sardana*, Catalonia's folk dance. Watching the dancers executing their fussy little hops and steps in a large circle, it's hard to believe that *sardanes* were once banned as a vestige of pagan witchcraft. The music is similarly restrained; a reedy noise played by an 11-piece *cobla* band. The *sardana* is much harder than it looks, and the joy lies in taking part rather than watching.

To try Catalan folk dancing for yourself, check out the *sardanes* held in front of the cathedral (Jan-Aug, Dec noon-2pm Sun; Sept-Nov 6-8pm Sat, noon-2pm Sun) and in the Plaça Sant Jaume (Oct-July 6pm Sun).

Spanish Grand Prix

Circuit de Catalunya, Ctra de Parets del Vallès a Granollers, Montmeló (93 571 97 00, www.circuitcat.com). By car C17 north to Parets del Vallès exit (20km/13 miles). **Date** *May.*

Barcelona boasts one of the world's finest racing circuits at Montmeló and tickets for the Spanish Grand Prix can be hard to come by, so book well in advance.

Barcelona Poesia & Festival Internacional de Poesia

Various venues (93 316 10 00, lameva. barcelona.cat/barcelonapoesia). **Date** *1wk mid May.*

This poetry festival started in 1393 as the courtly Jocs Florals (Floral Games), named after the prizes: a silver violet for third prize; a golden rose as second; and, naturally, a real flower for the winner. The games died out in the 15th century but were resuscitated in 1859 as a vehicle for the promotion of the Catalan language. Prizes went to the most suitably florid paeans to the motherland; these days, though, many different languages can be heard at the festival – Spanish is permitted, as are Basque and Galician.

Festa Major de Nou Barris

Nou Barris (lameva.barcelona.cat/ noubarris). Metro Virrei Amat. **Date** *mid May.*

What the humble neighbourhood of Nou Barris lacks in landmark architecture, it makes up for with vim. Along with some great cultural programming, it has a very lively *festa major*, attracting top-notch local bands, along with the usual parades and street fairs. The Nou Barris flamenco festival runs concomitantly, and also brings in some big names.

Ciutat Flamenco

CCCB, Raval (see p114, 93 443 43 46, ciutatflamenco.com). Metro Catalunya. **Date** *mid May.* **Map** *p109 G8.*

Although there are plenty of traditional performers featured in this four-day festival, hard-line flamenco purists should be warned that it includes DJs fusing the Andalucian music with anything from electronica to jazz and rock.

Dia Internacional dels Museus

Various venues (icom.museum/activities/ international-museum-day). **Date** *mid May.*

Masterminded by the International Council of Museums, this worldwide day of free museum entrance has an annual theme with related activities. La Nit dels Museus is a newer initiative, where 21 museums free entry on the previous night from 7p 1am (lameva.barcelona.cat/lanitdelsmuse

Festa dels Cors Muts de la Barceloneta

Barceloneta. Metro Barceloneta. **Date** *Whitsun weekend.*

In a Pentecostal tradition dating back 150 years, more than 20 choirs of workers parade through the streets of the *barrio* in elaborate costumes garlanded with objects typical of their profession – nets and oars for a fisherman, cereal boxes and sausages for a grocer – on the Saturday morning before Whitsun. They then pile into coaches and take off on a weekend jolly, returning for more parading, fireworks and revelry on Monday evening.

Sant Joan *p218*

La Tamborinada

Parc de la Ciutadella, Born (see p94, 93 414 72 01, www.fundaciolaroda.cat). Metro Ciutadella-Vila Olímpica. **Date** *early June.* **Map** *p90 K10*

Aimed at children, this vibrant one-day festival fills the Ciutadella park with concerts, workshops and circus performances. Games and entertainments run from snakes and ladders to a towering wall for rock-climbing.

L'Ou Com Balla

Barri Gòtic (www.bcn.cat/icub). Metro Jaume I. **Date** *Corpus Christi.* **Map** *p71 H9*

L'Ou Com Balla (the 'dancing egg') is a local Corpus Christi tradition dating from 1637: a hollowed-out eggshell is set spinning and bobbing in apparent *perpetuum mobile* on the spout of various fountains, garlanded for the occasion with flowers. The Sunday Corpus Christi procession leaves from the cathedral in the early evening; on the Saturday, there's free entry to the Ajuntament, the Palau Centelles behind it and the Museu d'Història de Barcelona, along with *sardanes* (circle dances) at 7pm by the cathedral.

Sónar

Various venues (93 320 81 63, www.sonar.es). **Date** *mid June.*

This three-day festival of what they term 'advanced music' and 'multimedia art' remains a must for anyone into electronic music, urban art and media technologies. The event is divided into two parts. SónarDay

comprises multimedia art, record fairs, conferences, exhibitions and sound labs, while DJs play. Later, SónarNight means a scramble for the desperately overcrowded shuttle bus from the bottom of La Rambla out to the vast hangars of the site in Hospitalet (tip: a cab between four costs the same), to soak up copious concerts and DJs.

Sant Joan★
Throughout the city. **Date** *night of 23 June.*

In the weeks leading up to the feast of St John, the streets become a terrifying war zone of firecrackers and cowering dogs. This is mere limbering up for the main event – on the night of 23 June there are bonfires and firework displays all over the city, but especially at the beach, running until dawn. Cava is the traditional tipple, and piles of *coca* – flat, crispy bread topped with candied fruit – are consumed. The 24th is a much-needed holiday.

Gran Trobada d'Havaneres
Passeig Joan de Borbó, Barceloneta (www. amicsdeleshavaneres.com). Metro Barceloneta. **Date** *last Sat in June.* **Map** *p124 J10.*

The barnacled legacy of Catalonia's old trade links with Cuba, *havaneres* are melancholy 19th-century shanties accompanied by accordion and guitar. The main event is at the port town of Calella de Palafrugells, but the Barcelona satellite is no less fun. Performances by groups dressed in stripy shirts, with salty sea-dog names such as *Peix Fregit* (fried fish) and *Xarxa* (fishing net), are followed by *cremat* (flaming spiced rum) and fireworks.

Música als Parcs
Various venues (ajuntament.barcelona.cat/ ecologiaurbana). **Date** *June-Aug.*

This series of free, weekly alfresco concerts runs throughout the summer months in some of Barcelona's loveliest parks. It comprises two cycles; there's jazz from June to August on Wednesdays and Fridays at 10pm in Ciutadella park in front of the fountain and, in July, young musicians perform a varied classical concert programme from Thursday to Saturday in various parks. A municipal band boosts the programme on occasional Thursdays with crowd-pleasers from Gershwin, *West Side Story* and the like.

Grec Festival de Barcelona
Various venues (lameva.barcelona.cat/grec). **Date** *late June-early Aug.*

Named after the Greek amphitheatre (Teatre Grec) that forms such an integral part of its programming, this is the major cultural festival of the year. It brings together dozens of shows from around the world, encompassing dance, music, theatre and circus, drawing over 150,000 spectators. Increasingly there are performances in English, with Catalan surtitles. The free four-day festival Dies de Dansa (Festival of Dance, www.marato.com) runs within the Grec Festival in early July.

Cruïlla BCN
Parc del Fòrum (www.cruillabarcelona.com). Metro El Maresme-Fòrum. **Date** *2 days mid July.*

Cruïlla has lost a little of its oompf in recent years, but still bags some good acts for its small two-day festival of world music, R&B, rap, reggae and various other genres. Acts lined up for 2017 include Youssou N'Dour and The Lumineers.

Festa Major del Raval
Raval. Metro Drassanes or Liceu. **Date** *mid-late July.*

Over three days, entertainments include giants, a flea market, children's workshops and free concerts on the Rambla del Raval. This particular *festa major* prides itself on multiculturalism, with music from around the world and ethnic food stalls.

Nits d'Estiu CaixaForum
CaixaForum, Montjuïc (see p141, 93 476 86 00, obrasociallacaixa.org). Metro Plaça Espanya. **Date** *every Wed in July, Aug.* **Map** *139 B8.*

Many museums hold a Nits de Estiu (Summer Nights) programme in July and August, but CaixaForum has one of the best. All exhibitions are open until midnight, and there are concerts of varying stripes, films and other activities.

Sala Montjuïc
Castell de Montjuïc, Montjuïc (see p141, www. salamontjuic.org). Metro Paral·lel. **Date** *July-early Aug.* **Map** *p139 C11.*

A blend of classics and recent independent cinema is shown three times a week throughout July, transforming the grassy moat of the castle into an outdoor

---

In the know
Festes majors

Each year, every neighbourhood in Barcelona holds their own *festa major*, or 'big party'. Unless a specific website is given, information on each *festa major* can be found at lameva.barcelona.cat/ culturapopular in the lead-up to the event.

nema. Bring a picnic and turn up arly for the live music; deckchairs are available for €3. There is a free shuttle bus service from Plaça Espanya.

San Miguel Mas i Mas Festival

Various venues (www.masimas.com). Date Aug.

This tasteful music festival has gone from concentrating on Latin sounds to providing a little bit of everything. Concerts take place at five venues, including the Palau de la Música (*see p98*).

Gandules

CCCB, Raval (see p114, 93 306 41 00, www. cccb.org). Metro Universitat. Date 10pm Tue-Thur in Aug. Map p109 G8.

A series of films is screened in the deckchair-strewn patio of the CCCB. It gets extremely crowded, so make sure you arrive early if you want any chance of getting a seat.

Festa de Sant Roc

Various venues around Plaça Nova, Barri Gòtic. Metro Jaume I. Date 12-16 Aug. Map p71 H9.

The Festa de Sant Roc, which has been celebrated every year since 1589, is the Barri Gòtic's street party. It's hard to beat for lovers of Catalan traditions: there are parades with the giants and fat heads, *sardana* dancing and 19th-century street games. The festivities, which centre on the Plaça Nova

in front of the cathedral, conclude with a *correfoc* and fireworks.

Festa Major de Gràcia

Gràcia (93 459 30 80, www. festamajordegracia.cat). Metro Fontana. Date 3rd wk in Aug.

The main event at Gràcia's extravagant *festa major* is its street competition, where residents transform some 25 streets into pirate ships, rainforests and Jurassic landscapes. The festival opens with giants and castles in Plaça Rius i Taulet, and climaxes with a *correfoc* and a *castell de focs* (castle of fireworks). In between, there are some 600 activities, from concerts to *sardanes* and bouncy castles. Recent years have been marred by vandalism and late-night scuffles with the police.

Festa Major de Sants

Sants (93 490 62 14, www.festamajordesants. net). Metro Plaça de Sants or Sants Estació. Date late Aug.

One of the lesser-known *festes majors*, Sants has a traditional flavour, with floral offerings to images of St Bartholomew at the local church and the market. Major events, such as the *correfoc* on the night of the 24th, can be found in the Parc de l'Espanya Industrial; others are held at Plaça del Centre, C/Sant Antoni, Plaça de la Farga and Plaça Joan Peiro, behind Sants station.

Festes de la Mercè p221

Autumn

Diada Nacional de Catalunya★
Throughout the city. **Date** *11 Sept.*

Catalan National Day commemorates Barcelona's capitulation to the Bourbon army in the 1714 War of the Spanish Succession, a bitter defeat that led to the repression of many Catalan institutions. It's lost some of its vigour but is still a day for national re-affirmation, with the Catalan flag flying on buses and balconies. There are marches throughout the city, the centre being the statue of Rafael Casanova (who directed the resistance) on the Ronda Sant Pere.

Festival L'Hora del Jazz
Various venues (93 268 47 36, www.amjm. org). **Date** *Sept.*

A month-long festival of local jazz acts, with free concerts taking place in the Plaça Vilà de Gràcia on Sunday lunchtimes and various venues during the week at night. Some night-time concerts are also free of charge.

Festival Asia
Various venues (www.festivalasia.es). **Date** *during the Festes de la Mercè, Sept.*

This week of twirling saris, Chinese acrobats, music, workshops and stalls from 13 Asian countries, includes over 150 artists in eight venues, including the MACBA (*see p111*) and the CCCB (*see p114*).

Barcelona Acció Musical (BAM)
Various venues (lameva.barcelona.cat/bam). **Date** *during the Festes de la Mercè, Sept.*

BAM stages free concerts, often showcasing jazz and singer-songwriters, on Plaça del Rei; more famous names perform outside the cathedral. Running for over 20 years, BAM promotes leftfield *mestissa* (vaguely ethnic fusion) in its mission to inspire the city to explore new sounds.

Festa Major de la Barceloneta
Barceloneta. Metro Barceloneta. **Date** *late Sept/early Oct.*

This tightly knit maritime community throws itself into the local *festes* with incredible gusto. The fun kicks off with fireworks on the beach, a 24-hour football tournament, *falcons* (acrobatic groups), *sardana* dancing and a free tasting of traditional crispy *coca* bread washed down with muscatel, and ends with more of the same ten days later. In between, expect parades, music, fire-breathing dragons, open-air cinema and bouncy castles. Look out, too, for a character called General Bum Bum, who parades with a wooden cannon but stops periodically to fire sweets into crowds of scrabbling children.

LEM Festival
Various venues, Gràcia (lemfestival. wordpress.com). **Date** *Oct.*

The main focus of the dynamic Gràcia Territori Sonor collective is the month-long LEM festival during autumn. Held in various venues, it's a rambling series of musical happenings, many experimental, improvised and electronic; most are free.

Sitges Festival Internacional de Cinema de Catalunya
Sitges (see p203, 93 894 99 90, www. sitgesfilmfestival.com). **Date** *2wks Oct.*

If rattling doorknobs, piercing screams, spilling guts and headless wraiths are your thing, then there's only one place for you to be when October comes around. What began modestly in 1968 as a week of fantasy and horror movies has become one of the most well-respected genre festivals in the world. It now attracts A-list stars, while at the same time staying small and intimate enough to attract local fans. Fans and stars mix in the bar and garden of the Hotel Meliá, the festival's focal point.

Caminada Internacional de Barcelona
Around the city (93 402 30 00/010, www. euro-senders.com/internacional). Starting point Auditori del Centre Cívic Cotxeres de Sants. Metro Plaça de Sants. **Date** *Oct.* **Map** *Fold-out A6*

The International Walk is conducted along two routes (one is 20km/12 miles and the other, 30km/19 miles).

Open House BCN
Throughout the city (www.48hopenhousebarcelona.org). **Date** *2 days late Oct.*

In line with the Open House weekend held in many countries, Open House BCN opens over 150 architecturally important or historically interesting buildings to the

EVENTS

Top 20

❤ Festes de la Mercè

Plaça Sant Jaume, Barri Gòtic (lameva.barcelona.cat/merce).
Metro Jaume I. **Date** *week of 24 Sept.* **Map** *p71 H9.*

This week-long event held around 24 September in honour of
the patron saint of the city, Our Lady of Mercy, marks the end
of the long hot summer, and is a time when friends reconnect
after the holidays and the kids are allowed a couple more late
nights before the term begins in earnest. It's a dizzying affair,
with more than 600 events taking place all over the city.

It kicks off with giants, dragons and *capgrosses* in the Plaça
Sant Jaume, and though the schedule varies according to which
day the 24th falls on, there are generally pyrotechnic displays
on the beach on the Friday, Saturday and Sunday nights, and
these are usually preceded by some incredible augmented-reality
video projections on the buildings of the Plaça Sant Jaume.
This is the Mercè's ground zero, and where you'll see the *castells*
(human castles) on the Sunday.

There are also displays of *sardanes* and *correfocs* (a tamer
version for children, followed by the biggest and wildest of the
year on the Saturday night), and the Parc de la Ciutadella is filled
with music and dance. Other highlights include a seafront air
show, sporting events including a swim across the port and a
regatta, and a heap of activities for children. The pressure on the
centre has been eased of late: many events are now staged up
at Montjuïc castle or in the former textile factory, Fabra i Coats,
in Sant Andreu. Even so, around 100,000 people have been
known to descend on the Barri Gòtic to watch the final parade.
Alongside the Mercè, a free three-day street arts festival takes
place, and includes family theatre and circus acts. Detailed
information is available at lameva.barcelona.cat/merce in the
lead-up to the festival.

public, but be warned that queues are very long. Arrive early to put your name on a list.

In-Edit Beefeater Festival
Various venues, Eixample (www.in-edit. beefeater.es). Metro Universitat. **Date** *2wks Oct/Nov.*

This highly regarded cinema festival focuses on musical documentaries and features a wide range of genres from jazz to flamenco.

Festival Internacional de Jazz de Barcelona
Various venues (93 481 70 40, www.jazz. barcelona). **Date** *Oct-Nov.*

One of Europe's most well-respected jazz festivals has grown to embrace everything from bebop to gospel. Venues include the Palau de la Música (*see p98*), Luz de Gas (*see p240*) and L'Auditori (*see p248*).

MPB
Various venues (www.festivalmpb.eu). **Date** *Oct-Dec.*

Not to be confused with Brazilian pop genre MPB, the festival of Música Popular de Barcelona celebrates every kind of music (except classical) in the city. Venues including Harlem Jazz Club (*see p235*) reverberate to sounds from gypsy punk to *cumbia*.

AvuiMúsica
Various venues (www.accompositors.com). Metro Jaume I. **Date** *Oct-Dec.*

Not so much a festival as a season of small-scale contemporary concerts run by the Association of Catalan Composers and held at various venues around the city. Members of the association are well represented and include local Grammy-nominated composer Joan Albert Amargós.

La Castanyada*
Throughout the city. **Date** *31 Oct-1 Nov.*

All Saints' Day and the evening before are known as the Castanyada, after the traditional treats of *castanyes* (roast chestnuts) – consumed along with *moniatos* (roast sweet potatoes) and *panellets* (small almond balls covered in pine nuts). The imported tradition of Halloween has grown in popularity of late, and there are now several celebrations around town. Tots Sants (All Saints') is also known as the Dia dels Difunts (Day of the Dead); the snacks switch to white, bone-shaped *ossos de sant* cakes. Thousands visit local cemeteries over the weekend to sprinkle the graves with holy water, leave flowers, hold vigils, and honour and pray for the dead.

L'Alternativa
Various venues (alternativa.cccb.org). **Date** *Nov.*

A week-long festival that showcases independent, mostly European cinema.

La Cursa de l'Amistat
www.cursadelamistat.com. Starting point Castell de Montjuïc. Metro Paral·lel. **Date** *Nov.* **Map** *p139 C11.*

Arduous but hugely popular 16km (ten-mile) uphill run from Montjuïc to the top of Tibidabo.

Winter

Buff Epic Run
Castell de Montjuïc, Montjuïc (www. buffepicrun.com). Metro Paral·lel. **Date** *Dec.* **Map** *p139 C11.*

Fancy dress attire is de rigueur for the participants in this fun- and mud-packed six-mile obstacle course around Montjuïc Castle.

Els Grans del Gospel
Various venues (www.theproject.es). **Date** *Dec.*

La Castanyada

This three-week festival of international gospel music, born of the gospel section of the International Jazz Festival, has now become popular enough to go it alone.

Festa dels Tres Tombs
Sant Antoni. Metro Sant Antoni. **Date** *around 17 Jan.* **Map** *p139 E8.*

St Anthony's day, naturally enough, also marks the *festa major* of the district; all the usual ingredients of music and *gegants* here include a monstrous, symbolic, fire-breathing pig – the form the devil took when tempting the saint. Anthony is patron saint of animals, and on his feast day it's still the custom to bring pets to the church of St Anthony to be blessed. Afterwards, horsemen ride three circuits (*tres tombs*) in a formal procession from Ronda Sant Antoni, through Plaça Catalunya, down La Rambla and along C/Nou de la Rambla.

Tradicionàrius
Centre Artesà Tradicionàrius, Travessia de Sant Antoni 6-8 & various venues in Gràcia (93 218 44 85, www.tradicionarius.cat). Metro Fontana. **Date** *mid Jan-mid Mar.* **Map** *p175 J3.*

A spirited folk festival that is held mainly in the auditorium listed above, even though some concerts take place in public squares and market places dotted around Gràcia. Acts are mostly local but there are occasional visits from international musicians or dance troupes.

Foguerons de Sa Pobla a Gràcia
Gràcia. Metro Fontana. **Date** *late Jan.*

Two days of Balearic folk festivities in honour of St Anthony see street bonfires, parades of dragons and giants, and candlelit singing (in *mallorquín*) in the Plaça del Diamant.

Santa Eulàlia
Throughout the city (lameva.barcelona.cat/ santaeulalia). **Date** *around 12 Feb.*

The city's blowout winter festival is in honour of Santa Eulàlia (Laia), who met her end at the hands of the Romans after enduring terrible tortures. Barcelona's

---

EVENTS

In the know
Tears of Santa Eulàlia

Almost without fail, the clear blue skies of a Barcelona September fill with clouds over the few days of the Mercè festival. These raindrops are known as the 'Tears of Santa Eulalia' and are said to express her sadness that, as joint patron saint of the city, she was overlooked and Mercè chosen for the big bash of the year.

Christmas & New Year Celebrations

A myriad of festivities culminating in the Kings' Parade

Nadal★ (Christmas Day, 25 Dec) begins with the *missa del gall* (cockerel's mass), held at dawn. Later, the whole family enjoys a traditional Christmas feast of *escudella i carn d'olla* (a meaty stew), seafood and roast truffled turkey, finishing off with great ingots of *turrón*. **Sant Esteve★** (Boxing Day, 26 Dec) is then followed by **El Dia dels Sants Innocents** on 28 December. The name is an incongruous reference to King Herod's Massacre of the Innocents, but in fact this is a cheerful local version of April Fool's Day, with cut-out newspaper figures attached to the backs of unsuspecting victims. The media also introduces fake stories into the day's coverage.

There are numerous Christmas fairs dotted around the city over the festive period, including the **Fira de Santa Llúcia** (en.firadesantallucia.cat) in the Barri Gòtic, which dates from 1786. You'll find more than 300 stalls, selling all manner of handcrafted Christmas decorations and gifts, along with mistletoe, poinsettias and Christmas trees. Other notable fairs include **Fira de Sant Eloi**, in Born, with handmade crafts and musical performances.

The most popular figure on sale for Nativity scenes at these fairs is the curious Catalan figure of the *caganer* (crapper), a small figure crouching over a steaming turd with his trousers round his ankles. Kids line up for a go on the giant *caga tió*, a huge, smiley-faced 'shitting log' that poops out pressies upon being beaten viciously by a stick; smaller versions are on sale at the stalls. There's also a Nativity scene contest, musical parades and exhibitions, including the popular life-size Nativity scene in Plaça Sant Jaume.

Cap d'Any★ (New Year's Eve, 31 December) tends to be a time for family dinners, with most people emerging to party after midnight, but there is always a group of revellers to be found in Plaça Catalunya. The drill is to wear red underwear for luck in the coming year, and to eat 12 grapes, one for each chime of the clock, at midnight. It's harder than you'd think, and tinned, pre-peeled versions are available. During the day, look out for L'Home dels Nassos, the man who has as many noses as days the year has left (it being the last day, the sly old fox has only one), who parades and throws sweets to the children.

Epiphany (*Cavalcada dels Reis*) on 5 January is the big Christmas event here, and is marked by the Kings' Parade. Melchior, Gaspar and Balthasar arrive aboard the Santa Eulàlia boat at the bottom of La Rambla before beginning a grand parade around town with a retinue of acrobats, circus clowns and child elves. The route is published in the newspapers, but normally starts at the lower entrance of Ciutadella, running up C/ Marquès de l'Argentera and Via Laietana. Later that night, children leave their shoes out on the balcony stuffed with hay for the kings' camels; in the morning, they're either full of presents or edible sugar coal depending on their behaviour the previous year. The following day is a holiday.

▶ *See lameva.barcelona.cat/ca/nadal for more information on Christmas fairs and celebrations in Barcelona.*

In the know
It could be you

Spaniards love their lotteries, but the favourite of them all is the Christmas El Gordo, the largest in the world and one of the most anxiously anticipated events of the year; the average Spaniard spends €20 a year on it. Tickets are on sale at every street corner from August, and the results are drawn on 22 December.

co-patron saint, she is a particular favourite with children. Her feast day on 12 February kicks off with a ceremony in Plaça Sant Jaume, followed by music, *sardanes* and parades, with masses and children's choral concerts held in the churches and cathedral. In the evening, the female giants gather in Plaça Sant Josep Oriol, then go to throw flowers on the Baixada de Santa Eulàlia before a final boogie in the Plaça Sant Jaume. The Ajuntament and the cathedral crypt (where she's buried) are open to the public and free, as are more than 30 museums. The festival closes on Sunday evening with *correfocs* (for adults and children) centred on the cathedral.

Carnaval (Carnival)

Throughout the city (www.bcn.cat/carnaval).
Date *Shrove Tuesday & Ash Wednesday.*

The city drops everything for this last big hurrah of overeating, overdrinking and underdressing prior to Lent. The celebrations begin on Shrove Tuesday with the appearance of pot-bellied King Carnestoltes – the masked personification of the carnival spirit. That's followed by the grand weekend parade, masked balls, *fartaneres* (neighbourhood feasts, typically with lots of pork), food fights and a giant *botifarrada* (sausage barbecue) on La Rambla, with most of the kids and market traders in fancy dress.

Carnaval

Film

Reel life

The city provides a popular backdrop for filmmakers of all stripes, most memorably, perhaps, for Woody Allen's *Vicky Cristina Barcelona*, while a rather grittier portrayal of Barcelona, showing its seedy underbelly, was on view in Alejandro González Iñárritu's *Biutiful*. The key figure in Spanish cinema continues to be Pedro Almodóvar, whose films invariably shoot to the top of the charts. However, Barcelona-born Isabel Coixet has also found international success and many of her films feature Hollywood-friendly actors and an English script (*My Life Without Me, The Secret Life of Words*). Alejandro Amenábar (*The Others, The Sea Inside*) has also found global recognition through English-language movies, and even genre-hopping wild child Álex de la Iglesia (*Perdita Durango, El Crime Perfecto, El Bar*) returned to the language of Shakespeare for *Oxford Murders*.

Vicky Cristina Barcelona (Woody Allen, 2008)

From the next generation of filmmakers, Fernando León de Aranoa (*Barrio, Mondays in the Sun, Princesas*) has built an impressive body of work as a Loach-esque social realist, though with greater doses of well-observed naturalist comedy. Equally distinctive are the many ethereal dreamscapes created by director Julio Medem, in films including *Cows, Lovers of the Arctic Circle, Sex and Lucia* and *Chaotic Ana*. One Barcelona-born director worth looking out for is José Luis Guerín, whose film, *In the City of Sylvia*, and documentary, *Work in Progress*, both met with worldwide acclaim.

Information and tickets

Release dates vary widely. Blockbusters are usually released more or less simultaneously worldwide, but smaller productions can take up to three years to arrive at cinemas, long after they're available to stream or out on DVD. The dubbing of films into Catalan often plays a part in delays.

Newspapers carry full details of screenings, as does www.butxaca.com. Subtitled (as opposed to dubbed) films are marked VO or VOSE (for '*versió original subtitulada en espanyol*'). Some of the larger cinemas open at 11am, but most have their first screenings around 4pm. Evening showings start around 7.30pm to 8.30pm; later screenings usually begin at 10.15pm to 10.45pm. On Fridays and Saturdays, many cinemas have a late-night session starting around 1am. Weekend evenings can be very crowded, especially for recent releases, so turn up early.

You can buy tickets for cinemas via their websites, which occasionally makes it cheaper.

Cinemas

Balmes Multicines

C/Balmes 422-424, Sant Gervasi (93 215 95 70, www.grupbalana.com). FGC El Putxet. **Tickets** *€7.50 Mon, Thur, Sun; €8.50 Fri, Sat.* **Map** *Fold-out G1.*

A 12-screen cinema in the uptown district of Sant Gervasi, this screens all the latest Hollywood blockbusters and international releases in their original language. The picture and sound quality are among the best in the city.

Cinema Maldà

C/Pi 5, Barri Gòtic (93 301 93 50, www.cinemamalda.com). Metro Catalunya or Liceu. **Tickets** *(all day) €5 Mon, Tue, Thur; €4.50 Wed; €9 Fri-Sun; (evening only) €5 Fri-Sun. No cards.* **Map** *p71 H9.*

In its latest incarnation, the well-loved Maldà shows a curious hotchpotch of indie and arthouse films, alongside mainstream fare and cult films of recent years. Tickets (except evening-only tickets) are valid for all of that day's screenings, so you could see up to seven films for one price.

Cinemes Méliès

C/Villarroel 102, Eixample (93 451 00 51, www.meliescinemes.com). Metro Urgell. **Tickets** *€4 Mon; €6 Tue-Thur; €7 Fri-Sun. No cards.* **Map** *p152 F6.*

This small, two-screen cinema is the nearest that Barcelona comes to an arthouse theatre, with an idiosyncratic roster of accessible classics alongside more recent films that aren't quite commercial enough for general release. This is the place to bone up on your Wilder, Antonioni, Hitchcock and others.

Filmoteca de Catalunya

Plaça Salvador Seguí 1-9, Raval (93 567 10 70, www.filmoteca.cat). Tickets €4; €3 reductions; €50 for 20 films. No cards. **Map** *p109 G9.*

The government-funded Filmoteca is a little dry for some tastes, offering comprehensive seasons of cinema's more recondite auteurs alongside better-known classics. Overlapping cycles last two to three weeks, with each film screened at least twice at different times. Adult films are subtitled, and the children's screenings at weekends often include non-speaking cartoons (*Tom & Jerry, Popeye* and so on) suitable for non-Catalan speakers. Books of 20 tickets bring down the price per film to a negligible amount. The 'Filmo' also runs an excellent library of film-related books, videos and magazines.

Essential Barcelona Films

Filmed in the city: six of the best

Barcelona

Whit Stillman 1994
Director Stillman casts an affectionate eye over the foibles of two preppy American cousins all at sea in the sexual, moral and political whirl of a changing Old World. Ted is a young, serious car-company exec getting over a failed affair, his recovery hardly helped when Fred – a brash naval officer – turns up uninvited to stay in his Barcelona flat. Wonderful shots of the city.

Todo Sobre mi Madre (All About my Mother)

Pedro Almodóvar 1999
After the death of her beloved teenage son in an accident, Cecilia Roth leaves Madrid for Barcelona to cope with her grief, hook up with old friends, and – just maybe – contact the long-estranged father the boy never knew. Almodóvar piles on the coincidences, contrivances and twists, but shows a depth and maturity lacking in earlier work.

En Construcción

José Luis Guerín 2001
Fascinating semi-documentary tracing the gentrification of a block of flats in a rundown corner of Barcelona. Guerín shot more than 100 hours of footage, then edited it down to focus on a squatting couple, a tramp, the workers and their foreman.

Perfume: The Story of a Murderer

Tom Tykwer 2006
Tom Tykwer and Andrew Birkin's adaptation of Patrick Süskind's novel chronicling the olfactory perversions of Jean-Baptiste Grenouille, a fictional serial killer in pre-revolutionary France with a particular nose for young women, offers obvious obstacles to any filmmaker. But Barna came to the rescue in terms of location – much of the film was shot in the Barri Gòtic and at the Poble Espanyol.

Vicky Cristina Barcelona

Woody Allen 2008
Woody Allen's European tour heads south to Spain for this funny, lusty film. Allen is liberal with the Spanish and Catalan clichés – Gaudí, Miró, long-haired lotharios with guitars – but in return provides a witty exchange of views on flirting, relationships, commitment and the ongoing clash of lifestyles in the Old and New Worlds.

Biutiful

Alejandro González Iñárritu 2010
Cannes Film Festival juries may have made some poor decisions over the years, but giving Javier Bardem the Best Actor award for his career-high performance as Uxbal, a backstreet Barcelona grafter who confronts a sea of troubles while doing his best for his kids, wasn't one of them.

Todo Sobre mi Madre

Renoir Floridablanca

*C/Floridablanca 135, Eixample (91 542 27 02, www.cinesrenoir.com). Metro Sant Antoni. **Tickets** €7.50 Mon, Tue-Thur; €4.50 Wed; €9.20 Fri-Sun. **Map** p152 F8.*

This screens up to 12 films a day, ranging from international blockbusters to offbeat, independent offerings. Membership, at €15 or €25 and including two or four free tickets, is a good deal. Tickets are cheaper online at www.pillalas.com.

Sala Phenomena

*C/Sant Antoni Maria Claret 168, Eixample (93 252 77 43, www.phenomena-experience. com). Metro Sant Pau or Dos de Maig. **Tickets** €8-€9. **Map** p152 M4.*

One of Barcelona's plushest cinemas, this shows everything from cult favourites (*Jaws, The Big Lebowski, Alien*) to the latest Hollywood releases on an enormous screen. It also has film programmes dedicated to specific genres, directors or actors, as well as talks, kids' films and fabulous double bills. Note that some films are dubbed.

Texas

*C/Bailén 205, Gràcia (93 348 77 48, www. cinemestexas.cat). Metro Verdaguer. **Tickets** €3. No cards. **Map** p175 K4.*

Locals love this four-screen cinema, which shows all the biggest films from around the world in their original language with Catalan subtitles. Most films are screened some months after their main release date, which means the tickets are a bargain.

Verdi

*C/Verdi 32, Gràcia (93 238 79 90, www. cines-verdi.com). Metro Fontana. **Tickets** €6 Mon; €8 Tue-Fri; €9 Sat, Sun (1st screening €6). **Map** p175 J3.*

The five-screen Verdi and Verdi Park, a four-screen annexe on the next street, have transformed this corner of Gràcia with a programme of independent, mainly European and Asian cinema. At peak times, chaos reigns; arrive early and make sure you don't confuse the queue to enter for the queue to buy tickets. Non-Spanish cards are not accepted.
Other locations Verdi Park, C/Torrijos 49, Gràcia (93 238 79 90).

Yelmo Icària Cineplex

*C/Salvador Espriú 61, Vila Olímpica (information 93 221 75 85, tickets 902 220 922, www.yelmocines.es). Metro Ciutadella-Vila Olímpica. **Tickets** €6.80 Mon; €4.90 Wed; €8.60 Tue, Thur-Sun; €6.80 reductions. **Map** Fold-out M1.*

This vast multiplex has all the atmosphere of the near-empty mall that surrounds it. But what it lacks in charm, it makes up for in choice, with 15 screens offering blockbusters, plus mainstream foreign and Spanish releases.

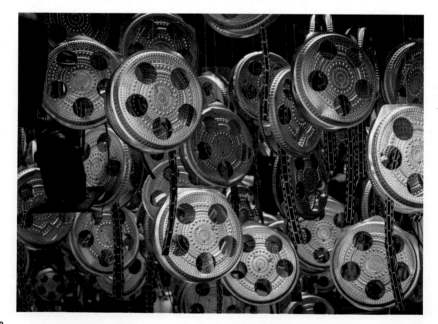

Sala Phenomena

Nightlife

Put on your dancing shoes

Barcelona makes no claims to be a party capital, despite a somewhat unwarranted reputation as such, but there is a reason that stag parties and night owls from around the globe head here in such numbers. There isn't the 24-hour, seven-days-a-week party vibe that you'll encounter in Ibiza, but there's an energy and creativity in the local nightlife that isn't found anywhere else.

It's a mood that's made and fostered by a population who party well, know when to go for it and when to call it quits, when to buy you a beer and when to leave you alone, when to clap and when to soft-shoe – but who most of all understand that going out is a necessary part of life that should be done right if it's to be done at all.

233

...l scene

...of words have been spent
...ng the clubs and bars that have
...victim to the municipal government's
...oise campaign, but visitors don't lack
...rtunities for after-dark indulgence.
...re are superclubs hosting superstar
...s and tiny venues playing the latest
...ectro. There are lounge clubs and gilded
...allrooms, *salsatecas* and Brazilian samba
bars, seductive tango emporiums and
alternative nights offering anything from
northern soul to Bollywood bhangra. There
is a thriving gay scene, confined to the part
of the Eixample known as the 'Gaixample'
(*see p242*), and clubs that are friendly to
every other sexual and gender orientation.

Going out happens late here, with people
rarely meeting for a drink much before
11pm – if they do, it's a pre-dinner thing.
Bars tend to close around 2am, or 3am at
weekends, and it's only after this that the
clubs get going, so many offer reduced
entrance fees or free drinks to those willing
to be seen inside before 1am. And if you're
still raring to go at 6am, just ask around –
more often than not there'll be an after-
party party catering to the truly brave.

Live music

While the licensing battles between club
owners and the town hall continue to
inspire apocalyptic images in the local
media, the rumours of the death of the city's
music scene are gradually fading away. In a
long-awaited move, officials have simplified
convoluted licensing laws and offered
financial support to those owners willing to
go some way towards meeting the objections
of local residents by soundproofing
their spaces.

There's further evidence that all is not as
bad as it seems: local acts continue to pop
up, their success and profligacy attesting
to Barcelona's tenacious relevancy on the
wider Spanish music scene. Electro group
Love of Lesbian, indie band Mishima,
techno DJ John Talabot, Catalan folk
popsters Manel, and the chirpy Pinker
Tones are a few of the names to look out for.
There are also more active metal-core bands
than you can shake a death rattle at, if that's
your thing, and a slew of internationally
minded musicians drawing from a blend
of rock, flamenco, hip hop and various
South American, Asian and African styles
of music; the best known among them are
Ojos de Brujo, CaboSanRoque, Maria del Mar
Bonet, Mayte Martín and the Raval's 08001.

Advance information

For concert information, see *Time Out
Barcelona* or the Friday papers, which
usually include listings supplements. Look
in bars and music shops for free magazines
such as Barcelona Metropolitan (in English),
Go, Mondo Sonoro (all mostly independent
pop/rock/electronica), *Batonga!* (which
covers world music) and *Suite* (good for
keeping abreast of the club scene).

For more, see www.infoconcerts.cat,
www.atiza.com, www.barcelonarocks.com,
and www.clubbing spain.com. For more on
the city's many music festivals, try www.
festivales.com.

♥ Best places to party

Arena *p245*
Good-time muscle Marys.

BARTS *p238*
Top-notch soundsystem.

City Hall *p239*
Hands-in-the-air action.

Heliogabal *p240*
Hang with the cool kids in Gràcia.

Sala Apolo *p239*
Theme nights in a 1940s dancehall.

La Terrrazza *p239*
Glamour and glitter within the Poble
Espanyol.

Sala Apolo *p239*

VENUES

Traditionally, you had to head uptown to hit the posh clubs, but the Port Olímpic is putting on some serious competition with places such as **Club Catwalk** (*see p238*) and **CDLC** (*see p238*) luring the *pijos* (well-groomed uptowners) downtown. There are also nightly beach parties running up and down the coast from Bogatell to Mataró through the summer. Meanwhile, you'll find smaller venues pulsating with life in the Barri Gòtic, particularly around the Plaça Reial and C/Escudellers. Across La Rambla, in the Raval, you can skulk in the grittier, grungier places, though even this neighbourhood hasn't proven impervious to gentrification, and a number of upmarket nightspots have sprung up on C/Joaquín Costa and between the kebab joints of the Rambla del Raval. If street beers, dogs and vintage sweaters are your thing, Gràcia is heaven – though in truth it's better for drinking than it is for dancing.

Some of the main music venues for seeing international names (as well as hotly tipped unknowns and locals) are the multi-faceted **Razzmatazz** (*see p241*), **Bikini** (*see p245*) and the old dancehall **Sala Apolo** (*see p239*). The first hosts both cutting-edge live and electronic music, while the latter specialises in feel-happy DJs and special theme nights. You can catch occasional visits by pop-rock superstars in the city's sports stadiums, at **Vall d'Hebron**, the **Palau Sant Jordi** or even way out in Badalona's **Palau Olímpic**.

Barri Gòtic

Café Royale
C/Nou de Zurbano 3 (93 318 89 56, www. royalebcn.com). Metro Liceu. **Open** *8.30pm-2.30am Tue-Sat.* **Admission** *free.* **Map** *p71 G10.*

Just off Plaça Reial, Café Royale offers a little more conversation, a little less action. Early in the evening it's a chilled place to slump on sofas, but later, when Fred Guzzo's funk, soul and jazz-driven beats are cranked up, the youngish crowd seems happier rubbing against each other at the bar than on the dancefloor. It's working on upgrading its image with tapas and a proper wine list.

Harlem Jazz Club
C/Comtessa de Sobradiel 8 (93 310 07 55, www.harlemjazzclub.es). Metro Jaume I. **Open** *July-Sept 8pm-4am Tue-Thur; 8pm-5am Fri, Sat. Oct-June 8pm-4am Tue-Thur, Sun; 8pm-5am Fri, Sat.* **Gigs** *10pm Tue-Thur, Sun; 11pm Fri, Sat. Closed 2wks Aug.* **Admission** *€7 Tue-Thur, Sun; €9 Fri, Sat.* **Map** *p71 H10.*

A hangout for not-so-c. buffs and students alike. has gone down at Harlem v century or so, and some of t. talents have emerged here. Ja funk and flamenco get a run in holds no musical prejudices.

Jamboree/Los Tarantos
Plaça Reial 17 (93 319 17 89, www.ma. com). Metro Liceu. **Open** *midnight-5am Thur, Sun; midnight-6am Fri, Sat. Shov Jamboree 8pm, 10pm daily. Los Tarantos 8.30pm, 9.30pm, 10.30pm daily.* **Admissic** *Shows Jamboree varies; Los Tarantos €15 daily. Club €10.* **Map** *p71 G10.*

Every night, the cave-like Jamboree hosts jazz, Latin or blues gigs by mainly Spanish groups – on Mondays, in particular, the popular WTF jazz jam session is crammed with a young local crowd. Upstairs, slicker sister venue Los Tarantos stages flamenco performances, then joins forces with Jamboree to become one fun, cheesy club later on in the evening. You'll need to leave the venue and pay again, but admission serves for both spaces.

La Macarena
C/Nou de Sant Francesc 5 (93 301 30 64). Metro Drassanes. **Open** *midnight-4.30am Mon-Thur, Sun; midnight-5am Fri, Sat.* **Admission** *free before 1.30am; €6 afterwards (but can vary). No cards.* **Map** *p71 H10.*

La Macarena is smaller than your apartment but has big-club pretensions in the best sense. The music is minimal electro selected by resident DJs and the occasional big-name guests, and is complemented by a kicking sound system. Be warned that you should watch your bag and your drink.

Marula Café
C/Escudellers 49 (93 318 76 90, www. marulacafe.com). Metro Liceu. **Open** *11pm-5am Mon-Thur, Sun; 11.30pm-6am Fri; 9.30pm-6am Sat.* **Admission** *free-€10 (incl 1 drink).* **Map** *p71 H10.*

Grown-up clubbers were thrilled when the popular Marula Café in Madrid announced it was opening a sister club in Barcelona,

In the know
Early doors

If you turn up at Barcelona clubs much before about 1am, you'll probably have the place to yourself. On the other hand, you're also more likely to get in for free, and drinks are occasionally cheaper, depending on the time.

...ed. The musical
...n in Spain, somewhat
...úsica negra – a fairly
...n this case ranges from
...y Stone to Michael Jackson
...it is a byword for quality and
...On Saturday nights musicians
...out 9.30pm. Admission is fairly
...charged, but seems not to apply if
...o queue.

...araigua
*...as de l'Ensenyança 2 (93 302 11 31, www.
...paraigua.com). Metro Jaume I or Liceu.
Open noon-midnight Mon-Wed, noon-2am
Thur; noon-3am Fri, Sat. Admission free.
Map p71 H9.*

Upstairs is a beautifully elegant Modernista
cocktail bar, whereas downstairs is a cosy
vaulted space framed by bare-brick walls,
which sees some of Barcelona's most
promising new bands performing on Friday
and Saturday nights. The music programme
in any given month might include an Irish
soul singer, a British funk band and a mixed-
nationality a cappella group.

Sidecar Factory Club
*Plaça Reial 7 (93 302 15 86,
sidecarfactoryclub.com). Metro Liceu. Open
7pm-5am Mon-Thur; 7pm-6am Fri, Sat.
Admission €5-€12. Map p71 H10.*

The Sidecar Factory Club still has all the
ballsy attitude of the spit 'n' sawdust rock club
that it used to be. Its programming, which
includes breakbeat, indie, electro and live
performances, has changed a bit over recent
times, but continues to pack in the local
indie kids and Interrailers to its bare-bricked,
barrel-vaulted basement.

Born & Sant Pere

Magic
*Passeig Picasso 40 (93 310 72 67). Metro
Barceloneta. Open 11pm-5.30am Thur;
11pm-6.30am Fri, Sat. Admission Club
(incl 1 drink) €12. Gigs varies. No cards.
Map p90 K10.*

There's magic in the air but there's not a lot
of air in Magic, an awkward basement rock
club whose big pull is the music: blistering
Northern Soul, rare grooves and raucous funk
for a tattooed crowd of ex- and aspirant mods.

The Mix
*C/Comerç 21 (93 319 46 96, www.mixbcn.
com). Metro Jaume I. Open Apr-Sept
9pm-3am Tue-Sat. Oct-Mar 9pm-3am Wed,
Thur; 9pm-3.30am Fri, Sat. Admission
free. Map p90 K9.*

With an interior designed by local tastemaker
Silvia Prada, a fashionable postcode and a
menu of delicate finger foods, Mix attracts a
professional, stylish crowd who enjoy both
an after-work cocktail and an after-dinner
piss-up. DJs play funk, soul and world beat on
Thursdays, and safe and sophisticated rare
groove the rest of the time. There's live bossa
nova and jazz on Tuesdays.

Rubí
*C/Banys Vells 6 (mobile 647 737 707). Metro
Jaume I. Open 7.30pm-2.30am Mon-Thur,
Sun; 7.30pm-3am Fri, Sat. Admission free.
No cards. Map p90 J10.*

A long and narrow bar with stone walls,
suffused with a womb-like red glow that can
make it hard to leave. The speciality at Rubí
is pocket-friendly (€4) mojitos, home-made
gins and tasty bar snacks.

Raval

23 Robadors
*C/Robador 23 (no phone, 23robadors.
wordpress.com). Metro Liceu. Open
8pm-2.30am daily. Admission free-€4.
No cards. Map p109 G9.*

Inside this stone-walled and smoke-filled
lounge, Raval denizens dig the jazz jam on
Wednesdays, jazz bands on Thursdays, the
flamenco (€4) on Tuesdays, Saturdays and
Sundays and, in between times, DJs playing
a genre-defying range of music (Joy Division
and DJ Shadow on the same night). A manga-
style mural on the back wall adds to the
underground appeal.

Bar Pastís
*C/Santa Mònica 4 (mobile 634 938 422,
www.barpastis.es). Metro Drassanes. Open
7.30pm-2.30am daily. Admission free.
Map p109 G10.*

This quintessentially Gallic bar once served
pastis to visiting sailors and denizens of
the Chino underworld. It still has a louche
feel, with floor-to-ceiling clippings and oil
paintings, Piaf on the stereo and paper cranes
swaying from the ceiling. There's live music
from Wednesday to Sunday.

Big Bang
*C/Botella 7 (93 329 65 96, www.bigbangbcn.
com). Metro Liceu or Sant Antoni.
Open 9.30pm-2.30am Tue-Thur, Sun;
9.30pm-3am Fri, Sat. Admission free. No
cards. Map p109 F9.*

Big Bang is decked out like a New York jazz
club, circa 1930, with the low-lit smokiness
and bar stool seating that this implies. The
diner-style tiled floor leads from the bar

t plans to sample Barcelona's
erratic nightlife, it's important to
ır *cul* (arse) from your *chulo* (arrogant
ıghtlife slang can be coarse and
ıg. Both Catalan and Spanish terms
ıed willy-nilly and sometimes combined.
ly expressions such as (*no*) *sóc gay* are
ıersally understood. So if you still '*tens
ınas*' (are up for it), here are a few pointers to
ıt you on your way.

Expressing intentions

sortir	to go out
anar de festa/juerga	to go out partying
anar de farra	to go on a big night out
agafar un pet	to get totally drunk
lligar	to pull
intentar lligar	chat up, or try to pull
fer un clau	(very vulgar indeed) to have sex

The venue – el lloc

brut	dirty
cutre	shabby
guarro (Sp)	seedy
de moda	trendy/flashy

de gom a gom (Cat)/ a tope (Sp)	packed
una estafa (Cat)/ un timo (Sp)	a rip-off

The clientele

golfo/golfa (Sp)	shameless/ up for anything/slapper
friqui	freak
pijo (Sp)	stuck-up
cursi (Sp)	cheesy
hortera (Sp)	flashy, tasteless

The experience

chupitos (Sp)	shots
dos per un	cheap drinks (lit. 'two for one')
un pitillo (Sp)	a cigarette
un after	a late-night/ early-morning bar

The post-mortem

nit en blanc	sleepless night
liarse	to get 'lost' in the night
tornar de dia	get back in daylight
empalmar	to stay out all night

to the tiny stage, where groups of talented musicians play swing, rock 'n' roll, bebop and every other vintage genre that should never have gone out of style. Bring your Stetson and a few euros for beer; shows are almost always free. There are concerts on Wednesdays, open mic rock, pop and blues sessions on Thursdays and Sundays and jam sessions followed by DJs on Fridays and Saturdays.

La Concha

*C/Guàrdia 14 (93 302 41 18). Metro Drassanes. **Open** 5pm-2.30am Mon-Thur, Sun; 5pm-3am Fri, Sat. **Admission** free. No cards. **Map** p109 G10.*

Papered with posters of vintage Spanish sexpot Sara Montiel and filled with the sounds of Bollywood balladry, La Concha is a gem of dusty fabulousness that stands in direct contrast to all the slick and pretentious glamour of most of the newer late-night bars. The venue is under Moroccan ownership and serves mint tea in the afternoons.

Jazz Sí Club

*C/Requesens 2 (93 329 00 20, tallerdemusics. com/jazzsi-club). Metro Sant Antoni. **Open** 8.30-11pm Mon, Wed-Fri; 7.45-10.30pm Tue; 7.45-11pm Sat; 6.30-10pm Sun.*

Admission (incl 1 drink) €5-€10. No cards. Map p109 F8.

Tucked into a Raval side street, with cheap shows every night and cheap bar grub, this truly authentic place is worth seeking out. Since it functions as both a venue for known-in-the-scene locals and an auditorium for students of the music school across the street, it's packed to the brim with students, teachers, music-lovers and players. Nights vary between jazz, flamenco and Cuban, and there are jam sessions on Tuesdays and Saturdays.

Moog

*C/Arc del Teatre 3 (93 319 17 89, www. masimas.com/moog). Metro Drassanes. **Open** midnight-5am daily. **Admission** €10. Map p109 G10.*

Moog is a curious club: long, narrow and enclosed, with the air-con pumping; the experience of partying here is like dancing in a dimly lit aeroplane. The two floors are rather hilariously divided along gender lines: girls shake to pop and 1980s music upstairs, while boys tune in to non-stop hard house and techno downstairs. The Moog is packed seven days a week, and Angel Molina, Laurent Garnier and Jeff Mills have all played here at some point.

Barceloneta & the Ports

Around the quayside of the Port Olímpic, you will find dance bars interspersed with seafood restaurants and mock-Irish pubs, with video screens and go-gos in abundance.

CDLC

Passeig Marítim 32 (93 224 04 70, www. cdlcbarcelona.com). Metro Ciutadella-Vila Olímpica. **Open** *noon-3.30am daily.* **Admission** *free.* **Map** *p124 L10.*

Carpe Diem Lounge Club, to give the venue its full name, remains at the forefront of Barcelona's splash-the-cash, see-and-be-seen celeb circuit: the white beds flanking the dancefloor, guarded by a clipboarded hostess, are perfect for showing everyone who's the daddy. Alternatively, for those not celebrating recently signed, six-figure record deals, funky house and a busy terrace provide an opportunity for mere mortals (and models) to mingle and discuss who's going to finance their next drink and, secondly, how to get chatting to whichever member of the Barça team has just walked in.

Club Catwalk

C/Ramón Trias Fargas s/n (93 224 07 40, www.clubcatwalk.net). Metro Ciutadella-Vila Olímpica. **Open** *Oct-Apr 11pm-6am Tue-Sun. May-Sept 11am-6pm daily.* **Admission** *(incl 1 drink) €10-€20.* **Map** *p124 M10.*

Maybe it's the name or maybe it's the location, but most of the Catwalk queue seems to think they're headed straight for the VIP room – that's crisp white collars and gold for the boys and short, short skirts for the girls. Inside it's suitably snazzy; upstairs there's R&B and hip hop, but the main house room is where most of the action is, with everything from electro-house to minimal beats.

Opium Mar

Passeig Marítim 34 (93 414 63 62, www. opiummar.com). Metro Ciutadella-Vila Olímpica. **Open** *11.45pm-5am Mon-Thur, Sun; 11.45pm-6am Fri, Sat.* **Admission** *(incl 1 drink) €20.* **Map** *p124 L10.*

It's tempting to dismiss Opium Mar as just another homogeneous upmarket beachside club, but beyond the zealous bouncers and the hefty entrance fee there is a surprisingly creative and eclectic vibe that belies the club's location. From chocolate fountains to live saxophonists, much is done to distinguish Opium Mar from the competition, but by far its most popular feature is the beach terrace, which provides a perfect spot to catch the sunrise.

Montjuïc, Poble Sec & Sant Antoni

La [2]

C/Nou de la Rambla 111 (93 441 4[0] sala-apolo.com). Metro Paral·lel. [Open] 8pm daily. **Club** *midnight-6am Mo[n] 12.30-6am Wed-Sat.* **Admission** *€6-* **Map** *p139 F10.*

The underground extension of Sala Apo[llo] *(see p239)*, La [2] has excellent sound and intimate layout. The live music is reliably good, with performances by more cultish artists than those that play upstairs, but increasingly the space is used for club nights.

Barcelona Rouge

C/Poeta Cabanyes 21 (mobile 666 25 15 56). Metro Paral·lel. **Open** *7pm-2.30am Wed, Sun; 7pm-3am Thur-Sat.* **Admission** *free. No cards.* **Map** *p139 E9.*

Ah – comfy. This is a pretty place done up with throw rugs, vintage lamps that don't do a whole lot (the lighting concept is the uncomplicated 'dark') and dusty sofas. Later in the night it gets packed with singing, decked-out thirtysomethings who don't mind getting tipsy in a place where it costs quite a bit of coin to do so. There are occasional live shows (normally Sundays).

❤ BARTS

Avda Paral·lel 62 (93 324 84 92, www.barts. cat). Metro Paral·lel. Box office 5pm-8pm Wed-Fri and 2hrs before shows start. **Admission** *free-€25.* **Map** *p139 F10.*

BARTS hasn't been around long, but has rapidly become the best place in the city to see rock and pop acts from around the world, such as Lucinda Williams, Matthew Herbert, LCD Soundsystem and John McLaughlin. Its success is thanks to its great acoustics, state-of-the-art sound system, comfortable seating (for those who don't want to dance downstairs) and eclectic programming.

Maumau

C/Fontrodona 35 (93 441 80 15, www. maumaubarcelona.com). Metro Paral·lel. **Open** *9pm-2.30am Thur; 9pm-2.30am Fri, Sat. Closed Aug.* **Admission** *free.* **Map** *p139 E10.*

Ring the bell by the anonymous grey door. You no longer have to pay to get in, but the membership card gets some good discounts for cinemas and clubs (see the website). Inside, a large warehouse space is humanised with colourful projections, IKEA-style sofas and scatter cushions, and a friendly, laid-back crowd. These days, Maumau has moved upmarket and is more of a lounge bar, and its latest speciality is the G&T, with 25 different types of gin offered.

♥ Sala Apolo

*C/Nou de la Rambla 113 (93 441 40 01, www. sala-apolo.com). Metro Paral·lel. **Club** 12.30-5am Mon-Thur; 12.30-6am Fri, Sat. **Concerts** varies. **Admission** Concerts varies. Club €10-€18. **Map** p139 F10.*

This 1940s dancehall is one of Barcelona's most popular clubs, with all that implies for atmosphere (good) and acoustics (bad). Live acts range from Toots & the Maytals to Killing Joke, but note that buying gig tickets doesn't include admission to the club night: you'll need to re-enter for that, and pay extra. On Wednesdays, the DJs offer African and Latin rhythms; on Thursdays, it's funk, Brazilian, hip hop and reggae; and Fridays and Saturdays are an extravaganza of bleeping electronica.

♥ La Terrrazza

*Poble Espanyol, Avda Francesc Ferrer i Guàrdia 13 (93 272 49 80, www.laterrrazza. com). Metro Espanya. **Open** June-mid Sept 12.30-5.45am Thur; 12.30-6.45am Fri, Sat. **Admission** €5-€20. **Map** p139 B8.*

Gorgeous, glamorous and popular (with the young, hair-gel-and-heels brigade), La Terrrazza is a nightclub that Hollywood might dream of. Wander through the night-time silence of Poble Espanyol to the starry patio that is the dancefloor for one of the more surreal experiences that it's possible to have with a highly priced G&T in your hand. Gazebos, lookouts and erotic paintings add to the magic, and if the music is mostly crowd-pleasing house tunes (the occasional big-

name DJ, though no one truly fabulous), so what? That's not really what you came for.

Tinta Roja

*C/Creu dels Molers 17 (93 443 32 43, www. tintaroja.cat). Metro Poble Sec. **Open** 8.30pm-1am Wed; 8.30pm-2am Thur; 8.30pm-3am Fri, Sat. Closed 2wks Aug. **Admission** free. Concerts €6-€10. No cards. **Map** p139 E9.*

A smooth and mysterious bar, once a dairy farm, lent a Buenos Aires bordello/theatre/circus/cabaret vibe by plush red velvet sofas, smoochy niches and an ancient ticket booth. It's an atmospheric place to go for a late-ish drink, and it's open 8-10.30pm for *milonga* classes on the first and third Wednesday of the month. The theatre at the back hosts performances including comedy improv (sometimes in English), poetry readings and live music; check the website for programming.

Eixample

Antilla BCN Latin Club

*C/Aragó 141 (93 451 45 64, www.antillasalsa. com). Metro Urgell. **Open** 10pm-5am Wed; 11pm-5am Thur; 11pm-6am Fri, Sat; 7pm-1am Sun. **Gigs** 12.30am Wed, Thur. **Admission** free Wed, Thur, Sun; (incl 1 drink) €10 Fri, Sat. **Map** p152 E6.*

This Caribbean cultural centre hosts exhibitions, publishes its own magazine (*Antilla News*) and offers Latin dance classes. But when the sun goes down all cultural pretensions go out the window – it's a hedonistic jungle in there. Salsa shows by entire orchestras and DJs playing rumba, merengue and *son* until the early hours will spin your head and parch your throat until the only word you can croak is 'mojito'.

♥ City Hall

*Rambla Catalunya 2-4 (93 238 07 22, www. cityhallbarcelona.com). Metro Catalunya. **Club** midnight-5am Mon-Thur, Sun; midnight-6am Fri, Sat. **Concerts** varies. **Admission** free before 1am; after 1am (incl 1 drink) €12-€18. **Map** p152 H7.*

City Hall ain't big, but it is popular. The music is mixed, from deep house to electro rock, and there's an older post- (pre-?) work crowd joining the young, tanned and skinny to show the dancefloors some love. Outside, the terrace is a melting pot of tourists and locals, who rub shoulders under the watchful (and anti-pot-smoking) eye of the bouncer. Earlier in the evening it operates as an excellent mid-sized live music venue.

Luz de Gas

C/Muntaner 246 (93 209 77 11, www. luzdegas.com). FGC Muntaner. **Club** *midnight-6am Wed-Sat.* **Gigs** *daily, times vary.* **Admission** *Club (incl 1 drink) €20. Gigs varies.* **Map** *p152 F4.*

This lovingly renovated old music hall, garnished with chandeliers and classical friezes, is a mainstay on the live music scene and is one classy joint. In between visits from international artists and benefit concerts for local causes, you will find nightly residencies: blues on Mondays, Dixieland jazz on Tuesdays, disco on Wednesdays, pop-rock on Thursdays, soul on Fridays and vintage and Spanish rock on weekends.

Soho

C/Aribau 195 (93 209 65 62, www.sohobcn. com). FGC Provença. **Open** *11.45pm-6am Thur-Sat.* **Admission** *free Thur; (incl 1 drink) €15 Fri, Sat.* **Map** *p152 G4.*

Looking a tad jaded, Soho's white leather sofas and pouffes still manage to pull a crowd of glamour pusses, who stalk their prey from the mezzanine. There's chill-out and jazz in the bar at the front and house for the dancefloor at the back. Drinks are a couple of euros more expensive if you're sitting at a table. Dress code is smart.

Gràcia

♥ Heliogàbal

C/Ramón y Cajal 80 (www.facebook.com/ heliogabal). Metro Joanic. **Open** *10pm-2am Wed-Sun.* **Admission** *free-€10. No cards.* **Map** *p175 K4.*

Loved by habitués of the Gràcia arts scene, this low-key bar and performance venue is filled to bursting with neighbourhood cutie pies in cool T-shirts who just really adore live poetry. Events change nightly, running from live music to film screenings, art openings and readings, and programming focuses mostly on local talents. On concert nights arrive early for an 'at-least-I'm-not-standing' folding chair.

Otto Zutz

C/Lincoln 15 (93 238 07 22, www.ottozutz. com). FGC Gràcia. **Open** *midnight-6am Tue, Thur-Sat; midnight-5am Wed.* **Admission** *(incl 1 drink) €15 Fri.* **Map** *p175 H3.*

Otto Zutz should have been great. Located away from the maddening crowds of the old quarter in a three-floor former textile factory that oozes character, the initial concept held potential in abundance. But it got lost somewhere among the pretentious staff, mediocre house and bad R&B music. Fortunately, the crowd doesn't seem to notice – this place sure can pack in the punters, especially when it comes to those who are young and dolled-up.

Bikini

Razzmatazz

Other districts

Bikini

Avda Diagonal 547, Les Corts (93 322 08 00, www.bikinibcn.com). Metro Les Corts or Maria Cristina. **Open** *midnight-5am Wed-Sat.* **Admission** *(incl 1 drink) €12-€17.* **Map** *Fold-out D3.*

This legendary music venue frequently changes hands, and programming – for both concerts and the after-show club nights – has become quite unpredictable. At its best, it has hosted some of the best concerts seen in the city, so although it seems to have been in another slump in recent years, it's worth watching this space.

Mirablau

Plaça Doctor Andreu, Tibidabo (93 418 58 79). FGC Avda Tibidabo then Tramvia Blau. **Open** *11am-4.30am Mon-Wed, Sun; 11am-6am Thur-Sat.* **Admission** *free.*

It doesn't get any more uptown than this, geographically and socially. Located at the top of Tibidabo, this small bar is packed with the high rollers of Barcelona, from local footballers living on the hill to international businessmen on the company card. They're drawn here for the view and the artificial wind that sweeps through the tropical shrubbery outside on hot summer nights.

Razzmatazz

C/Almogàvers 122, Poblenou (93 320 82 00, www.salarazzmatazz.com). Metro Bogatell or Marina. **Club** *midnight-5am Wed, Thur; 1-6am Fri, Sat.* **Concerts** *varies.* **Admission** *Concerts varies. Club (incl 1 drink) €15-€17.* **Map** *Fold-out N9.*

This monstrous club's five distinct spaces form the night-time playground of seemingly all young Barcelona. There's indie rock in Razz Club, tech-house in the Loft, techno pop in Lolita, electro pop in the Pop Bar and electro rock in the Rex Room. Live acts run from Arctic Monkeys to Bananarama, and concerts can get rammed, with queues so long that it's worth arriving early so that you don't miss the beginning of the show. The price of admission will get you into all five rooms, though the gigs are normally ticketed separately.

Sala BeCool

Plaça Joan Llongueras 5, Les Corts (93 362 04 13, www.salabecool.com). Metro Hospital Clínic. **Club** *midnight-6am Thur-Sat.* **Gigs** *varies.* **Admission** *Gigs varies. Club (incl 1 drink) €10-€15.* **Map** *Fold-out E3.*

The latest from Berlin's minimal electro scene reaches Barcelona via this uptown concert hall. After the live shows by local rock stars or international indie success stories, a packed and music-loving crowd throbs to sophisticated electronica and its bizarre attendant visuals. Upstairs, in the Red Room, DJs playing indie pop rock provide an alternative to the pounding beats of the main room.

Sala Salamandra

Avda Carrilet 235, L'Hospitalet (93 337 06 02, www.salamandra.cat). Metro Avda Carrilet. **Concerts** *9.30pm.* **Club** *1-6am Fri, Sat.* **Admission** *Gigs varies. Club (incl 1 drink) €8.*

If you're willing to travel 30 minutes on the metro to L'Hospitalet, do it for a night at this

Doing the Circuit

Barcelona's biggest gay festival has it all covered

Get the shirts off and the baby oil on: it's time for Barcelona's biggest gay festival. But this one is about much more than showing off your six-pack on the dancefloor. Hitting its tenth anniversary in 2017, the **Circuit Festival** (www.circuitfestival.net) has grown so popular that it now stretches over nine days (usually in late July and early August) and includes parties, cinema and cultural offerings from flamenco to gay art.

Circuit encompasses no fewer than three festivals in one: Circuit for gay men, Girlie Circuit for lesbians and bisexuals, and Circuit Bear, for the bears and chasers out there. All three are open to any homo-friendly person who is sufficiently buffed, hairy or brave enough to give it a go. Circuit, Girlie and Bear each have their own specific programme of after-dark clubs, parties and shows but share many of the daytime events. Among them is the notorious Circuit Water Park Day, when some 10,000 participants take over the Illa Fantasia water park for 24 hours of aquatic madness and DJs. Circuit was born as an initiative of the entrepreneurial Matinée Group. With over 50,000 participants from 50 countries, the event has become the most international LGBT festival in Europe, and no wonder: it's a smooth operation, with user-friendly packages including hotels, apartments, a flight selector and private transport to events. Parties are scattered among a variety of iconic gay venues in and around the city, ranging from Gaixample clubs to Mar Bella beach and the nearby town of Sitges.

The festival is also gaining ground away from the dancefloor, with sports events organised by the Panteres Grogues (Yellow Panthers, the local LGBT sports association), and theatre and movie screenings. On the more serious side, there are workshops on the prevention of HIV or homophobic bullying, and art exhibitions on topics such as the body as a creative space and the history of homosexuality.

500-person venue-cum-nightclub, which regularly hosts the best local artists, including Macaco, Muchachito Bombo Infierno and Kinky Beat. Local and visiting DJs take over after the shows; the music stays fun, the crowd local and the drinks fairly cheap.

Universal
*C/Marià Cubí 182 bis, Les Corts (93 201 35 96, www.grupocostaeste.com). FGC Muntaner. **Open** 11pm-5.30am Mon-Sat. **Admission** free Mon-Thur; free before 1am, (incl 1 drink) €12 after 1am Fri, Sat. **Map** Fold-out F3.*

One of the few clubs in Barcelona that caters to an older, well-dressed crowd, Universal doesn't charge admission until 1am, but the drink prices are pretty steep. Upstairs is a chill-out area, complete with aquatic slide projections, while downstairs sports a sharper look.

LGBT Barcelona

The gay scene – *el ambiente* in Spanish – is mostly limited to a small and otherwise unremarkable area in the Eixample. Bordered by the streets Diputació, Villarroel, Aragó and Balmes, it's delightfully if dizzily called the **Gaixample**. Here's where you'll find the majority of gay sex shops and saunas, and gay fashion, such as **Ovlas** (C/Aribau 31, 93 268 76 91, www.ovlas.com). But there are also shops and bars throughout the Old City, along with alfresco cruising behind Plaça d'Espanya in the leafy shadows of Montjuïc. There's also the aesthetically challenged 'Chernobyl beach': take the train or tram to **Sant Adrià de Besòs** and wander about in front of the three huge cooling towers.

Most of the city's nightlife is pretty mixed, and there's a lot of fun to be had off the official scene – a keen ear to the ground and the occasional flyer will often deliver an embarrassment of riches. Don't worry about dress codes: you can wear anything or almost nothing. The summer's fiestas at shacks on gay-friendly **Mar Bella** beach (*map p124 Q10*) are a fine example of minimum advertising, maximum raving.

In the know
Gay festivals throughout the year

For **Carnaval** in February, head to Sitges (see *p202*), but Barcelona takes over in summer. The **Mostra Internacional de Cinema Gai i Lesbià** film festival (www.cinemalambda.com) is usually held in June. At the end of June, **Gay Pride** (www.pridebarcelona.org) usually centres on the Plaça Universitat, with parades and concerts.

Pick up free copies of gay rag *Shanguide* in bars and gay shops around town, or have a look on: shangay.com, www.infogai. info, www.60by80.com/barcelona, www. guiagaybarcelona.es, www.bolloandbutter. com and catalunya-lgbt.catalunya.com.

Bookshops are also useful fonts of information: try **Antinous Libreria Café** (C/Casanova 72, Eixample, 93 301 90 70, www.antinouslibros.com) and **Complices** (C/Cervantes 4, Barri Gòtic, 93 412 72 83, www.libreriacomplices.com).

Gay bars

The Gaixample bars mentioned below have proved more durable than most, given the fickle nature of the local scene in Barcelona. However, we advise you to ask around about a venue before shelling out on a cab fare and making a special journey. Beyond the Gaixample, **La Concha** (*see p237*), **Schilling** (C/Ferran 23, 93 317 6787, www.cafeschilling. com), and **Zelig** (C/Carme 116, www.zelig-barcelona.com), though not exclusively gay, are all worth a visit. During the long summer months, though, the action moves to the shore. The *xiringuitos* (beach bars) on Mar Bella are the essential places to hang out, especially the first on this stretch (with the sea to your right): it's called **Be Gay** (chiringuitobegay.com).

Bacon Bear Bar
C/Casanova 64 (no phone). Metro Universitat. Open 6pm-2.30am Mon-Thur, Sun; 6pm-3am Fri, Sat. Admission free. Map p152 F7.

It's hard to maintain an attitude in a bar that has teddies as a theme, and so it is with the Bacon Bear Bar, a down-to-earth bare-bricked place for bears and those who go down to the woods to find them.

El Cangrejo
C/Villarroel 86 (mobile 625 779 393). Metro Universitat or Urgell. Open 10.30pm-3am Mon-Thur, Sun; 11pm-3am Fri, Sat. Admission free. Map p152 F7.

If you can ignore first impressions based on the decor (which looks as if Gaudí sneezed violently), you'll find a lively and friendly bar at El Cangrejo. It tends to attract a younger crowd, similar to that of the original Cangrejo in the Raval (C/Montserrat 9, 93 301 29 78).

Col·lectiu Gai de Barcelona
Ptge Valeri Serra 23 (93 453 41 25, www. colectiugai.org). Metro Universitat or Urgell. Open 7-9.30pm Tue-Thur; 7pm-3am Fri; 8pm-3am Sat. Admission free. No cards. Map p152 F7.

This is a good place to find out information about the city; the headquarters of this local gay association is home to an easygoing, quiet and unpretentious bar, with cheap drinks and few tourists.

Museum Bar
C/Sepúlveda 178 (933 25 18 31). Metro Universitat. Open 11pm-3am Fri, Sat. Admission free. Map p152 G7.

Over-the-top, tongue-in-cheek and fabulously faux baroque is the theme at this trendy music bar, where the video screens are surrounded by huge gilded frames. Rihanna, Beyoncé and other lamé-clad divas will get you warmed up for the long night ahead.

New Chaps
Avda Diagonal 365 (93 215 53 65, www. newchaps.com). Metro Diagonal or Verdaguer. Open 9pm-3am Mon-Wed; 7pm-3am Thur, Sun; 9pm-3.30am Fri, Sat. Admission free. No cards. Map p152 J5.

The more mature clientele that frequents this sex bar avoids studying the rather bizarre collection of objects hung around the place and instead heads directly for the busy darkroom downstairs. If you're tempted to join them, make sure that you check in your valuables first.

People Lounge
C/Villarroel 71 (93 532 77 43, www. peoplebcn.com). Metro Universitat or Urgell. Open 8pm-3am Mon-Thur; 8pm-3.30am Fri, Sat; 7pm-3am Sun. Admission free. No cards. Map p152 F7.

People Lounge offers a good alternative if you're tired of trekking around from bar to bar listening to non-stop Europop. Decked out as a facsimile of a posh English pub, with plush sofas and chandeliers, it attracts a mature, smartly dressed crowd.

Plata Bar
C/Consell de Cent 233 (93 452 46 36, www. platabar.com). Metro Universitat. Open 8pm-1.30am Wed, Thur; 8pm-3am Fri, Sat. Admission free. Map p152 F6.

This lively cocktail bar comes into its own on warm evenings, when the bar is completely

In the know
Taxiiii!

Taxi Pride (mobile 656 53 23 72, www. taxipridebarcelona.com) is more than a taxi service, it also acts as an information service for its LGBT clients. Just jump in, tell the driver what tickles your fancy, and he or she will whisk you to the ideal place.

Essential Barcelona Albums
Sounds of the city

Els Èxits de Lluís Llach (Lluís Llach, 1969)

With an impressive 33 albums to his name, Lluís Llach has long been a figurehead of Catalan nationalism, and his song 'L'Estaca' was the protest anthem par excellence in the dying years of Franco's reign. As a result, he was forced into exile in Paris, where he was to gain international recognition.

Bondia (Els Pets, 1997)

The predominant sound of the 1980s and '90s was *rock català*, which took over from Nova Cançó but shared many of its political sentiments, and Els Pets (The Farts) were its poster boys (along with Sopa de Cabra and Sau). Their biggest success came in 1997 with the Britpop-influenced *Bondia*, which sold 85,000 copies.

Barí (Ojos de Brujo, 2002)

Rumba catalana, which began in the gypsy slums in the 1940s, is another hugely popular genre in Barcelona. Bands influenced by it are too numerous to mention, but Ojos de Brujo brought the sound into the modern age (and brought it global renown), throwing flamenco, hip hop and a touch of reggae into the mix.

Barcelona Raval Sessions (2003)

A compilation of sounds produced in, or influenced by, Barcelona's edgiest *barrio*. It includes all the happening bands of the noughties, from electro-popsters The Pinker Tones to ethnic Raval supergroup 08001. Look out for ska- and rumba-influenced Cheb Balowski and eminently danceable band Polvorosa.

Barcelona (Montserrat Caballé & Freddie Mercury, 2012)

A curious grab-bag of styles and songs, headed up by the soaring title track that has become the city's de facto anthem and celebrates its spectacular reinvention with the 1992 Olympics. This edition of the album sees tracks remastered and given symphonic accompaniment.

Fin (John Talabot, 2012)

Known to his mother as Oriol Riverola, house DJ and producer John Talabot has seen a sudden and phenomenal success in the past few years, particularly with his debut album *Fin*. Despite his new-found international fame, though, he's still to be found spinning the discs in various venues around town.

open to the street. Take your pick from the standard cocktail menu, grab a seat and watch the world pass by.

Punto BCN
C/Muntaner 63-65 (no phone, www. grupoarena.com). Metro Universitat. **Open** *6pm-2.30am daily.* **Admission** *free. No cards.* **Map** *p152 F6.*

Punto BCN is a Gaixample staple. It's fiercely unstylish, but friendly and down to earth. It's also one of the few places where you'll find anybody early on. Tables on the mezzanine give a good view of the crowd, so you can take your pick before the object of your affections heads off into the night.

Gay clubs

Check local press for the latest on gay nights held in otherwise straight clubs, such as **The Black Room** at City Hall (*see p239*) on Saturdays, which has funky house downstairs and a darkroom upstairs.

❤ Arena
Classic *C/Diputació 233, Eixample.* **Open** *12.30-5am Fri, Sat.* **Map** *p152 G7*
Madre *C/Balmes 32, Eixample.* **Open** *2.30-6am daily.* **Map** *p152 G7.*
VIP *Gran Via de les Corts Catalanes 593, Eixample.* **Open** *1-6am Fri, Sat.* **Map** *p152 F7.*
All *93 487 83 42, www.grupoarena.com. Metro Universitat.* **Admission** *(incl 1 drink) €6 Mon-Fri, Sun; €12 Sat. No cards.*

The Arena clubs are still packing them in every week, with a huge variety of punters. The unique selling point is that you pay once, get your hand stamped and can then flit between all three clubs. Madre is the biggest and most full-on venue of the trio, with thumping house music and a darkroom. There are shows and strippers at the beginning of the week, but Wednesday's semi-riotous foam parties in July and August are where all the action takes place. VIP doesn't take itself too seriously and is popular with just about everyone, from mixed gangs of Erasmus students to parties of thirtysomethings in from the suburbs, all getting busy to Snoop Dogg and vintage Mariah Carey. Classic is similarly mixed, if even cheesier, playing mostly handbag hits.

Metro
C/Sepúlveda 185, Eixample (93 323 52 27, www.metrodiscobcn.com). Metro Universitat. **Open** *12.30-5am Mon-Thur, Sun; 12.30-6am Fri, Sat.* **Admission** *(incl 1 drink) €20.* **Map** *p152 G7.*

Metro's popularity seldom wanes, whatever the time of year. The club is particularly packed at the weekends, which makes the smaller of the two dancefloors, specialising in Latin beats, something of a challenge for more flamboyant dancers to navigate. The larger one is a space to dance to more traditional house music. The corridor-like darkroom is where the real action takes place, though. Among other nocturnal delights there are strippers, drag queen acts and, yes, bingo.

Lesbian bars & clubs

Barcelona's lesbian scene doesn't seem to have much consistency, with bars struggling to survive amid constant changes of ownership. You'll find lesbians in some of the spots favoured by gay men, such as **Arena** or **Metro**. The second *xiringuito* on Mar Bella beach functions as a lesbian meeting place – at its liveliest on Sunday evenings. Admission to the bars listed below is free, unless otherwise stated.

Aire
C/València 236, Eixample (93 454 63 94, wwwgrupoarena.com). Metro Passeig de Gràcia. **Open** *11pm-2.30am Thur-Sat.* **Admission** *(incl 1 drink) €5 Fri; €6 Sat. No cards.* **Map** *p152 G7.*

The girly outpost of the Arena group is the city's largest lesbian club, and as such sees a decent variety of girls (and their male friends, by invitation) head down to shoot pool and dance to pop, house and 1980s classics. On the first Sunday of the month, there's a women-only strip show.

La Sue
C/Villarroel 60, Eixample (93 323 61 53). Metro Universitat. **Open** *7pm-2am Thur-Sat.* **Admission** *free. No cards.* **Map** *p152 F7.*

The newest addition to the city's lesbian scene is a friendly, no-nonsense affair with bare-brick walls and flattering lighting, and draws in girls of many stripes. There are games to play, a large-screen TV that shows Barça matches and bar snacks.

Performing Arts

The city in stages, from full-scale opera to postmodern circus

Barcelona has a remarkable musical heritage, and now, finally, it has performance venues to match. Funding for the arts has dried up significantly as a result of the Spanish economic crisis – at one point even the prestigious Liceu opera house was forced to close for two months to cut costs. Despite this, the Liceu, and two more of the city's most venerable institutions – the Auditori concert hall and the extraordinary, century-old Palau de la Música Catalana – continue to attract audiences with increasingly diverse programming. And the rich pickings are not restricted to Spanish- or Catalan-speakers, thanks to the tradition of physical spectacle that began in the Franco years when the Catalan language was banned.

DE BIEN

CLASSICAL MUSIC & OPERA

Although the canon still reigns at the **Gran Teatre del Liceu**, contemporary productions, local works and some adventurous formats add a bit of risk to its classical repertoire. The **Conservatori** – the prestigious music school attached to the Liceu – offers its own programme of chamber operas, recitals and contemporary compositions in a subterranean auditorium. Smaller venues, such as **Auditori Axa** in L'Illa shopping centre (*see p187*), host fewer regular concerts, although those that are staged are generally of a high standard.

The main musical season runs from September to June (see below for exceptions). During this time, the city orchestra, the **Orquestra Simfònica de Barcelona** (OBC, *see p251*), plays weekly at the **Auditori**, which also regularly hosts resident contemporary orchestra **BCN 216** (*see p250*). The Liceu stages a different opera every three or four weeks. Both the Auditori and the **Palau de la Música Catalana** hold several concert cycles of various genres, either programmed by the venues or by independent promoters (Ibercàmera and Promoconcert are the most high-profile).

From June to August, many concerts take place outdoors. **Música als Parcs** (*see p218*) is a programme of some 50 evening concerts hosted in a number of parks across the city. Additionally, various museums, among them the **Fundació Joan Miró** (*see p143*) and the **CaixaForum** (*see p141*), also hold occasional small outdoor concerts.

Information and tickets

Weekly entertainment guide *Guía del Ocio* (in Spanish) has a music section, as does the weekly *Time Out Barcelona* (www. timeout.cat), in Catalan; both *El País* and *La Vanguardia* list forthcoming concerts. For children's events try www.socpetit.cat

---

♥ Best culture for kids

CosmoCaixa *p184*
Interactive museum for little ones.

La Mercè *p221*
A festival full of fireworks.

Palau de la Música Catalana *p249*
Family shows in a Modernista masterpiece.

La Puntual *p251*
Language-barrier-breaking puppet shows.

---

or www.kidsinbarcelona.com. The council website, www.bcn.cat/cultura, also has details of many forthcoming events. Tickets for most major venues can be bought by phone or online from venues, or from telendrada.com or www.ticketmaster.com.

Venues

In addition to the venues listed over the next few pages, several churches also hold concerts. Not only are the acoustics (usually) excellent, but also the spaces suit sacred music. The most popular church is **Santa Maria del Mar** (*see p100*) in the Born, where Handel's Messiah draws the crowds at Christmas, but more atmospheric are smaller chapels such as **Santa Maria del Pi** (*see p73*), **Sant Felip Neri** (*see p72*) and **Santa Anna** (*see p73*), as well as the gorgeous Gothic convent in **Pedralbes** (*see p185*). Concerts run from Renaissance music to gospel, with everything in between.

Ateneu Barcelonès

C/Canuda 6, Barri Gòtic (93 343 61 21, www.ateneubcn.org). Metro Liceu. **Open** *9am-10pm daily.* **Tickets** *vary. No cards.* **Map** *p71 H8.*

This fine old library hosts occasional concerts, either in its leafy central patio or in an auditorium. The '30 Minuts de Música' programme offers half-hour concerts on Friday, Saturday and Sunday evenings at 6pm, 7pm and 8pm. Organised by the Fundació Mas i Mas (www.fundaciomasimas. org), they feature mostly chamber music, with promising young musicians and the odd big name.

L'Auditori

C/Lepant 150, Eixample (93 247 93 00, www. auditori.cat). Metro Marina. **Box office** *5-9pm Tue-Fri; 10am-1pm, 5-9pm Sat; 1hr before performance Sun. Closed Aug.* **Tickets** *vary.* **Map** *p152 M8.*

Designed by architect Rafael Moneo, L'Auditori tries to offer something to everyone. The 2,400-seat Pau Casals hall, dedicated to the Catalan cellist, provides a stable home for city orchestra OBC, now under the baton of conductor Kazushi Ono (although it frequently performs with guest conductors). A more intimate 600-seat chamber space, which is dedicated to choir leader Oriol Martorell, has a more diverse programme incorporating contemporary and world music. Experimental and children's work is staged in a 350-seat space named after jazz pianist Tete Montoliu. **L'Auditori**, also houses the newly reopened **Museu de la Música** (*see p161*).

❤ Gran Teatre del Liceu

La Rambla 51-59, Barri Gòtic (93 485 99 00, www.liceubarcelona.cat). Metro Liceu. **Box office** *9.30am-8pm Mon-Fri; 9.30am-6pm Sat, Sun. Closed 2wks Aug.* **Tickets** *vary.* **Map** *p71 G9.*

Since it opened in 1847, two fires, a bombing and a financial crisis have failed to quash the spirit and splendour of the Liceu, one of the most prestigious venues in the world. A restrained façade opens into a 2,292-seat auditorium of red plush, gold leaf and ornate carvings. The latest mod cons include seat-back subtitles in various languages that complement the Catalan surtitles above the stage. Under the stewardship of artistic director Christina Scheppelmann and musical director Josep Pons, the Liceu has consolidated its programming, mixing co-productions with leading international opera houses with in-house productions. Classical, full-length opera is the staple –Wagner's *The Flying Dutchman*, Verdi's *Il Trovatore* and Mozart's *Don Giovanni*, for example – but pocket opera and even pop also feature.

A large basement bar hosts pre-performance talks and recitals, as well as children's shows (Le Petit Liceu) and other musical events. The **Espai Liceu** is a 50-seat auditorium with a regular programme of screenings of past operas, while the swish six-floor **Conservatori** (C/Nou de la Rambla 82-88, 93 327 12 00, www.conservatoriliceu. es), which is part of the Liceu, lends its 400-seater basement auditorium to classical and contemporary concerts, small-scale operas and jazz.

❤ Palau de la Música Catalana

C/Palau de la Música 4-6, Sant Pere (93 295 72 00, www.palaumusica.org). Metro Urquinaona. **Box office** *9.30am-9pm Mon-Sat; 10am-3pm Sun. Closed Aug for concerts.* **Tickets** *vary.* **Map** *p90 J8.*

This extraordinary visual explosion of Modernista architectural flights of fancy is a UNESCO World Heritage Site. Built in 1908 by Lluís Domènech i Montaner, it's certainly one of the most spectacular music venues anywhere in the world, and much work has been done to improve its acoustics.

A 21st-century extension has added a terrace, a restaurant and a subterranean hall. Now directed by the affable Joan Oller, the Palau has welcomed some of the finest performers from around the globe over the years, including the likes of Leonard Bernstein and Daniel Barenboim. For guided tours of the Palau, *see p98*.

Orchestras & ensembles

BCN 216
93 487 87 81, www.bcn216.com.

This small but prolific ensemble is resident in L'Auditori and maintains a strong commitment to contemporary music of all types, from solo works to pieces requiring 40 musicians.

La Capella Reial de Catalunya, Le Concert des Nations & Hespèrion XXI
93 594 47 67, www.alia-vox.com.

The popularity of Catalonia's rich heritage in early music is due in no small part to the efforts of the indefatigable Jordi Savall, the driving force behind these three interlinked musical groups which, between them, play around 300 concerts a year worldwide. La Capella Reial specialises in Catalan and Spanish Renaissance and Baroque music; Le Concert des Nations is a period instrument ensemble playing orchestral and symphonic work from 1600 to 1850; and Hespèrion XXI performs pre-1800 European music.

Ensemble Diapasón
mobile 605 081 060.

Diapasón is a septet specialising in Erik Satie and the more playful works of contemporary classical music. The group is led by composer/performer Domènec González de la Rubia.

Grup21
93 285 14 87, www.grup21music.com.

A contemporary music ensemble led by American flautist Peter Bacchus. The group has premiered international works as well as promoting Spanish and Catalan composers.

Orfeó Català
93 295 72 00, www.orfeocatala.cat.

The Orfeó Català began life as one of 150 choral groups that sprang up as part of the patriotic and social renewal movements in the late 19th century and, due to its success, was banned by Franco after the Civil War as a possible focus of Catalan nationalism. No longer as pre-eminent as it once was, the group still stages around 25 performances a year, giving a cappella concerts, as well as providing a choir for the Orquestra Simfònica and other Catalan orchestras. The largely amateur group also includes a small professional nucleus, the Cor de Cambra del Palau de la Música, which gives 50 performances a year.

Orquestra Simfònica de Barcelona i Nacional de Catalunya (OBC)

93 247 93 00, www.obc.cat.

The Orquestra Simfònica de Barcelona is the busiest orchestra in the city, performing at the Auditori almost every weekend of the season. The orchestra provides a fairly standard gallop through the symphonic repertoire, although the programme has become increasingly eclectic under the direction of Kazushi Ono. The orchestra is also committed to new Catalan composers, commissioning two works a year.

Orquestra Simfònica del Vallès

93 727 03 00, www.osvalles.com.

This provincial orchestra, based in the nearby town of Sabadell, performs regularly in Barcelona, often at the Palau de la Música Catalana, where it plays about ten symphonic concerts each season.

Orquestra Simfònica i Cor del Gran Teatre del Liceu

93 485 99 00, www.liceubarcelona.cat.

As well as a roster of operas every season, there's also a programme of concerts and recitals, and half a dozen colourful mini operas aimed at children (or their bigger brethren), including *The Little Magic Flute* and *The Houseboat*.

Trio Kandinsky

Mobile 690 603 984, www.triokandinsky.com.

Formed in 1999, the Trio Kandinsky has an excellent reputation, performing contemporary repertoire as well as the classical canon.

THEATRE & DANCE

Catalan theatre was banned under Franco. After his death, troupes surged on to the streets. However, the excitement of the 1980s fizzled out in the '90s, when groups became tired of the nomadic life and despondent with the lack of funding and dearth of performance spaces. The survivors were those companies such as **Els Comediants** and **La Fura dels Baus**, who stuck to the attention-seeking style of street theatre. The 21st century began more promisingly with a city council that put culture as a process and not just a product back on the agenda. This led to the availability of public cash for organisations that support creation, such as **L'Estruch** (www.lestruch.cat) and **La Caldera** (www.lacaldera.info), and theatre groups such as **Conservas** (conservas.tk). Unfortunately, with austerity measures introduced in response to the economic crisis, arts funding has been drastically reduced. Today, most Barcelona theatre is in Catalan, although Spanish-language productions tour, and **Teatre Lliure** (*see p253*) offers surtitles in English for major productions.

In the world of dance, performers such as the **Compañía Nacional de Danza**, directed by José Carlos Martínez (cndanza.mcu.es), fill grand venues such as the **Teatre Nacional** (*see p253*) and the **Liceu** (*see p249*). Companies such as **Sol Picó** and **Erre que Erre** usually run a new show every year, as do **Mudances** and **Gelabert-Azzopardi**.

Information and tickets

Main shows start around 9-10pm. On Sundays, there are morning matinées aimed at families and earlier evening shows at

In the know
Child-friendly shows

English-language children's theatre is rare, with the exception of the Christmas pantomime. **La Puntual** (C/ Allada Vermell 15, Born, mobile 639 305 353, www.lapuntual.info) is a little puppet theatre that often has language-free shows.

Pure Spectacle

The visual glory of Catalan theatre

In a city so proud of its language and culture, it's no surprise that the majority of plays are performed in Catalan. However, that's no reason for visiting theatre buffs who don't speak the lingo to miss curtain up.

Catalan theatre is famously visual as a result of groups like **La Fura dels Baus** and **Els Comediants** *(see p254)* finding new ways to tell their stories when Catalan was banned under Franco. Both companies are often away from Barcelona on tour, but if you get the chance to see them perform, expect big, ballsy, punch-you-in-the-face spectacle

and little or no dialogue. Meanwhile, **Teatro de los Sentidos** (www.teatrodelossentidos. com) performances take audiences on a memorable, though sometimes odorous, journey of the senses.

Professional English-language theatre is thin on the ground, but an enthusiastic amateur scene fills the void, especially during June and November. Look out for productions from **Jocular Theatre** (www. joculartheatre.com), known for its dark comedies and for being the most prolific of the English-language companies.

Els Comediants

around 5-6.30pm; most theatres are dark on Monday. The **Grec Festival** (*see p218*) attracts major international acts in theatre and dance.

Advance bookings are best made through Ticketmaster or Telentrada (*see p240*). The best places to find information about performances are *Guía del Ocio*, *Time Out Barcelona* magazine and the *cartelera* (listings) pages of the newspapers. Online, check www.teatral.net and www.butxaca. com; for dance, try www.dansacat.org. You can also visit Canal Cultura at www.bcn. cat/cultura.

Major venues

Large-scale commercial productions are shown in **Teatre Condal** (Avda Paral·lel 91, Poble Sec, 93 442 31 32, www.teatrecondal. com), **Teatre Apolo** (Avda Parallel 59, Poble Sec , 93 299 7081, www.teatreapolo. com) **Teatre Borràs** (Plaça Urquinaona 9, Eixample, 93 412 15 82), and the **Tívoli** (C/Casp 8-10, Eixample, 93 412 20 63). For information on these two latter venues, see www.grupbalana.com. Advance tickets for most major venues are also available from the Palau de la Virreina (*see p80*).

Mercat de les Flors

Plaça Margarida Xirgú, C/Lleida 59, Poble Sec (93 256 2600, mercatflors.cat). Metro Poble Sec. ***Box office*** *2hr before show. Advance tickets also available from Palau de la Virreina, see p80.* ***Tickets*** *vary. No cards.* ***Map*** *p139 C9.*

British theatre director Peter Brook is credited with transforming this former flower market into a venue for the performing arts in 1985, when he was looking for a place to stage his legendary production of the *Mahabharata*. After decades of fairly diffuse programming, the Mercat has finally focused on national and international contemporary dance, and offers a strong programme that experiments with unusual formats and mixes in new technologies and live music.

Teatre Lliure

Passeig Santa Madrona 40-46, Poble Sec (93 289 27 70, www.teatrelliure.com). Metro Poble Sec. ***Box office*** *9am-8pm Mon-Fri; 2hrs before show Sat, Sun.* ***Map*** *p139 C9.*

Under its director, Lluís Pasqual, the Teatre Lliure's main and mini stages host an adventurous array of theatre and dance that occasionally spills on to the square outside. Bigger theatre shows are surtitled in English on Thursdays and Saturdays.

Teatre Nacional de Catalunya (TNC)

Plaça de les Arts 1, Eixample (93 306 57 00, www.tnc.cat). Metro Glòries. ***Box office*** *5-8pm Wed-Fri; 3-8pm (9.30pm double performance days) Sat; 3-6pm Sun. Closed Aug.* ***Tickets*** *vary.* ***Map*** *p152 M8.*

The Generalitat-funded theatre, which was designed by Ricardo Bofill in a neo-classical style, boasts a vast airy lobby and three fabulous performance spaces. Director Xavier Albertí has opted for a good mix of contemporary and classical pieces and incorporated a fine contemporary dance programme, divided between a main stage and smaller stage.

Teatre Poliorama

La Rambla 115, Barri Gòtic (93 317 75 99, www.teatrepoliorama.com). Metro Catalunya. ***Box office*** *2hrs before start of show. Closed 2wks Aug.* ***Tickets*** *vary.* ***Map*** *p71 H8.*

Run by private producers 3xtr3s, this once adventurous theatre now puts on mainstream comedies and musicals such as *Spamalot*, along with the occasional piece of serious theatre. It also stages a long-running and very popular opera and flamenco show.

Teatre Romea

C/Hospital 51, Raval (93 301 55 04, www. teatreromea.cat). Metro Liceu. ***Box office*** *5.30pm until start of show Mon-Fri; 4.30pm until start of show Sat, Sun.* ***Tickets*** *vary.* ***Map*** *p109 G9.*

Artistic director Borja Sitjà looks to contemporary theatre from around the world for inspiration, even though most works are performed in Catalan.

Alternative theatres

There are a number of smaller theatres in Barcelona struggling to secure funding and audiences. Survivors are **Tantarantana** (C/Flors 22, Raval, 93 441 70 22, www. tantarantana.com), **La Seca Espai Brossa** (C/Flassaders 40, Born, 93 310 13 64, www. laseca.cat) and the **L'Antic Teatre** (C/ Verdaguer i Callis 12, Born, 93 315 23 54, www.anticteatre.com). Additionally, **Versus Teatre** (C/Castlllejos 179, Eixample, 93 603 51 52, www.versusteatre.com), **Teatreneu** (C/ Terol 26, Gràcia, 93 285 37 12, www. teatreneu.com) and **Sala Muntaner** (C/ Muntaner 4, Eixample, 93 451 57 52, www.salamuntaner.com) often produce interesting work. The **Cafè-Teatre Llantiol** (C/Riereta 7, Raval, 93 329 90 09, www. llantiol. com) occasionally holds Giggling Guiri comedy nights in English, which in

La Fura dels Baus

early 2017 included a run of small shows with Eddie Izzard.

Sala Beckett

C/Pere IV 228-232, Poblenou (93 284 53 12, www.salabeckett.cat). Metro Poblenou. **Box office** *2 hrs before start of show.*

This small but important theatre was founded by the Samuel Beckett-inspired Teatro Fronterizo group, which is run by playwright José Sanchís Sinisterra. Although he is no longer based at the theatre, his influence continues to prevail. Check the website for updates.

In the know
Seaside sounds

In summer, as the city empties out and the Catalans head to their (many, many) second homes, countless music festivals take place along the Costa Dorada and, particularly, the Costa Brava. Especially worth checking out are the festivals in the towns of Vilabertran, Perelada, Cadaqués and Torroella de Montgrí.

Theatre companies

As well as those reviewed below, companies to watch out for include the satirical troupe **The Chanclettes** (www.thechanclettes.com) and **Dagoll Dagom** (www.dagolldagom. com). **Els Joglars** (www.elsjoglars.com) was founded 50 years ago by Albert Boadella, who was imprisoned by Franco for his political stance and then decided to exile himself from Catalonia after some high-profile spats regarding the regional government's linguistic policy.

Els Comediants

www.comediants.com.

Els Comediants has its roots in *commedia dell'arte* and street performance; its mix of mime, circus, music, storytelling and fireworks is as likely to appear on the street to celebrate a national holiday as at any major theatre festival.

La Fura dels Baus

www.lafura.com.

This ostentatious troupe started out on the streets of Barcelona in the 1980s with a donkey, a cart and nihilistic ideas, but now tours the world with high-tech, polemical productions. Former founder member – and ex-abattoir employee – Marcel·li Antúnez Roca follows a similar vein in his solo shows.

Tricicle
93 317 4747, www.tricicle.com.

Local boys Carles Sans, Paco Mir and Joan Gràcia founded this mime trio some 35 years ago. The goofy, clean-cut humour appeals to the Spanish taste for slapstick, and children love it as well. They are regulars at El Petit Liceu and have, among other feats, managed to bring Monty Python's *Spamalot* to a local audience.

Dance companies

For an extensive list of groups, check www. companyiesdansa.info.

Compañia Mar Gómez
www.ciamargomez.com.

Compañia Mar Gómez provides an excellent mix of contemporary dance and theatre with a wicked sense of humour and good music.

Erre que Erre
www.errequeerredanza.net.

This excellent collective of younger dancers transforms complex ideas into contemplative performances, complete with well-measured doses of theatre and original music.

Gelabert-Azzopardi
www.gelabertazzopardi.com.

Expect fluid, poetic performances from Barcelona's Cesc Gelabert and Londoner Lydia Azzopardi.

Mal Pelo
www.malpelo.org.

Maria Munoz and Pep Ramis incorporate images and text into their shows.

Marta Carrasco
www.martacarrasco.com.

Veteran dancer Marta Carrasco has choreographed many plays and musicals over the years. Lavish costumes and extravagant set designs define her elegant performances.

Mudances
www.margarit-mudances.com.

Director Àngels Margarit and his dancers create melodic work drawing on world music and dance. The company produces pieces for family audiences.

Sol Picó
www.solpico.com.

Charismatic Sol Picó mixes up the genres and adds a touch of humour.

Flamenco

Local *cantaors* (flamenco singers), such as Miguel Poveda, play to sell-out crowds at the **Palau de la Música** or smaller venues such as **Luz de Gas** (*see p240*), as do singers and guitarists from the south such as Diego de Cigala and Vicente Amigo. Dancers, including Rafael Amargo and Sara Baras, appear at the **Liceu**.

While flamenco is not native to Catalonia, there are still plenty of shows on offer if you don't mind rubbing elbows with a largely foreign crowd. The Friday night flamenco performances that take place at the restaurant **Nervion** (C/Princesa 2, Born, 93 315 21 03, www. restaurantenervion. com, closed end Aug, 1st wk Sept) seem to be aimed at tourists, but they are a cheaper night out than the established *tablaos*: if you don't eat at the venue, entry is €16.90 and includes a drink; €27.90 gets you dinner and a show. **Flamenco Barcelona** (www.flamencobarcelona.com) organises flamenco events along with flamenco guitar, singing and dance courses.

El Tablao de Carmen
Poble Espanyol, Avda Francesc Ferrer i Guàrdia 13, Montjuïc (93 325 68 95, www. tablaodecarmen.com). Metro Espanya. **Open** *6-11pm Tue-Sun. Shows 6.30pm, 8.30pm Tue-Sun.* **Admission** *show & 1 drink €43; show & tapas €55; show & dinner €75 or €95.* **Map** *p139 B8.*

This rather sanitised version of the flamenco *tablao* resides in faux-Andalucían surroundings in the Poble Espanyol (*see p146*). You will find stars and young talent here on a regular basis, showcasing flamenco singing, dancing and music. It's advisable to book (up to a week ahead in summer). The admission fee includes entry to the Poble Espanyol.

Los Tarantos
Plaça Reial 17, Barri Gòtic (93 319 17 89, www.masimas.com/tarantos). Metro Liceu. **Open** *8-11pm daily. Shows 8.30pm, 9.30pm, 10.30pm daily.* **Admission** *€15.* **Map** *p71 G10.*

This flamenco *tablao* has presented many top stars to a wide audience over the years, as well as offering some *rumba catalana*. Now Los Tarantos caters mainly to the tourist trade.

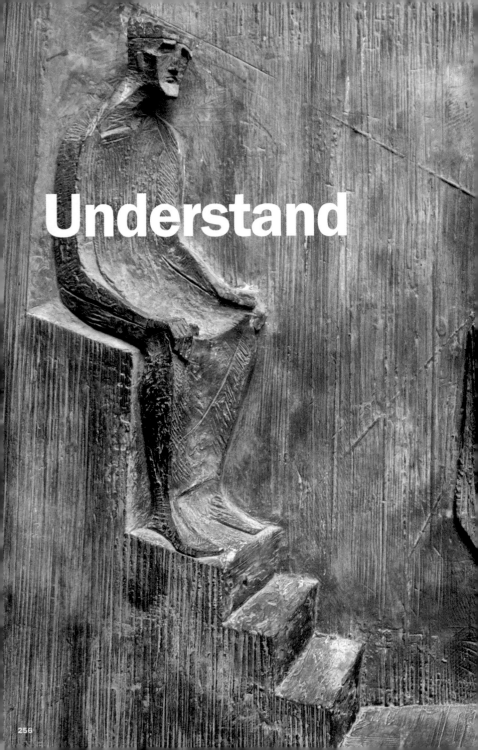

Understand

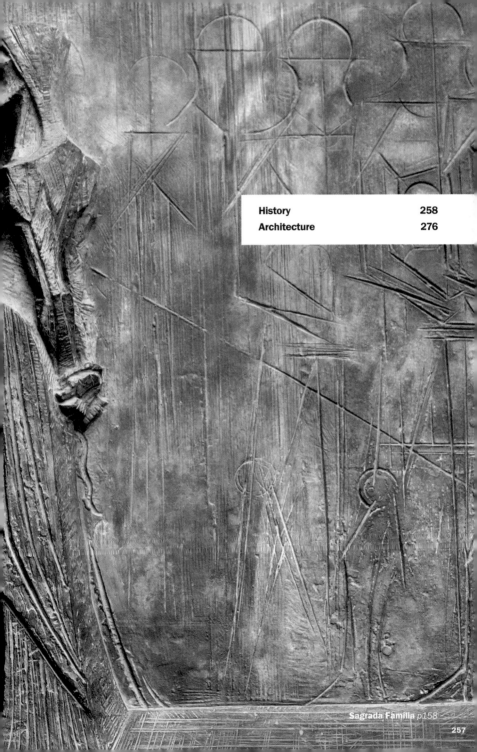

Sagrada Família *p158*

History

The fall and rise of Barcelona

Cultural, political and social diversity flourish in today's Barcelona, but things haven't always been that way. For long periods of its history, the city was the victim of attempts by governments in Madrid to absorb Catalonia within a unified Spanish state. Under several leaders, notably Philip V in the 17th century and Franco in the 20th, these attempts resulted in a policy aimed at stamping out any vestige of Catalan culture or independence. However, the region always re-emerged from such persecutions stronger and more vibrant, with a heightened desire to show the world its distinctive character – both socially and culturally.

Plaça de Ramon Berenguer el Gran

In the beginning

The Romans founded Barcelona in about 15 BC on the Mons Taber, a hill between two streams that provided a good view of the Mediterranean; today, it's crowned by a cathedral. At the time, the plain around it was sparsely inhabited by the Laetani, an Iberian people who produced grain and honey, and gathered oysters. Then called Barcino, it was smaller than Tarraco (Tarragona), the capital of the Roman province of Hispania Citerior, but had the only harbour between there and Narbonne.

Like virtually every other Roman new town in Europe, Barcino was a fortified rectangle with a crossroads at its centre (where the Plaça Sant Jaume is today). It was an unimportant provincial town, but the rich plain provided it with a produce garden and the sea gave it an incipient maritime trade. It acquired a Jewish community soon after its foundation and became associated with Christian martyrs; among them was Santa Eulàlia, Barcelona's first patron saint. Eulàlia was supposedly executed at the end of the third century via a series of revolting tortures that included being rolled naked in a barrel full of glass shards down the alley called Baixada ('Descent') de Santa Eulàlia.

The city's massive stone walls made the stronghold desirable to later warlords

The people of Barcino accepted Christianity in AD 312, together with the rest of the Roman Empire, which by then was under growing threat of invasion. In response, the town's rough defences were replaced in the fourth century with massive stone walls, many sections of which can still be seen today. It was these ramparts that ensured Barcelona's continuity, making the stronghold so desirable to later warlords.

Nonetheless, such defences could not prevent the empire's disintegration. In 415, Barcelona, as it became known, briefly became capital of the kingdom of the Visigoths, under their chieftain Ataülf. They soon moved on southwards to extend their control over the whole of the Iberian peninsula, and for the next 400 years the town was a neglected backwater. The Muslims swept across the peninsula after 711, crushing Goth resistance; they made little attempt to settle Catalonia, but much of the Christian population retreated into the Pyrenees, the first Catalan heartland.

Then, at the end of the eighth century, the Franks drove south, against the Muslims, from across the mountains. In 801, Charlemagne's son, Louis the Pious, took Barcelona and made it a bastion of the Marca Hispanica (Spanish March), which was the southern buffer of his father's empire. This gave Catalonia a trans-Pyrenean origin entirely different from that of the other Christian states in Spain; equally, it's for this reason that the closest relative of the Catalan language is Provençal, not Castilian.

When the Frankish princes returned to their main business further north, loyal counts were left behind to rule sections of the Catalan lands. At the end of the ninth century, Count Guifré el Pilós (Wilfred

Ataulf King of the Visigoths (Vincenzo Carducci, 1635)

Death of the Count Wilfred the Hairy
(Pablo Antonio Béjar y Novella)

'the Hairy') managed to gain control over several of these Catalan counties from his base in Ripoll. By uniting them under his rule, he laid the basis for a future Catalan state, founding the dynasty of the Counts of Barcelona, which reigned in an unbroken line until 1410. His successors made Barcelona their capital, setting the seal on the city's future.As a founding patriarch, Wilfred is the stuff of legends, not least of which is that he was the creator of the Catalan flag. The story goes that he was fighting the Saracens alongside his lord, the Frankish emperor, when he was severely wounded. In recognition of Wilfred's heroism, the emperor dipped his fingers into his friend's blood and ran them down the count's golden shield; thus, the Quatre Barres, four bars of red on a yellow background, also known as La Senyera was created. Recorded facts make this story highly unlikely, but whatever its origins, the four-stripe symbol was first recorded on the tomb of Count Ramon Berenguer II in 1082, making it the oldest national flag in Europe. What is not known is exactly in what way Wilfred was so notably hairy.

Laying the foundations

In the first century of the new millennium, Catalonia was consolidated as a political entity, and entered an age of cultural richness. This was the great era of Catalan Romanesque art, with the building of the magnificent monasteries and the churches of northern Catalonia, such as Sant Pere de Rodes near Figueres, and the painting of the glorious murals now housed in the Museu Nacional on Montjuïc. There was a flowering of scholarship, reflecting Catalan contacts with northern Europe and with Islamic and Carolingian cultures. In Barcelona, shipbuilding and trade in grain and wine grew, and a new trade developed in textiles. The city expanded both inside its old Roman walls and outside them, with vilanoves (new towns) appearing at Sant Pere and La Ribera.

The most significant addition, however, occurred in 1137, when Ramon Berenguer IV (1131-62) wed Petronella, heir to the throne of Aragon. In the long term, the marriage bound Catalonia into Iberia. The uniting of the two dynasties created a powerful entity known as the Crown of Aragon: each element retained its separate institutions and was ruled by monarchs known as the Count-Kings. Ramon Berenguer IV also extended Catalan territory to its current frontiers in the Ebro valley. At the beginning of the next century, however, the dynasty lost virtually all its land north of the Pyrenees to France, when Count-King Pere I 'the Catholic' was killed at the Battle of Muret in 1213. This proved a blessing in disguise. In future years, the Catalan-Aragonese state became oriented decisively towards the Mediterranean and the south. It was then able to embark on two centuries of imperialism that would be equalled in vigour only by Barcelona's burgeoning commercial enterprise.

Empire-building

Pere I's successor was the most expansionist of the Count-Kings. Jaume I 'the Conqueror' (1213-76) joined the campaign against the Muslims to the south, taking Mallorca in 1229, Ibiza in 1235 and, at greater cost, Valencia in 1238 (which he made another separate kingdom, the third part of the Crown of Aragon). Barcelona became the centre of an empire spanning the Mediterranean.

Barcelona contains the most important collection of historic Gothic civil architecture anywhere in Europe

The city grew tremendously. In the middle of the 13th century, Jaume I ordered the building of a second wall along the line of La Rambla, roughly encircling the area between there and what is now the Parc de la Ciutadella; in doing so, La Ribera and the other *vilanoves* were brought within the city. In 1274, Jaume also gave Barcelona a form of representative self-government: the Consell de Cent, a council of 100 chosen citizens, an institution that would last for more than 400 years. In Catalonia as a whole, royal powers were strictly limited by a parliament, the Corts, with a permanent standing committee known as the Generalitat.

In 1282, Pere II 'the Great' sent his armies into Sicily; Catalan domination over the island would last for nearly 150 years, as the Catalan empire reached its greatest strength under Jaume II 'the Just' (1291-1327). Corsica (1323) and Sardinia (1324) were added to the Crown of Aragon, although the latter would never submit to Catalan rule and would, from then on, be a constant focus of revolt.

The Golden Age

The Crown of Aragon was often at war with Arab rulers, but its capital flourished through commerce with every part of the Mediterranean, Christian and Muslim. Catalan ships also sailed into the Atlantic, to England and Flanders.

Unsurprisingly, this age of power and prestige was also the great era of building in medieval Barcelona. The Count-Kings' imperial conquests may have been ephemeral, but their talent for permanence in building can still be seen today. Between

1290 and 1340, the construction of most of Barcelona's best-known Gothic buildings was initiated. Religious edifices such as the cathedral, Santa Maria del Mar, Capella de Santa Àgata and Santa Maria del Pi were matched by civil buildings such as the Saló del Tinell and the Llotja, the old market and the stock exchange. As a result, Barcelona contains the most important collection of historic Gothic civil architecture anywhere in Europe.

The ships of the Catalan navy were built in the monumental Drassanes (shipyards), begun by Pere II and completed under Pere III, in 1378. In 1359, Pere III also built the third, final city wall along the line of the modern Paral·lel, Ronda Sant Pau and Ronda Sant Antoni. This gave the Old City of Barcelona its definitive shape. La Ribera, 'the waterfront', was the centre of trade and industry in the 14th-century city. Just inland, the C/Montcada was where newly enriched merchants displayed their wealth in opulent Gothic palaces. All around were the workers of the various craft guilds, grouped together in their own streets. The Catalan Golden Age was also an era of cultural greatness. Catalonia was one of the first areas in Europe to use its vernacular language, as well as Latin, in written form and as a language of culture.

Revolt and collapse

But the prosperity of the medieval period did not last. The Count-Kings had over-extended Barcelona's resources, and overinvested in far-off ports. By 1400, the effort to maintain their conquests, especially Sardinia, had exhausted both the spirit and the coffers of the Catalan imperialist drive. The Black Death, which arrived in the 1340s, had a devastating impact on Catalonia, intensifying the bitterness of social conflicts between the aristocracy, the merchants, the peasants and the urban poor.

In the 1460s, the effects of war and catastrophic famine led to a sudden collapse into violent and destructive civil war and peasant revolt. The population was depleted to such an extent that Barcelona would not manage to regain the numbers it had had in 1400 (40,000) until the 18th century.

In 1469, an important union for Spain initiated a woeful period in Barcelona's history; dubbed by some Catalan historians the Decadència, it led to the end of Catalonia as a separate entity. In that year, Ferdinand of Aragon (1452-1516) married Isabella of Castile (1451-1504), thereby uniting the different Spanish kingdoms, even though they would retain their separate institutions for another two centuries.

Palau Reial Major and the Capella de Santa Àgata p72

As Catalonia's fortunes declined, so those of Castile rose. In 1492, Granada, the last Muslim foothold in Spain, was conquered; Isabella decreed the expulsion of all Jews from Castile and Aragon; and Columbus discovered America. It was Castile's seafaring orientation towards the Atlantic, as opposed to the Mediterranean, that confirmed Catalonia's decline. The discovery of the New World was a disaster for Catalan commerce: trade shifted away from the Mediterranean, and Catalans were officially barred from participating in the exploitation of the new empire until the 1770s. Castile soon became the clear seat of government.

In 1516, the Spanish crown passed to the House of Habsburg, in the shape of Ferdinand and Isabella's grandson, Holy Roman Emperor Charles V. His son, Philip II of Spain, established Madrid as the capital of all his dominions in 1561. Catalonia was managed by viceroys, and the power of its institutions increasingly restricted, with a down-at-heel aristocracy and a meagre cultural life.

Fear the reapers

While Castilian Spain went through its 'Golden Century', Catalonia was left out on the margins. However, worse was to come in the next century, with the two national revolts, both heroic defeats that have since acquired a central role in Catalan mythology.

The problem for the Spanish monarchy was that Castile was an absolute monarchy and thus could be taxed at will, but in the former Aragonese territories, and especially Catalonia, royal authority kept coming up against a mass of local rights and privileges. As the Habsburgs' empire became entrenched in wars and expenses that not even American gold could meet, the Count-Duke of Olivares, the great minister of King Philip IV (1621-65), resolved to extract more money and troops from the non-Castilian dominions of the Crown. But the Catalans felt they were taxed enough already.

In 1640, a mass of peasants, later dubbed Els Segadors (the Reapers), gathered on La Rambla in Barcelona, outside the Porta

Ferrissa (Iron Gate) in the second wall. The peasants rioted against royal authority, surged into the city and murdered the viceroy, the Marquès de Santa Coloma. This began the general uprising known as the Guerra dels Segadors, or the 'Reapers' War'. The authorities of the Generalitat, led by its president, Pau Claris, were fearful of the violence of the poor; lacking the confidence to declare Catalonia independent, they appealed for protection from Louis XIII of France. French armies, however, were unable to defend Catalonia adequately, and in 1652 a destitute Barcelona capitulated to the exhausted army of Philip IV. In 1659, France and Spain made peace with a treaty that gave the Catalan territory of Roussillon, around Perpignan, to France. Following the revolt, Philip IV and his ministers were magnanimous, allowing the Catalans to retain what was left of their institutions despite their disloyalty.

The reign in Spain

Fifty years later came the second of the great national rebellions – the War of the Spanish Succession. In 1700, Charles II of Spain died without an heir, and Castile accepted the grandson of Louis XIV of France, Philip of Anjou, as King Philip V of Spain (1700-46). But the alternative candidate, Archduke Charles of Austria, promised that he would restore the traditional rights of the former Aragonese territories, and won their allegiance. He also had the support, in his fight against France, of Britain, Holland and Austria.

But Catalonia had backed the wrong horse. In 1713, Britain and the Dutch made a separate peace with France and withdrew their aid, leaving the Catalans stranded, with no possibility of victory. After a 13-month siege in which every citizen was called to arms, Barcelona fell to the French and Spanish armies on 11 September 1714. The most heroic defeat of all, the date marked the most decisive political reverse in Barcelona's history, and is now commemorated as Catalan National Day, the Diada. Some of Barcelona's resisters were buried next to the church of Santa Maria del Mar in the Born, in the Fossar de les Moreres (Mulberry Graveyard), now a memorial.

In 1715, Philip V issued his decree of Nova Planta, abolishing all the remaining separate institutions of the Crown of Aragon and so, in effect, creating 'Spain' as a single, unitary state. Large-scale 'Castilianisation' of the country was initiated, and Castilian replaced the Catalan language in all official documents. In Barcelona, extra measures were taken to keep the city under control. The crumbling medieval walls and the

castle on Montjuïc were refurbished with new ramparts, and a massive new citadel was built on the eastern side of the Old City, where the Parc de la Ciutadella is today. To make space, thousands were expelled from La Ribera and forcibly rehoused in the Barceloneta, Barcelona's first-ever planned housing scheme, with its barrack-like street plan unmistakably provided by French military engineers. The citadel became the most hated symbol of the city's subordination.

Urban renaissance

Politically subjugated and without a significant ruling class, Catalonia nevertheless revived in the 18th century. Shipping picked up again, and Barcelona started a booming export trade to the New World in wines and spirits from Catalan vineyards, and textiles, wool and silk. Catalan trade with Spanish America quadrupled; Barcelona's population had grown from 30,000 in 1720 to around 100,000 by the end of the 18th century.

The citadel became the most hated symbol of the city's subordination

The prosperity was reflected in a new wave of building in the city. Neoclassical mansions appeared, notably on C/ Ample and La Rambla, but the greatest transformation was La Rambla itself, turned from a dusty riverbed to a paved promenade with the destruction of the city wall that had hitherto flanked it. Beyond La Rambla, the previously semi-rural Raval was swiftly becoming densely populated.

Barcelona's expansion was briefly slowed by the French invasion of 1808. Napoleon sought to appeal to Catalans by offering them national recognition within his empire, but was met with curiously little response. After six years of turmoil, Barcelona's growing business class resumed its many projects in 1814, with the restoration of the Bourbon monarchy in the shape of Ferdinand VII (1808-33).

Getting up steam

Ferdinand VII attempted to reinstate the absolute monarchy of his youth and reimpose his authority over Spain's American colonies, but failed to do either. On his death he was succeeded by his three-year-old daughter Isabella II (1833-68), but the throne was also claimed by his brother Carlos, who was backed by the country's most reactionary sectors.

To defend Isabella's rights, the Regent, Ferdinand's widow Queen María Cristina, was obliged to seek the support of liberals, and so granted a very limited form of constitution. Thus began Spain's Carlist Wars, which had a powerful impact in conservative rural Catalonia, where Don Carlos's faction won a considerable following, in part because of its support for traditional local rights and customs.

While this struggle went on around the country, a liberal-minded local administration in Barcelona, freed from subordination to the military, was able to engage in city planning, opening up the soon-to-be fashionable C/Ferran and Plaça Sant Jaume in the 1820s and later adding the Plaça Reial. A fundamental change came in 1836, when the government in Madrid decreed the Desamortización (or the 'disentailment') of Spain's monasteries. In Barcelona, where convents and religious houses still took up great sections of the Raval and La Rambla, a huge area was freed for development. La Rambla took on the appearance it roughly retains today, while the Raval, the main district for new industry in a city still contained within its walls, filled up with tenements and textile mills several storeys high.

In 1832, the first steam-driven factory in Spain was built on C/Tallers, sparking resistance from hand-spinners and weavers. Most of the city's factories were still relatively small, however, and the Catalan manufacturers were aware that they were at a disadvantage in competing with the industries of Britain and other countries to the north. Complicating matters further, they didn't even have the city to themselves. Not only did the anti-industrial Carlists threaten from the countryside, but Barcelona also soon became a centre of radical ideas. Its people were notably rebellious, and liberal, republican, free-thinking and even utopian socialist groups proliferated between bursts of repression.

By this time, the Catalan language had been relegated to secondary status, spoken in every street but rarely written or used in cultured discourse. Then, in 1833, Bonaventura Carles Aribau published his *Oda a la Pàtria*, a romantic eulogy in Catalan of the country, its language and its past. The poem had an extraordinary impact and is still traditionally credited with initiating the Renaixença (Renaissance) of Catalan heritage and culture.

Diada Nacional de Catalunya

Setting an Eixample

The optimism of Barcelona's new middle class was counterpointed by two persistent obstacles: the weakness of the Spanish economy as a whole; and the instability of their own society, which was reflected in atrocious labour relations. No consideration was given to the manpower behind the industrial surge: the underpaid, overworked men, women and children who lived in appalling conditions in high-rise slums within the cramped city.

One response to the city's problems that had almost universal support was the demolition of the city walls, which had imposed a stifling restriction on its growth. For years, however, the Spanish state had refused to relinquish its hold on the city. To find space, larger factories were established in villages around Barcelona, such as Sants and Poblenou, and in 1854 permission finally came for the demolition of the citadel and the walls. The work began with enthusiastic popular participation, crowds of volunteers joining in at weekends. Barcelona at last broke out of the space it had occupied since the 14th century and spread outwards into its new *eixample* (extension), built to a controversial plan by Ildefons Cerdà.

In 1868, Isabella II, once a symbol of liberalism, was overthrown by a progressive revolt. During the six years of upheaval that followed, power in Madrid would be held by the provisional government, a constitutional monarchy under an Italian prince and subsequently a federal republic. However, workers were free to organise.

Giuseppe Fanelli brought the first anarchist ideas, and two years later, the first Spanish workers' congress took place in Barcelona. The radical forces were divided between many squabbling factions, whereas the established classes of society felt increasingly threatened and called for the restoration of order. The Republic proclaimed in 1873 was unable to establish its authority, and succumbed to a military coup less than a year later.

The Midas touch

In 1874, the Bourbon dynasty, in the person of Alfonso XII, son of Isabella II, was restored to the Spanish throne. Workers' organisations were again suppressed. The middle classes, however, felt their confidence renewed. The 1870s saw a frenzied boom in stock speculation, known as the *febre d'or* (gold fever), and the real take-off of building in the Eixample. From the 1880s, Modernisme became the preferred style of the new district, the perfect expression of the confidence and impetus of the industrial class. The first modern Catalanist political movement was founded by Valentí Almirall.

Barcelona felt it needed to show the world all that it had achieved, and that it was more than just a 'second city'. In 1885, a promoter named Eugenio Serrano de Casanova proposed to the city council the holding of an international exhibition, such as had been held successfully in London, Paris and Vienna. Serrano was a highly dubious character who eventually made off with large amounts of public funds, but by the time that this became clear, the city fathers had fully committed themselves to the event.

Modernisme became the perfect expression of the confidence and impetus of the industrial class

The Universal Exhibition of 1888 was used as a pretext for the final conversion of the Ciutadella into a park. Giant efforts had to be made to get everything ready in time, a feat that led the mayor, Francesc Rius i Taulet, to exclaim that, 'The Catalan people are the Yankees of Europe.' The first of Barcelona's three great attempts to prove its status to the world, the 1888 Exhibition signified the consecration of the Modernista style, as well as marking the end of dowdy, provincial Barcelona and its establishment as a modern-day city on the international map.

The city of the new century

The 1888 Exhibition left Barcelona with huge debts, a new look and many reasons to believe in itself as a paradigm of progress. The Catalan Renaixença continued, and acquired a more political tone. A truly decisive moment came in 1898, when the underlying weakness of the Spanish state was made plain over the superficial prosperity of the first years of the Bourbon restoration. It was then that Spain was forced into a short war with the United States, in which it lost its remaining empire in Cuba, the Philippines and Puerto Rico.

Industrialists were horrified at losing the lucrative Cuban market, and despaired of the ability of the state ever to reform itself. Many swung behind a conservative nationalist movement: the Lliga Regionalista (Regionalist League), founded in 1901 and led by Enric Prat de la Riba and the politician-financier Francesc Cambó, promised both national revival and modern, efficient government.

At the same time, however, Barcelona continued to grow, fuelling Catalanist optimism. Above all, it had a vibrant artistic community, centred on Modernisme, which consisted of great architects and established painters such as Rusiñol and Casas, but also the penniless bohemians who gathered round them, among them the young Picasso. They were drawn to the increasingly wild nightlife of the Raval, where cabarets, bars and brothels multiplied at the end of the 19th century. Located around the cabarets, though, were the poorest of the working classes, for whom conditions had only continued to decline; Barcelona had some of the worst overcrowding and highest mortality rates in Europe. Local philanthropists called for something to be done, but Barcelona was more associated with revolutionary politics and violence than with peaceful social reform.

In 1893, more than 20 people were killed in a series of anarchist terrorist attacks, which included the notorious incident in which a bomb was hurled into the wealthy audience at the Liceu. The perpetrators acted alone, but the authorities seized the opportunity to round up the usual suspects – mainly local anarchists and radicals. Several of them, known as the 'Martyrs of Montjuïc', were later tortured and executed in the castle above the city. Retaliation came in 1906, when a Catalan anarchist tried to kill King Alfonso XIII on his wedding day.

Anarchism was still only in a fledgling state among workers during the 1900s. However, rebellious attitudes, along with growing republican sentiment and a fierce hatred of the Catholic Church, united the underclasses and led them to take to the barricades. The Setmana Tràgica (Tragic Week) of 1909 began as a protest against the conscription of troops for the colonial war in Morocco, but degenerated into a general

Barricades during the Setmana Tràgica, 1909

riot, accompanied by the destruction of churches by excited mobs. Suspected culprits were summarily executed, as was the anarchist educationalist Francesc Ferrer, who was accused of 'moral responsibility', despite the fact that he wasn't even in Barcelona at the time.

These events dented the optimism of the Catalanists of the Lliga. However, in 1914, they secured from Madrid the Mancomunitat, or administrative union, of the four Catalan provinces, the first joint government of any kind in Catalonia in 200 years. Its first president was Prat de la Riba, who would be succeeded on his death in 1917 by the architect Puig i Cadafalch. However, the Lliga's plans for an orderly Catalonia were to be obstructed by a further surge in social tensions.

Champagne and socialists

Spain's neutral status during World War I gave a huge boost to the Spanish, and especially Catalan, economy. Exports soared as Catalonia's manufacturers made millions supplying uniforms to the French army. Barcelona's industry was at last able to diversify from textiles into engineering, chemicals and other more modern sectors. The war also set off massive inflation, driving people in their thousands from rural Spain into the big cities. Barcelona doubled in size in 20 years to become the largest city in Spain, and also the fulcrum of Spanish politics. Workers' wages, meanwhile, had lost half their real value.

The chief channel of protest in Barcelona was the anarchist workers' union, the Confederación Nacional del Trabajo (CNT), constituted in 1910, which gained half a million members in Catalonia by 1919. The CNT and the socialist Union General de Trabajadores (UGT) launched a joint general strike in 1917, roughly co-ordinated with a campaign by the Lliga and other liberal politicians for political reform. However, the politicians soon withdrew at the prospect of serious social unrest. Inflation continued to intensify and, in 1919, Barcelona was paralysed for more than two months by a CNT general strike over union recognition. Employers refused to recognise the CNT, and the most intransigent among them hired gunmen to get rid of union leaders. Union activists replied in kind, and virtual guerrilla warfare developed between the CNT, the employers and the state. More than 800 people were killed on the city's streets over five years.

In 1923, in response both to the chaos in the city and a crisis in the war in Morocco, the Captain-General of Barcelona, Miguel Primo de Rivera, staged a coup and established a military dictatorship under King Alfonso XIII. The CNT was already exhausted, and it was suppressed. Conservative Catalanists, longing for an end to disorder and the revolutionary threat, initially supported the coup, but were rewarded by the abolition of the Mancomunitat and a vindictive campaign by the Primo regime against the Catalan language and national symbols.

This, however, achieved the opposite of the desired effect, helping to radicalise and popularise Catalan nationalism. Following the terrible struggles of the previous years, the 1920s were actually a time of notable prosperity for many in Barcelona, as some of the wealth recently accumulated filtered through the economy. It was also, though, a highly politicised society, in which new magazines and forums for discussion – despite the restrictions of the dictatorship – found a ready audience.

A prime motor of Barcelona's prosperity in the 1920s was the International Exhibition of 1929, the second of the city's great showcase events. It had been proposed by Cambó and Catalan business groups, but Primo de Rivera saw that it could also serve as a propaganda event for his regime. A huge number of public projects were undertaken in association with the main event, including the post office in Via Laietana, the Estació de França and Barcelona's first metro line, from Plaça Catalunya to Plaça d'Espanya. By 1930, Barcelona was very different from the place it had been in 1910; it contained more than a million people, and its urban sprawl had crossed into towns such as Hospitalet and Santa Coloma.

The Republic suppressed

Despite the Exhibition's success, Primo de Rivera resigned in January 1930, exhausted. The king appointed another soldier, General Berenguer, as prime minister, with the mission of restoring stability. The dictatorship, though, had fatally discredited the old regime, and a protest movement spread across Catalonia against the monarchy. In early 1931, Berenguer called local elections as a first step towards a restoration of constitutional rule. The outcome was a complete surprise, for republicans were elected in all of Spain's cities. Ecstatic crowds poured into the streets, and Alfonso XIII abdicated. The Second Spanish Republic was proclaimed on 14 April 1931.

The Republic arrived amid real euphoria, especially in Catalonia, where it was associated with hopes for both social change and national reaffirmation. The clear winner of the elections in the country had

EXPOSICION INTERNACIONAL

International Exhibition of 1929

BARCELONA

been the Esquerra Republicana, a leftist Catalanist group led by Francesc Macià. A raffish, elderly figure, Macià was one of the first politicians in Spain to win genuine affection from ordinary people. He declared Catalonia to be an independent republic within an Iberian federation of states, but later agreed to accept autonomy within the Spanish Republic.

The Generalitat was re-established as a government that would, potentially, acquire wide powers. All aspects of Catalan culture were then in expansion, and a popular press in Catalan achieved a wide readership. Barcelona was also a small but notable centre of the avant-garde. Miró and Dalí had already made their mark in painting;

under the Republic, the Amics de l'Art Nou (ADLAN, Friends of New Art) group worked to promote contemporary art, while the GATCPAC architectural collective sought to bring rationalist architecture to the city.

In Madrid, the Republic's first government was a coalition of republicans and socialists led by Manuel Azaña, its overriding goal to modernise Spanish society through liberal-democratic reforms. However, as social tensions intensified, the coalition collapsed, and a conservative republican party, with support from the traditional Spanish right, secured power shortly after new elections in 1933. For Catalonia, the prospect of a return to right-wing rule prompted fears that it would

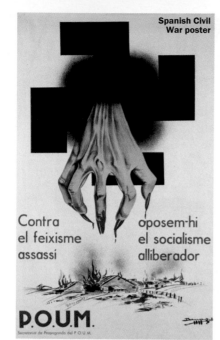

Spanish Civil
War poster

Contra
el feixisme
assassi

oposem-hi
el socialisme
alliberador

P.O.U.M.
Secretariat de Propagando del P.O.U.M.

Up in arms

In Barcelona, militants from the unions and leftist parties, on alert for weeks, poured into the streets to oppose the troops in fierce fighting. Over the course of 19 July, the military were worn down, and finally surrendered in the Hotel Colón on Plaça Catalunya (by the corner with Passeig de Gràcia, the site of which is now occupied by the Radio Nacional de España building). Opinions have always differed as to who could claim most credit for this remarkable popular victory: workers' militants have suggested it was the 'people in arms' who defeated the army, while others stress the importance of the police remaining loyal to the Generalitat throughout the struggle. A likely answer is that they actually encouraged each other.

Barcelona became a magnet for leftists from around the world

Tension released, the city was taken over by the revolution. Militias of the CNT, different Marxist parties and other left-wing factions marched off to Aragon, led by streetfighters such as the Durruti and García Oliver, to continue the battle. The army rising had failed in Spain's major cities but won footholds in Castile, Aragon and the south, although in the heady atmosphere of Barcelona in July 1936 it was often assumed their resistance could not last and the people's victory was near inevitable.

Far from the front, Barcelona was the chief centre of the revolution in republican Spain, the only truly proletarian city. Its middle class avoided the streets, where, as Orwell recorded in his *Homage to Catalonia*, everyone you saw wore workers' clothing. It became a magnet for leftists from around the world, drawing writers André Malraux, Ernest Hemingway and Octavio Paz. All kinds of industries and public services were collectivised, including cinemas, the phone system and food distribution. Ad hoc 'control patrols' of the revolutionary militias roamed the streets supposedly checking for suspected right-wing agents and sometimes carrying out summary executions, although this was condemned by many leftist leaders.

The alliance between the different left-wing groups was unstable and riddled with tensions. The communists, who had some extra leverage because the Soviet Union was the only country prepared to

immediately abrogate the Generalitat's hard-won powers. On 6 October 1934, while a general strike was launched against the central government in Asturias and some other parts of Spain, Lluís Companys, leader of the Generalitat since Macià's death the previous year, declared Catalonia independent. The 'uprising' turned out to be something of a farce, however: the Generalitat had no means of resisting the army, and the new 'Catalan Republic' was rapidly suppressed. The Generalitat was suspended and its leaders imprisoned.

Over the following year, fascism seemed to become a real threat for the left, as political positions became polarised. Then, in February 1936, elections were won by the Popular Front of the left across the country. The Generalitat was reinstated, and in Catalonia the next few months were peaceful. In the rest of Spain, though, tensions were close to bursting point; right-wing politicians, refusing to accept the loss of power, talked openly of the need for the military to intervene. In July, the stadium on Montjuïc was to be the site of the Popular Olympics, a leftist alternative to the 1936 Olympics in Nazi Germany. On 18 July, the day of the Games' inauguration, army generals launched a coup against the Republic and its left-wing governments, expecting no resistance.

give the Spanish Republic arms, demanded the integration of these loosely organised militias into a conventional army under a strong central authority. The following months saw continual political infighting between the discontented CNT, the radical Marxist party Partit Obrer d'Unificació Marxista (POUM) and the communists. Co-operation broke down totally in May 1937, when republican and communist troops seized the telephone building in Plaça Catalunya (on the corner of Portal de l'Àngel) from a CNT committee, sparking the confused war-within-the-civil-war witnessed by Orwell from the roof of the Teatre Poliorama. A temporary agreement was patched up, but shortly after the POUM was banned, and the CNT excluded from power. A new republican central government was formed under Dr Juan Negrín, a socialist allied to the communists.

After that, the war gradually became more of a conventional conflict. This did little, however, to improve the Republic's position, for the nationalists under General Francisco Franco and their German and Italian allies had been continually gaining ground throughout it all. Madrid was under siege, and the capital of the Republic was moved to Valencia, and then to Barcelona, in November 1937.

Catalonia received thousands of refugees, as food shortages and the lack of armaments ground down morale. Barcelona also had the sad distinction of being the first major city in Europe to be subjected to sustained intensive bombing – to an extent that has rarely been appreciated – with heavy raids throughout 1938, especially by Italian bombers based in Mallorca. The Basque Country and Asturias had already fallen to Franco and, in March 1938, his troops reached the Mediterranean near Castellón, cutting the main Republican zone in two. The Republic had one last throw of the dice, in the Battle of the Ebro in the summer of 1938, when for months the Popular Army struggled to retake control of the river. After that, the Republic was exhausted. Barcelona fell to the Francoist army on 26 January 1939. Half a million refugees fled to France, to be interned in barbed-wire camps along the beaches.

The Franco years

In Catalonia, the Franco regime was iron-fisted and especially vengeful. Thousands of Catalan republicans and leftists were executed, among them Generalitat president Lluís Companys; exile and deportation were the fate of thousands more. Publishing, teaching and any other public cultural expression in Catalan, including even speaking it in the street, were prohibited, and every Catalanist monument in the city was dismantled. All independent political activity was suspended, and the entire political and cultural development of the country was brought to an abrupt halt.

The epic nature of the Spanish Civil War is known worldwide; more present in the collective memory of Barcelona, though, is the long *posguerra* or post-war period,

General Francisco Franco

which lasted for nearly two decades after 1939. During those years, the city was impoverished, and food and electricity were rationed; Barcelona would not regain its prior standard of living until the mid 1950s. Nevertheless, migrants in flight from the still more brutal poverty of the south flowed into the city, occupying precarious shanty towns around Montjuïc and other areas in the outskirts.

In Catalonia, the Franco regime was iron-fisted and especially vengeful: thousands of republicans and leftists were executed

The Franco regime was subject to a UN embargo after World War II. Years of international isolation and attempted self-sufficiency came to an end in 1953, when the country was at least partially re-admitted to the western fold. Even a limited opening to the outside world meant that foreign money finally began to enter the country, and the regime relaxed some control over its population. In 1959, the Plan de Estabilización ('Stabilisation Plan'), drawn up by Catholic technocrats of Opus Dei, brought Spain definitively within the western economy, throwing its doors wide open to tourism and foreign investment. After years of austerity, tourist income at last brought the Europe-wide 1960s boom to Spain and set off change at an extraordinary pace.

After the years of repression and the years of development, 1966 marked the beginning of what became known as *tardofranquisme*, 'late Francoism'. Having made its opening to the outside world, the regime was losing its grip, and labour, youth and student movements began to emerge from the shroud of repression. Nevertheless, the Franco regime never hesitated to show its strength. Strikes and demonstrations were dealt with savagely, and just months before the dictator's death, the last person to be executed in Spain by the traditional method of the garrotte, a Catalan anarchist named Puig Antich, went to his death in Barcelona. In 1973, however, Franco's closest follower, Admiral Carrero Blanco, was assassinated by a bomb planted by the Basque terrorist group ETA, leaving no one to guard over the core values of the regime.

Generalísimo to Generalitat

When Franco died on 20 November 1975, the people of Barcelona took to the streets in celebration; by evening, there was not a bottle of cava left in the city. But no one knew quite what would happen next. The Bourbon monarchy was restored under King Juan Carlos, but his attitude and intentions were not clear. In 1976, he charged a little-known Francoist bureaucrat, Adolfo Suárez, with leading the country to democracy.

The first years of Spain's 'transition' were difficult. Nationalist and other demonstrations continued to be repressed by the police with considerable brutality, and far-right groups threatened less open violence. However, political parties were legalised, and June 1977 saw the first democratic elections since 1936. They were won across Spain by Suárez's own new party, the Union de Centro Democratico (UCD), and in Catalonia by a mixture of socialists, communists and nationalists.

It was, again, not clear how Suárez expected to deal with the demands of Catalonia, but shortly after the elections he surprised everyone by visiting the president of the Generalitat in exile, veteran pre-Civil War politician Josep Tarradellas. His office was the only institution of the old Republic to be so recognised, perhaps because Suárez astutely identified in the old man a fellow conservative. Tarradellas was invited to return as provisional president of a restored Generalitat; he arrived amid huge crowds in October 1977.

The following year, the first free council elections since 1936 were held in Barcelona. They were won by the Socialist Party, with Narcís Serra appointed as mayor. In 1980, elections to the restored Generalitat were won by Jordi Pujol and his party, Convergència i Unió (CiU), which held power for 23 years.

Inseparable from the restoration of democracy was a change in the city's atmosphere after 1975. New freedoms – in culture, sexuality and work – were explored, and energies released in a multitude of ways. Barcelona began to look different too, as the dowdiness of the Franco years was swept away by a new Catalan style: postmodern, high-tech, comic-strip, minimalist and tautly fashionable. This emphasis first began underground, but it was soon taken up by public authorities and, above all, the Ajuntament, in a drive to reverse the policies of the regime. The technocrats in the socialist city administration began to restore the city from its neglected state, and in doing so enlisted the support of the Catalan artistic elite. No one epitomises this more than

Ghosts of the Past

The vestiges of war are still visible in the city

It takes a leap of imagination to picture Barcelona during the Civil War. Decades of dictatorship and a democracy that chose until very recently to forget the events have erased most remains, but a hidden city begins to emerge if you know where to look.

The most dramatic site in the old centre is undoubtedly Plaça de Sant Felip Neri, its walls pitted by shrapnel. On 30 January 1938, a bomb dropped by Mussolini's planes fell on the church, where dozens of children were taking shelter below the sacristy. A couple of hours later, as rescue services, teachers and children were pulling out victims from the rubble, another bomb fell in the square. In total, 42 people were killed, including 30 children. A plaque commemorates the event. Nearby, in Plaça del Sant Josep Oriol, look on the church wall for the old painted sign of Plaça del Milicià Desconegut (Square of the Unknown Militiaman), covered up in 1939, which miraculously survived the Franco years unscathed and was recently rediscovered during restoration work.

Anyone hoping to walk in Orwell's footsteps should head for the Hotel Continental (La Rambla 138), where he stayed when he arrived in December 1936. Later, during the tragic May Days, he found himself perched on the roof of the Teatre Poliorama (La Rambla 115), defending the Workers' Party of Marxist Unification (POUM) headquarters opposite. There, a plaque on the side of the plush Hotel Rivoli Rambla (La Rambla 128) reminds us of the arrest and murder of POUM leader Andreu Nin by Stalin's agents. Further down (La Rambla 30-32) is the Andreu Nin public library, installed in what was the Gran Hotel Falcón, used as a residence by the POUM and later turned into a Stalinist prison.

Montjuïc, too, has its fair share of reminders of Barcelona's bloody past. A guided tour of Refugi 307 (see p148), a restored air raid shelter, is highly recommended, as is a visit to Fossar de La Pedrera in Montjuïc. The cemetery's peaceful beauty belies its past as the mass grave of some 1,900 Republicans and anarchists shot by the Franco regime in Barcelona. Today, it functions as a memorial for all sides of the anti-Francoist opposition, and is perhaps the most remarkable such site in Spain.

▶*Nick Lloyd is author of* Forgotten Places: Barcelona and the Spanish Civil War *and runs Civil War tours in the city (www.iberianature.com).*

Plaça de Sant Felip Neri

Oriol Bohigas, the architect and writer who was long the city's head of culture and chief planner. A programme of urban renewal was initiated, beginning with the open spaces, public art and low-level initiatives, such as the campaign in which hundreds of historic façades were given an overdue facelift.

Endgames

This ambitious, modern approach to urban problems acquired greater focus after Barcelona's bid to host the 1992 Olympic Games was accepted, in 1986. Far more than just a sports event, the Games were to be Barcelona's third great effort to cast aside suggestions of second-city status. The exhibitions of 1888 and 1929 had seen developments in the Ciutadella and on Montjuïc; the Olympics provided an opening for work on a citywide scale. Taking advantage of the investment the Games would attract, Barcelona planned an all-new orientation towards the sea, in a programme of urban renovation of a scope unseen in Europe since the years after World War II.

The Olympic Games were held in July and August 1992 and universally hailed as a success. The cultural legacy of the Games remains strong, with landmarks such as Frank Gehry's *Fish* now major attractions. Popular former Mayor Pasqual Maragall went on to become Socialist candidate for President of the Generalitat in 1999, but he would not succeed until 2003, when he enjoyed muted triumph in the regional elections, after which he had some success in pushing through an Autonomy Statute. He stood down in 2006 and a tripartite government was elected, led by new Socialist leader José Montilla, who was in turn replaced by CiU's Artur Mas. In the wake of the massive pro-independence march on 11 September 2012, Mas called a snap election, presenting himself as the embodiment of the Catalan nation and promising a referendum on independence if the electorate gave him an overall majority. It declined, and Mas came out of it 12 seats worse off than when he started. At the end of 2012, he concocted an informal pro-independence coalition, in return for calling for an unofficial referendum on the future political status of Catalonia by 2014 – a popular consultation that would land him in hot water after the event when the central Spanish government declared it 'unconstitutional'. After infighting and accusations of corruption, he lost support within the then coalition and stepped down in January 2016, to be replaced by Carles Puigdemont after an agreement between fiercely separatist Junts pel Si (Together for Yes) and the far-left CUP (Popular Unity Candidacy). See Barcelona Today (*pp26-33*) for more on the referendum debate.

Over at City Hall, the Socialist run of 32 years ended in 2011 with the election of CiU candidate Xavier Trias, and then – in 2014 – with the victory of current incumbent Ada Colau. Colau heads up an anti-austerity 'citizens movement', Barcelona en Comú, born out of the 2011 protests of the *indignados*, a prototype for the Occupy Wall Street movement and others around the world. She runs on a progressive, anti-corruption platform, with a focus on housing and education, as well as environmental issues. Her determination to control the suffocating numbers of tourists that swamp the city every year has won her many enemies in the hospitality industries, and many fans elsewhere.

Fish (Frank Gehry, 1992)

Key Events

Barcelona in brief

15 BC Town of Barcino founded by Roman soldiers.

AD 350 Roman stone city walls built.

719 Muslims seize Barcelona.

801 Barcelona taken by the Franks.

985 Muslims sack Barcelona; Count Borrell II renounces Frankish sovereignty.

1035-76 Count Ramon Berenguer I of Barcelona extends his possessions into southern France.

1137 Count Ramon Berenguer IV marries Petronella of Aragon, uniting the two states in the Crown of Aragon.

1213 Pere I is killed; his lands north of the Pyrenees are seized by France.

1229 Jaume I conquers Mallorca, then Ibiza (1235) and Valencia (1238); second city wall built in Barcelona.

1274 Consell de Cent, municipal government of Barcelona, established.

1282 Pere II captures Sicily.

1298 Work begins on Gothic cathedral.

1323-34 Conquest of Corsica, Sardinia.

1347-48 Black Death kills thousands.

1462-72 Catalan civil war.

1479 Ferdinand II inherits Crown of Aragon, and with his wife Isabella unites the Spanish kingdoms.

1492 Final expulsion of Jews.

1640 Catalan national revolt, the Guerra dels Segadors.

1652 Barcelona falls to Spanish army.

1702-14 War of Spanish Succession.

1714 Barcelona falls to Franco-Spanish army after siege.

1715 Nova Planta decree abolishes Catalan institutions; new ramparts and citadel built around Barcelona.

1808-13 French occupation.

1814 Restoration of Ferdinand VII.

1833 Aribau publishes *Oda a la Pàtria*, beginning of Catalan cultural renaissance. Carlist wars begin.

1836-37 Dissolution of the monasteries.

1842-44 Barcelona bombarded for the last time from Montjuïc, to quell Jamancia revolt.

1854 Demolition of city walls.

1855 First general strike suppressed.

1859 Cerdà plan for the Eixample is approved.

1868 September: revolution overthrows Isabella II. November: first anarchist meetings held in Barcelona.

1873 First Spanish Republic.

1874 Bourbon monarchy restored.

1882 Work begins on Sagrada Família.

1888 Barcelona Universal Exhibition.

1899 Electric trams introduced.

1909 Setmana Tràgica, anti-church and anti-army riots.

1910 CNT workers' union founded.

1921 First Barcelona metro line begins service.

1923 Primo de Rivera establishes dictatorship in Spain.

1931 Second Spanish Republic.

1934 Generalitat attempts revolt against new right-wing government in Madrid, and is then suspended.

1936 February: Popular Front wins elections; Catalan Generalitat restored. 19 July: military uprising against left-wing government is defeated.

1939 Barcelona taken by Franco.

1959 Stabilisation Plan opens up the Spanish economy.

1975 Franco dies.

1977 First democratic general elections in Spain since 1936; provisional Catalan Generalitat re-established.

1978 First democratic local elections in Barcelona won by Socialists.

1980 Generalitat fully re-established under Jordi Pujol.

1992 Olympic Games.

2003 Coalition of left-wing parties wins control of Generalitat.

2011 Artur Mas becomes President of the Generalitat.

2011 PP wins Spanish elections.

2011 'Indignados' anti-austerity protests.

2014 Ada Colau takes control of City Hall.

2014 Informal referendum on Catalan independence.

2016 Carles Puigdemont becomes President of the Generalitat.

Architecture

Gaudí grabs the headlines, but he didn't build the city alone

Architecture is sometimes seen as Catalonia's greatest contribution to art history. Catalan craftsmen have been famed for their skills since the Middle Ages, while the region's architects have long been both artists and innovators. Traditional Catalan brick-vaulting techniques, for example, were the basis of visionary structural innovations that allowed later architects to span ever larger spaces and build higher structures, and modern Catalan architects such as Ricardo Bofill and Enric Miralles inherited the international prestige of their forebears. Contemporary buildings are often daringly constructed alongside or even within old ones, a mix of old and new that characterises some of the most successful recent projects, such as Arato Isozaik's Louvre-style entrance plaza to the Casaramona textile factory at the CaixaForum.

Edifici Gas Natural (Enric Miralles, 2005)

Roman to Gothic

The Roman citadel of Barcino was founded on the hill of Mons Taber, just behind the cathedral, which to this day remains the religious and civic heart of the city. It left an important legacy in the fourth-century city wall, fragments of which are visible at many points around the Old City. Barcelona's next occupiers, the Visigoths, left little, although a trio of fine Visigothic churches survives in Terrassa.

When the Catalan state began to form under the Counts of Barcelona from the ninth century, its dominant architecture was Romanesque. The Pyrenean valleys hold hundreds of fine Romanesque buildings, notably at Sant Pere de Rodes, Ripoll, Sant Joan de les Abadesses and Besalú, but there are very few in Barcelona. On the right-hand side of the cathedral (if you're looking at the main façade) sits the 13th-century chapel of Santa Llúcia, eventually incorporated into the later building; the church of Santa Anna is tucked away near Plaça Catalunya; and the Born district is home to the Capella d'en Marcús, a tiny travellers' chapel. But the city's greatest Romanesque monument is the beautifully plain 12th-century church and cloister of **Sant Pau del Camp** (*see p114*), part of a larger monastery.

By the 13th century, Barcelona was the capital of a trading empire and had started to grow rapidly. The settlements – called *ravals* or *vilanoves* – that had sprung up outside the Roman walls were brought within the city by the building of Jaume I's second set of walls, which extended west to La Rambla. This commercial growth and political eminence set the scene for the great flowering of the Catalan Gothic style, which saw the construction of many of the city's most important civic and religious buildings. The cathedral was begun in 1298, in place of an 11th-century building. Work began on the **Ajuntament** (Casa de la Ciutat; *see p76*) and the **Palau de la Generalitat** (*see p79*), which was later subject to extensive alteration, in 1372 and 1403 respectively. Major additions were made to the **Palau Reial Major** (*see p72*) of the Catalan-Aragonese kings, especially the **Saló del Tinell** of 1359-62. And the great hall of **La Llotja** (the Stock Exchange, *see p96*) was built between 1380 and 1392.

The Catalan Gothic style is clearly distinguished from classic northern Gothic by its relative simplicity. It also gives more prominence to solid, plain walls between towers and columns, rather than the empty spaces between intricate flying buttresses that were the hallmarks of the great French cathedrals, with the result that Catalan buildings appear much larger. On the façades, as much emphasis is given to horizontals as to verticals; octagonal towers end in cornices and flat roofs, not spires. And the decorative intricacies are mainly confined to windows, portals, arches and

Sant Pau del Camp

gargoyles. Many churches have no aisles but only a single nave; the classic example of this style is the beautiful **Santa Maria del Pi** (*see p73*) in Plaça del Pi, built between 1322 and 1453.

The Catalan Gothic style went on to establish a historic benchmark for Catalan architecture: simple and robust, yet elegant and practical. Sophisticated techniques were developed as part of the style: the use of transverse arches supporting timber roofs, for instance, allowed the spanning of great halls uninterrupted by columns, a system that was used in Guillem Carbonel's Saló del Tinell. The **Drassanes**, built from 1378 as the royal shipyards (and now the Museu Marítim; *see p134*), is really just a very beautiful shed, but its enormous parallel aisles make it one of the city's most imposing spaces.

Església de Betlem

The Pyrenean valleys hold hundreds of fine Romanesque buildings, notably at Sant Pere de Rodes, Ripoll, Sant Joan de les Abadesses and Besalú, but there are very few in Barcelona

Around this time, La Ribera (nowadays known as Sant Pere and the Born) was the commercial centre of the city. Its pre-eminence resulted in the construction of **Santa Maria del Mar** (*see p100*), the magnificent masterpiece of Catalan Gothic built between 1329 and 1384. The building's superb proportions are based on a series of squares imposed on one another, with three aisles of almost equal height. The interior is staggering in its austerity. The architecture of medieval Barcelona, at least that of its noble and merchant residences, can be seen at its best along **C/Montcada**, running up from the rear entrance to Santa Maria del Mar. Built by the city's merchant elite at the height of its confidence and wealth, this line of buildings conforms to a very Mediterranean style of urban palace and makes maximum use of space. A plain exterior faces the street with heavy doors opening into an imposing patio; on one side, a grand external staircase leads to the main rooms on the first floor (*planta noble*), which often have elegant open loggias.

Marking time

By the beginning of the 16th century, a period of political and economic downturn, the number of patrons for new city buildings declined. The next 300 years saw plenty of construction, but rarely in any distinctively Catalan style; as a result, these structures have often been disregarded.

The Church also built lavishly around this time. Of the Baroque convents and churches along La Rambla, the **Betlem** (1680-1729), at the corner of C/Carme, is the most important survivor. Later Baroque churches include **Sant Felip Neri** (1721-52, *see p72*) and **La Mercè** (1765-75, *see p76*). Another addition, after the siege of Barcelona in 1714, was new military architecture, since the city was encased in ramparts and fortresses. Examples include the **Castell de Montjuïc** (*see p141*, the buildings in the Ciutadella, and Barceloneta.

Another positive 18th-century alteration was the conversion of La Rambla into a paved promenade, a project that began in 1775 with the demolition of Jaume I's second wall. Neoclassical palaces were built alongside: **La Virreina** and the **Palau Moja** (at the corner of C/Portaferrisa) both date from the 1770s. Also from that time, but in a less classical style, is the **Gremial dels Velers** (Candlemakers' Guild) at Via Laietana 50, with its two-colour stucco decoration.

However, it wasn't until the closure of the monasteries in the 1820s and '30s that major rebuilding on La Rambla could begin.

Most of the new constructions were in international, neoclassical styles. The site that now holds the **Mercat de la Boqueria** was first remodelled in 1836-40 as Plaça Sant Josep to a design by Francesc Daniel Molina, based on the English Regency style of John Nash; it's now buried beneath the 1870s market building, but its Doric colonnade can still be detected. Molina also designed the **Plaça Reial** (*see p76*), begun in 1848. Other fine examples include the colonnaded **Porxos d'en Xifré**, blocks built in 1836 opposite the Llotja on Passeig Isabel II by the Port Vell.

Birth of the modern city

In the 1850s, Barcelona was able to expand physically, with the demolition of the walls, and psychologically, with economic expansion and the cultural reawakening of the Catalan Renaixença. One of the characteristics of modern Barcelona was clearly visible from the start: audacious planning. The city eventually expanded outwards and was connected to Gràcia and other outlying towns via the **Eixample** (*see pp150-171*), designed by Ildefons Cerdà. An engineer by trade, Cerdà was influenced by socialist ideas, and concerned with the poor condition of the workers' housing in the Old City.

With its straight lines and grids, Cerdà's plan was closely related to the visionary rationalist ideas of its time, as was the idea of placing two of its main avenues along a geographic parallel and a meridian. Cerdà's central aim was to alleviate overpopulation while encouraging social equality by using quadrangular blocks of a standard size, with strict building controls to ensure they were built only on two sides, to a limited height, and with a garden. Each district would consist of 20 blocks, with all community necessities.

However, this idealised use of space was rarely achieved, with private developers regarding Cerdà's restrictions as pointless interference. New buildings exceeded planned heights, and all the blocks from Plaça Catalunya to the Diagonal were enclosed. Even the planned gardens failed to withstand the onslaught of construction. Still, the development of the Eixample did see the refinement of a specific type of building: the apartment block, with giant flats on the principal floor (first above the ground), often with large glassed-in galleries for the drawing room, and small flats above. In time, the interplay between the Eixample's straight lines and the disorderly tangle of the older city became an essential part of the city's identity.

Modernisme

The art nouveau style was the leading influence in the decorative arts in Europe and the US between 1890 and 1914. In Barcelona, its influence merged with the cultural and political movement of the Catalan Renaixença to produce what became known as Modernisme (used here in Catalan to avoid confusion with 'modernism' in English, which refers to 20th-century functional styles).

For all Catalonia's traditions in building and the arts, no style is as synonymous with Barcelona as Modernisme. This is due to the enormous modern popularity of Antoni Gaudí, its most famous practitioner (*see pp52-p59* Gaudí & Modernisme), and also to its mix of decoration, eccentric unpredictability, dedicated craftsmanship and practicality. Modernisme can also be seen as matching certain archetypes of Catalan character, as a passionately nationalist expression that made use of Catalan traditions of design and craftwork. Artists strove to revalue the best of Catalan art, showing interest in the Romanesque and Gothic of the Catalan Golden Age; Domènech i Montaner combined iron-frame construction with distinctive brick Catalan styles from the Middle Ages, regarding them as an 'expression of the Catalan earth'.

Art nouveau had a tendency to look at both the past and future, combining a love of decoration with new industrial techniques and materials. Even as they constructed a nostalgic vision of the Catalan motherland, Modernista architects experimented with new technology. Encouraged by wealthy patrons, they designed works made of iron and glass, introduced electricity, water and gas piping to building plans, were the first to tile bathroom and kitchen walls, made a point of allowing extensive natural light and fresh air into all rooms, and toyed with the most advanced, revolutionary expressionism.

Catalan Modernista creativity was at its peak from 1888 to 1908. The Eixample is the style's display case, with the greatest concentration of art nouveau in Europe, but Modernista buildings can be found in innumerable other locations: in streets behind the Avda Paral·lel and villas on Tibidabo, in shop interiors and dark hallways, in country town halls and in the cava cellars of the Penedès.

Huge international interest in Gaudí often eclipses the fact that many other remarkable architects and designers worked at the same time. Indeed, Modernisme was much more than an architectural style: the movement also included painters such as Ramon Casas, Santiago Rusiñol and Isidre

Passion façade, Sagrada Família

Nonell, sculptors Josep Llimona, Miquel Blay and Eusebi Arnau, and furniture-makers such as the superb Mallorcan Gaspar Homar. More than any other form of art nouveau, Modernisme extended into literature, thought and music, marking a whole generation of Catalan writers, poets, composers and philosophers. It found its most splendid expression in architecture, but Modernisme was an artistic movement in the fullest sense of the word. In Catalonia, it took on a nationalistic element.

Gaudí's vision

Although Antoni Gaudí i Cornet is widely regarded as the genius of the Modernista movement, he was really an unclassifiable one-off. His work was a product of the social and cultural context of the time, but also of his individual perception of the world, together with a deep patriotic devotion to anything Catalan.

Gaudí worked first as assistant to Josep Fontseré in the 1870s on the building of the **Parc de la Ciutadella** (see p94); the gates and fountain are attributed to him. Around the same time, he designed the lamp-posts in the Plaça Reial, but his first major commission was for **Casa Vicens** (see p174) in Gràcia, built between 1883 and 1888. An orientalist fantasy, the building is structurally conventional, but Gaudí's use of surface material stands out in the

neo-Moorish decoration, multicoloured tiling and superbly elaborate ironwork on the gates. His **Col·legi de les Teresianes** convent school (1888-89, see p184) is more restrained, but the clarity and fluidity of the building are very appealing.

In 1878, Gaudí met Eusebi Güell, heir to one of the largest industrial fortunes in Catalonia. The pair shared ideas on religion, philanthropy and the socially redemptive role of architecture, and Gaudí produced several buildings for Güell. Among them were **Palau Güell** (1886-88, see p113), an impressive, historicist building that established his reputation, and the crypt at **Colònia Güell** (see p196) outside Barcelona, one of his most structurally experimental and surprising buildings.

In 1882, Gaudí became involved in the design of the **Sagrada Família** (see p158), which had been started the previous year. From 1908 until his death in 1926, he worked on no other projects, a shabby, white-haired hermit producing visionary ideas that his assistants had to interpret into drawings (on show in the museum alongside). Gaudí was profoundly religious, and part of his obsession with the building came from a belief that it would help redeem Barcelona from the sins of secularism and the modern era.

Although he lived to see the completion of only the crypt, apse and Nativity façade, with its representation of 30 species

ants, the Sagrada Família became
testing ground for Gaudí's ideas on
 structure and form. As his work matured,
he abandoned historicism and developed
free-flowing, sinuous expressionist forms.
His boyhood interest in nature began to take
over from more architectural references,
and what had previously provided external
decorative motifs became the inspiration for
the actual structure of his buildings.

In his greatest years, Gaudí combined
other commissions with his cathedral. **La
Pedrera** (*see p160*), which he began in
1905, was his most complete project. The
building has an aquatic feel about it: the
balconies resemble seaweed, while the
undulating façade is reminiscent of the
sea, or rocks washed by it. The **Casa Batlló**
(*see p156*), on the other side of Passeig de
Gràcia, was an existing building that Gaudí
remodelled in 1905-07; the roof looks like
a reptilian creature perched high above
the street. The symbolism of the façade is
the source of speculation: some link it to
the myth of St George and the dragon, but
others say it's a celebration of carnival, with
its harlequin-hat roof, wrought-iron balcony
'masks' and confetti-like tiles. This last
element was the work of Josep Maria Jujol,
who many believe was an even more skilled
mosaicist than his master.

Gaudí's fascination with natural forms
found full expression in the **Park Güell**
(1900-14; *see p177*), for which he blurred
the distinction between natural and
artificial forms in a series of colonnades
winding up a hill. These paths lead up
to the large central terrace projecting
over a hall; a forest of distorted Doric
columns planned as the marketplace for
Güell's proposed 'garden city'. The terrace
benches are covered in some of the finest
examples of *trencadís* (broken mosaic work),
again mostly by Jujol.

Beyond the master

Modernista architecture received a vital,
decisive boost around the turn of the 19th
century from the Universal Exhibition
of 1888. The most important buildings
for the show were planned by Lluís
Domènech i Montaner (1850-1923), who
was both far more prominent than Gaudí
as a propagandist for Modernisme in all its
forms and far more of a classic Modernista
architect. Domènech was one of the first
Modernista architects to develop the idea of
the 'total work', working closely with teams
of craftsmen and designers on every aspect
of a building. His admirers dubbed him 'the
great orchestra conductor'.

Most of the Exhibition buildings no longer
exist, but the **Castell dels Tres Dragons**
in the Parc de la Ciutadella has survived.
Designed as the Exhibition restaurant
(it's now the Museu de Zoologia), the
building demonstrated many key features
of Modernista style: the use of structural
ironwork allowed greater freedom in the
creation of openings, arches and windows;
while plain brick, instead of the stucco
usually applied to most buildings, was used
in an exuberantly decorative manner.

Domènech's greatest creations are the
Hospital de la Santa Creu i Sant Pau
(*see p157*), built as small 'pavilions'
within a garden to avoid the usual effect
of a monolithic hospital, and the **Palau
de la Música Catalana** (*see p98*), an
extraordinary display of outrageous
decoration. He also left impressive
constructions in Reus, notably the **Casa
Navàs** and **Casa Rull** mansions, and the
amazing pavilions of the **Institut Pere
Mata**, a psychiatric hospital and forerunner
of the Hospital de Sant Pau.

Third in the trio of leading Modernista
architects was Josep Puig i Cadafalch
(1867-1957), who combined traditional
Catalan arches with a neo-Gothic
influence in such buildings, as the **Casa
de les Punxes** ('House of Spikes', officially
the Casa Terrades; *see p157*) on Avda
Diagonal. Nearby on Passeig de Sant Joan,
at no.108, is another masterpiece, the
Casa Macaya, its inner courtyard inspired
by the medieval palaces of C/Montcada.

Sagrada Família

Pavelló Barcelona

Puig was also responsible for some of the most impressive industrial architecture of the time, an area in which Modernisme excelled. The **Fàbrica Casaramona**, near the Plaça Espanya, was built as a textile mill and now houses the **CaixaForum** (*see p141*); outside Barcelona, he also designed the extraordinary **Caves Codorníu** wine cellars. But his best-known work is the **Casa Àmatller** (*see p157*), between Domènech's **Casa Lleó Morera** and Gaudí's Casa Batlló in the extraordinary **Manzana de la Discòrdia** (*see p155*), a city block on Passeig de Gràcia with buildings by four Modernista architects.

Modernisme caught on with extraordinary vigour all over Catalonia, but some of its most engaging architects are little known internationally. Impressive apartment blocks and mansions were built in the Eixample by Joan Rubió i Bellver (**Casa Golferichs**, Gran Via 491), Salvador Valeri (**Casa Comalat**, Avda Diagonal 442) and Josep Vilaseca. North of Barcelona is La Garriga, where MJ Raspall built exuberant summer houses for the rich and fashionable families of the time; there are also some dainty Modernista residences in coastal towns, such as Canet and Arenys de Mar. Some of the finest Modernista industrial architecture is in Terrassa, designed by the municipal architect Lluís Moncunill (1868-1931). And Cèsar Martinell, another local architect, built co-operative cellars that are true 'wine cathedrals' in Falset, Gandesa and many other towns in southern Catalonia.

The 20th century

By the 1910s, Modernisme had become too extreme for Barcelona's middle classes; Gaudí's later buildings were met with derision. The new 'proper' style for Catalan architecture was Noucentisme, which stressed the importance of classical proportions. But it produced little of note: the main buildings that survive are those of the 1929 Exhibition, Barcelona's next 'big event' that served as the excuse for the bizarre, neo-Baroque **Palau Nacional** (now home to the MNAC; *see p144*). The Exhibition also brought the city one of the most important buildings of the century: Ludwig Mies van der Rohe's German Pavilion, the **Pavelló Barcelona**, rebuilt near its original location in 1986. Its impact at the time was extraordinary; even today, it seems modern in its challenge to conventional ideas of space.

Mies van der Rohe had a strong influence on the main new trend in Catalan architecture of the 1930s, which, reacting against Modernisme and nearly all earlier Catalan styles, was quite emphatically functionalist. Its leading figures were Josep Lluís Sert (1902-83) and the GATCPAC collective (Group of Catalan Architects and Technicians for the Progress of Contemporary Architecture), who struggled to introduce the ideas of Le Corbusier and of the International Style. Under the Republic, Sert built a sanatorium off C/ Tallers and the **Casa Bloc**, a workers' housing project at Passeig Torres i Bages 91-105 in Sant Andreu.

In collaboration with Le Corbusier, GATCPAC also produced a plan for the radical redesign of the whole of Barcelona as a 'functional city', the Pla Macià of 1933-34. Drawings for the scheme present a Barcelona that looks more like a Soviet-era new town in Siberia, and few regret that it

Edifici Fòrum

Barcelona placed itself at the forefront of international urban design.

Barcelona's renewal programme took on a more ambitious shape with the 1992 Olympics. The third and most spectacular of the city's great events, the Games were intended to be stylish and innovative, but they were also designed to provide a focus for a sweeping renovation of the city, with emblematic new buildings (such as Lord Foster's **Torre de Collserola**; *see p183*) and infrastructure projects linked by clear strategic planning.

Funds were initially concentrated on a string of modern parks and squares, many of which were to incorporate original artwork

The three main Olympic sites are quite different. The **Vila Olímpica** (*see p135*) had the most comprehensive masterplan: drawn up by Bohigas and MBM, it sought to extend Cerdà's grid right down to the seafront. The main project on **Montjuïc** (*see pp136-149*) was the transformation of the 1929 stadium, but there's also Arata Isozaki's Palau Sant Jordi and its space-frame roof. **Vall d'Hebron** was the least successful of the three sites, but Esteve Bonell's Velòdrom is one of the finest (and earliest) of the sports buildings, built in 1984 before the Olympic bid had even succeeded.

After the Olympics

Not content with the projects completed by 1992, the city continued to expand through the '90s. Post-1992, the focus shifted to the Raval and the Port Vell ('Old Port'), then to the Diagonal Mar area in the north of the city. Many of the striking buildings here are by local architects such as Helio Piñón and Albert Viaplana, whose work combines elegant lines with a strikingly modern use of materials. Examples range from the controversial 1983 **Plaça dels Països Catalans** to transformations of historic buildings such as the **Casa de la Caritat** (now the CCCB, *see p114*) and all-new projects including the **Maremagnum** in the port.

Other contributions to post-Olympic Barcelona were made by foreign architects: notable examples include Richard Meier's bold white building for the **MACBA** (*see*

never got off the drawing board. In 1937, Sert also built the Spanish Republic's pavilion for that year's Paris Exhibition, since rebuilt in Barcelona as the **Pavelló de la República** in the Vall d'Hebron. However, his finest work came much later in the shape of the **Fundació Joan Miró** (*see p143*), built in the 1970s after he'd spent many years in exile in the United States.

Barcelona's new style

The Franco years had an enormous impact on the city. As the economy expanded at breakneck pace during the 1960s, Barcelona received a massive influx of migrants, in a general context of unchecked property speculation and minimal planning controls; the city became ringed by a chaotic mass of high-rise suburbs. Another legacy of the era is some ostentatiously tall office blocks, especially on the Diagonal and around Plaça Francesc Macià.

When a democratic city administration took over at the end of the 1970s, there was much to be done. A generation of architects had been chafing at Francoist restrictions. However, the tone set early on – above all by Barcelona's chief planner Oriol Bohigas, who has continued to design individual buildings as part of the MBM partnership with Josep Martorell and David Mackay – was one of 'architectural realism', with a powerful combination of imagination and practicality. Budgets were limited, so the public's hard-earned funds were initially concentrated not on buildings but on the gaps between them: public spaces, a string of modern parks and squares, many of which were to incorporate original artwork. From this quiet beginning, *p111*) and Frank Gehry's **Fish** sculpture overlooking the beach (*photo p274*). More recently two venerable buildings have been remodelled: the last stage of Italian architect Gae Aulenti's interior redesign of the Palau Nacional on Montjuïc created the expanded **Museu Nacional d'Art de Catalunya** (*see p144*) and the **CosmoCaixa** building (*see p184*) in Tibidabo, which again converted a 19th-century hospice into a science museum. The Mudéjar-style arches of **Las Arenas** bullring have also been converted by Richard Rogers into a shopping and leisure centre.

Of late, architectural projects have become increasingly circumscribed by commercial imperatives, sometimes causing tensions between local traditions and the globalisation of commerce. The huge changes to the cityscape linked to the Fòrum Universal de les Cultures 2004 are a case in point. The area at the mouth of the Besòs river, near where Avda Diagonal meets the sea, was transformed for the occasion, most notably by the construction of a triangular building, the **Edifici Fòrum** (*see p189*), designed by Herzog and de Meuron (of Tate Modern fame). Nearby, Enric Miralles, also known locally for his redesign of the **Mercat de Santa Caterina** (*see p93*) and

the **Gas Natural building** (*photo p277*) in Barceloneta, created a fiercely modern and rather soulless park, the **Parc de Diagonal Mar** (*see p189*). **Parc Central del Poblenou** (*see p189*), the work of Jean Nouvel – who also designed the 38-storey **Torre Agbar** in the same neighbourhood – has been a much more popular addition to the area, and combines futurism with nature to provide playfulness and much-needed shade.

Whether this fourth stage in the re-imagining of the city can be linked to those outbursts of Barcelona's architectural creativity in the service of urban planning is debatable. While the value of many of these buildings is unquestionable, some see the dark hand of big business behind the latest developments and dismiss the new expansions connected to the Fòrum as more about making money than art. It's also telling that many of Barcelona's most recent landmark buildings are five-star hotels, such as Ricardo Bofill's **W Hotel** (*see p128*) or Dominique Perrault's 'slider phone' building to house the **Meliá Barcelona Sky** in Poblenou. Still, whatever the motives behind the city's latest reinvention, no one is denying the unique, dynamic air of its current urban fabric.

Torre Agbar

Plan

Telefèric de Montjuïc

Accommodation

Despite the best efforts of Airbnb.com, along with Mayor Ada Colau's determination to limit hotel licences, the accommodation scene has come on in leaps and bounds over the last few years, with style and innovation appearing at every level. The glut of top-end accommodation in Barcelona means that hotels are continually revising their rates, and bargains are there for the taking: it's well worth doing a little extra research before booking. At the budget end of the market, many *hostales* are situated in fabulous old buildings with elaborate doorways and grand staircases, though the rooms aren't always so elegant. There's also been a rise in boutique B&Bs – bright places with en-suite bathrooms, internet access and other modern essentials.

Market Hotel p293

Booking a room

With the city's growing niche as a conference capital, booking ahead is strongly advised. High season runs year round and finding somewhere to lay your head at short notice can be tough. Hotels generally require you to guarantee your booking with card details or a deposit; it's always worth calling a few days before arrival to reconfirm the booking (get it in writing if you can; many readers have reported problems) and check the cancellation policy. Often you will lose at least the first night. *Hostales* are more laid-back and don't always ask for a deposit.

To be sure of a room with natural light or a view, ask for an outside room (*habitació/ habitación exterior*), which will usually face the street. Many of Barcelona's buildings are built around a central patio or airshaft, and the inside rooms (*habitació/habitación interior*) around them can be quite gloomy, albeit quieter.

However, in some cases (especially in the Eixample), these inward-facing rooms look on to large, open-air patios or gardens, which benefit from being quiet and having a view.

Hotels listed under the expensive and moderate brackets all have air-conditioning as standard. Air-conditioning is increasingly common even in no-frills places, however, and around half the *hostales* in the budget listings are equipped with it.

The law prohibits smoking in communal areas in hotels. As a result, most hotels have banned smoking altogether, and the others will have the majority of floors/ rooms as non-smoking.

Theft can be a problem, especially in lower-end establishments. If you're sleeping cheap, you might want to travel with a padlock to lock your door, or at least lock up your bags. Check to see if youth hostel rooms have lockers if you're sharing. Use hotel safes where possible.

Star ratings and prices

Accommodation in Catalonia is divided into two official categories: hotels (H) and *pensiones* (P). To be a hotel (star-rated one to five), a place must feature en-suite bathrooms in every room. Ratings are based on physical attributes rather than levels of service; often the only difference between a three- and a four-star hotel is the presence of a meeting room. *Pensiones*, usually cheaper and often family-run, are star-rated one or two, and are not required to have en-suite bathrooms (though many do). *Pensiones* are also known as *hostales*, but, confusingly, are not youth hostels; those are known as *albergues*.

For a double room, expect to pay €50-€75 for a budget *pensión*, €80-€180 for a mid-range spot and €200 upwards for a top-of-the-range hotel. However, prices vary depending on the time of year; always check for special deals. All bills are subject to seven per cent IVA (value added tax) on top of the basic price; this is not

High season runs year round and finding somewhere to lay your head at short notice can be tough

normally included in the advertised rate, but we've factored it into the price categories here. Breakfast is not included as standard, but Wi-Fi is almost always free.

Where to stay

La Rambla is flanked by hotels ranging from no-frills to luxury, but the overwhelmingly touristy environment – not to mention the noise – may prove a bit too much for some people. The medieval labyrinth of the Barri Gòtic conceals some cheaper alternatives, but bear in mind that old buildings can often be grotty rather than charming. The well-to-do Born is home to plenty of restaurants, bars and boutiques and has an increasing number of hotels, while the Raval – the Barri Gòtic's edgy neighbour – is usefully central and well served for bars and restaurants.

The broad avenues forming the vast grid of streets of the Eixample district contain some of Barcelona's most expensive and fashionable hotels, along with some great budget options hidden away in Modernista buildings.

Hotels are springing up along the waterfront, particularly in the stretch between the Hotel Arts and the Fòrum that lies north of the city centre, and slightly inland in Poblenou. These are mostly aimed at business travellers, so rates tend to fall at weekends and during holiday periods.

Poble Sec is a fast-changing neighbourhood between Montjuïc hill and the Avda Paral·lel, close to the hipster enclave of Sant Antoni, while Gràcia is off the beaten tourist track, which only adds to its allure. Its narrow streets and leafy squares have a villagey feel, and there are more and more interesting restaurants, shops and night-time activities to test out.

Sants is convenient if you have an early train to catch, and it's pleasantly far from the crowds that fill the rest of the city, although it's not the most picturesque neighbourhood.

> The medieval labyrinth of the Barri Gòtic conceals some cheaper alternatives, but bear in mind that old buildings can often be grotty rather than charming

Apartment Rentals

A home from home

Short-term apartment rental is an expanding market. People who've visited the city several times, or who want to spend longer than a few days here, are increasingly opting for self-catering accommodation. Some firms rent their own apartments; others act as intermediaries between apartment owners and visitors.

When renting, it pays to check the small print (payment methods, deposits, cancellation fees, etc.) and what's included (cleaning, towels and so on) before booking. Note that apartments offered for rental tend to be small.

Airbnb.com is obviously the giant, but there are plenty of others:

barcelona-home.com
www.apartmentsbcn.net
www.destinationbcn.com
www.friendlyrentals.com
www.insidebarcelona.com
www.oh-barcelona.com
www.rentthesun.com

In addition to the outfits listed above, check the gay-operated www.outlet4spain.com.

Luxury

Casa Fuster

Passeig de Gràcia 132, Gràcia (93 255 30 00, www.hotelcasafuster. com). Metro Diagonal. Map p175 H4.

There was a great deal of talk about the Fuster when it first opened. Many complained that this historic Modernista building should have been preserved as a public space. The famed Café Vienés answers that demand somewhat, though when a cup of tea costs €8.25 you won't find many locals drinking it. What is so appealing to the luxury end of the market, however, is the air of exclusivity that envelops you on arrival. Service is spot on; rooms – while rather small – feel regal in their dove greys and purples. The rooftop pool has spectacular views, while the gourmet restaurant has a clubby, insider feel.

Cotton House Hotel

Gran Via de les Corts Catalanes 670, Eixample (93 450 50 45, www.hotelcottonhouse.com), Metro Girona. Map p152 J7.

After a stunning renovation, the former headquarters of the cotton guild is now a plush five-star, with snowy-white rooms that contrast with the deco splendour of the common areas. There is a plunge pool lined with day beds on the roof, but in winter the library bar is the place to be. Nods to the building's past are everywhere, from the spray of cotton bolls at reception to the small 'Atelier', filled with bolts of cotton, where you can have a shirt made.

Hotel Claris

C/Pau Claris 150, Eixample (93 487 62 62, www.derbyhotels. com). Metro Passeig de Gràcia. Map p152 J6.

Antiques and contemporary design merge behind the neoclassical exterior of the Claris, which contains the largest private collection of Ancient Egyptian art in Spain. Some bedrooms are on the small side, while others are duplex, but all have Chesterfield sofas and plenty of art. Residents get free entry into the Barcelona Egyptian Museum. The rooftop pool is just about big enough to swim in, with plenty of loungers, and a cocktail bar and DJ.

Hotel Neri

C/Sant Sever 5, Barri Gòtic (93 304 06 55, www.hotelneri.com). Metro Jaume I. Map p71 H9.

One of the coolest boutiques in town, this is the perfect treat for a naughty weekend, located in a former 18th-century palace. The vampish lobby-cum-library is decorated with flagstone floors, with crushed red velvet chaises longues and lashings of gold leaf, though the rooms are slightly more understated. Neutral tones, natural materials and rustic finishes (untreated wood and unpolished marble) stand in stylish contrast to lavish satins, sharp-edged design and high-tech perks (Bluetooth speakers, plasma-screen TVs). The lush rooftop garden features plenty of private nooks for dangerous liaisons.

Mandarin Oriental Barcelona

Passeig de Gràcia 38-40, Eixample (93 151 88 88, www. mandarinoriental.com/ barcelona). Metro Passeig de Gràcia. Map p152 H7.

Top Spanish designer Patricia Urquiola's high-design Mandarin Oriental oozes old-style glamour with a contemporary twist. It was originally a bank, and life in the hotel centres on the old trading floor – now a seafood bistro – and the slick Bankers Bar, peopled by Catalan TV celebs downing designer cocktails. Foodies get their kicks at two-Michelin-starred MO ments, an all-Catalan eatery managed by multi-Michelin-starred Carme Ruscalleda and her son Raül Balam, then relax on the pretty Mimosa patio or the rooftop Terrat. Rooms are as plush as you could hope for, big on bespoke Urquiola pieces like 'Fat' sofas, cylindrical bathtubs and 'Caboche' chandeliers.

Soho House Barcelona

Plaça del Duc de Medinaceli 4, Barri Gòtic (93 220 46 00, www. sohousebarcelona.com) Metro Drassanes. Map p71 H10.

The latest outpost of the London members' club for creative types, this is a blissfully

Casa Camper

comfortable place that feels fun and unpretentious for all its cool credentials. The style is 'English country house', and facilities include a rooftop pool and terrace with views second to none, a plush Italian restaurant, the Cowshed spa, a small cinema, sunny gym and, of course, the relaxed but elegant members' bar (also open to guests).

Other top options include **H1898** (www.hotel1898.com), a dapper luxury hotel in the Barri Gòtic, and the **W Hotel** (www.whotels. com/barcelona), a handsome building in Barceloneta with incredible views of the sea and city.

Expensive
Casa Camper
C/Elisabets 11, Raval (93 342 62 80, www.casacamper.com). Metro Catalunya. **Map** *p109 G8.*
Devised by the Mallorcan footwear giant, this is a wonderfully quirky concept-fest of a hotel. One of its unique selling points is a bedroom-living room arrangement, giving two

spaces for the price of one. Less cleverly, the living rooms are across the corridor from the bedrooms, so in order to enjoy the cinema-sized TV screen, hammock and balcony you'll need to pack respectable pyjamas or risk the dash of shame. There are no minibars, but you can help yourself to free (great) snacks and drinks in the café whenever you fancy, including breakfast. The 'jungle shower' on the roof is a fun place to cool down in summer.

Grand Hotel Central
Via Laietana 30, Born (93 295 79 00, www.grandhotelcentral. com). Metro Jaume I. **Map** *p90 J9.*
Another of the recent wave of Barcelona hotels to adhere to the unwritten design protocol that grey is the new black. The Central's shadowy, almost Hitchcockian corridors open up on to sleekly appointed, understated rooms with interiors that feature flat-screen televisions, a media hub and Gilchrist & Soames toiletries. But the real charm of this establishment lies on the roof. Here you can sip a cocktail and

admire the wonderful views while floating in the vertiginous infinity pool. There's also a swish cocktail bar and Mediterranean restaurant on the ground floor.

Hotel Duquesa de Cardona
Passeig Colom 12, Barri Gòtic (93 268 90 90, www. hduquesadecardona.com). Metro Drassanes or Jaume I. **Map** *p71 H10.*
This elegantly restored 16th-century palace retains many original features and is furnished with natural materials – wood, leather, silk and stone – that are complemented by a soft colour scheme reflecting the paintwork. The cosy bedrooms make it ideal for a romantic stay, particularly the deluxe rooms and junior suites on the higher floors, with views out across the harbour. Guests can sunbathe and linger over lunch on the decked roof terrace and then cool off in the mosaic-tiled plunge pool. The arcaded hotel restaurant serves a menu of modern Catalan dishes, and offers local produce fresh off the terrace barbeque.

Hotel Granados 83
C/Enric Granados 83, Eixample (93 492 96 70, www.derbyhotels. com). Metro Diagonal. **Map** *p152 G5.*
The original ironwork structure of this former hospital contrives to lend an unexpectedly industrial feel to the Granados 83. The hotel's variety of bare-bricked rooms includes details of African zebrawood and Italian leather sofas. There are duplex and triplex versions, some with their own terraces and plunge pools. For mortals in the standard rooms, there's a rooftop pool and sun deck with cocktail bar.

Hotel Petit Palace Boquería
C/Boquería 10, Barri Gòtic (93 302 07 53, www.petitpalace. com). Metro Liceu. **Map** *p71 H9.*
A private mansion was completely gutted to create this minimalist hotel on a busy street just off La Rambla. The rooms are white and futuristic, and lamps and chairs lend a 1960s air. Some bathrooms have hydro massage showers,

others Jacuzzi baths, and you can borrow an iPad on request. Only breakfast is served in the chic dining room. There's also a little-known public garden at the back: a delightful luxury in this densely packed area of town. The hotel offers free bike rental for residents.

Hotel Pulitzer

*C/Bergara 8, Eixample (93 481 67 67, www.hotelpulitzer.es). Metro Catalunya. **Map** p152 G8.*
Situated just off Plaça de Catalunya, the Hotel Pulitzer has become a popular place to meet before going on a night out. A discreet façade reveals an impressive lobby that's stuffed with comfortable white leather sofas, a reading area overflowing with glossy picture books and a swanky bar and restaurant. The rooftop terrace is a fabulous spot for a cocktail, with squishy loungers, scented candles and tropical plants, and spectacular views across the heights of the city. The rooms themselves are not big, but they are sumptuously decorated and come complete with cool grey marble, fat fluffy pillows and kinky leather trim.

Other options include **Villa Emilia** (www.hotelvillaemilia. com), a great-value hotel in the Eixample, and **Advance Hotel** (www.advancehotelbarcelona. com), a welcome retreat from the madness of the town centre.

Moderate
Ciutat de Barcelona

*C/Princesa 33, Born (93 269 74 75, www.ciutathotels.com). Metro Jaume I. **Map** p90 J9.*
The Ciutat de Barcelona is a jolly, primary-coloured affair, which offers a refreshing contrast to the chocolate and charcoal shades of most of Barna's smart hotels. Retro shapes prevail in the furnishings and decorations, and rooms are very compact but reasonably comfortable. The big draw, however, is a wood-decked roof terrace that is complete with shaded tables and a decent-sized plunge pool.

Hotel Constanza

*C/Bruc 33, Eixample (93 270 19 10, www.hotelconstanza. com). Metro Urquinaona. **Map** p152 J7.*
This quiet and pleasant boutique hotel has been around for a few years now and continues to please. Rooms are contemporary and simple, with warm, earthy colour palette. The best rooms are at the back, some with smart walled-in terraces, and it has comfortable single rooms. The Constanza also does a good buffet breakfast.

Hotel España

*C/Sant Pau 9-11, Raval (93 550 00 00, www.hotelespanya.com). Metro Liceu. **Map** p109 G9.*
First opened in 1859, the España has a chequered history but has now been sympathetically

restored, in keeping with its status as a Modernista gem. You take your buffet breakfast in the Mermaid Salon, surrounded by breathtaking ceramic sea-life murals designed by Ramon Casas, and sip cocktails in front of an elaborate fireplace by architect Lluís Doménech i Montaner. Contemporary designs are used, too, notably in the Patio de las Monjas quadrangle, on the terrace and in the comfortably stylish taupe rooms. Ask for a room on the fourth floor – far enough up to give some distance from the occasional street noise and with slightly higher ceilings.

Hotel Mesón Castilla

*C/Valldonzella 5, Raval (93 318 21 82, www.mesoncastilla. com). Metro Universitat. **Map** p109 G8.*
If you want a change from modern design, check into this chocolate-box hotel, which opened in 1952. Before then, it belonged to an aristocratic Catalan family. The communal areas are full of antiques and artworks, while all rooms have tiled floors and are decorated with hand-painted furniture from Olot in northern Catalonia. The best rooms have terraces, and there is also a delightful plant-filled terrace off the breakfast room.

Market Hotel

C/Comte Borrell 68, Eixample (93 325 12 05, www.andilanahotels.

Hotel España

com). *Metro Sant Antoni.* **Map** *p139 E8. Photo 288.*

The people who brought us the wildly successful Quinze Nits chain of restaurants (*see p82*) have gone on to apply their low-budget, high-design approach to this hotel. The monochrome rooms with pops of colour, though not huge, are comfortable and stylish for the price, and downstairs is a handsome and keenly priced restaurant, typical of the group. For now, the nearby Mercat Sant Antoni is still undergoing a lengthy renovation, thus ensuring you won't be woken at dawn by shouting stallholders.

Room Mate Emma
C/Rosselló 205, Eixample (93 238 56 06, www.room-matehotels. com). Metro Diagonal. **Map** *p152 G5.*

The arrival of 'Emma' was a boon for the design-conscious and cash-strapped. The hotel reflects a fictional personality, as do all in the chain, in this case a graphic designer with aspirations to create the next space hotel. The hotel's undulating ceilings, walls studded with sequins and mood lighting add va-va-voom. Rooms are small – if you value space, check into the penthouse suite with a private terrace and hot tub – but the pay-off is soft, bouncy beds, power showers and a proper breakfast served until noon.

Other mid-range hotels include **Barceló Raval** (www.barceloraval.com), whose modern, cylindrical building dominates the Rambla del Raval, and **Abba Rambla Hotel** (www.abbaramblahotel.com), making a comfortable and friendly Barcelona base – also in the Raval.

Budget
Bonic Guesthouse
C/Josep Anselm Clavé 9, 1º-4ª, Barri Gòtic (mobile 626 053 434, www.bonic-barcelona.com). Metro Drassanes. **Map** *p71 G10.*

Bonic is painted in daisy-fresh colours and sunlight streams

through the windows onto meticulously restored original features. Attention to detail is exceptional for the price. Free newspapers and magazines, tea, coffee and water, and flowers in the three immaculate, communal bathrooms all add up to an experience that raises the bar considerably.

Casa Gràcia
Passeig de Gràcia 116, Gràcia (93 174 05 28 www.casagraciabcn. com). Metro Diagonal. **Map** *p175 H5.*

A cut above the regular youth hostel experience, Casa Gràcia is located in a lovely Modernista building, where natural light abounds through high windows and antiques dot the corridors. It offers an array of apartments, private rooms and dorm beds, and there are numerous common areas, including a library, bar, terrace and buzzy restaurant (that serves a rather rare unpasteurised beer). Regular events held here include daily yoga classes (free for guests), salsa lessons and live music.

Chic&Basic Born
C/Princesa 50, Born (93 295 46 52, www.chicandbasic.com). Metro Arc de Triomf or Jaume I. **Map** *p90 K9.*

Set in a building that's over a hundred years old, this hotel takes the white-on-white theme to extremes (until you choose from the array of coloured lighting options, that is). Rooms come with white cotton sheets, white floors, white walls, mirrored cornicing and glassed-in wet rooms in the centre for hosing yourself down. There's a comfortably furnished, relaxed lounge room with bar, and complimentary tea and coffee. There are similarly designed apartments.

Hostal Girona
C/Girona 24, 1º-1ª, Eixample (93 265 02 59, www.hostalgirona. com). Metro Urquinaona. **Map** *p152 J8.*

A gem of a *hostal*, filled with antiques, chandeliers and oriental

rugs. The rooms may be on the simple side, but all have charm to spare, with tall windows, pretty paintwork (gilt detail on the ceiling roses) and tiled floors. Rooms are available with or without en-suites. Brighter, outward-facing rooms have small balconies overlooking C/Girona or bigger balconies on to a huge and quiet patio.

Hostal Grau Barcelona
C/Ramelleres 27, Raval (93 301 81 35, www.hostalgrau.com). Metro Catalunya. **Map** *p109 G8.*

This charming, family-run eco-hostal oozes character, with a tiled spiral staircase and fabulous rustic communal areas, including a comfortable lounge and lively café. Rooms are stylish and fairly quiet, with sustainable wooden furniture and Coco-Mat and Naturalmat beds. All paint used in the *hostal* is chemical-free. Guests can enjoy complimentary tea, coffee and homemade cake every morning, as well as a glass of wine in the early evening.

Hostal Sol y K
C/Cervantes 2, 2º-1ª, Barri Gòtic (93 318 81 48, www.solyk.es). Metro Jaume I or Liceu. **Map** *p71 H10.*

Bright and cheerful with some nice aesthetic touches (slate bathrooms and arty, bold bedheads), this *hostal* is a bargain for those who don't need any frills. Not all rooms are en-suite, but all have washbasins, and the traditional patterned tiles and exposed wood beams give the Sol y K plenty of character. There's no breakfast, but free tea and coffee are available. Light sleepers would benefit from bringing a pair of earplugs with them, as noise carries from the street, and towels are for the skinny.

Other affordable options include **Itaca Hostel** (www.itacahostel. com), a laid-back place with a homely atmosphere, and **Pensión Hostal Mari-Luz** (www. pensionmariluz.com), with its characterful hotchpotch design and quiet rooms – both in the Barri Gòtic.

Getting Around

Barcelona's centre is compact and easily explored on foot. Bicycles are good for the Old City and port; there is a decent network of bike lanes across the city. The metro and bus systems are best for longer journeys. Cars can be a hindrance: there's little parking, and most of the city is given over to an array of one-way systems.

ARRIVING & LEAVING

By air
Aeroport de Barcelona
902 40 47 04, 91 321 10 00, www.aena.es.
Barcelona's airport is at El Prat, south-west of the city. There are 2 main terminals: Terminal 1 (known as T1), and Terminal 2 (T2). The latter comprises the old terminals formerly called A, B and C, and now called T2A, T2B and T2C. Tourist information desks can be found in T1 and T2B, and currency exchanges are in both terminals. The map (download it from www.emt-amb.com) details all bus and train routes to and from the airport.

Note that passengers travelling from T1 to countries outside the Schengen Agreement (including the UK and Ireland) cannot access the shopping and restaurant areas once they've passed through passport control. However, there is a café that's accessible to all.

Aerobús 010 *www.aerobusbcn.com.*
The airport bus runs 2 routes to and from Plaça Catalunya: bus A1 from T1, and bus A2 from T2 (which makes 2 stops: at T2B and T2C; it's a 5-10min walk to T2A). From the airport, both services stop at Plaça Espanya, Gran Via Urgell, Plaça Universitat and

Plaça Catalunya. On your return to the airport, both services depart from Plaça Catalunya (in front of El Corte Inglés), with stops at C/Sepúlveda and Plaça Espanya. The A1 bus runs every 5-10mins, departing the airport 5.35am-1.05am daily; and departing Plaça Catalunya 5am-12.30am daily. The A2 bus runs every 10mins, departing the airport 5.35am-1am daily; and departing Plaça Catalunya 5am-1am daily. Journey time (A1 and A2) is 35-45mins. Single €5.90; return (valid 15 days) €10.20.

Airport trains The long overhead walkway between T2A and T2B leads to the train station. The Cercanías train (R2 Nord) leaves the airport at 08 and 38 mins past the hr (except the first train, which leaves at 5.42am) until 11.38pm, stopping at Barcelona Sants and Passeig de Gràcia. Trains to the airport leave Barcelona Sants at 09 and 39 mins past the hr (except the first two trains, which leave at 5.13am and 5.35am), until 11.14pm daily (7mins earlier from Passeig de Gràcia, departing at 02 and 32 mins past the hr). Journey time 17-25mins and costs €2.15 one way (no return tickets). Tickets are valid only for 2hrs after purchase (902 32 03 20). The T-10 Zone 1 metro pass (*see p296*) is also valid.

City buses Bus 46 runs between Plaça Espanya and the airport every 30mins. The service leaves from Plaça Espanya 4.50am-11.50pm daily. From the airport the first is at 5.30am and the last at 11.50pm. Journey time 45mins.

At night, the N17 runs every 20mins between both airport

terminals (from 9.55pm T1, from 10.01pm T2) and Plaça Catalunya (from 11pm), with several stops on the way, including Plaça d'Espanya and Plaça Universitat. Last departures are 4.45am from T1, 5am from T2. Journey time 50mins from T2, 1hr from T1.

Metro A new metro line, the orange L9, runs from T1 and T2 to Zona Universitària, in the west of the city, where it hooks up with the green L3, which will take you into the heart of the city. Tickets cost €4.50, which includes the ongoing leg, by metro, bus or FGC train. The T-10 (*see p296*) is not valid on this service. The journey takes 32mins and trains run every 7mins, subject to the regular metro timetable (*see p296*).

Taxis The basic taxi fare to town should be €25-€30, including a €3.10 airport supplement (the minimum fare from the airport is €20 including all supplements). Fares are about 15% higher after 8pm and at weekends. There is a €1 supplement for each large piece of luggage placed in the car boot. All licensed cab drivers use the ranks outside the terminals.

By bus
Most long-distance coaches (national and international) stop or terminate at **Estació d'Autobusos Barcelona-Nord** (C/Alí Bei 80, 902 26 06 06, www.barcelonanord.com, map p152 L*). The **Estació d'Autobusos Barcelona-Sants** at C/Viriat (*fold-out map C5*) is only a secondary stop for many coaches, though some international Eurolines services (93 367 44 00, www.eurolines.es) both begin and end at Sants.

By rail

Most long-distance services run by the Spanish state railway company RENFE leave from **Barcelona-Sants** station, easily reached by metro. A few services from the French border or south to Tarragona stop at the **Estació de França** in the Born, which is otherwise sparsely served. Many trains stop at **Passeig de Gràcia**, which can be the handiest for the city centre and also has a metro stop.

RENFE operates the high-speed service **AVE** (Alta Velocidad) between Barcelona Sants station and Madrid, via Zaragoza, Lleida and Camp de Tarragona. Travelling at speeds averaging 300kmph, the AVE whisks travellers to the capital in about 2hrs 30mins. A single ticket to Madrid starts from €105 but there are special deals if you book online and in advance.

RENFE *902 32 03 20, www.renfe. com.* **Open** *24hrs daily.* Some English-speaking operators. RENFE tickets can be bought online, at stations and travel agents, or reserved over the phone, and either collected from machines at the train station or delivered for a small fee.

By road

The easiest way to central Barcelona from almost all directions is the **Ronda Litoral**, the coastal half of the ring road. Take exit 21 (Paral·lel) if you're coming from the south, or exit 22 (Via Laietana) from the north. Motorways also feed into Avda Diagonal, Avda Meridiana and Gran Via, which all lead to the city centre. Tolls are charged on most of the main approach routes, payable in cash (the lane marked 'manual'; motorbikes are charged half) or by card ('automatic'). For more, *see p298* Driving.

By sea

Balearic Islands ferries dock at the Moll de Barcelona quay, at the bottom of Avda Paral·lel. **Acciona Trasmediterránea** (902 45 46 45, www.trasmediterranea.es) is the main operator.

Grimaldi Lines runs a ferry a day Mon-Sat (also on Sun in Aug) between Barcelona and Civitavecchia (near Rome), which also stops at Porto Torres in Sardinia, as well as a service to Livorno (Tuscany) 3 times a week (902 53 13 33, www.grimaldi-ferries.com).

Cruise ships use several berths around the harbour. The **PortBus** shuttle service (93 415 60 20) runs every 15mins between them and the bottom of La Rambla when ships are in port.

MAPS

For a street map of Barcelona, see the fold-out map at the back of this guide, and also detailed maps at the beginning of each Explore area. Tourist offices also provide a reasonable free street map, or a better-quality map for €1. There's also an excellent interactive street map at www.bcn.cat/guia.

For Barcelona's metro map, see the fold-out map. Metro maps (ask for *un plano/un plànol del metro*) are also available free at all metro stations; bus maps can be obtained from the main Oficines d'Informació Turística (*see p308*).

PUBLIC TRANSPORT

Barcelona's public transport is now highly integrated, with units on multi-journey tickets valid for up to 3 changes of transport (within 75mins) on bus, tram, local train and metro lines. The metro is generally the quickest way of getting around the city. All metro lines operate 5am-midnight Mon-Thur, Sun and public holidays; 5am-2am Fri; and nonstop on Sat. Buses run all night to areas not covered by the metro system. Local buses and the metro are run by the city transport authority (TMB). Various underground lines connect with the metro, run by Catalan government railways, the FGC. Most run north from Plaça Catalunya; the others west from Plaça d'Espanya to Cornellà. There are 6 tramlines following 2 main routes (www.trambcn.com), though they're of limited use to visitors.

Public transport is free for under-4s. An increasing number of metro stations have lifts. Officially, pushchairs are supposed to be folded on the metro, but most people just grapple with the obstacle course and the guards don't interfere. All buses are low enough to wheel buggies straight on.

FGC information *Vestibule, Plaça Catalunya FGC station (93 205 15 15, www.fgc.net).* **Open** *8am-8pm Mon-Fri.* **Map** *p152 H8.*
Other locations *FGC Plaça d'Espanya.* **Open** *9am-2pm, 4pm-6.30pm Mon-Fri.*

TMB information *Main vestibule, Metro Universitat, Eixample (902 07 50 27, www.tmb. cat).* **Open** *8am-8pm Mon-Fri.* **Map** *p152 G7.*
Other locations *Vestibule, Metro Diagonal, Metro Sagrera.*

Fares & tickets

Journeys in the Barcelona urban area have a flat fare of €2.15, but multi-journey tickets (*targetes/ tarjetas*) are better value. The basic 10-trip *targeta* is the **T-10** (*Te-Deu* in Catalan, *Te-Diez* in Spanish), which can be shared by any number of people travelling simultaneously; the ticket is validated in the machines on the metro, train or bus once per person per journey.

Along with the other integrated *targetes* listed below, the T-10 offers access to all 5 of the city's main transport systems (local RENFE and FGC trains within the main metropolitan area, the metro, the tram and buses). To change transport type using the same unit, insert your card into a machine a second time; unless 75mins have elapsed since your last journey, no other unit will be deducted. Single tickets do not allow free transfers.

You can buy T-10s in newsagents and Servi-Caixa cashpoints, as well as on the metro and train systems (from machines or the ticket office), but not on buses. More expensive versions of all *targetes* take you to the outer zones of the metropolitan region, but the prices listed below will get you anywhere in central Barcelona, and to the key sights on the outskirts of the city itself.

Integrated targetes
T-10 Valid for 10 trips; each ticket can be shared by 2 or more people. €9.95.
T-Día 1-day travelcard. €8.40.
T-Mes Valid for any 30-day period. €52.75.
T-Trimestre Valid for 3 mths. €142.
T-50/30 50 trips in any 30-day period; but can only be used by 1 person. €42.50.
T-70/30 70 trips in any 30-day period; can be shared. €59.50.
T-Jove Valid for 3 mths; for under-25s. €105.

Other targetes
2, 3, 4 & 5 Dies 2-, 3-, 4- and 5-day travelcards on the metro, buses and FGC trains. Also sold at tourist offices. €14, €20.50, €26.50 and €32 (10% discount available if purchased online).
Barcelona Card A tourist scheme offering unlimited use of public transport for up to 5 days (www.barcelonacard.com).

Buses
Many bus routes originate in or pass through Plaça Catalunya, Plaça Universitat and Plaça Urquinaona. However, they often run along parallel streets, due to the city's one-way system. Not all stops are labelled, and street signs are not always easy to locate.

Most routes run 5.30am-11pm daily except Sun. There's usually a bus every 10-15mins, but they're less frequent before 8am, after 9pm and on Sat. On Sun, buses are less frequent still; a few do not run at all. Only single tickets can be bought from the driver; if you have a *targeta*, insert it into the machine behind the driver as you board.

Night buses There are 17 urban night bus (*Nitbus*) routes (010, or EMT), most running from around 10.15-11.30pm to 4.30-6am nightly, with buses every 20-30mins, plus an hourly bus to the airport (*see p295* By

air). Most pass through Plaça Catalunya. Fares and *targetes* are as for daytime buses. Plaça Catalunya is also the terminus for all-night bus services linking Barcelona with more distant parts of its metropolitan area.

Local trains
Regional trains to Sabadell, Terrassa and other towns beyond Tibidabo depart from FGC Plaça Catalunya, those for Montserrat from FGC Plaça d'Espanya.

All trains on the RENFE local network ('Rodalies/Cercanías') stop at Sants but can also be caught at either Plaça Catalunya and Arc de Triomf (for Vic and the Pyrenees, Manresa, the Penedès and Costa del Maresme) or Passeig de Gràcia (for the southern coastal line to Sitges and the Girona-Figueres line north).

Metro
The metro is the easiest way to get around Barcelona. There are 9 lines, each colour coded. For tickets and running times, *see left*; for a map, see the fold-out map.

Trams
Lines T1, T2 and T3 go from Plaça Francesc Macià, Zona Alta, to the outskirts of the city. T4 is the most useful line for visitors and runs from Ciutadella to Vila Olímpica (also a metro stop), via Glòries and the Fòrum. T5 and T6 run north to Badalona.

All trams are fully accessible for wheelchair-users and are part of the integrated TMB *targeta* system. You can buy integrated tickets and single tickets from the machines at tram stops.

Tram information *Trambaix (901 70 11 81, www.trambcn.com). Open July, Aug 8am-3pm Mon-Fri. Sept-June 9am-7pm Mon-Fri.*

TAXIS

It's usually easy to find a taxi. There are ranks at railway and bus stations, in main squares and throughout the city, but taxis can also be hailed on the street when they show a green light on the

roof and a sign saying *lliure/libre* ('free') behind the windscreen. Information on taxi fares, ranks and regulations can be found at www.taxi.ambcat.

Fares
Current rates and supplements are shown inside cabs on a sticker on the rear side window (in English). The basic fare for a taxi hailed in the street is €2.10, which is what the meter should register when you set off. The basic rates (€1.10/km) apply 8am-8pm Mon-Fri; at other times, including public holidays, the rate is €1.30/km.

There are supplements for luggage (€1), for the airport (€3.10), Sants train station (€2.10), and the port (€3.10), and for nights such as New Year's Eve (€3.10), as well as a waiting charge. There is also a €2.10 supplement midnight-6am Fri-Sun. And if a public holiday falls on one of these days, there's an additional €3.10 supplement. Taxi drivers are not required to carry more than €20 in change; few accept cards.

Radio cabs
These companies take bookings 24hrs daily. Phone cabs start the meter when a call is answered but, by the time it picks you up, it should not display more than €3.40 (€4.20 at night, weekends or public holidays). Note that a minimum fare applies for radio cabs (€7). Supplements are added at the end of the journey.
Fono-Taxi 93 300 11 00.
Ràdio Taxi '033' or 93 303 30 33.
Servi-Taxi 93 330 03 00.
Taxi Miramar 93 433 10 20.

Receipts & complaints
To get a receipt, ask for *un rebut/un recibo*. It should include the fare, the taxi number, the driver's NIF (tax) number, the licence plate, the driver's signature and the date; if you have a complaint, insist on all these, and the more details (time, route) the better. Complaints must be filed in writing to the **Institut Metropolità del Taxi** (93 223 51 51, www.taxi.amb.cat).

DRIVING

For information on driving in Catalonia, call the local government's information line (012), which has English speakers; or see www.gen cat.net/ transit. Driving in the city can be intimidating. If you do drive:
• Keep your driving licence, vehicle registration and insurance documents with you at all times.
• Do not leave anything of value, including car radios, in your car. Foreign plates can attract thieves.
• Be on your guard at motorway service areas, and take care to avoid thieves in the city who may try to make you stop, perhaps by indicating you have a flat tyre.

Breakdown services

If you're planning to take a car, join a motoring organisation such as the **AA** (www.theaa.com) or the **RAC** (www.rac.co.uk) in the UK, or the **AAA** (www.aaa.com) in the US, which usually have reciprocal agreements.

RACE (Real Automóvil Club de España) *900 100 992, 24hr help 900 112 222, or 91 593 33 33 from abroad, www.race.es.*

Car & motorbike hire

Car hire is relatively pricey, but it's a competitive market, so shop around. Ideally, you want unlimited mileage, VAT (IVA) included and full insurance cover *(seguro sense risc/seguro todo riesgo)* rather than the 3rd-party minimum *(seguro obligatori/ seguro obligatorio)*. You'll need a credit card as a guarantee. Most companies require you to have had a licence for at least a year; many also enforce a minimum age limit.

Europcar *Plaça dels Països Catalans, Sants (902 10 50 55, www.europcar.com). Metro Sants Estació.* **Open** *6am-midnight Mon-Fri; 7am-11.30pm Sat, Sun.* **Map** *Fold-out C5.*
Other locations *Airport T1 and T2B (902 105 055); C/Viladomat 214, Eixample (93 439 84 03); Gran Via de les Corts Catalanes 680, Eixample (93 302 05 43).*

Motíssimo *C/Comandante Benítez 25, Sants (93 490 84 01, www.motissimo.es). Metro Badal.* **Open** *9am-2pm, 4-8pm Mon-Fri; 9am-1.30pm Sat.* **Map** *Fold-out A4.*
Vanguard *C/Londres 31, Eixample (93 439 38 80, www.vanguardrent.com). Metro Hospital Clínic.* **Open** *8.30am-1.30pm, 4-7pm Mon-Fri; 9am-1pm Sat, Sun.* **Map** *p152 E4.*

Legal requirements

For driving laws and regulations (in Spanish), see the **Ministry of Interior**'s website (www.dgt.es).

Parking

Parking is fiendishly complicated and municipal police are quick to hand out tickets or tow cars. In some parts of the Old City, access is limited to residents for much of the day. In some Old City streets, time-controlled bollards pop up, meaning your car may get stuck. Never park in front of doors marked '*Gual Permanent*', indicating an entry with 24hr right of access.

Pay & display areas The Àrea Verda contains zones only for use of residents (most of the Old City and centre of Gràcia – look out for *Àrea residents* signs). Elsewhere in central Barcelona, non-residents pay €2.50 or €2.25/ hr with a 1- or 2hr maximum stay.
   If you overstay by no more than half the time you've already paid for, you can cancel the fine by paying an extra €7; to do so, press *Anul·lar denúncia* on the machine, insert €7, then press Ticket. Some machines accept cards; none accept notes or give change. For information, check www.areaverda.cat or call 010. There's a drop-in centre for queries at C/Calàbria 66, open 8am-8pm Mon-Fri.

Car parks Car parks (*parkings*) are signalled by a white 'P' on a blue sign. Those run by **SABA** (902 28 30 80, www.saba.es) cost around €3.05/hr. Discount and long-stay passes (6-12hrs) are available in packs of 10 units. The municipal parking network

B:SM has 40 car parks in the city, costing €3.07/hr (www.bsmsa. cat/activitats/mobilitat). Long-stay and motorhome parking available.

Towed vehicles If police tow your car, they should leave a triangular sticker on the pavement where it was. The sticker should let you know to which pound it's been taken. If not, call 901 513 151; staff generally don't speak English. Recovering your vehicle within 4 hrs costs €147.69, after which it's €1.99/hr, or €19.86/ day. You'll also have to pay a fine. You'll need your passport and documentation, or rental contract, to prove ownership. You can find information in Catalan, Spanish, English and French at www.gruabcn.cat.

CYCLING

There's a network of bike lanes (*carrils bici*) along major avenues and alongside the seafront; local authorities are very keen to promote cycling. Be warned that bike theft is rife: always carry a good lock. For information see www.bcn.cat/bicicleta. There are bike hire shops all over the city; also, *see below* Un Cotxe Menys.

TOURS

Another way to get around is to hire a Trixi rickshaw (www.trixi. com). Running 9am-8pm, Apr-Nov, and costing €30/hr for 2 people, they can be hailed on the street, or by calling mobile 677 732 773. There are several tours, including a 30min Barri Gòtic tour (€18 for 2 people) and a 2hr Gaudí tour (€50 for 2 people).

By bike
Un Cotxe Menys *C/Esparteria 3, Born (93 268 21 05, www. bicicletabarcelona.com). Metro Jaume I.* **Open** *10am-7pm daily.* **Tours** *11am daily, plus Apr-Sept 4.30pm Mon, Fri-Sun.* **Tickets** *€23. €5/1hr; €10/4hrs; €12/1-day; €60/wk. No cards.* **Map** *p90 J10.*
Meet in Plaça Sant Jaume and then head to the shop for bikes

and helmets followed by a 3hr English-speaking tour.

Fat Tire Bike Tours *C/Marlet 4 (93 342 92 75, fattirebiketours. com/barcelona). Metro Drassanes. Tours Feb-mid Apr, Nov-mid Dec 11am daily. Mid Apr-Oct 11am, 4pm daily. Rates €24. Map p71 H9.*
Tours meet in Plaça Sant Jaume and last over 4hrs, taking in the Old City, Sagrada Família, Ciutadella park and the beach.

By bus

Barcelona City Tours
93 317 64 54, www.barcelonacity tour.cat. Tours Oct-Jan 11am-6pm daily; every 15-20mins. June-Oct 11am-8pm daily; every 8-10mins. Tickets 1 day €28; 2 days €39. Free under-4s. Available on bus.
Though more frequent, off-season, than rival Bus Turístic, there are no discounts offered to attractions. There are 2 routes: the East route takes in Sagrada Família, Park Güell and Port Olímpic; the West route takes in the seafront and the Fòrum, Montjuïc and Camp Nou. Both circuits take around 2hrs.

Bus Turístic *93 285 38 32, www. tmb.net. Tours Apr-Oct 9am-8pm daily; every 5-10mins. Nov-Mar 9am-7pm daily; every 25mins. Tickets 1 day €28; 2 days €39. Free under-4s. Available from tourist office or on bus. No cards.*
Bus Turístic (white and blue, with colourful images of the sights) runs 3 circular routes. Tickets are valid for all routes and ticket-holders get discount vouchers for a range of attractions.

Bus Turístic de Nit *93 285 38 32, www.tmb.net. Tours June-Sept 9.30pm (boarding from 9.10pm) Sat, Sun. Tickets €19; €10 reductions. Available from tourist offices or on bus. No cards.*

Travel Advice

For up-to-date information on travel to a specific country – including the latest on safety and security, health issues, local laws and customs – contact your home country government's department of foreign affairs. Most have websites with useful advice for would-be travellers.

Australia
www.smartraveller.gov.au

Republic of Ireland
foreignaffairs.gov.ie

Canada
www.voyage.gc.ca

UK
www.fco.gov.uk/travel

New Zealand
www.safetravel.govt.nz

USA
www.state.gov/travel

The night tour bus (with guided commentary) is designed to show off the illuminations of the city.

On foot

Barcelona Walking Tours *93 285 38 32, www. barcelonaturisme.com. Tours (in English) Gothic 9.30am daily. Picasso Apr-Oct 3pm Tue-Sat; Nov-Mar 3pm Tue, Thur, Sat. Modernisme April-Oct 6pm Wed, Fri; Nov-Mar 3.30pm Wed, Fri. Gourmet 10.30am Mon-Fri. Tickets Gothic, Modernisme €16. Picasso, Gourmet (reservations essential) €22.*
Tours take 90mins-2hrs, excluding the museum trip. Modernisme and Picasso tours start in the underground tourist office in Plaça Catalunya; Gothic tour starts at the tourist office in the Ajuntament, Plaça Sant Jaume; Gourmet tour starts at the tourist office in C/Ciutat 2. There is a 10% discount for booking online. Also offers shopping tours, literary tours, a guided tour of Park Güell, night tours of the Gothic Quarter, and a scenic Collserola tour; check website for details.

My Favourite Things *mobile 637 265 405, www.myft.net.*

Unusual outings (€26) that include walking tours for families with children, urban design tours, and romantic tours, plus a 1-day wine tasting tour in the Priorat (€155).

Ruta del Modernisme *93 317 76 52, www.rutadelmodernisme.com. Rates €12.*
Not so much a route as a guidebook to 120 Modernista buildings, giving discounts on entry. Available at the Plaça Catalunya tourist office (see p308), the Hospital Sant Pau and the Pavellons Güell.

By scooter

Barcelona Scooter Tours *Cooltra Motos, Via Laietana 6, Barceloneta (93 221 40 70, www.cooltra.com). Metro Barceloneta. Tours & rates €50 4hr BCN Fun and Beach tour (11am Fri, Sun); €50 4hr min Modernista Gaudí tour (2.30pm Fri, Sun); €40 3hr 360° Panoramic Tour (4pm Sat, 10.30pm Thur). Hire €37 for 24hrs, incl basic insurance and helmet. Map p71 J10.*
Note that you must have at least 3 yrs' driving experience. Book 24hrs ahead.

Resources A-Z

ACCIDENT & EMERGENCY

Emergency numbers
Emergency services *112*.
Police, fire or ambulance.
Ambulance *Ambulància 061*.
For hospitals *see below* and other health services, *see p302* Health.
Fire service *Bombers/ Bomberos 080*.
Police *Mossos d'Esquadra 088*.
Catalan police force.

A&E departments

In a medical emergency, go to the casualty department (*Urgències*) of any of the main public hospitals in the city (including those below). All are open 24hrs daily. The most central are the Clínic and Perecamps. Call 061 or 112 for an ambulance. For more information *see p302* Health.

Centre d'Urgències Perecamps *Avda Drassanes 13-15, Raval (93 441 06 00). Metro Drassanes or Parallel.* **Map** *p109 G10.*

Hospital Clínic *C/Villarroel 170, Eixample (93 227 54 00). Metro Hospital Clínic.* **Map** *p152 F5.*

Hospital Dos de Maig *C/Dos de Maig 301, Eixample (93 507 27 00). Metro Sant Pau-Dos de Maig.* **Map** *p152 N5.*

Hospital del Mar *Passeig Marítim 25-29, Barceloneta (93 248 30 00). Metro Ciutadella-Vila Olímpica.* **Map** *p124 L10.*

Hospital de Sant Pau *C/Sant Quintí 89, Eixample (93 291 90 00). Metro Hospital de Sant Pau-Guinardó.* **Map** *p152 N4.*

ADDRESSES

Most apartment addresses consist of a street name followed by a street number, floor level and flat number, in that order. So, to go to C/València 246, 2º 3ª, find No.246, go to the second floor and find the door marked 3 or 3ª. Ground-floor flats are usually called *baixos* or *bajos* (often abbreviated bxs/ bjos); one floor up is the *entresol/ entresuelo* (entl), and the next is often the *principal* (pral). Confusingly, numbered floors then start: 1st, 2nd, up to the *àtic/ático* at the top. Addresses occasionally point out whether a property number is on the left- or right-hand side of the street; 'right' is *dreta/derecha* (dta/dcha) and 'left' is *esquerra/izquierda* (esq/izq).

AGE RESTRICTIONS

Buying/drinking alcohol 18.
Driving 18.
Smoking 18.
Sex (*hetero- and homosexual*) 16.

ATTITUDE & ETIQUETTE

The Catalans are generally less guarded about personal space than people in Britain or the US. The common greeting between members of the opposite sex and between two women, even the first time that the two parties have met, is a kiss on both cheeks. Men usually greet each other by shaking hands. Don't be surprised if people bump into you on the street, or crowd or push past you on the bus or metro without apologising: it's not seen as rude.

Contrary to appearances, Catalans have an advanced queuing culture. They may not stand in an orderly line, but they're normally very aware of when it's their turn, particularly at market stalls. The standard drill is to ask when you arrive, *¿Qui es l'últim/la última?* ('Who's last?'), and say *jo* ('me') to the next person who asks.

CLIMATE

Barcelona is usually agreeable year-round. Spring is unpredictable: warm, sunny days can alternate with winds and showers. Temperatures in May and June are pretty much perfect and 23 June marks the beginning of summer. July and Aug can be unpleasant, as the summer heat kicks in and many locals leave town. Public transport and cinemas can overcompensate for the heat with bracing air-conditioning. The summer humidity can be debilitating, particularly when it's overcast. Autumn weather is generally warm and fresh, with heavy downpours common around Oct. Crisp, cool sunshine is normal Dec-Feb. Snow is very rare. *See also p301* Weather Chart.

EMBASSIES & CONSULATES

The contact details for all embassies in Spain and for Spanish embassies around the world are available on embassy. goabroad.com. Embassies are located in Madrid, but several countries also have consulates in Barcelona.

British Consulate *Avda Diagonal 477, 13º, Eixample (93 366 62 00, www.gov.uk/ government/world/spain). Metro Hospital Clínic.* **Open** *8.30am-1.30pm Mon-Fri (telephone hours 9am-5pm).* **Map** *p152 F4.*

Canadian Consulate *Plaça Catalunya 9, 1º, Eixample (93 270 36 14, www.espana.gc.ca). Metro Catalunya.* **Open** *9am-12.30pm Mon-Fri.* **Map** *p152 H7.*

Irish Consulate *Gran Via Carles III 94, 10º, Les Corts (93 491 50 21, www. embassyofireland.es). Metro Maria Cristina.* **Open** *10am-1pm Mon-Fri.* **Map** *Fold-out B3.*

New Zealand Consulate *Travessera de Gràcia 64, 2º, Gràcia (93 209 50 48). Metro Diagonal.* **Open** *9am-2pm, 4-5pm Mon-Fri.* **Map** *Fold-out G4.*

US Consulate *Passeig Reina Elisenda 23, Sarrià (93 280 22 27, barcelona.usconsulate.gov). FGC Reina Elisenda.* **Open** *by appt 9am-1pm Mon-Fri.*

CONSUMER

Ask for a complaint form (*full de reclamació/hoja de reclamación*), which many businesses and all shops, bars and restaurants are required to keep. Leave one copy with the business. Take the other forms to the consumer office.
Oficina Municipal d'Informació al Consumidor *Ronda de Sant Pau 43-45, Sant Antoni (93 402 78 41, ajuntament.barcelona.cat/omic). Metro Paral·lel or Sant Antoni.* **Open** *9am-3pm Mon-Thur; 9am-2pm Fri.* **Map** *p139 E9.*
The official centre for consumer advice and complaints follow-up.
Telèfon de Consulta del Consumidor *012.* **Open** *24hrs.* Consumer advice.

CUSTOMS

Custom declarations are not usually necessary if you arrive from another EU country and are carrying legal goods for personal use (regardless of whether you are an EU citizen). The amounts given below are guidelines only: if you come close to the maximums in several categories, you may have to explain your personal habits.
• 800 cigarettes, 400 small cigars, 200 cigars or 1kg loose tobacco.
• 10 litres of spirits (more than 22% alcohol), 20 litres of spirits (less than 22% alcohol), 90 litres of wine (or 60 litres of sparkling wine) or 110 litres of beer.
    Coming from a non-EU country or the Canary Islands, you can bring:
• 200 cigarettes, 100 small cigars, 50 regular cigars or 250g (8.82oz) of tobacco.
• 1 litre of spirits (more than 22% alcohol) or 2 litres of spirits or similar beverages (less than 22% alcohol) or 4 litres of wine (less than 22% alcohol) or 16 litres of beer.
• Personal goods to a value of €430.
    Visitors can also carry up to €10,000 in cash without having to declare it. Non-EU residents can reclaim VAT (IVA) on some large purchases when they leave. For details, *see p305.*

DISABLED

Although many sights claim to be accessible, you may still need assistance. Phoning ahead to check is always a good idea. A useful resource is the Catalan government's website www.turismeperatothom.com, which describes accessible accommodation, sights, and transport in Barcelona and throughout Catalonia.
    The website www.accessiblebarcelona.com, run by a British wheelchair-user who used to live in Barcelona, is a little out of date, but still a useful resource. It also provides reviews of accessible accommodation, attractions and restaurants.
Institut Municipal de Persones amb Discapacitat *C/València 344, Eixample (93 413 27 75, ajuntament.barcelona.cat/ accessible). Metro Girona.* **Open** *9am-2pm Mon-Fri.* **Map** *p152 K6.*
The official city organisation for the disabled has information on access to venues and transport, and can provide a map with wheelchair-friendly itineraries. Call in advance to make an appointment. There are some English speakers available.

Transport
Access for disabled people to local transport is improving but still leaves much to be desired. For wheelchair-users, buses and taxis are usually the best bet. For transport information, call **TMB** (902 075 027) or 010. Transport maps, which can be picked up from transport information offices and some metro stations, indicate wheelchair access points and adapted bus routes.

Buses All the Aerobús airport buses, night buses, standard buses and the open-topped tourist buses are fully accessible, though you may need assistance with the steep ramps. Press the blue button with the wheelchair symbol to alert the driver before your stop. Visual and audio assistance is also in place for blind passengers.

FGC Accessible FGC stations include Provença, Muntaner

Weather Chart

Average temperatures and monthly rainfall in Barcelona

	Temp (°C/°F)	Rainfall (mm/in)	Sun (hrs/day)
January	10/50	44/1.7	5
February	10/50	36/1.4	7
March	12/54	48/1.9	7
April	13/55	51/2.0	8
May	16/61	57/2.2	8
June	20/68	38/1.5	9
July	23/73	22/0.9	10
August	24/75	66/2.6	9
September	22/72	79/3.1	8
October	18/64	94/3.7	6
November	13/55	74/2.9	5
December	11/52	50/2.0	4

d Avda Tibidabo. The FGC
infrastructures at Catalunya and
Espanya stations are accessible,
but interchanges with metro lines
are not. The Montjuïc funicular
railway is fully wheelchair-
adapted.

Metro For a list of accessible
metro stations and bus lines,
check www.tmb.cat/en/
barcelona/metro/lines and
select a line to view accessibility
information, or see the TMB map
on the fold-out map. Only L2, L9,
L10 and L11 have lifts and ramps
at all stations. On L1, L3, L4 and
L5 some stations have lifts. There
is usually a step on to the train,
the size of which varies; some
assistance may be required.

RENFE trains Sants and
Plaça Catalunya stations are
wheelchair-accessible, but the
trains are not. If you go to the
Atenció al Viajero office ahead of
time, help on the platform can be
arranged.

Taxis All taxi drivers are
officially required to transport
wheelchairs and guide dogs for
no extra charge, but cars can
be small, and the willingness
of drivers to co-operate varies
widely. Special minibus taxis
adapted for wheelchairs can
be ordered from the **Taxi Amic**
service (93 420 80 88, www.
taxi-amic-adaptat.com, open
7am-11pm Mon-Fri; 8am-10pm
Sat, Sun). Fares are the same
as for regular cabs, but there
is a minimum fare of €12.90
for Barcelona city (€14.40 at
weekends), and more for the
surrounding areas.

Trams All tram lines throughout
Barcelona are fully accessible for
wheelchair-users, with ramps
that can access all platforms.
Look for the symbol on each
platform that indicates where the
wheelchair-accessible doors will
be situated.

Wheelchair-friendly museums & galleries

All of the below should be
accessible to wheelchair-users:
CCCB; CaixaForum; Disseny
Hub Barcelona; Espai Gaudí – La

Pedrera; Fundació Joan Miró;
Fundacío Antoni Tàpies; MNAC;
Museu Barbier-Mueller d'Art
Precolombi; Museu Frederic
Marès; Museu d'Arqueologia
de Catalunya; Museu de Cera;
Museu del Temple Expiatori
de la Sagrada Família; Museu
d'Història de Catalunya; Museu
d'Història de Barcelona; Museu de
la Ciència – CosmoCaixa; Museu
de la Xocolata; Museu Picasso;
Palau de la Música; Palau de
la Virreina.

DRUGS

Many people smoke cannabis
fairly openly in Spain, but
possession or consumption in
public is illegal. In private, the
law is contradictory: smoking
is OK, but you can be nabbed
for possession or distribution.
Enforcement is often not the
highest of police priorities, but
you could theoretically receive a
fine. Larger amounts entail a fine
and, in extreme cases, prison.
Smoking in bars is also prohibited.
Cocaine is also common in Spain,
but if you are caught in possession
of this or any other Class A drug,
you are looking at a hefty fine, and
possibly a long prison sentence.

ELECTRICITY

The standard voltage in Spain is
220V. Plugs are of the 2-round-
pin type. You'll need a plug
adaptor to use British-bought
electrical devices. If you have US
(110V) equipment, you will need
a current transformer as well as
an adaptor.

HEALTH

For general details on healthcare,
check the website catsalut.gencat.
cat or get health advice over the
phone by calling 061.
Visitors can obtain emergency
care through the public health
service, Servei Catalá de la Salut
(*see p300 Accident & emergency*).
EU nationals are entitled to free
basic medical attention if they
have the European Emergency
Health Card (Tarjeta Sanitaria
Europea), also known as the
European Health Insurance Card
(EHIC). Contact the health service
in your country of residence for

details. If you don't have one but
can get one sent or faxed within
a few days, you will be exempt
from charges. Citizens of certain
other countries that have a special
agreement with Spain, among
them several Latin American
states, can also have access to
free care.
For non-emergencies it's
usually quicker to use private
travel insurance (*see p303*)
rather than the state system.
Similarly, non-EU nationals
with private medical insurance
can also make use of state
health services on a paying
basis, but private clinics are
generally simpler.
Tap water is drinkable in
Barcelona, but tastes faintly
of chlorine.

Contraception

All pharmacies sell condoms
(*condoms/preservativos*) and other
forms of contraception including
pills (*la píndola/la píldora*),
which can be bought without a
prescription, as can the morning-
after pill (*la píndola de l'endemà/
la píldora del día siguiente*)
but som health centres will
dispense it free themselves. Many
bars and clubs have condom
vending machines.
**Centre Jove d'Anticoncepció
i Sexualitat** *C/La Granja 19-21,
Gràcia (93 415 10 00, www.
centrejove.org). Metro Lesseps.
Open 11am-7pm Mon-Thur;
10am-5pm Fri. Closed 2wks Aug.
Map p175 K2.*
A family-planning centre aimed
at young people (under-25s).

Dentists

Most dentistry is not covered
by the Spanish public health
service (to which EU citizens have
access). Check the classified ads
in *Metropolitan* (*see right*) for
English-speaking dentists.
Institut Odontològic Calàbria
*C/Calàbria 236, Eixample (902
119 321, www.ioa.es). Metro
Entença. Open 10am-1pm, 3-8pm
Mon-Fri. Map p152 E5.*
These well-equipped clinics
provide a complete range of
dental services. Some staff
speak English.
Other locations Institut
Odontològic Sagrada Família,

C/Sardenya 319, Eixample (93 457 04 53); Institut Odontològic, C/Diputació 238, Eixample (93 342 64 00).

Hospitals

See *p300* Accident & emergency.

Opticians

+Visión El Triangle *Plaça Catalunya 4, Eixample (93 304 16 40, www.masvision.es). Metro Catalunya. Open 10am-10pm Mon-Sat. Map p152 H8.* There are some English-speaking staff at this handy optical superstore. It's occasionally possible to get a test without an appointment.

Pharmacies

Pharmacies (*farmàcies/farmàcias*) are signalled by large green and red neon crosses. About a dozen operate around the clock, while more have late opening hours. The full list of pharmacies that stay open late and/or all night is posted on every pharmacy door and in the local papers. You can also call two helplines, 010 and 098, for information.
Farmàcia Álvarez *Passeig de Gràcia 26, Eixample (93 302 11 24). Metro Passeig de Gràcia. Open 24hrs daily. Map p152 H6.*
Farmàcia Cervera *C/Muntaner 254, Eixample (93 200 09 96). Metro Diagonal/FGC Gràcia. Open 24hrs daily. Map p152 E4.*
Farmàcia Clapés *La Rambla 98, Barri Gòtic (93 301 28 43). Metro Liceu. Open 24hrs daily. Map p71 H9.*
Farmàcia Vilar *Vestibule Estació de Sants, Sants (93 490 92 07). Metro Sants Estació. Open 6.30am-10.30pm Mon-Fri; 8am-10.30pm Sat, Sun. Map Fold-out C5.*

STDs, HIV & AIDS

Free, anonymous blood tests for HIV and other STDs are given at the Unidad de Infección de Transmisión Sexual (93 441 46 12) at **CAP Drassanes** (Avda Drassanes 17-21, Raval, open 8am-8pm Mon-Fri; emergencies only 9am-5pm Sat). HIV tests are also available at the Asociación Ciutadana Antisida de Catalunya (C/Lluna 11, Raval, 93 317 05 05,

www.acasc.info) and at BCN Checkpoint (C/Comte Borrell 164-166, 93 318 20 56, www. bcncheckpoint.com).
AIDS Information Line *(Freephone 900 21 22 22) Open 24hrs daily.*

ID

From the age of 14, Spaniards are legally obliged to carry their DNI (identity card). Foreigners are also meant to carry an ID card or passport, and are in theory subject to a fine for not doing so – in practice, you're more likely to get a warning. If you don't want to carry it around with you (wisely, given the prevalence of petty crime), it's a good idea to carry a photocopy or a driver's licence instead: technically, it's not legal, but usually acceptable. ID is needed to check into a hotel, hire a car and – very occasionally – when you pay with a card in shops.

INSURANCE

For health care for EU nationals, see *p302*Health. Some non-EU countries also have reciprocal health-care agreements with Spain. Regardless of your nationality, you are strongly advised to take out private travel insurance, which will cover you in case of theft and flight problems as well as medical emergencies.

LANGUAGE

Over a 3rd of Barcelona residents prefer to speak Catalan as their everyday language, around 70% speak it fluently, and more than 90% understand it. Everyone in the city can also speak Spanish, and will switch to it if visitors show signs of linguistic jitters. If you take an interest and learn a few phrases in Catalan, it is likely to be appreciated.
Most signage is written in Catalan by default, though you will also see Spanish and – occasionally – English, particularly in tourist areas. See *p309* Spanish Vocabulary and *p310* Catalan Vocabulary. For classes, see *p306* Language classes.

LEFT LUGGAGE

Look for signs to the *consigna*.
Aeroport del Prat *Open Terminal 1 24hrs daily; Terminal 2 6am-10pm daily. Rates €6 for 2hrs, €10 for every 24hrs thereafter.*
Estació d'Autobusos *Barcelona-Nord C/Alí Bei 80, Eixample. Metro Arc de Triomf. Open 24hrs daily. Rates €3.50-€5.40/day. Map p152 L8.*
Sants-Estació *Open 24hrs daily. Rates €3-€5/day. Map Fold-out C5.* Some smaller railway stations also have left-luggage lockers.

LEGAL HELP

Consulates (*see pxxx*) can help tourists in emergencies and recommend lawyers.
Martí & Associats *Avda Diagonal 584, pral 1ª, Eixample (93 201 62 66, www. martilawyers.com). Bus 6, 7, 15, 33, 34. Open Sept-July 9am-8pm Mon-Thur; 9am-7pm Fri. Aug 9am-2pm, 4-7pm Mon-Thur; 9am-2pm Fri. Map p152 F4.*

LGBT

Casal Lambda *Avda Marques de Argentera 22, Born (93 319 55 50, www.lambda.cat). Metro Barceloneta. Open 5-9pm Mon-Sat. Closed Aug. Map p90 K10.* Gay cultural organisation.
Front d'Alliberament Gai de Catalunya *C/Verdi 88, Gràcia (93 217 26 69, www.fagc.org). Metro Fontana. Open 7-9pm Mon-Fri. Map p175 J3.* A vocal group that produces the *Debat Gai* information bulletin.

LIBRARIES

There's a network of public libraries around the city that offer free internet access, some English-language novels and information on cultural activities. Membership is free. Opening times are generally 10am-2pm, 4-8.30pm Mon-Sat. See www.bcn. cat/icub/biblioteques or call 93 316 10 00 for details.

LOST PROPERTY

If you lose something at the airport, report it to the lost property centre (Oficina d'Objectes Perduts, in T1, 93 259 64 40). If you have mislaid anything on a train, look for the Atenció al Passatger desk or Cap d'Estació office at the nearest station to where your property went astray. Call ahead to the destination station, or call station information and ask for *objetos perdidos*.

Oficina de Troballes *Plaça Carles Pi i Sunyer 8-10, Barri Gòtic (010). Metro Catalunya or Jaume I. Open 9am-2pm Mon-Fri. Map p71 H8*
All documentation or valuables found on city public transport and taxis, or picked up by the police in the street, should eventually find their way to this Ajuntament office, just off Avda Portal de l'Àngel.

TMB Lost Property Office *Diagonal metro station L5 entrance (902 075 027, www. tmb.cat). Open 8am-8pm Mon-Fri. Map p152 H5.*
Items found on most public transport services are sent to this office, then transferred to the municipal office (see above) on Wed. If the item was lost on a tram, call 900 701 181; on FGC trains, 93 205 15 15; for taxis, call 902 101 564.

MEDIA

Spanish and Catalan newspapers tend to favour serious and lengthy political commentary. There are no sensationalist tabloids in Spain: for scandal, the *prensa rosa* ('pink press', or gossip magazines) is the place to look. Television channels, though, go straight for the mass market, with junk television (*telebasura*) prevalent. Catalan is the dominant language on both radio and TV, less so in print and online.

Daily newspapers
Free daily papers of reasonable quality, such as *20 Minutos* and *Metro*, are handed out in the city centre every morning. The dailies tend to the highbrow. Spanish

readers can try *ABC, El Mundo, El País* and *La Vanguardia*; those conversant in Catalan have *Avui* and one of the editions of *El Periódico*.

English-language
Foreign newspapers are available at most kiosks on La Rambla and Passeig de Gràcia.
Barcelona Connect *www. barcelonaconnect.com.*
A small free magazine with tips for travellers.
Barcelona Metropolitan *www. barcelona-metropolitan.com.*
A free monthly magazine for English-speaking locals, distributed in bars and other anglophone hangouts.
Catalonia Today *www. cataloniatoday.cat.*
English-language monthly with a round-up of local news and cultural events. A PDF version is available for €36 a year.

Listings & classifieds
Most of the main papers have daily 'what's on' listings, some of which are also online, with entertainment supplements on Fridays (most run TV schedules on Saturdays). For monthly listings, see *Metropolitan (left)* or the handy *Butxaca* (www.butxaca. com), which can be picked up in cultural information centres, such as Palau de la Virreina on La Rambla; and freebies such as *Mondo Sonoro* (www. mondosonoro.com), which can be found in bars and music shops. Of the dailies, *La Vanguardia* has the best classifieds; you can also consult it at www.clasificados.es.
Guía del Ocio *www. guiadelocio.com/barcelona.*
A weekly listings magazine, published every Fri, in Spanish, with the odd page in English.
Time Out Barcelona *www. timeout.com/barcelona/time-out-barcelona-magazine.*
A free monthly listings magazine available in English, found in newsstands around the city.

Radio
There are vast numbers of local, regional and national stations, with the Catalan language having a high profile. **Catalunya Mùsica**

(101.5 FM) is mainly classical and jazz, while **Flaix FM** (105.7 FM) provides news and music. For something a little more alternative, try **Radio Bronka** (104.5 FM) or **Radio 3** (98.6 FM), which has a wonderfully varied music policy.

Television
The emphasis of Spanish television is on mass entertainment, with Catalan channels only marginally better. Films are mainly dubbed and advertising is interminable. The best of the bunch may be **Barcelona TV**, which produces the city's most groundbreaking viewing. Also worth a look is **La2** ('La Dos'), which is often compared to BBC2, with good late-night movies and documentaries.

MONEY

Spain's currency is the euro. Each euro (€) is divided into 100 cents (¢), known as *céntims/céntimos*. Notes come in denominations of €500, €200, €100, €50, €20, €10 and €5. Due to the increasing circulation of counterfeit notes, smaller businesses may be reluctant to accept anything larger than €50.

Banks & currency exchanges
Obtaining money through ATMs with a debit or credit card is the easiest option, despite the fees often charged. Banks (*bancos*) and savings banks (*caixes d'estalvis/ cajas de ahorros*) usually accept euro travellers' cheques for a commission, but they tend to refuse any kind of personal cheque except one issued by that bank. Some bureaux de change (*cambios*) don't charge commission, but rates are worse.
Bank hours Banks are normally open 8.30am-2pm Mon-Fri. Oct-Apr, most branches also open 8.30am-1pm Sat. Oct-May, many savings banks (normally beginning 'Caixa' or 'Caja') are also open 4.30-7.45pm Thur.
Out-of-hours banking Foreign exchange offices at the airport are in T1 (open 7am-10pm) and T2B (open 7am-8.30pm). Others in the centre open late: some on La Rambla open until midnight,

later July-Sept. At Sants, you can change money at La Caixa (8am-8pm daily); there's another change point at Plaça Catalunya 7. At the airport and outside some banks are automatic exchange machines that accept notes in major currencies.

Credit & debit cards

Major credit cards are accepted in hotels, shops, restaurants and other places (metro ticket machines and pay-and-display parking machines, for instance). American Express cards are less frequently accepted than MasterCard and Visa. Many debit cards from other European countries may also be accepted. You can withdraw cash with major cards from ATMs, and banks will also advance cash against a credit card.

Note: occasionally you need photographic ID (a passport, driving licence or something similar) when using a credit or debit card in a shop, but it's usually not required for payment in a restaurant.

Lost/stolen cards All lines have English-speaking staff and are open 24hrs daily. Maestro does not have a Spanish helpline.
American Express *902 375 637*.
Diners Club *902 401 112*.
MasterCard *900 971 231*.
Visa *900 991 124*.

Tax

The standard rate for sales tax (IVA) is 21%; this drops to 10% in hotels and restaurants, and 4% on some books. IVA may or may not be included in listed prices at restaurants, and it usually isn't included in rates quoted at hotels. If it's not, the expression *IVA no inclòs/incluido* (sales tax not included) should appear after the price. Beware of this when getting quotes on expensive items.

In shops displaying a 'Tax-Free Shopping' sticker, non-EU residents can reclaim tax on large purchases when leaving the country.

The *tasa turística* ('tourist tax') is now levied on hotel stays, and varies from 65¢ to €2.25 a night, depending on the star rating of

the hotel. Children under 16 are exempt, and the tax is applicable for a maximum of 7 nights.

OPENING TIMES

Note that in summer, many of Barcelona's shops and restaurants shut for all or part of Aug (we have noted this where possible in our listings). Some businesses also work a shortened day June-Sept, 8/9am-3pm. Many museums close one day each week, usually Mon.

Shops Most shops are open 9/10am-1/2pm, and then 4/5pm-8/9pm Mon-Sat. Many smaller businesses don't reopen on Sat pm. All-day opening (10am-8/9pm) is becoming more common, especially for larger and more central establishments.

Markets Markets open at 7/8am; most stalls are shut by 2pm, although many stay open on Fri and Sat until 8pm.

POLICE

Barcelona has several police forces: the **Mossos d'Esquadra** (in a uniform of navy and light blue with red trim), the **Guàrdia Urbana** (municipal police – navy and pale blue), the **Policía Nacional** (national police – darker blue uniforms and white shirts, or blue, combat-style gear). The Mossos are the Catalan government's police force and are taking over from the other two police forces but the GU and the PN will keep control of certain matters, like immigration and terrorism, which are dealt with by central government.

The **Guàrdia Civil** is a paramilitary force with green uniforms, policing highways, customs posts, government buildings and rural areas.

Reporting a crime

If you're robbed or attacked, report the incident as soon as possible at the nearest police station (*comisaría*), or dial 112 (*see p300* Accident & emergency). In the centre, the most convenient is the 24-hr **Guàrdia Urbana** station (La Rambla 43, Barri Gòtic, 112 or 93 300 22 96), which often

has English-speaking officers on duty; they may transfer you to the **Mossos d'Esquadra** (C/ Nou de la Rambla 76-80, Raval, 088 or 93 306 23 00) to report the crime formally. To do this, you'll need to make an official statement (*denuncia*). It's highly improbable that you will recover your property, but you need the *denuncia* to make an insurance claim. You can also make this statement over the phone or online (902 102 112, www.policia.es), apart from for crimes involving violence, or if the perpetrator has been identified. You'll still have to go to the *comisaría* within 72 hrs to sign the *denuncia*, but you'll be able to skip some queues.

POSTAL SERVICES

Letters and postcards weighing up to 20g cost 45¢ within Spain; €1.15 to the rest of Europe; €1.30 to the rest of the world; prices normally rise on 1 Jan. It's usually easiest to buy stamps at *estancs* (*see below*). Mail sent abroad is slow: 5-6 working days in Europe, 8-10 to the USA. Postboxes in the street are yellow, sometimes with a white or blue horn insignia. For information on postal services, call 902 197 197 or see www.correos.es.

Correus Central *Plaça Antonio López, Barri Gòtic (93 486 83 02). Metro Barceloneta or Jaume I.* **Open** *8.30am-9.30pm Mon-Fri; 8.30am-2pm Sat.* **Map** *p71 J10.* Take a ticket from the machine as you enter and wait your turn. Apart from the typical postal services, fax-sending and receiving is offered (with the option of courier delivery in Spain, using the Burofax option). To send something express delivery, ask for *urgente*.
Other locations *Ronda Universitat 23 & C/Aragó 282, Eixample (both 8.30am-8.30pm Mon-Fri, 9.30am-1pm Sat); and throughout the city.*

Estancs/estancos

Government-run tobacco shops, which are known as *estancs/ estancos* (at times, just *tabac*) and identified by a brown-

and-yellow sign, are important institutions in Spain. As well as tobacco – still popular in the country – they supply postage stamps, public transport *targetes* and phonecards.

Poste restante Poste restante letters should be sent to Lista de Correos, 08080 Barcelona, Spain. Pick-up is from the main post office; you'll need your passport when coming to claim your mail.

PUBLIC HOLIDAYS

Most shops, banks and offices, and many bars and restaurants, close on public holidays (*festius/ festivos*), and public transport is limited or runs on a Sun service. Many Spaniards take long weekends whenever a major holiday comes along. If the holiday falls on, say, a Tue or a Thur, many people will take the Mon or Fri off: this is what is known as a *pont/puente* (bridge).

New Year's Day *Any Nou* 1 Jan
Epiphany/Three Kings *Reis Mags* 6 Jan
Good Friday *Divendres Sant*
Easter Monday
Dilluns de Pasqua
May (Labour) Day *Festa del Treball* 1 May
Whit Monday *Segona Pascua* 1 June
Sant Joan 24 June
Assumption *Verge de l'Assumpció* 15 Aug
Diada de Catalunya 11 Sept
La Mercè 24 Sept
Dia de la Hispanitat 12 Oct
All Saints' Day *Tots Sants* 1 Nov
Constitution Day *Día de la Constitución* 6 Dec
La Immaculada 8 Dec
Christmas Day *Nadal* 25 Dec
Boxing Day *Sant Esteve* 26 Dec

RELIGION

Anglican:
St George's Church *C/Horaci 38, Zona Alta (93 417 88 67, www. st-georges-church.com). FGC Avda Tibidabo. **Main service** 11am Sun.*
An Anglican/Episcopalian church with a mixed congregation.

Roman Catholic:
Parròquia de Maria Reina *Avda d'Esplugues 103, Zona Alta (93 203 55 39). Metro Maria Cristina. **Mass** in English 10.30pm Sun. Closed Aug.*

Jewish Orthodox:
Sinagoga de Barcelona & Comunitat Israelita de Barcelona *C/Avenir 24, Zona Alta (93 200 85 13). FGC Gràcia. **Prayers** call for times.*

Muslim:
Mosque Islamic Cultural Council of Catalunya *C/Nou de Sadurní 9, entl, Raval (93 301 08 31, www.consellislamic.org). Metro Liceu. **Map** p109 G9.*
Phone or see website for information on local services.

SAFETY & SECURITY

Pickpocketing and bag-snatching are epidemic in Barcelona, with tourists a prime target. Be especially careful around the Old City, particularly La Rambla, as well as at stations and on public transport, the airport train being a favourite. However, thieves go anywhere tourists go, including parks, beaches and internet cafés. Most street crime is aimed at the inattentive and can be avoided by taking precautions:

• Avoid giving invitations: don't keep wallets in accessible pockets, keep your bags closed and in front of you. When you stop, put bags down where you can always see them (or hold them on your lap).
• Don't flash wads of cash, fancy cameras and phones.
• In busy streets or crowded places, keep an eye on what is happening around you. If you're suspicious of someone, move somewhere else.
• As a rule, Barcelona street thieves tend to use stealth and surprise rather than violence. However, muggings and knife threats do sometimes occur. Avoid deserted streets in the city centre if you're on your own at night, and offer no resistance when threatened.
• Don't carry more money and valuables than you need: use your hotel's safe deposit facilities, and take out travel insurance.

SMOKING

Smoking is banned in enclosed public areas. Most hotels have a non-smoking policy.

STUDY

Catalonia is generally well disposed towards the European Union, and the vast majority of foreign students who come to Spain under the EU's Erasmus scheme are studying at Catalan universities or colleges. Catalan is usually the language spoken in these universities, although some lecturers are more relaxed than others about the use of Castilian in class for the first few months.
Oficina Jove *C/Calabria 147, Eixample (93 483 83 84, www.oficinajove.cat). Metro Rocafort. **Open** 9am-2pm, 3-6pm Mon-Thur; 9am-2pm Fri. **Map** p152 D6.*
Generalitat-run centre with a number of services: information for young people on travel, work and study.

Language classes

If you plan to stay in bilingual Barcelona for a while, you may want (or need) to learn some Catalan. The city is also a popular location for those coming to the country to study Spanish. See acreditacion.cervantes.es for schools recommended by Spain's official language institute, the Instituto Cervantes.
Consorci per a la Normalització Lingüística *Carrer d'en Quintana 11, Barri Gòtic (93 412 72 24, www. cpnl.cat). Metro Drassanes. **Open** 9am-noon Mon, Wed-Fri; 9am-noon, 4-8pm Tue. **Map** p71 H9.*
The Generalitat organisation for the promotion of the Catalan language has centres around the city offering Catalan courses for non-Spanish speakers at very low prices or even for free (level 1). The basic classes are held at the C/ Avinyó venue.
Other locations *C/Avinyó 52, Barri Gòtic (933 428 080); C/ Mallorca 115, entl 1ª, Eixample (93 451 24 45); and throughout the city.*

Escola Oficial d'Idiomes de Barcelona – Drassanes

Avda Drassanes 14, Raval (93 324 93 30, www.eoibd.cat). Metro Drassanes. **Open** *Sept-June 8am-9pm Mon-Thur; 8.30am-8pm Fri. July 9am-8pm Mon-Fri.* **Map** *p109 G10.*

This state-run school has semi-intensive 4-mth courses, starting in Oct and Feb (enrolment tends to be in either Sept or Jan, check the website for details), at all levels in Spanish, Catalan, French and other languages.

Other locations *Escola Oficial, Avda del Jordà 18, Vall d'Hebrón (93 418 74 85, 93 418 68 33).*

Estudios Hispánicos de la Universitat de Barcelona

Gran Via de les Corts Catalanes 585, Eixample (93 403 55 19, www.eh.ub.es). Metro Universitat. **Open** *information (Pati de Ciències entrance) Aug 9am-3pm Mon-Fri, shut 1 wk Aug. Sept-July 10am-2pm, 4pm-8pm Mon-Thur; 10am-2pm Fri.* **Map** *p152 G7.*

Intensive fortnight, 1-mth, 3-mth and year-long Spanish language and culture courses.

International House

C/Trafalgar 14, Eixample (93 268 45 11, www.ihes.com/bcn). Metro Urquinaona. **Open** *8am-10pm Mon-Thur; 8am-9.30pm Fri; 9.30am-1.30pm Sat.* **Map** *p152 M8.*

Intensive Spanish courses run year round.

TELEPHONES

Dialling & codes

Normal Spanish phone numbers have 9 digits; the area code (93 in the province of Barcelona) must be dialled with all calls, both local and long-distance. Spanish mobile numbers usually begin with 6, and, very occasionally, 7. Numbers starting 900 are freephone lines, while other 90 numbers are special-rate services. Those starting with 80 are high-rate lines and can be called only from within Spain.

International & long-distance calls

To phone Spain from abroad, dial 00, followed by 34, followed

by the number. To make an international call from Spain, dial 00 and then the country code, followed by the area code (omitting the first 0 in UK numbers), and then the number. Country codes are as follows:
Australia 61.
Canada 1.
Irish Republic 353.
New Zealand 64.
South Africa 27.
United Kingdom 44.
USA 1.

Mobile phones

Mobile phone, or *móvil* calls are paid for either through direct debit or by using prepaid phones, topped up with vouchers. Most mobiles from other European countries can be used in Spain, but you may need to set this up before you leave. You may be charged international roaming rates even when making a local call, and you will be charged for incoming calls. Not all US handsets are GSM-compatible; check with your service provider before you leave.

If you're staying more than a few weeks, it may work out cheaper to buy a pay-as-you-go package when you arrive or buy a local SIM card for your own phone.

Phone centres, payphones & phonecards

Phonecards and phone centres give cheaper call rates, especially for international calls. Phone centres (*locutoris*) are full of small booths where you can sit down and pay at the end. They offer cheap calls and avoid the need for change. Find them particularly in streets such as C/Sant Pau and C/Hospital in the Raval, and along C/Carders-C/Corders in Sant Pere. The most common type of payphone in Barcelona accepts coins (5¢ and up), phonecards and credit cards. Telefónica phonecards (*targetes telefónica/tarjetas telefónica*) are sold at newsstands and *estancs* (*see p305*). Other cards sold at phone centres, shops and newsstands give cheaper rates on all but local calls.

Operator services & useful phone numbers

Operators normally speak Catalan and Spanish only, except for international operators, most of whom speak English.
General information (Barcelona) *010 (24hrs daily).* From outside Catalonia, but within Spain, call 807 117 700.
International directory enquiries *11825.*
International operator for reverse charge calls *1408.*
National directory enquiries *11888 (Yellow Pages, free on www.paginasamarillas.com), among others.*
National operator for reverse charge calls *1409.*
Telephone faults service *(Telefónica) 1002.*

TIME

The local time is Central European Time: 1 hr ahead of Greenwich Mean Time, 6 hrs ahead of US Eastern Standard Time and 9 hrs ahead of Pacific Standard Time. Daylight saving time runs concurrently with the United Kingdom: clocks go back in Oct and forward in Mar.

TIPPING

There are no rules for tipping in Barcelona, but locals don't tip much. It's fair to leave 5-10% in restaurants, unless the service has been bad. People sometimes leave a little change in bars. In taxis, tipping is not standard, but many people round up to the nearest 50¢. It's usual to tip hotel porters.

TOILETS

There are 24-hr public toilets in Plaça del Teatre, just off La Rambla, and more at the top of C/dels Àngels, opposite the MACBA. Most of the main railway stations have clean toilets. Parks such as Ciutadella and Güell have a few dotted about, but you sometimes need a 20¢ coin to use them. The beach at Barceloneta has 6 (heavily in demand) Portaloos; there are 5 further up at the beach at Sant Sebastià, and in season there are also toilets open under the boardwalk, along the beach towards the Port Olímpic. Most bar and café owners don't mind if you use their toilets (you may have to ask for the key), although some in the centre and at the beach are less amenable.

Toilets are known as *serveis, banys* or *lavabos* (in Catalan) or *servicios, aseos, baños* or *lavabos* (in Spanish).

In bars or restaurants, the ladies' is generally denoted by a D (*dones/damas*), and occasionally by an M (*mujeres*) or S (*señoras*) on the door; while the men's mostly say H (*homes/hombres*) or C (*caballeros*).

TOURIST INFORMATION

010 phoneline *Open 24hrs daily.*

This city-run information line is aimed mainly at locals, but it does an impeccable job of answering all kinds of queries. There are sometimes English-speaking operators available. Call 807 117 700 from outside Catalonia but within Spain.

Centre d'Informació de la Virreina *Palau de la Virreina, La Rambla 99, Barri Gòtic (93 316 10 00, www.barcelona. cat/barcelonacultura). Metro Liceu.* **Open** *10am-8.30pm daily (information office and ticket sales).* **Map** *p71 G9.*

The information office of the city's culture department has details of shows, exhibitions and special events.

Oficines d'Informació Turística *Plaça Catalunya 17, Eixample (information 93 285 38 34, bookings 93 285 38 33, www. bcn.cat, www.barcelonaturisme. com). Metro Catalunya.* **Open** *Office 8.30am-8.30pm daily. Call centre 8am-8pm Mon-Fri.* **Map** *p152 H8.*

The main office of the city tourist board is underground on the El Corte Inglés/south side of the square: look for the big red signs with 'i' superimposed in white. It has information, a shop and a hotel booking service, and sells phonecards and tickets for shows, sights and public transport.

Other locations *C/Ciutat 2 (ground floor of Ajuntament),*

Barri Gòtic; C/Sardenya (opposite the Sagrada Família), Eixample; Plaça Portal de la Pau (opposite Monument a Colom), Port Vell; Sants station; La Rambla 115, Barri Gòtic; corner of Plaça d'Espanya and Avda Maria Cristina, Eixample; airport.

Palau Robert *Passeig de Gràcia 107, Eixample (93 238 80 91/ 92/93, www.gencat.net/probert, www.catalunya.com). Metro Diagonal.* **Open** *10am-7pm Mon-Sat; 10am-2.30pm Sun.* **Map** *p152 H5.*

The Generalitat's centre for tourists is at the junction of Passeig de Gràcia and Avda Diagonal. It has maps and other essentials for Barcelona, but its speciality is a huge range of information in different media for attractions to be found elsewhere in Catalonia. It also sometimes hosts interesting exhibitions on local art, culture, gastronomy and nature and has a pleasant garden out back.

VISAS & IMMIGRATION

UK and Irish nationals will need a valid passport to enter Spain. Due to the Schengen Agreement, most other European Union citizens, as well as Norwegian and Icelandic nationals, need only a national identity card.

Visas are not required for citizens of the United States, Canada, Australia and New Zealand who are arriving for stays of up to 90 days and not for work or study. Citizens of South Africa and other countries need visas to enter Spain; approach Spanish embassies in your home country for information (see http://embassy.goabroad.com). Visa regulations do change, so check before leaving home.

WORK

Common recourses for English speakers in Barcelona are to find work in the tourist sector (often seasonal and outside the city), in a downtown bar or teaching English in the numerous language schools. For the latter, it helps to have the TEFL (Teaching English as a Foreign Language)

qualification; this can be gained in reputable institutions in the city as well as in your home country. Bear in mind that teaching work dries up from June until the end of summer, usually Sept, although it's possible to find intensive teaching courses during July. The number of jobs in call centres for English speakers and other foreigners has also rocketed of late.

EU citizens

EU citizens living in Spain for more than 3 mths need a resident's card (*tarjeta de residencia*), as well as ID or a passport from their own country.

Non-EU citizens

While in Spain on a tourist visa, you are not legally allowed to work. Those wanting a work permit officially need to be made a job offer while still in their home country. The process is lengthy and not all applications are successful. If you do get lucky, you can then apply for residency at a Spanish consulate in your home country.

Spanish Vocabulary

Spanish is generally referred to as *castellano* (Castilian) rather than *español*. The Spanish familiar form for 'you' – *tú* – is used very freely, but it's safer to use the more formal *usted* with older people and strangers (verbs below are given in the *usted* form). For menu terms, *see p310*.

Pronunciation

- **c** before an **i** or an **e** and **z** are like **th** in **th**in
- **c** in all other cases is as in **c**at
- **g** before an **i** or an **e** and **j** are pronounced with a guttural **h**-sound that doesn't exist in English – like **ch** in Scottish 'lo**ch**', but much harder
- **g** in all other cases is as in **g**et
- **h** at the beginning of a word is normally silent
- **ll** is pronounced like a **y**
- **ñ** is like **ny** in ca**ny**on
- a single **r** at the beginning of a word and **rr** elsewhere are heavily rolled
- **v** is more like an English **b**
- In words ending with a vowel, **n** or **s**, the penultimate syllable is stressed: eg *barato, viven*.
- In words ending with any other consonant, the last syllable is stressed: eg *exterior, universidad*
- An accent marks the stressed syllable in words that depart from these rules: eg *estación, tónica*

Basics

- **please** *por favor*; **thank you (very much)** *(muchas)* **gracias**; **very good/great/OK** *muy bien*, **you're welcome** *de nada*
- **hello** *hola*; **hello** (when answering the phone) *hola, diga*
- **goodbye/see you later** *adiós/ hasta luego*
- **excuse me/sorry** *perdón*; **excuse me, please** *oiga* (the standard way to attract attention, politely; literally, 'hear me')
- **OK/fine/that's enough** (to a waiter) *vale*
- **open** *abierto*; **closed** *cerrado*
- **entrance** *entrada*; **exit** *salida*
- **very** *muy*; **and** *y*; **or** *o*; **with** *con*; **without** *sin*; **enough** *bastante*

More expressions

- **good morning/good day** *buenos días*; **good afternoon/ good evening** *buenas tardes*; **good evening** (after dark)/**good night** *buenas noches*
- **do you speak English?** *¿habla inglés?*; **I'm sorry, I don't speak** Spanish *lo siento, no hablo castellano*; **I don't understand** *no lo entiendo*; **speak more slowly, please** *hable más despacio, por favor*; **wait a moment** *espere un momento*; **how do you say that in Catalan?** *¿Cómo se dice eso en catalán?*
- **what's your name?** *¿cómo se llama?* **my name is...** *me llamo...*
- **Sir/Mr** *señor* (sr); **Madam/Mrs** *señora* (sra); **Miss señorita** (srta)
- **where is...?** *¿dónde está...?*; **why?** *¿porqué?*; **who?** *¿quién?*; **when?** *¿cuándo?*; **what?** *¿qué?*; **where?** *¿dónde?*; **how?** *¿cómo?*; **who is it?** *¿quién es?*; **is/are there any...?** *¿hay...?*
- **what time does it open/close?** *¿a qué hora abre/cierra?*
- **pull** *tirar*; **push** *empujar*
- **I would like** *quiero*; **how many would you like?** *¿cuántos quiere?*; **how much is it?** *¿cuánto vale?*
- **price** *precio*; **free** *gratis*; **discount** *descuento*; **do you have any change?** *¿tiene cambio?*
- **I don't want** *no quiero*; **I like** *me gusta*; **I don't like** *no me gusta*
- **good** *bueno/a*; **bad** *malo/a*; **well/ badly** *bien/mal*; **small** *pequeño/a*; **big** *gran*, **grande**; **expensive** *caro/a*; **cheap** *barato/a*; **hot** (food, drink) *caliente*; **cold** *frío/a*
- **bank** *banco*; **to rent** *alquilar*; **(for) rent, rental** *(en) alquiler*; **post office** *correos*; **stamp** *sello*; **postcard** *postal*; **toilet** *el baño, el servicio, el lavabo*
- **airport** *aeropuerto*; **rail station** *estación de ferrocarril/ estación de RENFE* (Spanish railways); **metro station** *estación de metro*; **car** *coche*; **bus** *autobús*; **train** *tren*; **bus stop** *parada de autobus*; **the next stop** *la próxima parade*
- **a ticket** *un billete*; **return** *de ida y vuelta*
- **excuse me, do you know the way to...?** *¿oiga, señor/señora, sabe cómo llegar a...?*
- **left** *izquierda*; **right** *derecha*
- **here** *aquí*; **there** *allí*; **straight**

on *recto*; **near** *cerca*; **far** *lejos*; **at the corner** *a la esquina*; **as far as** *hasta*; **towards** *hacia*; **it is far?** *¿está lejos?*

Time

- **now** *ahora*; **later** *más tarde*
- **yesterday** *ayer*; **today** *hoy*; **tomorrow** *mañana*; **tomorrow morning** *mañana por la mañana*
- **morning** *la mañana*; **midday** *mediodía*; **afternoon/evening** *la tarde*; **night** *la noche*
- **at what time...?** *¿a qué hora...?* **in an hour** *en una hora*; **at 2** *a las dos*

Numbers

0 cero; **1** un, uno, una; **2** dos; **3** tres; **4** cuatro; **5** cinco; **6** seis; **7** siete; **8** ocho; **9** nueve; **10** diez; **11** once; **12** doce; **13** trece; **14** catorce; **15** quince; **16** dieciséis; **17** diecisiete; **18** dieciocho; **19** diecinueve; **20** veinte; **21** veintiuno; **22** veintidós; **30** treinta; **40** cuarenta; **50** cincuenta; **60** sesenta; **70** setenta; **80** ochenta; **90** noventa; **100** cien; **200** doscientos; **1,000** mil; **1,000,000** un millón

Dates & seasons

- **Monday** *lunes*; **Tuesday** *martes*; **Wednesday** *miércoles*; **Thursday** *jueves*; **Friday** *viernes*; **Saturday** *sábado*; **Sunday** *domingo*
- **January** *enero*; **February** *febrero*; **March** *marzo*; **April** *abril*; **May** *mayo*; **June** *junio*; **July** *julio*; **August** *agosto*; **September** *septiembre*; **October** *octubre*; **November** *noviembre*; **December** *diciembre*
- **spring** *primavera*; **summer** *verano*; **autumn** *otoño*; **winter** *invierno*

Catalan Vocabulary

Catalan phonetics are different from those of Spanish, with a wider range of vowel sounds and soft consonants. Catalans use the familiar (*tu*) rather than the polite (*vosté*) forms of the second person freely, but for convenience, verbs are given here in the polite form.

Pronunciation

- In Catalan, words are run together, so *si us plau* (please) is more like sees-plow
- **ç**, and **c** before an **i** or an **e**, are like a soft **s**, as in s**i**t; **c** in all other cases is as in **c**at
- **e**, when unstressed as in *cerveses* (beers), or Jaume I, is a weak sound, like centr**e** or comfortabl**e**
- **g** before **i** or **e** and **j** are pronounced like **s** in plea**s**ure; **tg** and **tj** are similar to **dg** in ba**dg**e
- **g** after an **i** at the end of a word (Pu**ig**) is a hard **ch** sound, as in wat**ch**; otherwise, **g** is as in **g**et
- **h** is silent
- **ll** is somewhere between the **y** in **y**es and the **lli** in mi**lli**on
- **l·l** has a slightly stronger stress on a single **l** sound; paral·lel sounds similar to the English paral**l**el
- **o** at the end of a word is like the u sound in fl**u**; **ó** at the end of a word is similar to the **o** in tomat**o**; **ò** is like the **o** in h**o**t
- **r** beginning a word and **rr** are heavily rolled; but at the end of many words is almost silent, so *carrer* (street) sounds like carr-ay
- **s** at the beginning and end of words and **ss** between vowels are soft, as in s**i**t; a single **s** between two vowels is a **z** sound, as in la**z**y
- **t** after **l** or **n** at the end of a word is almost silent
- **v** is more like an English **b**
- **x** at the beginning of a word, or after a consonant or the letter **i**, is like the **sh** in **sh**oe, at other times like the English e**x**pert
- **y** after an **n** at the end of a word or in **nys** is not a vowel but adds a nasal stress and a y-sound to the n

Basics

- **please** *si us plau*; **thank you (very much)** (*moltes*) *gràcies*; **very good/great/OK** *molt bé*; **you're welcome** *de res*
- **hello** *hola*; **hello** (when answering the phone) *hola, digui'm*
- **goodbye/see you later** *adéu/fins després*
- **excuse me/sorry** *perdoni/disculpi*; **excuse me, please** *escolti* (literally, 'listen to me')
- **OK/fine** *val/d'acord*
- **open** *obert*; **closed** *tancat*
- **entrance** *entrada*; **exit** *sortida*
- **very** *molt*; **and** *i*; **or** *o*

More expressions

- **good morning, good day** *bon dia*; **good afternoon/evening** *bona tarda*; **good evening** (after dark), **good night** *bona nit*
- **do you speak English?** *parla anglès?*; **I'm sorry, I don't speak Catalan** *ho sento, no parlo català*; **I don't understand** *no ho entenc*; **speak more slowly, please** *parli més a poc a poc, si us plau*
- **what's your name?** *com es diu?*; **my name is...** *em dic...*
- **Sir/Mr** *senyor* (sr); **Madam/Mrs** *senyora* (sra); **Miss** *senyoreta* (srta)
- **where is...?** *on és...?*; **why?** *per què?*; **who?** *qui?*; **when?** *quan?*; **what?** *què?*; **where?** *on?*; **how?** *com?*; **who is it?** *qui és?*; **is/are there any...?** *hi ha...?/ n'hi ha de...?*
- **what time does it open/close?** *a quina hora obre/tanca?*
- **I would like...** *vull...* (literally, 'I want'); **how many would you like?** *quants en vol?*; **how much is it?** *quant val?*
- **price** *preu*; **free** *gratuït/de franc*
- **I don't want** *no vull*; **I like** *m'agrada*; **I don't like** *no m'agrada*
- **good** *bo/bona*; **bad** *dolent/a*; **well/badly** *bé/malament*; **small** *petit/a*; **big** *gran*; **expensive** *car/a*; **cheap** *barat/a*; **hot** (food, drink) *calent/a*; **cold** *fred/a*
- **bank** *banc*; **to rent** *lloguer*; **post office** *correus*; **stamp** *segell*; **postcard** *postal*; **toilet** *el bany/el servei/el lavabo*

- **airport** *aeroport*; **rail station** *estació de tren/estació de RENFE* (Spanish railways); **metro station** *estació de metro*; **car** *cotxe*; **bus** *autobús*; **train** *tren*; **bus stop** *parada d'autobús*
- **a ticket** *un bitllet*; **return** *d'anada i tornada*
- **excuse me, do you know the way to...?** *disculpi, saps com anar a...?*
- **left** *esquerra*; **right** *dreta*
- **here** *aquí*; **there** *allà*

Time

- **now** *ara*; **later** *més tard*
- **yesterday** *ahir*; **today** *avui*; **tomorrow** *demà*; **tomorrow morning** *demà pel matí*
- **morning** *el matí*; **midday** *migdía*; **afternoon** *la tarda*; **evening** *el vespre*; **night** *la nit*; **late night** (roughly, 1-6am) *la matinada*
- **at what time...?** *a quina hora...?*; **in an hour** *en una hora*; **at 2** *a les dues*

Numbers

0 *zero*; 1 *u, un, una*; 2 *dos, dues*; 3 *tres*; 4 *quatre*; 5 *cinc*; 6 *sis*; 7 *set*; 8 *vuit*; 9 *nou*; 10 *deu*; 11 *onze*; 12 *dotze*; 13 *tretze*; 14 *catorze*; 15 *quinze*; 16 *setze*; 17 *disset*; 18 *divuit*; 19 *dinou*; 20 *vint*; 21 *vint-i-u*; 22 *vint-i-dos, vint-i-dues*; 30 *trenta*; 40 *quaranta*; 50 *cinquanta*; 60 *seixanta*; 70 *setanta*; 80 *vuitanta*; 90 *noranta*; 100 *cent*; 200 *dos-cents, dues-centes*; 1,000 *mil*; 1,000,000 *un milló*

Dates & seasons

- **Monday** *dilluns*; **Tuesday** *dimarts*; **Wednesday** *dimecres*; **Thursday** *dijous*; **Friday** *divendres*; **Saturday** *dissabte*; **Sunday** *diumenge*
- **January** *gener*; **February** *febrer*; **March** *marÇ*; **April** *abril*; **May** *maig*; **June** *juny*; **July** *juliol*; **August** *agost*; **September** *setembre*; **October** *octubre*; **November** *novembre*; **December** *desembre*
- **spring** *primavera*; **summer** *estiu*; **autumn** *tardor*; **winter** *hivern*

Menu Glossary

CATALAN	SPANISH	ENGLISH	CATALAN	SPANISH	ENGLISH

Essential terminology

CATALAN	SPANISH	ENGLISH
una cullera	una cuchara	a spoon
una forquilla	un tenedor	a fork
un ganivet	un cuchillo	a knife
una ampolla de	una botella de	a bottle of
un/a altre/a	otro/otra	another (one)
més	más	more
pa*pan*		bread
oli d'oliva	aceite de oliva	olive oil
sal i pebre	sal y pimienta	salt and pepper
amanida	ensalada	salad
truita	tortilla	omelette

(note: **truita** can also mean 'trout')

CATALAN	SPANISH	ENGLISH
la nota	la cuenta	the bill
un cendrer	un cenicero	an ashtray
vi negre	vino tinto	red wine
rosat	rosado	rosé
blanc	blanco	white
bon profit	que aproveche	enjoy your meal
sóc...	soy...	I'm a...
vegetarià/ana	vegetariano/a	vegetarian
diabètic/a	diabético/a	diabetic

Cooking terms

CATALAN	SPANISH	ENGLISH
a la brasa	a la brasa	chargrilled
a la graella/planxa	a la plancha	cooked on a hot plate
a la romana	a la romana	fried in batter
al forn	al horno	baked
al vapor	al vapor	steamed
fregit	frito	fried
rostit	asado	roast
ben fet	bien hecho	well done
a punt	medio hecho	medium
poc fet	poco hecho	rare

Carn i aviram	Carne y aves	Meat & poultry
ànec	pato	duck
bou	buey	beef
cabrit	cabrito	kid
colomí	pichón	pigeon
conill	conejo	rabbit
embotits	embutidos	cold cuts
fetge	hígado	liver
gall dindi	pavo	turkey
garrí	cochinillo	suckling pig
guatlla	codorniz	quail
llebre	liebre	hare
llengua	lengua	tongue
llom	lomo	loin (usually pork)
oca	oca	goose
ous	huevos	eggs
perdiu	perdiz	partridge
pernil (serrà)	jamón serrano	dry-cured ham
pernil dolç	jamón york	cooked ham
peus de porc	manos de cerdo	pigs' trotters
pintada	gallina de Guinea	guinea fowl
pollastre	pollo	chicken
porc	cerdo	pork
porc senglar	jabalí	wild boar
vedella	ternera	veal
xai/be	cordero	lamb

Peix i marisc	Pescado y mariscos	Fish & seafood
anxoves	anchoas	anchovies
bacallà	bacalao	salt cod
besuc	besugo	sea bream
caballa	verat	mackerel
calamarsos	calamares	squid
cloïsses	almejas	clams
cranc	cangrejo	crab

311

MENU GLOSSARY

CATALAN	SPANISH	ENGLISH	CATALAN	SPANISH	ENGLISH
escamarlans	cigalas	crayfish	**enciam**	lechuga	lettuce
escopinyes	berberechos	cockles	**endívies**	endivias	chicory
espardenyes	espardeñas	sea cucumbers	**espinacs**	espinacas	spinach
gambes	gambas	prawns	**mongetes**	judías blancas	haricot beans
llagosta	langosta	spiny lobster	**blanques**		
llagostins	langostinos	langoustines	**mongetes**	judías verdes	French beans
llamàntol	bogavante	lobster	**verdes**		
llenguado	lenguado	sole	**pastanagues**	zanahorias	carrots
llobarro	lubina	sea bass	**patates**	patatas	potatoes
lluç	merluza	hake	**pebrots**	pimientos	peppers
moll	salmonete	red mullet	**pèsols**	guisantes	peas
musclos	mejillones	mussels	**porros**	puerros	leeks
navalles	navajas	razor clams	**tomàquets**	tomates	tomatoes
percebes	percebes	barnacles	**xampinyons**	champiñones	mushrooms
pop	pulpo	octopus			
rap	rape	monkfish	**Postres**	**Postres**	**Desserts**
rèmol	rodaballo	turbot			
salmó	salmón	salmon	**flam**	flan	crème caramel
sardines	sardinas	sardines	**formatge**	queso	cheese
sípia	sepia	cuttlefish	**gelat**	helado	ice-cream
tallarines	tallarinas	wedge clams	**música**	música	dried fruit and
tonyina	atún	tuna			nuts, with
truita	trucha	trout			muscatel

(note: **truita** can also mean 'omelette')

			pastís	pastel	cake
			tarta	tarta	tart

Verdures **Legumbres** **Vegetables**

Fruita **Fruta** **Fruit**

CATALAN	SPANISH	ENGLISH	CATALAN	SPANISH	ENGLISH
albergínia	berenjena	aubergine	**figues**	higos	figs
all	ajo	garlic	**gerds**	frambuesas	raspberries
alvocat	aguacate	avocado	**maduixes**	fresas	strawberries
bolets	setas	wild mushrooms	**pera**	pera	pear
			pinya	piña	pineapple
carbassons	calabacines	courgettes	**plàtan**	plátano	banana
carxofes	alcahofas	artichokes	**poma**	manzana	apple
ceba	cebolla	onion	**préssec**	melocotón	peach
cigrons	garbanzos	chickpeas	**prunes**	ciruelas	plums
col	col	cabbage			

Further Reference

BOOKS

Food & drink

Colman Andrews *Catalan Cuisine (Grub Street, 1997)*. A mine of information on food and more – with usable recipes.

Anya von Bremzen *The New Spanish Table (Workman Publishing, 2006)*. A guide to Spanish staples with some entertaining anecdotes.

Alan Davidson *Tio Pepe Guide to the Seafood of Spain and Portugal (Santana Books, 2002)*. An excellent pocket-sized guide to Spain's fishy delights.

Guides & walks

Xavier Güell *Gaudí Guide (Gustavo Gili, 1991)*. A handy guide, with good background on the architect's work.

Juliet Pomés Leiz & Ricardo Feriche *Barcelona Design Guide (Gustavo Gili, 1992)*. An engaging listing of everything ever considered 'designer' in BCN.

Context & culture

Jimmy Burns *Barça: A People's Passion (Bloomsbury, 2016)*. The first full-scale history in English of one of the world's most storied football clubs.

JH Elliott *The Revolt of the Catalans (Cambridge University Press, 1984)*. A fascinating, detailed account of the Guerra dels Segadors and the Catalan revolt of the 1640s.

Felipe Fernández Armesto *Barcelona: A Thousand Years of the City's Past (Sinclair-Stevenson, 1991)*. A solid history.

Ronald Fraser *Blood of Spain (Pimlico, 1994)*. A vivid oral history of the Spanish Civil War.

Gijs van Hensbergen *Gaudí (HarperCollins, 2002)*. A thorough account of his life.

Gijs van Hensbergen *The Sagrada Familia: Gaudí's Heaven on Earth (Bloomsbury, 2017)*. A definitive biography of the unfinished temple.

John Hooper *The New Spaniards (Penguin, 2006)*. An incisive and very readable survey of the changes in Spanish society since the death of Franco.

Robert Hughes *Barcelona (Vintage, 2001)*. The most comprehensive single book about Barcelona.

Temma Kaplan *Red City, Blue Period: Social Movements in Picasso's Barcelona (University of California Press, 1993)*. The interplay of avant-garde art and politics in the 1900s.

Sid Lowe *Fear and Loathing in La Liga: Barcelona vs Real Madrid (Yellow Jersey, 2014)*. More than a football book, covering modern history and the politics of the great rivalry.

George Orwell *Homage to Catalonia (Penguin Classics, 2000)*. Barcelona in revolution.

Abel Paz Durruti *The People Armed (Free Life Editions, 1977)*. The legendary Barcelona anarchist.

Ignasi Solà-Morales *Fin de Siècle Architecture in Barcelona (Gustavo Gili, 1992)*. A wide-ranging description of the city's Modernista heritage.

Colm Tóibín *Homage to Barcelona (Picador, 2010)*. An evocative and perceptive journey around the city.

Manuel Vázquez Montalbán *Barcelonas (Triangle Postals, 2001)*. Idiosyncratic, insightful reflections.

Rainer Zerbst *Antoni Gaudí (Taschen, 1991)*. A lavishly illustrated survey.

Literature

Pere Calders *The Virgin of the Railway and Other Stories (Aris & Phillips, 1991)*. Quirky stories by a Catalan writer who spent years in exile in Mexico.

Victor Català *Solitude (Editions Phébus, 2014)*. This masterpiece by female novelist Caterina Albert shocked readers in 1905 with its open, modern treatment of female sexuality.

Ildefonso Falcones *Cathedral of the Sea (Black Swan, 2009)*. A hugely popular historical novel, centred on the construction of Santa Maria del Mar in the Born.

Juan Marsé *The Fallen (Little, Brown, 1979)*. The classic novel of survival in the city during the long posguerra.

Joanot Martorell & Joan Martí de Gualba *Tirant lo Blanc (Alianza Editorial, 2006)*. The first European prose novel, from 1490: a rambling, bawdy, shaggy-dog story of travels, romances and chivalric adventures.

Eduardo Mendoza *City of Marvels (Thompson Learning, 1988)*. A sweeping saga of the city between its great Exhibitions in 1888 and 1929.

Eduardo Mendoza *Year of the Flood (The Harvill Press, 1995)*. A novel of passions in the city of the 1950s.

Maria-Antònia Oliver *Antipodes (Seal Press, 1989); Study in Lilac (Thorsons, 1989)*. Two adventures of Barcelona's first feminist detective.

Mercè Rodoreda *The Time of the Doves (Graywolf Press, 1989)*. A translation of Plaça del Diamant, the most widely read of all Catalan novels.

Carlos Ruiz Zafón *Shadow of the Wind (W&N, 2005)*. An enjoyable neo-Gothic melodrama set in post-war BCN.

Manuel Vázquez Montalbán *The Angst-Ridden Executive (Serpent's Tail, 1989); An Olympic Death (2008); Southern Seas (1999).* Three thrillers starring detective and gourmet Pepe Carvalho.

WEBSITES

www.barcelonarocks. com Music listings and news.

www.barcelonaturisme.com Official tourist authority info.
www.bcn.cat The city council's information-packed website.
www.bcn.cat/planol Excellent interactive Barcelona street maps.
www.enciclopedia.cat Contains the best English–Catalan online dictionary.

www.mobilitat.net Generalitat's website about getting from A to B in Catalonia, by bus, car or train.
www.renfe.es Spanish railways.
www.timeout.com/barcelona The online city guide.

▶ *For a list of Barcelona films, see p229; for Barcelona albums, see p244.*

Index